Hiking California's Desert Parks

Help Us Keep This Guide Up to Date

Every effort has been made by the authors and editors to make this guide as accurate and useful as possible. However, many things can change after a guide is published—trails are rerouted, regulations change, techniques evolve, facilities come under new management, etc.

We would love to hear from you concerning your experiences with this guide and how you feel it could be improved and kept up to date. While we may not be able to respond to all comments and suggestions, we'll take them to heart, and we'll also make certain to share them with the authors. Please send your comments and suggestions to the following address:

> The Globe Pequot Press
> Reader Response/Editorial Department
> P.O. Box 480
> Guilford, CT 06437

Or you may e-mail us at:

> editorial@GlobePequot.com

Thanks for your input, and happy trails!

Hiking California's Desert Parks

Second Edition

Bill and Polly Cunningham

FALCON GUIDE®

GUILFORD, CONNECTICUT
HELENA, MONTANA
AN IMPRINT OF THE GLOBE PEQUOT PRESS

A FALCON GUIDE®

Text design by Nancy Freeborn
All interior photos by the authors
Spine photo © 2004 Michael DeYoung
Maps created by XNR Productions Inc. and Bruce Grubbs
© Morris Book Publishing, LLC

ISSN: 1558-3732
ISBN-13: 978-0-7627-3545-7
ISBN-10: 0-7627-3545-7

Manufactured in the United States of America
Second Edition/First Printing

The authors and The Globe Pequot Press assume no liability for accidents happening to, or injuries sustained by, readers who engage in the activities described in this book.

To the thousands of citizens from California and elsewhere, past and present, who laid the groundwork for protection of a large portion of the California desert, to those who helped secure passage of the California Desert Protection Act, and to the dedicated state and federal park rangers and naturalists charged with stewardship of California's irreplaceable desert wilderness.

Contents

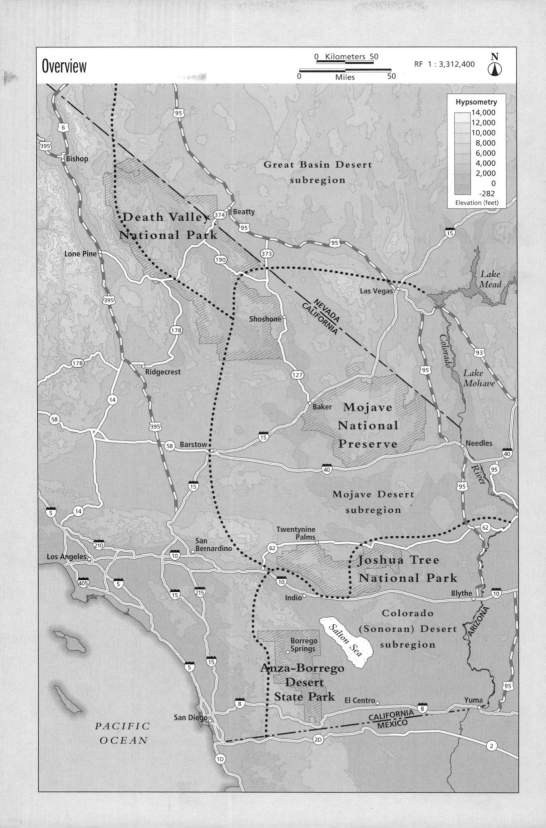

Overview

0 Kilometers 50

0 Miles 50

RF 1 : 3,312,400

N

Hypsometry

14,000
12,000
10,000
8,000
6,000
4,000
2,000
0
-282
Elevation (feet)

6

395

Bishop

95

Great Basin Desert
subregion

374 Beatty

**Death Valley
National Park**

95

Lone Pine

190

373

95

15

395

Shoshone

Las Vegas

*Lake
Mead*

NEVADA
CALIFORNIA

178

95

93

*Lake
Mohave*

Colorado

178

Ridgecrest

127

14

58

395

Baker

**Mojave
National
Preserve**

58 Barstow

15

40

Needles

40

95

15

**Mojave Desert
subregion**

95

River

5

14

62

210

Los Angeles

San
Bernardino

Twentynine
Palms

62

**Joshua Tree
National Park**

ARIZONA

405

5

10

15

215

10

Indio

Blythe

10

**Colorado
(Sonoran) Desert
subregion**

*Salton
Sea*

Borrego
Springs

5

15

**Anza-Borrego
Desert
State Park**

8

El Centro

Yuma

95

8

San Diego

CALIFORNIA
MEXICO

*PACIFIC
OCEAN*

1D

2D

2

Death Valley National Park

Acknowledgments

When we wrote the first edition of this comprehensive hiking guide nearly a decade ago, we received generous assistance from knowledgeable staffers from each of the four desert parks. The book could not have been written without their help, so it is fitting that they once again be given special thanks: Homer Townsend, chief ranger, and Mark Jorgensen, associate resource ecologist at Anza-Borrego Desert State Park; Charlie Callagan, interpretative ranger and still one of the leading authorities on wilderness hiking in Death Valley; Esy Fields, director of the Death Valley Natural History Association; Joe Zarki, chief of interpretation of the Joshua Tree Natural History Association, and his assistant Sandra Kaye, who provided an excellent review of the text; Kirsten Talken, district interpreter, at Mojave National Preserve; and Ramon Sanchez and Thom Thompson, interpretive rangers at Providence Mountains State Park/Mitchell Caverns National Preserve. Even after all this time, we fondly remember the wonderful hot shower Ramon provided for us during our visit to Providence, our first in several days of desert exploration. Our thanks also to all the hospitable folks who provided advice and insights during our treks in the desert. Please know that you are not forgotten.

When it came time to produce this major update, revision, and expansion of *Hiking California's Desert Parks,* we called upon two of the same rangers who had helped us so much with the first edition. Joe Zarki of Joshua Tree National Park and members of his ranger staff provided detailed updates for each of the Joshua Tree hikes. The effort they expended to ensure accurate information in this book is both commendable and deeply appreciated. We were also delighted to learn that Charlie Callagan is now on the permanent ranger staff for Death Valley National Park. He is a virtual fountain of information and enthusiasm for the park. He provided an in-depth review of our draft material time and again until he was satisfied that we finally had it right. But most of all, Charlie served as friend and guide on several of the new hikes, notably South Fork Hanaupah and Upper Hole-in-the-Wall.

During our most recent field trips, we had the pleasure of working with James Woolsey, chief of interpretation and outreach for Mojave National Preserve. Not only did he provide many helpful suggestions and ideas, but he also guided us to several magical places in Mojave that now appear in this updated book. These include Lava Tubes and Castle Peaks, which are only a couple of the new Mojave hikes we're proud to include. It was truly wonderful to hike into the Mojave wilderness with James as a companion, friend, and guide. In addition, MNP ranger Christina Burns provided an incredibly detailed review of our manuscript with numerous suggestions for improvements and updates.

Kathy Dice, supervising state park ranger for Anza-Borrego Desert State Park, also deserves special recognition. Kathy circulated our request for updated information to her rangers and forwarded a mountain of useful information back to us. Throughout our long revision process, Kathy was extremely helpful. Her enthusiasm and love for Anza-Borrego is especially appreciated.

Thanks to you all!

Introduction

The California desert covers the southeastern quarter of our most populous and most ecologically diverse state. And the four huge desert parks featured in this book encompass about a quarter of the California desert—from its southern- to northernmost extent. Incredibly, three of the four desert subregions that make up most of the arid southwest corner of North America are found within the California desert. These subregions—the Colorado (called the Sonoran in Mexico), Mojave, and Great Basin Deserts—differ by climate and distinct plant and animal communities.

The geographer's definition of a desert as a place with less than 10 inches average annual rainfall says little about what a desert really is. Deserts are regions of irregular and minimal rainfall, so much so that for most of the time, scarcity of water is limiting to life. Averages mean nothing in a desert region that may go one or two years without *any* rain only to receive up to three times the annual average the following year.

In the desert, evaporation far exceeds precipitation. Temperatures swing widely between night and day. This is because low humidity and intense sun heat up the ground during the day, but almost all of the heat dissipates at night. Daily temperature changes of 50 degrees or more are common—which can be hazardous to unprepared hikers caught out after dark.

Sparse rainfall means sparse vegetation, which in turn means naked geological features. Most of the California desert is crisscrossed with mountain ranges, imparting an exposed, rough-hewn, scenic character to the landscape. Rather than having been uplifted, the mountains were largely formed by an east-west collision of the earth's tectonic plates, producing a north-south orientation of the ranges. Some would call the result stark, but all would agree that these signatures on the land are dramatic and, at times, overpowering. This very starkness tends to exaggerate the drama of space, color, relief, and sheer ruggedness.

Despite sparse plant cover, the number of individual plant species in the California desert is amazing. At least 1,000 species are spread among 103 vascular plant families. Equally amazing is the diversity of bird life and other wildlife on this deceptively barren land. Many of these birds and animals are active only at night, or are most likely seen during the hotter months at or near watering holes. Hundreds of bird species and more than sixty kinds of reptiles and amphibians fly, nest, crawl, and slither in habitat niches to which they have adapted. Desert bighorn sheep and the rare mountain lion are at the top of the charismatic mega-fauna list, but at least sixty other species of mammals make the desert their home—from kit foxes on the valley floors to squirrels on the highest mountain crests. The best way to observe these desert denizens is on foot, far from the madding crowd, in the peace and solitude of desert wilderness.

Anza-Borrego Desert State Park is within the Colorado (Sonoran) Desert, which extends deep into Arizona and Mexico. This is the hottest and lowest of the desert types, with elevations from below sea level to 4,500 feet. Temperatures are among the highest in the United States, with summer highs of 120 degrees or more. Characteristic plants include jumping cholla, creosote bushes, ocotillo, and ironwood.

Joshua Tree National Park is in the transition zone between the Colorado and Mojave Deserts, accounting for much of its rich diversity of plant and animal life. The Mojave Desert is the smallest of the four North American deserts and lies mostly in southeastern California. Elevations range from below sea level to around 4,000 feet, with average elevations of 3,000 feet in the rugged eastern portion, which includes the Mojave National Preserve. The hottest temperature ever recorded in the United States—134 degrees—was in the Mojave Desert at Death Valley. Summer temperatures usually exceed 100 degrees, but winter can bring bitter cold, with temperatures sometimes dropping near zero in valleys where dense, frigid air settles at night. Plant cover is typified by Joshua trees, creosote bushes, white bursage, and indigo bushes.

Much of Death Valley National Park is on the southwestern edge of the vast Great Basin desert region, which also encompasses most of Nevada, much of Utah, and portions of Oregon, Idaho, and Wyoming. This is high, cold desert, largely above 4,000 feet, with snow and freezing temperatures during winter. The Great Basin is distinguished by sunken interior drainage basins bounded by hundreds of mountain ranges, created by shifting along fault lines. Rubber rabbitbrush, blackbrush, and big sagebrush characterize the plant cover.

Death Valley, Joshua Tree, and Anza-Borrego are included within the Colorado and Mojave Desert Biosphere Reserve, which was internationally designated in 1984. There are more than 265 biosphere reserves worldwide that protect lands within each of the earth's biogeographic regions. The parks are within the core of the biosphere reserve where human impact is kept to a minimum. The core is surrounded by a multiple-use area where sustainable development is the guiding principle. In Death Valley the "human connection" of the reserve is represented by members of the Timbisha Shoshone Indian tribe who live within the park.

Each of the desert parks receives many international visitors who are drawn to the desert because there is no desert in their homeland. Many come during the peak of summer to experience the desert at its hottest. Regardless of whether the visitor is from Europe, a nearby California town, or someplace across the nation, the endlessly varied desert offers something for everyone. Unlike snowbound northern regions, the California desert is a year-round hiker's paradise. There is no better place in which to actually see the raw, exposed forces of land-shaping geology at work. Those interested in history and paleoarchaeology will have a field day. And the list goes on. This book is designed to enhance the enjoyment of all who wish to sample the richness of California's desert parks on their own terms. Travel is best done on foot, with distance and destination being far less important than the experience of getting there.

The California Desert Protection Act of 1994

The California Desert Protection Act of 1994 was one of the last measures passed by the 103rd Congress. More than eight years of vigorous lobbying by a huge alliance of local concerned citizens, the California Desert Coalition, and national environmental groups culminated in this monumental legislation, the largest wilderness designation since the 1980 Alaska Lands Bill, and the largest ever in the lower forty-eight. The law upgraded Death Valley and Joshua Tree National Monuments to national park status and enlarged the territory of each of them. Death Valley National Park, at 3.3 million acres, is now the largest national park outside of Alaska. Joshua Tree was likewise enlarged to 793,955 acres from its original 560,000 acres. The 1.4 million acres of the East Mojave National Scenic Area became the Mojave National Preserve and was transferred from the commodity-oriented Bureau of Land Management (BLM) to the preservation-minded National Park Service. Wilderness areas were designated within these new national parks and preserve, and sixty-nine new wilderness areas were established on nearby BLM, national forest, and wildlife-refuge lands in the California desert.

The California Desert Protection Act had both friends and foes. To gain passage, it was necessary to compromise often. Thus, while federal wilderness protection was provided for six million acres, many preexisting uses are also permitted to continue under the act. Preexisting mining, grazing, and military overflights are allowed in Mojave National Preserve and in the expansion regions of Death Valley and Joshua Tree. A major last-minute concession to gain passage involved hunting in Mojave; thus, this region is not a national park (where hunting is not allowed), but instead, to permit continued hunting, was named a national preserve.

While passage of the Desert Protection Act was widely hailed both in California and throughout the nation, pockets of opposition to the new status of these desert wildlands continue. In the 104th Congress, local congressional hostility to the new regulations threatened to severely reduce funding for the Mojave National Preserve. Instead, political stalemate over the federal budget resulted in providing no funds for Mojave under the National Park Service's continuing resolution. During 1995 operations at Mojave were brought to a standstill, halting the implementation of the Desert Protection Act in one of the largest federally protected wilderness areas in the lower forty-eight states.

The 1994 law proclaimed that "federally owned desert lands of southern California constitute a public wildland resource of extraordinary and inestimable value for this and future generations." It is indeed noteworthy that it is in the nation's most populous state—and one of the fastest-growing states as well—that the recognition of wilderness protection as essential to preserve the quality of life for all citizens resulted in passage of this law. These desert lands are close to huge and rapidly expanding urban areas; this is exactly what makes these vast desert spaces even more valuable as protected wildlands.

Changing from national monument to national park status represents a gigantic step. While both monuments and parks are administered by the National Park Service and thus appear to be identical to the visitor, the permanence of these entities is different. A national monument is designated by executive order of the president. The original 1.6-million-acre Death Valley National Monument was created by President Herbert Hoover in 1933. Joshua Tree National Monument, 825,000 acres, was created by President Franklin Roosevelt's executive order in 1936. But what can be created by the stroke of a pen can also be removed, as the history of Joshua Tree illustrates. In 1950 and again in 1961 Joshua Tree's acreage was reduced by acts of Congress in response to demands of the mining industry. Now, as a national park, its boundaries are both expanded and more sacrosanct.

Although funding will always be a concern, these desert wildlands are safer from development and exploitation with park or preserve status. The proponents of desert protection worked for decades to achieve their goal. Much of the California desert, which took many thousands of years to form, is now assured a protected future. What Congress designates, however, Congress can also take away. Only through the continued support of the American people will these fragile lands remain protected.

The Meaning and Value of Wilderness

With millions of acres of California desert parks designated as wilderness in both the state and federal systems, visitors to these wildlands should appreciate the meaning and values of wilderness, if for no other reason than to better enjoy their visits with less impact on the wildland values, which is what attracted them in the first place. Nearly 14 percent of California (almost fourteen million acres) is designated federal wilderness, making the Golden State the premier wilderness state in the continental United States. The California Desert Protection Act of 1994 doubled the wilderness acreage in the state and tripled the amount of wilderness under National Park Service jurisdiction, increasing from two million to six million acres.

Those who know and love wild country have their own personal definition of wilderness, heartfelt and often unexpressed, which varies with each person. But since Congress reserved to itself the exclusive power to designate wilderness in the monumental Wilderness Act of 1964, it is important that we also understand the *legal* meaning of "wilderness." The California Wilderness Act, which applies to much of Anza-Borrego Desert State Park, is patterned largely after the federal statute, so the following applies to both federal and state of California wilderness.

The most fundamental purpose of the Wilderness Act is to provide an *enduring* resource of wilderness for this and future generations so that a growing, increasingly mechanized human population does not occupy and modify every last wild niche. Just as important as preserving the land is the preservation of natural processes, such as naturally ignited fire, erosion, landslides, and other forces that shape the land. Before 1964 the uncertain whim of administrative fiat was all that protected wilderness. During the 1930s the "commanding general" of the wilderness battle, Wilderness Society cofounder Bob Marshall, described wilderness as a "snowbank melting on a hot June day." In the desert the analogy might be closer to a sand dune shrinking on a windy day. Declassification of much of Joshua Tree National Monument prior to its present park status certainly illustrates lack of permanency for land lacking statutory protection.

The act defines wilderness as undeveloped federal lands (or state lands in the case of the California Wilderness System) "where the earth and its community of life are untrammeled by man, where man is a visitor who does not remain." In old English the word "trammel" means a net, so "untrammeled" conveys the idea of land that is unnetted or uncontrolled by humans. Congress recognized that no land is completely free of human influence, going on to say that wilderness must "generally appear to have been affected primarily by the forces of nature, with the imprint of man's work substantially unnoticeable." Further, a "wilderness" must have outstanding opportunities for solitude or primitive and unconfined recreation, and be at least 5,000 acres in size or large enough to preserve and use in an unimpaired condition. Also, wilderness may contain ecological, geological, or other features of scientific, educational, scenic, or historical value. The various stretches of California desert parks wilderness described in this book meet and easily exceed these legal requirements. Any lingering doubts are removed by the distant music of a coyote beneath a star-studded desert sky, or by the soothing rhythm of an oasis waterfall in a remote canyon.

In general, wilderness designation protects the land from development such as roads, buildings, motorized vehicles, and equipment, and from commercial uses except preexisting livestock grazing, outfitting, and the development of mining claims and leases validated before the 1984 cutoff date in the federal Wilderness Act. The act set up the National Wilderness System and empowered three federal agencies to administer wilderness: the Forest Service, the Fish and Wildlife Service, and the National Park Service. The Bureau of Land Management was added to the list with passage of the 1976 Federal Land Policy and Management Act. These agencies can and do make wilderness recommendations, as any citizen can, but only Congress can set aside wilderness on federal lands, or the state of California in the case of Anza-Borrego Desert State Park. This is where politics enters in, epitomizing the kind of grassroots democracy that eventually brought about passage of the landmark California Desert Protection Act. The formula for wilderness conservationists has been and continues to be "endless pressure endlessly applied."

But once designated, the unending job of wilderness stewardship is just beginning. The managing agencies have a special responsibility to administer wilderness in "such manner as will leave them (wilderness areas) unimpaired for future use and enjoyment *as wilderness.*" Unimpairment of wilderness over time can only be achieved through partnership between concerned citizens and the agencies.

Wilderness is the only truly biocentric use of land. It is off-limits to intensive human uses with an objective of preserving the diversity of nonhuman life, which is richly endowed in the California desert. As such, its preservation is our society's highest act of humility. This is where we deliberately slow down our impulse to drill the last barrel of oil, mine the last vein of ore, or build a parking lot on top of the last wild peak. The desert wilderness explorer can take genuine pride in reaching a remote summit under his or her power, traversing a narrow serpentine canyon, or walking across the uncluttered expanse of a vast desert basin. Hiking boots and self-reliance replace motorized equipment and push-button convenience, allowing us to find something in ourselves we feared lost.

Have Fun and Be Safe

Wandering in the desert has a reputation of being a dangerous activity, thanks to both the Bible and Hollywood. Usually depicted as a wasteland, the desert evokes fear. With proper planning, however, desert hiking is not hazardous. In fact, it is fun and exciting and is quite safe.

An enjoyable desert outing requires preparation. Beginning with this book, along with the maps suggested in the hike write-ups, you need to be equipped with adequate knowledge about your hiking area. Carry good maps and a compass, and know how to use them.

Calculating the time required for a hike in the desert defies any formula. Terrain is often rough; extensive detours around boulders, dry falls, and drop-offs mean longer trips. Straight-line distance is an illusion. Sun, heat, and wind likewise all conspire to slow down even the speediest hiker. Therefore, distances are not what they appear in the desert. Five desert miles may take longer than 10 woodland miles. Plan your excursion conservatively, and always carry emergency items in your pack (see appendix B).

While you consult the equipment list (appendix B), note that water ranks the highest. Carrying the water is not enough—take the time to stop and drink it. This is another reason why desert hikes take longer. Frequent water breaks are mandatory. It's best to return from your hike with empty water bottles. You can cut down on loss of bodily moisture by hiking with your mouth closed and breathing through your nose; reduce thirst also by avoiding sweets and alcohol.

Driving to and from the trailhead is statistically far more dangerous than hiking in the desert backcountry. But being far from the nearest 911 service requires knowledge about possible hazards and proper precautions to avoid them. It is not an oxymoron to have fun and to be safe. Quite to the contrary: If you're not safe, you won't have fun. At the risk of creating excessive paranoia, here are the treacherous twelve:

Dehydration

It cannot be overemphasized that plenty of water is necessary for desert hiking. Carry one gallon per person per day in unbreakable plastic screw-top containers. And pause often to drink it. Carry water in your car as well so you'll have water to return to. As a general rule, plain water is a better thirst-quencher than any of the colored fluids on the market, which usually generate greater thirst. It is very impor-tant to maintain proper electrolyte balance by eating small quantities of nutritional foods throughout the day, even if you feel you don't have an appetite.

Changeable Weather

The desert is well known for sudden changes in the weather. The temperature can change 50 degrees in less than an hour. Prepare yourself with extra food and cloth-ing, rain/wind gear, and a flashlight. When leaving on a trip, let someone know your exact route, especially if traveling solo, and your estimated time of return; don't for-get to let them know when you get back. Register your route at the closest park office or backcountry board, especially for longer hikes that involve cross-country travel.

Hypothermia/Hyperthermia

Abrupt chilling is as much a danger in the desert as heat stroke. Storms and/or night-fall can cause desert temperatures to plunge. Wear layers of clothes, adding or sub-tracting depending on conditions, to avoid overheating or chilling. At the other extreme, you need to protect yourself from sun and wind with proper clothing. The broad-brimmed hat is mandatory equipment for the desert traveler. Even in the cool days of winter, a delightful time in the desert, the sun's rays are intense.

Vegetation

You quickly will learn not to come in contact with certain desert vegetation. Cat-claw, Spanish bayonet, and cacti are just a few of the botanical hazards that will get your attention if you become complacent. Carry tweezers to extract cactus spines. Wear long pants if traveling off-trail or in a brushy area. Many folks carry a hair comb to assist with removal of cholla balls.

Rattlesnakes, Scorpions, Tarantulas

These desert "creepy crawlies" are easily terrified by unexpected human visitors, and they react predictably to being frightened. Do not sit or put your hands in dark places you can't see, especially during the warmer "snake season" months. Carry and know how to use your snakebite-venom-extractor kit for emergencies when help is far away. In the event of a snakebite, seek medical assistance as quickly as possible. Keep tents zipped and always shake out boots, packs, and clothes before putting them on.

Mountain Lions

The California desert is mountain-lion country. Avoid hiking at night when lions are often hunting. Instruct your children on appropriate behavior when confronted with a lion. Do not run. Keep children in sight while hiking; stay close to them in areas where lions might hide.

Mine Hazards

The California desert contains thousands of deserted mines. All of them should be considered hazardous. Stay away from all mines and mine structures. The vast majority of these mines have not been secured or even posted. Keep an eye on young or adventuresome members of your group.

Hanta Virus

In addition to the mines, there are often deserted buildings around the mine sites. Hanta virus is a deadly disease carried by deer mice in the Southwest. Any enclosed area increases the chances of breathing the airborne particles that carry this life-threatening virus. As a precaution, do not enter deserted buildings.

Flash Floods

Desert washes and canyons can become traps for unwary visitors when rainstorms hit the desert. Keep a watchful eye on the sky. Never camp in flash-flood areas. Check at a ranger station on regional weather conditions before embarking on your backcountry expedition. A storm anywhere upstream in a drainage can result in a sudden torrent in a lower canyon. Do not cross a flooded wash. Both the depth and the current can be deceiving; wait for the flood to recede, which usually does not take long.

Lightning

Be aware of lightning, especially during summer storms. Stay off ridges and peaks. Shallow overhangs and gullies should also be avoided because electrical current often moves at ground level near a lightning strike.

Unstable Rocky Slopes

Desert canyons and mountainsides often consist of crumbly or fragmented rock. Mountain sheep are better adapted to this terrain than us bipeds. Use caution when climbing; the downward journey is usually the more hazardous. Smooth rock faces such as in slick-rock canyons are equally dangerous, especially when you've got sand on the soles of your boots. On those rare occasions when they are wet, the rocks are slicker than ice.

Giardia

Any surface water, with the possible exception of springs where they flow out of the ground, is apt to contain *Giardia lamblia,* a microorganism that causes severe diarrhea. Boil water for at least five minutes or use a filter system. Iodine drops are not effective in killing this pesky parasite.

Zero-Impact Desert Etiquette

The desert environment is fragile; damage lasts for decades—even centuries. Desert courtesy requires us to leave no evidence that we were ever there. This ethic means no grafitti or defoliation at one end of the spectrum, and no unnecessary footprints on delicate vegetation on the other. Here are seven general guidelines for desert wilderness behavior:

    Avoid making new trails. If hiking cross-country, stay on one set of footprints when traveling in a group. Try to make your route invisible. Desert vegetation grows very slowly. Its destruction leads to wind and water erosion and irreparable harm to the desert. Darker crusty soil that crumbles easily indicates cryptogamic soils, which are a living blend of tightly bonded mosses, lichens, and bacteria. This dark crust prevents wind and water erosion and protects seeds that fall into the soil. Walking can destroy this fragile layer. Take special care to avoid stepping on cryptogamic soil.

Keep noise down. Desert wilderness means quiet and solitude, for the animal life as well as other human visitors.

Leave your pets at home. Most parks have regulations forbidding dogs on trails; check with park authorities before including your dog in the group. Share other experiences with your best friend, not the desert.

Pack it in/pack it out. This is more true in the desert than anywhere. Desert winds spread debris, and desert air preserves it. Always carry a trash bag, both for your trash and for any that you encounter. If you must smoke, pick up your butts and bag them. Bag and carry out toilet paper (it doesn't deteriorate in the desert) and feminine hygiene products.

Never camp near water. Most desert animals are nocturnal, and most, like the bighorn sheep, are exceptionally shy. The presence of humans is very disturbing, so camping near their water source means they will go without water. Camp in already-used sites if possible to reduce further damage. If none is available, camp on ground that is already bare. And use a camp stove. Ground fires are forbidden in most desert parks; gathering wood is also not permitted. Leave your campsite as you found it. Better yet, improve it by picking up litter, cleaning out fire rings, or scattering ashes of any inconsiderate predecessors. Contradictory though it may be, remember that artifacts fifty years old or older are protected by federal law, and must not be moved or removed.

Treat human waste properly. Bury human waste 4 inches deep and at least 200 feet from water and trails. Pack out toilet paper and feminine hygiene products; they do not decompose in the arid desert. Do not burn toilet paper; many wildfires have been started this way.

Respect wildlife. Living in the desert is hard enough without being harassed by human intruders. Remember this is the only home these animals have. They treasure their privacy. Be respectful and use binoculars for long-distance viewing. *Especially important:* Do not molest the rare desert water sources by playing or bathing in them.

Beyond these guidelines, refer to the regulations of the individual park areas for their specific rules governing backcountry usage. Enjoy the beauty and solitude of the desert, and leave it for others to enjoy.

How to Use This Book

This guide is *the* source book for those who wish to experience on foot the very best hikes and backcountry trips the vast and varied California desert has to offer. A broad array of hikes is presented here for each of California's four major desert parks. Hikers are given many choices from which they can pick and choose, depending on their wishes and abilities.

The maps in this book that depict a detailed close-up of an area use elevation tints, called hypsometry, to portray relief. Each gray tone represents a range of equal elevation, as shown in the scale key with the map. These maps will give you a good idea of elevation gain and loss. The darker tones are lower elevations and the lighter grays are higher elevations. The lighter the tone, the higher the elevation. Narrow bands of different gray tones spaced closely together indicate steep terrain, whereas wider bands indicate areas of more gradual slope.

Maps that show larger geographic areas use shaded, or shadow, relief. Shadow relief does not represent elevation; it demonstrates slope or relative steepness. This gives an almost 3-D perspective of the physiography of a region and will help you see where ranges and valleys are.

For a general geographic orientation, begin with the overview map of southeastern California near the front of this book. Here you'll find the relative sizes and locations of the four parks—from Anza-Borrego, just north of the Mexican border, northward to Death Valley. The book is divided into four chapters, one for each of the four major parks. The parks are presented from south to north, beginning with Anza-Borrego Desert State Park, followed by Joshua Tree National Park, Mojave National Preserve, and Death Valley National Park. The numbering of the individual hikes in each park also generally runs south to north, although this is sometimes altered by the clustering of hikes sharing common access. This south-to-north presentation roughly parallels the progression of seasons. For example, spring comes earlier in Anza-Borrego as compared to Death Valley, due to its lower average elevation. Thus, the desert hiker seeking comfortable hiking weather can start the season earlier in Anza-Borrego and work gradually to the more northern desert parks as the season advances.

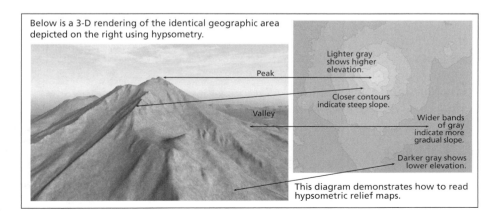

Below is a 3-D rendering of the identical geographic area depicted on the right using hypsometry.

Peak

Valley

Lighter gray shows higher elevation.

Closer contours indicate steep slope.

Wider bands of gray indicate more gradual slope.

Darker gray shows lower elevation.

This diagram demonstrates how to read hypsometric relief maps.

After selecting the park you'll be visiting, refer to the hike locator map at the beginning of the applicable section, along with the "Hikes at a Glance" matrix for a quick overview of all of the hikes presented for the park. After making your selections, turn to the specific hike descriptions for added detail. Each hike is numbered and named and begins with a general description. This overview briefly describes the type of hike and highlights the destination and key features.

The "start" is the approximate road distance from a nearby town or park visitor center to the trailhead. The idea is to give you a mental picture of where the hike is in relation to your prospective travels.

Hike "distance" is given in total miles for the described route. The mileage is in one direction for a loop, in which you return to the place where you started without retracing your steps, or for a one-way hike, in which you begin at one trailhead and end at another, requiring two vehicles, a shuttle bus, or another driver to pick you up or deposit you at either end. Round-trip mileage is provided for an out-and-back hike, in which you return to the trailhead the same way you came. A lollipop loop combines a stretch of out-and-back with a loop at one end. Mileages were calculated in the field and double-checked as accurately as possible with the most detailed topographic maps.

"Approximate hiking time" provides a best guess as to how long it will take the average hiker to complete the route. Always add more time for further exploration or for contemplation.

The "difficulty" rating is necessarily subjective, but it is based on the authors' extensive backcountry experience with folks of all ages and abilities. Easy hikes present no difficulty to hikers of all abilities. Moderate hikes are challenging to inexperienced hikers and might tax even experienced hikers. Strenuous hikes are extremely difficult and challenging, even for the most-seasoned hikers. Distance, elevation gain and loss, trail condition, and terrain were considered in assigning the difficulty rating. There are, of course, many variables. The easiest hike can be sheer torture if you run out of water in extreme heat—a definite no-no.

"Trail surfaces" are evaluated based on well-defined trail standards. Dirt trails have no obstructions and are easy to follow. Rocky trails may be partially blocked by slides, rocks, or debris but are generally obvious and easy to find. Primitive trails are faint, rough, and rocky and may have disappeared completely in places. In the desert some of the best hiking takes place on old four-wheel-drive mining roads that are now closed to vehicular use because of wilderness designation or to protect key values, such as wildlife watering holes. Many of the desert hikes are off-trail in washes, canyons, ridges, and fans. "Use trails" may form a segment of the route. A use trail is simply an informal, unconstructed path created solely by the passage of hikers.

The best "season" is based largely on the moderate-temperature months for the particular hike and is greatly influenced by elevation. Additional consideration is given to seasonal road access at higher altitudes. The range of months given is not necessarily the best time for wildflowers, which is highly localized and dependent on elevation and rainfall. Nor is it necessarily the best time to view wildlife, which may be during the driest and hottest summer months near water sources.

The maps listed are the best available for route-finding and land navigation: the relevant 7.5-minute topographic map (1:24,000 scale or 2.6 inches = 1 mile) with a 40-foot contour interval. These U.S. Geological Survey maps can usually be purchased at the park visitor centers, except at Mojave. They can also be purchased for $6.00 each (price as of this writing) directly from Map Distribution, USGS Map Sales, Box 25286, Federal Center, Building 810, Denver, CO 80225; by calling (800) ASK–USGS; or online at www.usgs.gov/pubprod/. See appendix C for a listing of other useful smaller-scale maps for each park.

For more information on the hike, the best available "trail contact" for the park management agency is listed. See appendix D for a complete listing of all agency addresses and phone numbers.

"Finding the trailhead" includes detailed up-to-date driving instructions to the trailhead or jumping-off point for each hike. For most hikes, there is no formal trailhead but rather a starting point where you can park. To follow these instructions, start with the beginning reference point, which might be the park visitor center, nearby town, or important road junction. Pay close attention to mileage and landmark instructions. American Automobile Association (AAA) map mileages are used when available, but in many instances we had to rely on our car odometer, which may vary slightly from other car odometers.

The text following the driving directions is a narrative of the actual route with general directions and key features noted. In some cases interpretation of the natural and cultural history of the hike and its surroundings is included. The idea is to provide accurate route-finding instructions, with enough supporting information to enhance your enjoyment of the hike without diminishing your sense of discovery—a fine line indeed. Some of these descriptions are augmented with photographs that preview a representative segment of the hike.

The trail itinerary, "Miles and Directions," provides detailed mile-by-mile instructions while noting landmarks, trail junctions, canyon entrances, dry falls, peaks, and historic sites along the way.

And last, please don't allow our value-laden list of "favorite hikes" (appendix A) to discourage you from completing any of the other hikes. They're all worth doing!

Map Legend

Boundaries

	National wilderness/ preserve boundary
	National park boundary
	State park boundary
	County park boundary
— · — · ·	State boundary

Transportation

15	Interstate
95	U.S. highway
62	State highway
522	Primary road
	Other road
	Unpaved road
= = = = =	Unimproved road
	Featured unimproved road
	Featured trail
·············	Optional trail
- - - - - - -	Other trail
┼┼┼┼┼┼	Railroad
·—·—·—	Power line

Hydrology

	Intermittent stream
℘	Spring
//	Fall
	Lake
	Dry lake
	Lava bed
	Sand/wash

Physiography

×	Spot elevation
) (	Pass
▲	Peak
∩	Cave
⊔⊔⊔	Cliff

Symbols

🚶	Trailhead
START	Trail start
❷	Trail locator
↻	Trail turnaround
P	Parking
🚻	Restroom/toilet
△	Campground
▲	Backcountry campground
♠	Lodging
❓	Visitor center
	Ranger station
☏	Telephone
⊞	Picnic area
○	Town
👁	Overlook
▪	Point of interest
⚒	Mine/prospect
•—•	Gate
⋈	Bridge
✈ ▬	Airport/ landing strip

Anza-Borrego Desert State Park

Anza–Borrego Desert State Park was set aside by the state of California in 1933, decades before the state's population expanded and desert junctions grew into cities. Anza–Borrego's irregular boundary encloses 600,000 acres, making it California's largest state park, 63 percent of which is protected in twelve wilderness areas. One thousand private inholdings are located within the park; the town of Borrego Springs is an island surrounded by it. The name Anza–Borrego, adopted in 1957, is a blend of the human and natural history of the San Diego desert: *Anza* for the Spanish explorer who traversed the region with a party of emigrants in 1774, and *Borrego,* a Spanish word meaning bighorn sheep, for those animals that still make these desert mountains and canyons their home.

Ten million years ago the Anza-Borrego region formed the floor of a great inland sea. As the mountains rose and the Colorado River delta expanded, the area was eventually blocked from the sea, and the water diminished. A million years ago mastodons and saber-tooths roamed the savannahs around the receding estuary. Early man arrived in the region at least 10,000 years ago and enjoyed the temperate climate of Southern California. The rivers, lakes, and grasslands provided a bountiful environment for humans and animals. Gradual warming began 8,000 years ago. Rising mountains to the west, driven upward by faults and earthquakes as tectonic plates collided, blocked the moisture-laden oceanic winds. Ancient ice-age lakes became playas. The desert began to form.

The earth's dynamics that created the landscape at Anza-Borrego are still at work. Like many desert regions, the park is a geology lab in action. The San Andreas Fault, to the north and east of the park, is constantly shifting. Park elevations range from 15 feet near Travertine Point (northeast corner of the park) to 6,193 feet at Combs Peak in the Bucksnort Mountains on the west. Vast valleys, badlands, canyons, oases, and mountain ranges are included in this varied geological wonderland.

Natural and Human History

Animals, plants, and man adapted to a changing climate as this Southern California region became a desert. The endangered desert pupfish are well-known residents of

Native California fan palm grove at the Borrego Palm Oasis.

Anza-Borrego that date from earlier times. As the prehistoric inland sea shrank and increased in salinity, this hardy member of the minnow family adapted to the new conditions. Pupfish can live within a broad range of temperatures (from 34 to more than 108 degrees F) and in water twice as saline as seawater. Ponds at the park's visitor center and the Borrego Palm Canyon trailhead harbor pupfish schools.

Of the famed Peninsular bighorn sheep, only about 400 of these rare animals remain. Researchers are actively engaged in finding the cause of their continued decline here in the park. Three groups live in the Santa Rosa Mountains, the Vallecitos Mountains, and Carrizo Gorge, while two more herds hang out in Coyote and Palm Canyons. Hikers may spot these elusive denizens of the desert in the rocky, high backcountry. Sheep also drop down to canyon water sources every few days for an early-morning drink. They can be seen in Borrego Palm Canyon or at other streams. Because the shrunken water sources of summer put pressure on the sheep

Pond near the beginning of the Borrego Palm Canyon trail ▶
provides a sanctuary for the endangered desert pupfish.

population, Coyote Canyon is closed to all human visitors from June 1 through September 30 to protect the sheep's access to water there.

In addition to these two celebrity species, nearly 60 mammal species, 270 bird species, 27 snake species, and 31 lizard species call Anza-Borrego home, dispelling the myth that there is no life in the desert. An evening coyote chorus is evidence of a flourishing rodent food chain. It does take a sharp eye to spot desert creatures. Many are nocturnal, and most are very shy. Do not camp, therefore, within 200 yards of a water source to allow the animals a chance to drink. The twenty-five oases in the park are the most likely locations for viewing wildlife.

In the botanical kingdom, Anza-Borrego is in the Colorado (Sonoran) Desert. California fan palms *(Washingtonia filifera)*, the only palm tree native to California, are numerous at the springs and oases and in the canyons of Anza-Borrego. The rare elephant tree *(Bursera microphylla)* exists here and nowhere else in California. Chaparral vegetation dominates the higher mountains on the western side of the park. At lower elevations creosote bushes and ocotillo are common. Twenty-two varieties of cacti, especially several of the ubiquitous cholla family, flourish, ranging from the 3-inch fishhook cactus to the barrel cactus, sometimes over 8 feet tall. Removing or disturbing any of these plants is forbidden by law.

The spectacular spring bloom of desert wildflowers attracts thousands of visitors annually. The flower season ranges from late February through April, depending on the weather. Park naturalists will notify you of the anticipated peak bloom. Send a self-addressed stamped postcard to WILDFLOWERS, Anza-Borrego Desert State Park, 200 Palm Canyon Drive, Borrego Springs, CA 92004, if you would like to be notified about two weeks before the peak. The park also maintains a flower hotline, (760) 767–4684, or can be visited on the Web at www.anzaborrego.statepark.org.

Man is a relative newcomer, arriving from 6,000 to 10,000 years ago. These early inhabitants left few artifacts. They left no pottery since they stored their food in rock-lined caches. They hunted with spears, not the more advanced bow and arrow. Beginning 2,000 years ago, the Kumeyaay people from the Colorado River, and the Cahuilla people from the Great Basin, migrated to the Anza-Borrego region. These were seminomadic hunter-gatherers. Sites of their *morteros,* pictographs, and petroglyphs are numerous, as are their fire rings and fire pits, their ancient trails, campsite middens, and fragments of pottery. All artifacts are protected by law and must not be altered or removed by visitors. Please leave these traces of prior inhabitants for future generations to enjoy.

Beginning in the eighteenth century with the Anza expedition, Spanish and American groups have traveled through this desert, heading for the coastal areas of Southern California. Several historical routes of emigrants and stages can be seen in the Blair Valley and Collins Valley areas. In the late nineteenth century, ranchers and farmers began to settle in Borrego Springs and the nearby valleys. Their efforts to make the desert productive had varied results. Today stock watering tanks can be found in remote corners of the park, remnants of the defunct cattle industry, whereas

Wilson Trail leading to the northwest at mile 1.3.

the green orchards of Borrego Valley indicate greater success for the growers. Unlike the other desert parks of Southern California, Anza-Borrego was never the scene of frenzied mining activity. Mine openings and tailings do not dot the mountainsides.

How and When to Get There

Anza-Borrego Desert State Park is 80 miles east of San Diego at the eastern border of San Diego County. Interstate 8 passes by the park's southern boundary on the way to El Centro. California Highway 78 is the major access route to the central region of the park. County Road S22 is the highway to Borrego Springs, where the park visitor center is located.

The nearest commercial airports are in San Diego and Palm Springs, although an airport in Borrego Springs provides facilities for private aircraft and refueling.

Although the summer is typically sizzling in Anza-Borrego, with temperatures well over 100 degrees F, the remainder of the year features highs from 70 to 85 degrees. Average annual rainfall at park headquarters is about 6 inches, but that figure can be misleading. Winter months may bring heavy downpours. The summer months also have occasional thunderstorms. Heavy rains in any season may result in flash flooding, washouts, and road closures. Always check the park Web site before heading to Anza-Borrego.

Park Regulations

Anza-Borrego Desert State Park has no entrance fee. It is also one of the few California parks that permit open camping. The open-camping policy has resulted in a tradition of care and consideration; roadside campsites are clean and well cared for. Vehicles must remain within one car-length of the road, and all fires must be enclosed in metal containers. Visitors should not camp within 200 yards of water sources to protect animals' access to water. Developed fee campgrounds are near the visitor center in Borrego Springs and at Tamarisk Grove; open camping is not permitted near these two sites. Several undeveloped no-fee campgrounds are also located throughout the park.

All vehicles must be highway legal and must stay on the 500 miles of established roads within the park. Drivers must be licensed. Ocotillo Wells State Vehicular Recreation Area is immediately east of the park on CA 78 for off-road-vehicle driving, where a driver's license is not required

In Anza-Borrego, bicycles too must remain on the paved and dirt roads. There are more than 500 miles of roads in the park open to bicycles. The park has published a new mountain-biking guide, available at any ranger station.

No dogs are permitted on the trails of Anza-Borrego. On roadways and in campgrounds, dogs must be on leashes no longer than 6 feet. It is advised that you leave your pet at home. Lack of water, heat, coyotes, cacti, and rattlesnakes all make the desert inhospitable to pets.

Backcountry permits are not required for backpacking. However, registering your trip plan with the ranger at the regional ranger station is recommended for safety.

All cultural and natural contents of the park are protected by state law. No collecting of any kind is permitted. Carrying a loaded weapon of any kind and hunting are likewise forbidden in the park.

The visitor center just west of Borrego Springs is open daily 9:00 A.M. to 5:00 P.M. from October through May. From June through September it is open only on weekends and holidays from 9:00 A.M. to 5:00 P.M. Maps, publications, slide and video shows, and informational exhibits are available here. There is also a signed nature trail featuring much of the variety of desert plants found in the Colorado (Sonoran) Desert. Check here for current regulations and road conditions. Several self-guided-hike brochures are available at the visitor center, providing information for hikes and auto tours throughout the park.

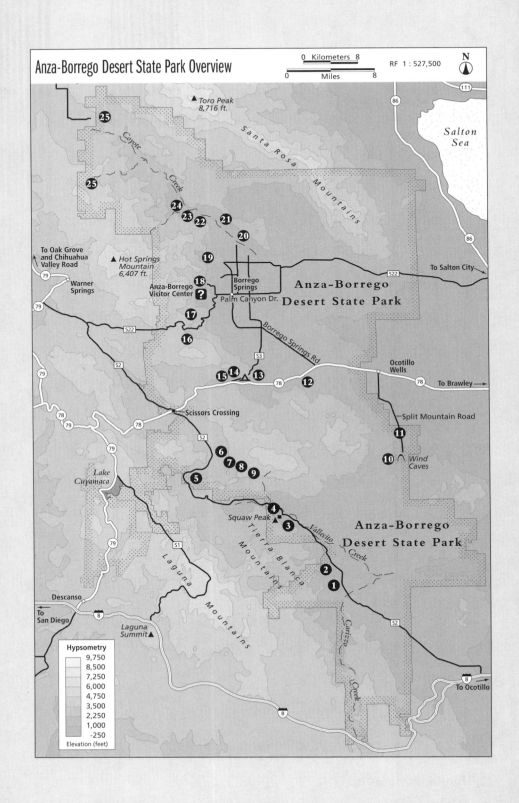

Anza-Borrego Desert State Park Overview

0　Kilometers　8

RF 1 : 527,500

0　Miles　8

N

▲ Toro Peak
8,716 ft.

Salton
Sea

Santa Rosa Mountains

Coyote Creek

25

25

24
23 **22**
21
20
19

86

86

111

To Salton City

S22

Anza-Borrego
Desert State Park

Borrego
Springs

To Oak Grove
and Chihuahua
Valley Road

▲ Hot Springs
Mountain
6,407 ft.

79

Warner
Springs

79

Anza-Borrego
Visitor Center

18
?

17

16

Palm Canyon Dr.

Borrego Springs Rd

S3

S22

S2

79

79

78

79

78

15 **14**
△ **13**
78
12

Scissors Crossing

S2

Ocotillo
Wells

78　To Brawley →

Split Mountain Road

11

10 ⌒ Wind
Caves

Lake
Cuyamaca

6
7 **8**
5 **9**

4
Squaw Peak ▲ **3**

Vallecito Creek

S1

Tierra Blanca Mountains

Anza-Borrego
Desert State Park

2

1

79

Laguna Mountains

Descanso

To
San Diego

8

Laguna
Summit ▲

Carrizo Creek

S2

8

8
To Ocotillo

Hypsometry

| |
| 9,750 |
| 8,500 |
| 7,250 |
| 6,000 |
| 4,750 |
| 3,500 |
| 2,250 |
| 1,000 |
| -250 |

Elevation (feet)

Anza-Borrego Desert State Park Hikes at a Glance

Hike (Number)	Distance	Difficulty*	Features	Page
Alcoholic Pass (20)	3.4 miles	M	vista	67
Borrego Palm Canyon Nature Trail (19)	3.5 miles	M	oasis	65
Box Canyon Overlook (5)	1.8 miles	E	historic site	34
Cactus Loop Trail (14)	1.0 mile	E	nature trail	54
California R & H Trail (17)	8.5 miles	S	vistas	59
Cougar Canyon (23)	3.0 miles	M/S	canyon	75
Elephant Trees Nature Trail (11)	1.0 mile	E	nature trail	48
Foot and Walker Pass (6)	0.2 mile	E	historic site	37
Ghost Mountain (7)	2.0 miles	M	historic site, vista	38
Indian Canyon (22)	4.5 miles	S	canyon	73
Kenyon Overlook Trail Loop (13)	1.0 mile	E	vista	51
Lower Willows (21)	4.0 miles	M	stream, canyon	70
Moonlight Canyon (3)	1.5 miles	M	canyon	29
The Morteros (8)	0.5 mile	E	archaeological site	41
Mountain Palm Springs Loop (1)	6.5 miles	M	oases	23
Narrows Earth Trail (12)	0.5 mile	E	geology	50
Pacific Crest Trail S. (25)	5.0 miles	S	mountain peak	81
Pacific Crest Trail N. (25)	5.0 miles	M	mountain peak	81
Panorama Overlook/Extended Overlook (18)	2.6 miles	S	vista	62
Pictograph Trail (9)	3.0 miles	E	archaeological site	43
Sheep Canyon (24)	3.0 miles	S	canyon, oasis	78
Squaw Peak/Pond (4)	1.9 miles	E	vista, oasis	32
Torote Canyon (2)	4.0 miles	M	elephant trees	27
Wilson Trail (16)	11.0 miles	M	vistas	56
Wind Caves (10)	1.4 miles	M	geology, archaeological site	45
Yaqui Well Nature Trail (15)	2.0 miles	E	nature trail	55

*E=easy, M=moderate, S=strenuous

1 Mountain Palm Springs Loop

This loop trail in the eastern Tierra Blanca Mountains has several short but steep climbs as it leads to two short forks. Here you will find several native palm groves at isolated oases. These hidden patches of greenery provide excellent birding sites.

Start: About 52 miles south of Borrego Springs.
Distance: 6.5-mile loop with two side trips.
Approximate hiking time: 5 hours.
Difficulty: Moderate.
Trail surface: Mostly clear trail with several clear wash stretches along with short, good sections of rocky cutoff trails.

Seasons: October through April.
USGS topo map: Sweeney Pass-CA (1:24,000).
Trail contact: Anza-Borrego Desert State Park (see appendix D).

Finding the trailhead: From the park visitor center, go 1.9 miles east on Palm Canyon Drive to Christmas Circle; from the circle, take Borrego Springs Road (S3) south for 5.6 miles to the Y intersection, where you bear right. Continue on S3 7.4 miles to the Tamarisk Grove intersection with California Highway 78. Go right (west) on CA 78 for 7.4 miles to Scissors Crossing. Turn left (south) on Park Route S2. Drive 31.8 miles south on S2. Shortly after mile marker 47, turn right (west) onto the dirt road for the Mountain Palm Springs Campground. Continue 0.5 mile to the trailhead and parking area.

The Hike

The Mountain Palm Springs oasis loop is really two separate hikes from the same trailhead to the end point of both hikes: the extensive Palm Bowl Grove. The resulting combination is a wonderful loop to all six of the captivating palm groves in the Mountain Palm Springs complex. Both trails lead up sandy washes, one westward and the other to the north. It is preferable to begin on the south leg of the loop by heading west to the Pygmy Grove, but it makes little difference which way you hike the loop.

The native California fan palm derives its name from the shape of its leaves. As the tree produces new leaves at the top of its trunk, skirts of older leaves die and droop over the lower part of the tree, giving it the distinctive full look characteristic of these palms. These groves are remnants of ancient savannahs. Here water and shade attract scores of bird species, such as the hooded oriole, which weaves its nest on the underside of palm fronds. You may also catch a glimpse of a great horned owl, mourning dove, cactus wren, or western bluebird. In the fall coyotes help regenerate the trees by eating their tiny fruits and leaving seed-laden droppings in new locations.

On the south end of the loop, head west up a sandy wash to the first small grove of four large palm trees at 0.4 mile. Continue up the main wash another 0.4 mile to Pygmy Grove, named after the larger grove of short, fire-scarred trees. The third

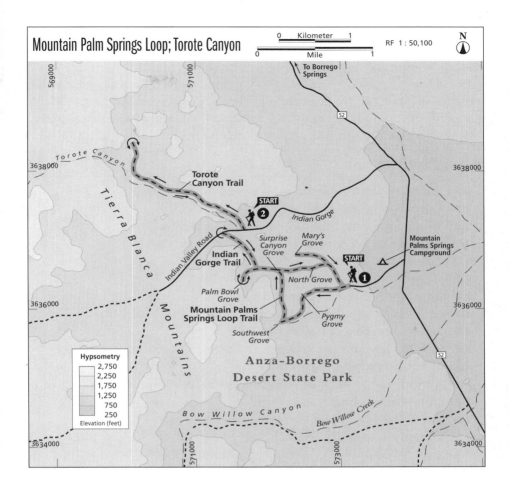

Mountain Palm Springs Loop; Torote Canyon

0   Kilometer   1

0   Mile   1

RF 1 : 50,100

N

To Borrego Springs

Torote Canyon

Torote Canyon Trail

START 2

Indian Gorge

Tierra Blanca

Indian Valley Road

Surprise Canyon Grove

Mary's Grove

Indian Gorge Trail

START 1

Mountain Palms Springs Campground

North Grove

Palm Bowl Grove

Mountain Palms Springs Loop Trail

Pygmy Grove

Southwest Grove

Mountains

Anza-Borrego Desert State Park

Hypsometry
2,750
2,250
1,750
1,250
750
250
Elevation (feet)

Bow Willow Canyon

Bow Willow Creek

S2

small grove consists of five trees in a tight cluster. From here a rocky ravine leads to the right another 0.2 mile to a single palm tree. Turn left up the main valley to a fork in the trail at 1.2 miles. Continue to the right another 0.3 mile to the sizable Southwest Grove, which can be seen straight ahead. Pools of water and nearby elephant trees make this peaceful oasis an enjoyable interlude during the loop hike.

From Southwest Grove, take a fairly distinct trail northward over a rocky ridge 1 mile to Surprise Canyon. From here turn left and walk up the canyon another 0.5 mile to the largest and most luxuriant grove in the complex, Palm Bowl. On the way back down from Palm Bowl Grove, look for the signed Indian Gorge Cutoff Trail leading to the north. This old Indian trail is signed 0.5 MILE TO INDIAN GORGE. The actual distance is closer to 0.7 mile. The narrow, rocky trail gains 200 feet to the top

◀ *The palms of Mary's Grove are tightly clustered on the north end of the Mountain Palm Springs Loop.*

of the ridge then angles down left into Indian Valley. The round-trip distance from Surprise Canyon to Indian Valley is 1.4 miles, providing yet more variety to this already diverse hiking loop.

To complete the loop from Surprise Canyon, continue down the wash to the parking area/trailhead. North Grove is reached 0.5 mile down the canyon, Mary's Grove is a 0.6-mile side trip to the left, and from this junction the trailhead is only another 0.5 mile.

Miles and Directions

0.0 From the trailhead, head west up the sandy wash.

0.8 Arrive at Pygmy Grove.

1.0 Turn left next to a single palm tree and head up the main wash.

1.2 Stay right at the fork in the trail.

1.5 Arrive at Southwest Grove.

2.5 At Surprise Canyon, turn left and walk up to Palm Bowl Grove.

3.0 This is Palm Bowl Grove, the turnaround point.

3.3 Turn left (north) on the signed Indian Gorge Trail.

4.0 Use the turnaround point at Indian Valley Road.

4.7 You're back at Surprise Canyon for completion of the 1.4-mile out-and-back side hike.

4.9 Turn left (east) at Surprise Canyon Grove.

5.4 At North Grove, turn left (north) for the short walk to Mary's Grove.

5.7 Use the turnaround point at Mary's Grove.

6.0 Back at North Grove, continue south to the trailhead.

6.5 Complete the loop back at the trailhead.

Option: If you start the hike on the northern leg of the loop, the trail leads north from the parking area up a sandy wash or, if you prefer firmer footing, up the right bank of the wash. Straight ahead you can catch a glimpse of palm trees 0.2 mile farther. The wash grows progressively rockier as you approach Mary's Grove, where huge 30- to 40-foot palms tower above the rocky gorge. Retrace your steps 0.3 mile back down the wash to the trailpost that marks the mouth of the wash that runs westward. The intersection is rocky, but this new wash becomes sandy as it gains slightly in elevation.

As you continue west up the new wash, you will pass North Grove, which consists of several clumps of palm trees, providing a delightful shady interlude in your journey. One spot to keep in mind for later is a distinctive row of palms (appropriately called Surprise Canyon Grove), for it is there that a marked cutoff trail climbs over the ridge to the south to the Southwest Grove. Meanwhile, however, keep moving west, because another lovely surprise awaits you: a huge array of majestic palms arranged like an orchestra in an amphitheater valley. This is the Palm Bowl Grove. Plan on allowing ample time to enjoy this magical place before hiking back down the wash.

2 Torote Canyon

Torote Canyon is a half-day out-and-back hike through a sandy wash and boulder-strewn canyon with intermittent wide basins ringed by rugged rock ridges. A sizable "herd" of elephant trees can be seen within the first 0.5 mile.

See map on page 25.
Start: About 50 miles south of Borrego Springs.
Distance: 4 miles out and back.
Approximate hiking time: 2 hours.
Difficulty: Moderate.
Trail surface: A use trail follows the main wash with easy routes over and around boulders.

Seasons: October through April.
USGS topo maps: Aqua Caliente Springs-CA; Arroyo Tapiado-CA; Sombrero Peak-CA; and Sweeney Pass-CA (1:24,000).
Trail contact: Anza-Borrego Desert State Park (see appendix D).

Finding the trailhead: From the park visitor center, drive east 1.9 miles to Christmas Circle, turn right on Borrego Springs Road (S3), and drive south for 5.6 miles to the Y intersection; turn right (south) on S3 and drive 7.4 miles to the junction with California Highway 78. Turn right on CA 78 and drive another 7.4 miles to Scissors Crossing. Turn left (south) on Park Route S2 and drive 29.6 miles to the signed Indian Valley Road. Turn right (southwest) and drive 1.8 miles up the sandy road to the mouth of Torote Canyon, which is marked with a small sign. A monument called "El Torote" faces away from the road into the canyon. Park and begin the hike here.

The Hike

Hike up the sandy-wash use trail of Torote Canyon, which, for the most part, makes a good and easy-to-follow trail. At times you will need to scramble up and over an occasional boulder-clogged segment of the wash, but in general the going is easy enough to allow enjoyment of the remote surroundings of the canyon. You'll come to the first elephant tree on the left slope (south side) in less than 0.4 mile, but keep going for a good look at a dense "herd" of elephant trees.

The Spanish word *torote* means "twisted," referring to the gnarled growth pattern of the elephant trees, which are widespread in Mexico. At about 0.6 mile (1,180 feet), a large group of trees clings to the steep, rocky slopes above the canyon floor. Take time to get better acquainted with Borrego's rarest tree: Feel its parchmentlike bark, take note of its small, feathery leaves, and breathe deeply of its pleasant cedar-like aroma. At about 0.9 mile the canyon opens up into the first wide valley, which stretches a good 0.5 mile to the northwest. At the head of the valley, the main Torote Canyon continues up a bouldery draw to the northwest. Instead of continuing up the main canyon, follow what appears to be the main valley northward to the right. This leads to a short, tight canyon that opens after about 300 yards to the second wide valley. Continue up the valley to a low pass straight ahead.

Elephant trees in Torote Canyon.

Although several cross-country routes are possible—eastward to Carrizo Valley or to the south toward the north fork of Indian Valley—the upper end of this second wide valley is a good turnaround point for this pleasant 4-mile round-trip journey. But go back only after you've given yourself enough time to savor the remote upper canyon's magic.

Miles and Directions

0.0 Start at the trailhead at the mouth of Torote Canyon (1,060 feet).

0.6 Arrive at a sizable "herd" of elephant trees.

1.0 This is the first wide basin you'll come to.

1.5 With the main Torote Canyon to the left, turn right (north) at the canyon junction.

2.0 At the turnaround point at a low pass above a second wide valley (1,600 feet), return to the trailhead by the same route.

4.0 Arrive back at the trailhead.

3 Moonlight Canyon

Moonlight Canyon is a colorful gem of a canyon within the state park, although its trailhead lies within Agua Caliente County Park.

Start: About 43 miles south of Borrego Springs, in Agua Caliente County Park.
Distance: 1.5-mile loop.
Approximate hiking time: 1 hour.
Difficulty: Moderate.
Trail surface: Clear sandy trail, clear wash.

Seasons: October through April.
USGS topo map: Agua Caliente Springs-CA (1:24,000).
Trail contact: Agua Caliente County Park and Anza-Borrego Desert State Park (see appendix D).

Finding the trailhead: From the park visitor center, drive east on Palm Canyon Drive 1.9 miles to Christmas Circle. Turn south at the circle on S3 (Borrego Springs Road) 5.6 miles to the Y intersection. Bear right and continue south on S3 for 7.4 miles to its intersection with California Highway 78 just beyond the Tamarisk Grove Campground. Turn right (west) on CA 78 and go 7.4 miles to Scissors Crossing. At the crossing turn left (south) on S2 and drive 22.3 miles to the turnoff to Agua Caliente Springs and Campground. Turn right and continue 0.5 mile to the trailhead at the parking area adjacent to the park gate. There is a daily park entrance fee; check with the county park, as the fee increases annually. The trailhead leaves from campsites no. 39 and 40 and returns near campsite no. 63.

The Hike

Although the trailhead lies outside of the Anza-Borrego boundary and there is an entry fee to the county park, it is definitely worth a visit. Interesting erosion formations, intermittent watery spots, and cozy side canyons combine for a series of discoveries as you follow the well-marked trail through its circular route in the canyon.

The trail begins inauspiciously by climbing to a low ridge; it quickly drops to the stream bottom, which goes up a rocky draw and into the canyon itself. Side washes and small canyons periodically invite further exploration as the main wash winds downward. There are occasional steep slopes requiring only simple scrambling on this otherwise easy hike. The rock formations, courtesy of centuries of water and earthquake activity, are endlessly fascinating. The variety of colors of the rocks is also noteworthy. Where water exists, sudden splashes of greenery—tamarisk and willow patches—punctuate the trip.

The canyon empties into a wide dry wash, leading to a rock-lined trail that winds through an ocotillo forest and back to the campground at site no. 63, down the hill from your starting point.

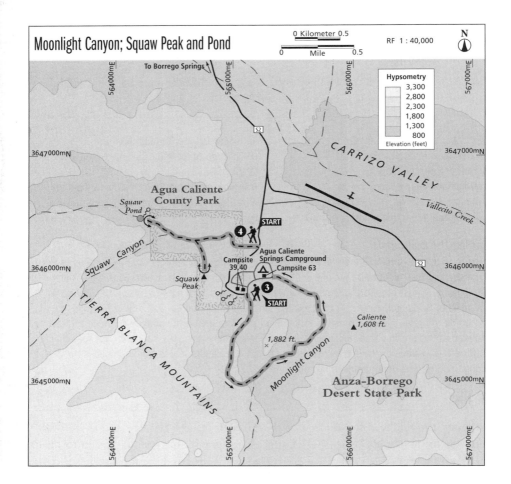

Moonlight Canyon; Squaw Peak and Pond

0 Kilometer 0.5

0 Mile 0.5

RF 1 : 40,000

N

Hypsometry
3,300
2,800
2,300
1,800
1,300
800
Elevation (feet)

To Borrego Springs

CARRIZO VALLEY

Vallecito Creek

Agua Caliente County Park

Squaw Pond

START

Squaw Canyon

Agua Caliente Springs Campground

Campsite 39,40

Campsite 63

Squaw Peak

START

Caliente 1,608 ft.

1,882 ft.

TIERRA BLANCA MOUNTAINS

Moonlight Canyon

Anza-Borrego Desert State Park

Miles and Directions

0.0 The trailhead is located at campsites no. 39 and 40.

1.0 The trail enters the main wash.

1.1 At the signposted junction, the short box canyon is a worthy side trip.

1.3 You'll see an open ocotillo forest as the canyon broadens.

1.5 End the hike near campsite no. 63.

Dropping into the narrow of Moonlight Canyon. ▶

4 Squaw Peak/Pond

This is a short climb on the edge of the Tierra Blanca Mountains to a scenic overlook of the Carrizo Valley and Vallecito Mountains, combined with a sandy-wash hike to a favored watering hole for wildlife.

See map on page 30.
Start: About 43 miles south of Borrego Springs, in Agua Caliente County Park.
Distance: 1.9 miles out and back.
Approximate hiking time: Between 1 and 2 hours.
Difficulty: Easy.

Trail surface: Clear sandy trail.
Seasons: November through April.
USGS topo map: Agua Caliente Springs-CA (1:24,000).
Trail contact: Agua Caliente Springs Regional County Park (see appendix D).

Finding the trailhead: From the Anza-Borrego visitor center, head east on Palm Canyon Drive for 1.9 miles to Christmas Circle. Turn south at the circle on S3 (Borrego Springs Road) 5.6 miles to the Y intersection; bear right at the Y and continue south on S3 for 7.4 miles to its intersection with California Highway 78 just beyond the Tamarisk Grove Campground. Turn right (west) on CA 78 and go 7.4 miles to Scissors Crossing. At the crossing turn left (south) on S2 and drive 22.3 miles to the turnoff to Agua Caliente Springs. Turn right and drive 0.5 mile to the trailhead at the parking area adjacent to the park entrance. There is a park entrance fee, which changes annually; contact the park for details. The trailhead is directly north of the ranger station. Cross the parking lot to a low ridge on the right next to the campfire circle and take the path that leads to the campground amphitheater and the Squaw Peak/Pond trailhead.

The Hike

From the Agua Caliente Springs parking area, pick up the Squaw Peak/Pond trail near the campfire circle just above the ranger station/park entrance. Climb 0.1 mile to the ridgetop trail junction. Take the left trail 0.25 mile to 1,450-foot Squaw Peak. From the junction, the trail makes switchbacks up 150 feet to this overlook of the Carrizo Valley and Badlands and the more distant Vallecito Mountains.

To reach Squaw Pond, drop back to the junction and continue left down to the sandy Squaw Canyon wash. Turn left up the well-traveled wash past clumps of honey mesquite, an important food staple for early-day Cahuilla Indians. Mesquite are adorned with cylindrical spikes of yellow flowers in late spring.

Squaw Pond is 0.5 mile up the wash. Tracks of coyote, bobcat, and a host of smaller animals tell the tale of their visitation to this desert spring oasis shaded by dense willow and a single palm tree. Bring your binoculars for excellent bird watching at Squaw Pond. The surrounding hillsides are dotted with barrel and cholla cactus.

After savoring this tranquil setting, the most direct return to the trailhead is to simply walk all the way back down the wash, which intersects the road just below

The Anza-Borrego Desert stretches to the north from Squaw Peak.

the parking area. In so doing, you'll avoid the additional climb back over the ridge to the trail junction.

After the hike you might enjoy a soak in the mineral hot springs of Agua Caliente. A shallow outdoor pool averages around ninety-five degrees and is open during the day. A larger indoor Jacuzzi pool is kept slightly warmer. The natural hot-water source is an offshoot of the Elsinore Fault.

Miles and Directions

0.0 Start at the trailhead.

0.1 At the trail junction, turn left to the Squaw Peak overlook.

0.35 Arrive at the Squaw Peak overlook (1,450 feet).

0.6 Return to the trail junction (1,290 feet) and turn left toward the pond.

0.7 Arrive at the Squaw Canyon wash (1,240 feet).

1.2 Use the turnaround point at Squaw Pond (1,280 feet).

1.9 Arrive back at the parking area trailhead.

5 Box Canyon Overlook

This historic mountain pass on the Old Southern Emigrant Trail was used by forty-niners and other emigrants, as well as the Butterfield Overland Stage. You can simply view it from the overlook or take a winding path down to the trail itself to get a real feel for the challenges that faced the early pioneers.

Start: About 31 miles south of Borrego Springs.
Distance: 1.8 miles out and back.
Approximate hiking time: Up to 2 hours.
Difficulty: Easy.
Trail surface: Clear trail, clear wash.

Seasons: October through April.
USGS topo map: Earthquake Valley-CA (1:24,000).
Trail contact: Anza-Borrego Desert State Park (see appendix D).

Box Canyon wash.

Box Canyon Overlook; Foot and Walker Pass

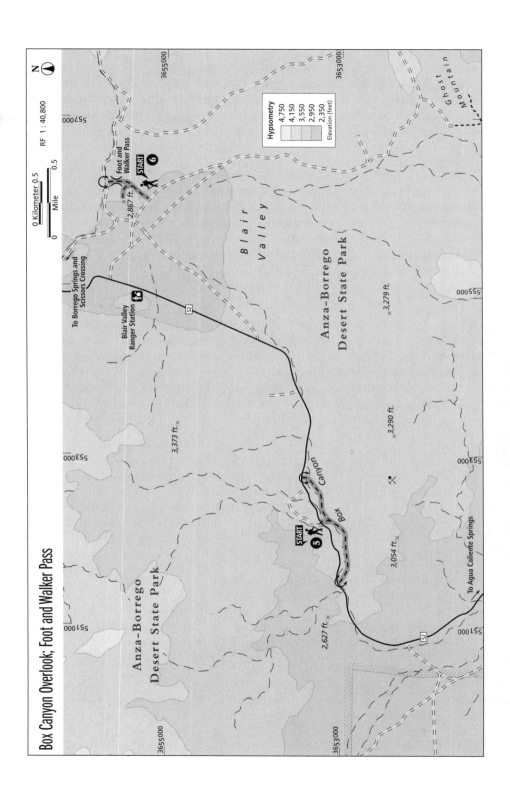

Finding the trailhead: From the visitor center, go east 1.9 miles to Christmas Circle in Borrego Springs; turn south on Park Route S3 and go 5.6 miles to the Y intersection. Bear right and continue on S3 7.4 miles to the intersection with California Highway 78. Turn right on CA 78 and go another 7.4 miles to Scissors Crossing. Turn left on Park Route S2 and continue south 9 miles. About 0.6 mile south of mile marker 25 on S2 is the Box Canyon parking pullout on the south side of the road.

The Hike

Much Anza-Borrego history coincides at this spot! The Southern Emigrant Trail, the Mormon Battalion, and the Butterfield Overland Mail Route used this arduous low mountain pass. The historical marker is right by the highway; the overlook of the trail below is 250 feet farther south.

By following the path down to the trail itself, you quickly get a feeling for the obstacle that this rocky ridge represented for early travelers. To follow a piece of the trail itself, hike the sloping path down to the right to a wooden post marked U.S. MORMON BATTALION TRAIL. At this point the trail coincides with the wash. The historic wash trail is marked with an occasional wooden post. Follow the gently graded wash down 0.7 mile to a pullout where S2 almost touches the wash. Your hike parallels the highway but is wholly hidden in the small canyon to provide a feeling of seclusion and communion with the hundreds of previous users of this trail segment.

Return to the overlook via the wash, not the highway. The narrow blind curves make it dangerous at this point.

6 Foot and Walker Pass

A short hike to an overlook at Blair Valley provides you with a view of the Butterfield Overland Stage's route over Puerta Pass. Here you may gain sympathy for both horses and passengers as they made their way through this rocky landscape.

See map on page 35.
Start: About 31 miles south of Borrego Springs.
Distance: 0.2 mile out and back.
Approximate hiking time: 30 minutes.
Difficulty: Easy.

Trail surface: Clear sandy and rocky trail.
Seasons: October through April.
USGS topo map: Earthquake Valley-CA (1:24,000).
Trail contact: Anza-Borrego Desert State Park (see appendix D).

The California Riding and Hiking Trail extends northward.

Finding the trailhead: From the park visitor center, go east 1.9 miles to Christmas Circle; turn south on Borrego Springs Road (S3) and go 5.6 miles to the Y intersection. Bear right and continue on S3 7.4 miles to the intersection with California Highway 78. Turn right on CA 78 and go another 7.4 miles to Scissors Crossing. Turn left on S2 and go 6.3 miles to the Blair Valley turnoff, on your left. The Foot and Walker Trail historical monument is 0.3 mile from the turnoff on the north side of the valley.

The Hike

This short trail provides an excellent orientation to the Blair Valley region, with its layers of human use, from prehistoric (pictographs and morteros) to historic (routes through Box Canyon and Foot and Walker Pass) to recent (the South home on Ghost Mountain) times.

Here at the entrance to the valley, the Butterfield Stage had difficulty with the pass, especially if the coach had a heavy load. Often passengers had to hop out and walk—hence the name of the pass.

From the pullout on the dirt road below the hill above you, a use trail goes up the rise to a historic marker. A second use trail goes through the pass itself. A brief hike in this area reminds us of the arduous conditions for nineteenth-century desert travelers.

7 Ghost Mountain: Marshal South Home

The steep rugged trail to the remains of a primitive adobe home built in 1932 on top of isolated Ghost Mountain rewards you with a spectacular view.

Start: About 31 miles south of Borrego Springs.
Distance: 2 miles out and back.
Approximate hiking time: 2 hours allows you to explore the homesite.
Difficulty: Moderate.

Trail surface: Clear but rocky trail up the mountain, with some constructed stone steps in steep places.
Seasons: October through April.
USGS topo map: Earthquake Valley-CA (1:24,000).
Trail contact: Anza-Borrego Desert State Park (see appendix D).

Finding the trailhead: From the visitor center, drive east 1.9 miles to Christmas Circle in Borrego Springs. Turn south on Park Route S3, then drive 5.6 miles to the Y intersection; bear right at the Y and continue on S3 7.4 miles to the intersection with California Highway 78. Turn right on CA 78 and go another 7.4 miles to the intersection with Park Route S2 at Scissors Crossing. Turn south (left) on S2. Blair Valley is 6.3 miles southeast of Scissors Crossing, on your left at mile 23. Turn left onto the dirt road. The road junctions in Blair Valley are clearly marked with signs. Go straight on the dirt road and turn right at the T intersection for the Ghost Mountain parking area, 3.2 miles from S2.

The stone remnants of the Marshal South home on Ghost Mountain.

The Hike

Poet Marshal South was an early refugee from civilization, fleeing with his family in the 1930s to this remote desert mountaintop, named Yaquitepec. This hike is an interesting mixture of scenic splendor and devastating squalor—the South home was primitive at best. The remains of the family's attempt to live atop a mountain peak in this valley create a striking contrast with the awesome views in every direction. No water is available; remains of a cistern system sit on the boulders near the cooking area. Fuel is also nonexistent. Living here was hard work.

The path snakes its way to the mountaintop with a series of steps and switchbacks. Marshal South built quite a trail; there are even steps on some of the steeper stretches. It is thought provoking to imagine what it would be like to transport essentials up this hillside and rear three children in such a location. When you arrive at the house site, the ruins reveal how basic life was for the South family. This was no castle. Of course, the dwelling has fallen into severe disrepair.

Ghost Mountain: Marshal South Home; The Morteros; Pictograph Trail

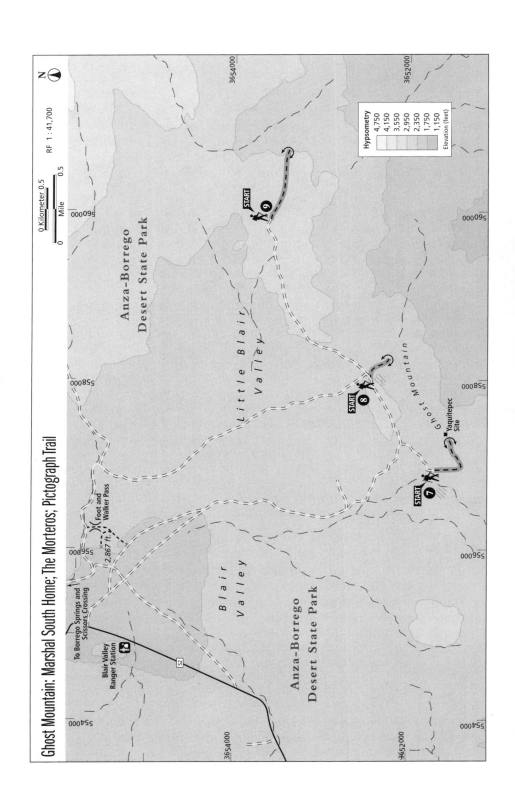

Since both sunrise and sunset are spectacular from Ghost Mountain, campers have used the two or three sites available here, apparently with no trouble from the ghost. However, to protect the homesite, the park does not encourage camping there. The South family surely enjoyed the view. Many interesting tales exist among local residents about the family and its escapades. According to one source, Marshal South eventually left his family and the mountain, going to live with a lady librarian in a nearby town.

8 The Morteros

An easy path leads to the site of a Native American settlement with ancient grinding holes cut into granitic boulders.

Several morteros were ground into this large flat rock at the end of the Morteros Trail.

See map on page 40.
Start: About 31 miles south of Borrego Springs.
Distance: 0.5 mile out and back.
Approximate hiking time: 30 minutes.
Difficulty: Easy.

Trail surface: Broad, clear dirt trail.
Seasons: October through April.
USGS topo maps: Earthquake Valley-CA (1:24,000) and Whale Peak-CA (1:24,000).
Trail contact: Anza-Borrego Desert State Park (see appendix D).

Finding the trailhead: From the visitor center, drive east on Palm Canyon Drive 1.9 miles to Christmas Circle. Turn south on Park Route S3. At 5.6 miles south of the circle, bear right at the Y intersection and continue 7.4 miles on S3 to the intersection with California Highway 78. Turn right on CA 78 and go 7.4 miles to Scissors Crossing. Turn left on S2 and go south 6.3 miles. At mile marker 23 is the Blair Valley road. Turn left onto the dirt road. At the stop sign at the first intersection in Blair Valley, a park sign indicates distances and directions to three trails. Follow the dirt road and turn left to the Morteros pullout, 3.7 miles from the stop sign.

The Hike

A broad, sandy trail leads from the parking lot up the rise to the site of a prehistoric village set against the rock-strewn hillside. The slight elevation gain provides a sweeping view of Little Blair Valley, stretching to the northwest. Huge obelisk-like boulders frame large horizontal granite stones, in which the *morteros,* or mortar stones, were worn over a thousand years of grinding by the Kumeyaay Indians. Fortunately the site has been respected by visitors and remains in the same condition as when the Indians departed, giving it a hallowed feeling.

9 Pictograph Trail

This short hike leads to a major pictograph site and an overlook of Vallecito Valley.

See map on page 40.
Start: About 31 miles south of Borrego Springs.
Distance: 3 miles out and back.
Approximate hiking time: 1 to 2 hours.
Difficulty: Easy.

Trail surface: Broad dirt path.
Seasons: October through April.
USGS topo map: Whale Peak-CA (1:24,000).
Trail contact: Anza-Borrego Desert State Park (see appendix D).

Finding the trailhead: From the visitor center, drive east on Palm Canyon Drive 1.9 miles to Christmas Circle. Turn south on Park Route S3. At 5.6 miles south of the circle, bear right at the Y intersection and continue 7.4 miles on S3 to the intersection with California Highway 78. Turn

Pictographs are found at mile 1 along the Pictograph Trail.

right on CA 78 and go 7.4 miles to Scissors Crossing. Turn left on S2 and go south 6.3 miles. At mile marker 23 is the Blair Valley road. Turn left (southeast) on the Blair Valley road. Follow this dirt road, turning left at the T intersection, 5 miles to the Pictograph Trail parking area/trailhead.

The Hike

Blair Valley has attracted human visitors for centuries. High above the desert, its temperatures are more moderate than those of its surroundings. Early inhabitants evidently found it comfortable, as do present-day hikers and campers.

A wide, sandy trail leads from the parking lot up a gradual slope to a saddle 160 feet higher than the parking area. The trail becomes more rocky as it climbs through piñon-juniper vegetation. Over the saddle, at 0.4 mile on your right, is a large boulder with the mysterious pictographs (identified as petroglyphs on the topographic map) left by prehistoric residents of this high valley. These striking artifacts of an ancient culture have been well preserved despite their remote, wild location. Hikers can pause to contemplate the meaning of these signs, which still puzzle archaeologists.

About 0.5 mile farther down the sandy-wash path is a sharply defined notch in a rocky ridge; through the notch is the overlook of Vallecitos Valley and the Vallecitos Mountains. Whale Peak (5,349 feet) is prominent to the northeast. There's an abrupt 100-foot precipice at the overlook, so keep an eye on overly adventurous members of your hiking party.

Your view of Little Blair Valley on the hike back to the parking area shows the value of this location to early desert dwellers. Residents enjoyed excellent visibility from this slope at the end of the valley. There's a sacred feeling about being in an area that was lived in so many centuries ago.

10 Wind Caves

Although it involves a long drive, this short hike features an interesting geologic and archaeological site located on a ridgetop, with a sweeping view of the Carrizo Badlands.

Start: About 38 miles southeast of Borrego Springs.
Distance: 1.4-mile out and back (add 0.5 mile for exploring the caves).
Approximate hiking time: 1 to 2 hours.
Difficulty: Moderate.

Trail surface: Dirt trail.
Seasons: October through April.
USGS topo map: Carrizo Mountain NE-CA (1:24,000).
Trail contact: Anza-Borrego Desert State Park (see appendix D).

Finding the trailhead: From the park visitor center in Borrego Springs, take Palm Canyon Drive 1.9 miles east to Christmas Circle; at the circle, turn south on Borrego Springs Road. In 5.6 miles, at the intersection with Park Route S3, continue straight on Borrego Springs Road 6.6 miles to the intersection with California Highway 78. Turn left on CA 78; go 6.7 miles east to Ocotillo Wells. At the main intersection in town, turn right (south) onto Split Mountain Road. Continue past Elephant Trees to the right turn onto Split Mountain or Fish Creek Wash at 10.8 miles. Drive up the sandy wash 5.1 miles to a small Wind Caves sign indicating the trail on your left. The trailhead is just south of the narrows of Split Mountain wash. The wash is not difficult for a passenger vehicle, but it should definitely be avoided in wet or threatening weather. This road often requires four-wheel drive. Check conditions at the visitor center before taking this road.

The Hike

The trip's excitement begins with the drive up the wash. Progressing upward from the valley floor, the wash approaches the rocky face of Split Mountain—then cuts through the mountain, with hardly any gain in elevation. The trailhead is beyond this narrow spot in the wash.

The first 0.2 mile of trail climbs from the floor of the wash to the ridge via a rocky but well-defined trail. The view of the Carrizo Badlands behind you is spectacular. A variety of worn footpaths lead from the edge of the wash into the lands above; some of these routes are believed to be remnants of prehistoric use of the area. They all converge on the caves, so it does not matter which one you choose.

Around 0.6 mile the caves come into view. A lower, smaller set of these fascinating sandstone wind-sculpted formations lies slightly below the larger set. There is an extraterrestrial quality about the site, due to both its ethereal appearance and the evidence that early Indians made use of these natural shelters. You may walk another 0.5 mile while exploring the caves. On your return trip down Split Mountain wash, watch for additional wind-cave formations high above the rim on the right.

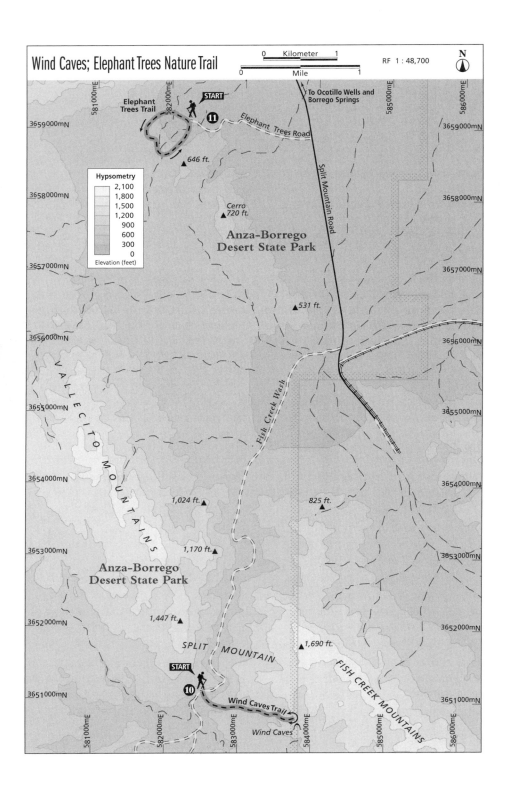

Wind Caves; Elephant Trees Nature Trail

0 Kilometer 1
0 Mile 1

RF 1 : 48,700

N

Elephant
Trees Trail

START

To Ocotillo Wells and
Borrego Springs

11

Elephant Trees Road

582000mE

581000mE

585000mE

586000mE

3659000mN

▲ 646 ft.

Hypsometry

| 2,100 |
| 1,800 |
| 1,500 |
| 1,200 |
| 900 |
| 600 |
| 300 |
| 0 |

Elevation (feet)

Cerro
▲720 ft.

**Anza-Borrego
Desert State Park**

Split Mountain Road

3658000mN

3658000mN

3657000mN

3657000mN

▲531 ft.

3656000mN

3656000mN

V A L L E C I T O   M O U N T A I N S

Fish Creek Wash

3655000mN

3855000mN

3654000mN

3654000mN

1,024 ft. ▲

825 ft.
▲

3653000mN

1,170 ft.▲

3653000mN

**Anza-Borrego
Desert State Park**

1,447 ft.▲

3652000mN

3652000mN

SPLIT   MOUNTAIN

▲1,690 ft.

F I S H   C R E E K   M O U N T A I N S

START

10

3651000mN

Wind Caves Trail

3651000mN

Wind Caves

581000mE

582000mE

583000mE

584000mE

585000mE

586000mE

The wind-eroded sandstone of Wind Caves forms an unearthly appearance high on the ridge above Split Mountain wash.

Miles and Directions

0.0 The trail climbs steeply from the wash to the plateau above.

0.3 Take any one of the variety of trails here, all of which head easterly.

0.7 Arrive at Wind Caves and the turnaround point (after exploring caves).

1.4 Return to the trailhead (add 0.5 mile for exploring the caves).

11 Elephant Trees Nature Trail

This easy self-guided loop displays the diverse plant community of an alluvial fan and desert wash. The name is deceiving since there remains only one of the rare and unusual elephant trees.

See map on page 46.
Start: About 32 miles southeast of Borrego Springs.
Distance: 1-mile loop.
Approximate hiking time: 1 hour.
Difficulty: Easy.

Trail surface: Broad dirt trail.
Seasons: October through April.
USGS topo map: Borrego Mountain SE-CA (1:24,000).
Trail contact: Anza-Borrego Desert State Park (see appendix D).

Elephant trees—Anza-Borrego's most unusual plant.

Finding the trailhead: From the park visitor center in Borrego Springs, go east 1.9 miles on Palm Canyon Drive to Christmas Circle. Take Borrego Springs Road south from the circle for 5.6 miles to Park Route S3. At the intersection with S3, go straight (southeast) on Borrego Springs Road toward Ocotillo Wells. Borrego Springs Road meets California Highway 78 in 6.6 miles. Go left (east) on CA 78 for 6.7 miles to Ocotillo Wells. Turn right (south) at the Ocotillo Wells intersection onto Split Mountain Road and drive 5.9 miles to Elephant Trees Road. Turn right (west) and follow the dirt road 1 mile to the parking area/trailhead.

The Hike

This well-signed self-guided nature trail climbs gently up a rock-lined wash to a solitary elephant tree. An informative brochure is available at the trailhead.

The unusual elephant tree of the Sonoran Desert was not discovered and identified by botanists until 1937. There used to be a herd of elephants, and now one rogue elephant remains. This example of the species was long thought to be the northernmost group of elephant trees in California. However, in 1987 another grove of almost 200 elephant trees was discovered on the western slopes of the Santa Rosa Mountains, 21 miles farther north. Numbering only in the hundreds, they cling precariously to boulders and steep side slopes. Desert Indians used their red sap as medicine and to bring good fortune. Elephant trees are common to Baja California and the Mexican state of Sonora but are found in only a few scattered canyons and washes of Anza-Borrego—the northernmost extension of their range.

An easy, educational loop winds up and down a rock-lined wash with thirteen plant identification stops keyed to the brochure. Most of the plants are common desert perennial shrubs such as burroweed, desert lavender, and brittlebush. Certainly the most fascinating plant is the trail's namesake elephant tree, *Bursera microphylla*. The species name means "small-leaved," a common adaptation by desert plants to conserve water. The common name reflects the folded "skin" of the main trunk, much like that of an elephant.

12 Narrows Earth Trail

Offering insights into the geologic forces that created these mountains, this ½-mile loop features a self-guiding brochure that explains the fault lines of the gorge and the power of erosion along the edge of an alluvial fan. Chuparosa and pencil cholla abound.

Start: About 20 miles south of Borrego Springs.
Distance: 0.5-mile loop.
Approximate hiking time: Up to 1 hour.
Difficulty: Easy.
Trail surface: Dirt trail.

Seasons: October through May.
USGS topo map: Borrego Sink-CA (1:24,000).
Trail contact: Anza-Borrego Desert State Park (see appendix D).

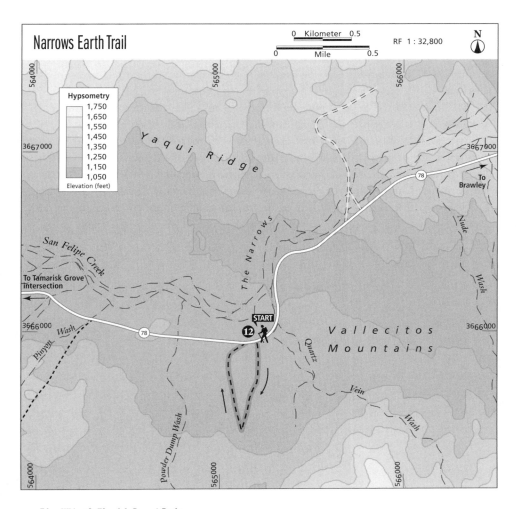

Finding the trailhead: From the park visitor center in Borrego Springs, go east on Palm Canyon Drive to Christmas Circle (1.9 miles); at the circle turn south onto Borrego Springs Road. Drive south-southeast 5.6 miles to the Y intersection; turn right onto S3. Go 7.4 miles to the intersection with California Highway 78 just beyond the Tamarisk Grove Campground. Turn left (east) on CA 78 and continue 4.7 miles to the Narrows Earth parking area, signed on.your right. The parking area is a wide spot on the right side of CA 78 immediately before the road takes a sharp right-angle turn (north) through the Narrows.

The Hike

The trailhead for this short nature trail is on a busy state highway, a major through route for trucks. It is immediately west of a narrow gap (labeled "The Narrows" on the topographic map) where Yaqui Ridge almost meets the Vallecitos Mountains.

The signed, self-guided trail begins directly east of the parking area to your left. It's easy to miss spot no. 1, which is important since the brochures are located there. The points along the trail focus on the geologic history of the region, revealed in the naked rock walls of this canyon. Fault lines, rock formation, and erosion are some of the lessons of the Narrows Earth Trail. The seven stops on the loop provide an introduction to the forces that created Anza–Borrego topography.

From the top of the loop, Powder Dump Wash continues another 0.2 mile to a sharp rise. For a longer hike, and to apply your newly acquired knowledge, you can continue up the wash before returning to the parking area.

13 Kenyon Overlook Trail Loop

From a rocky ridge in the central region of the park, this short loop trail provides a panoramic vista. On a clear day the expansive view extends beyond the Vallecitos Mountains as far as the Salton Sea.

Start: About 13 miles south of Borrego Springs.
Distance: 1-mile loop.
Approximate hiking time: Less than 1 hour.
Difficulty: Easy.
Trail surface: Dirt path.

Seasons: October through April.
USGS topo map: Borrego Sink-CA (1:24,000).
Trail contact: Anza-Borrego Desert State Park (see appendix D).

Finding the trailhead: From the visitor center in Borrego Springs, go east on Palm Canyon Drive 1.9 miles to Christmas Circle. At the circle take Borrego Springs Road south for 5.6 miles to the Y intersection. At the Y turn right (south) onto S3 (Yaqui Pass Road). Drive 5.8 miles and turn left into the Yaqui Pass Primitive Campground, the northern trailhead.

After hiking the point-to-point loop trail to the Kenyon Overlook parking pullout, walk back down the highway about 0.2 mile to the starting point at the Yaqui Pass Campground parking lot.

Kenyon Overlook Trail Loop; Cactus Loop Trail; Yaqui Well Nature Trail

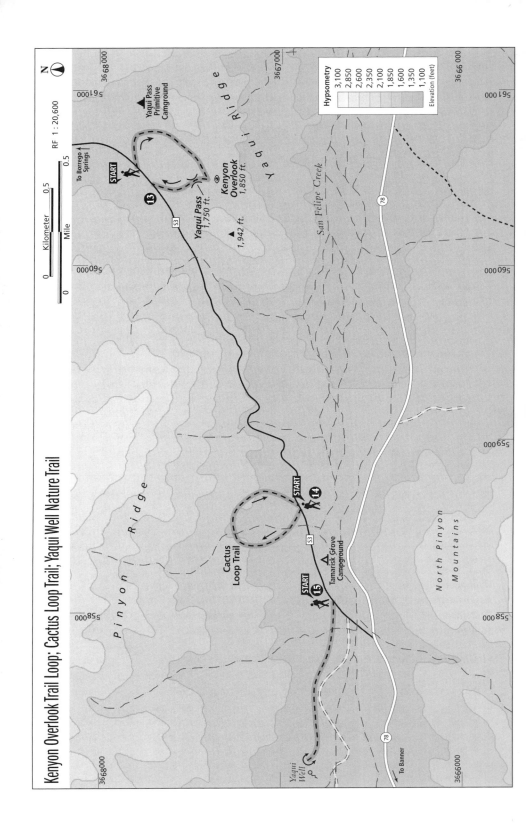

N

RF 1 : 20,600

Kilometer
0   0.5
Mile
0   0.5

561 000

To Borrego Springs

START

13

S3

Yaqui Pass
1,750 ft.

▲ 1,942 ft.

Yaqui Pass Primitive Campground ▲

Kenyon Overlook
1,850 ft.

Pinyon Ridge

Yaqui Ridge

San Felipe Creek

560 000

START

14

S3

Tamarisk Grove Campground ⛺

Cactus Loop Trail

START

15

Yaqui Well ♒

To Banner

78

North Pinyon Mountains

78

3668000

3667000

3666000

558000   559 000   560 000   561 000

Hypsometry

3,100
2,850
2,600
2,350
2,100
1,850
1,600
1,350
1,100

Elevation (feet)

Ocotillo (left) on the Kenyon Overlook trail.

The Hike

From the trailhead, take the signed trail uphill. The trail maintains a gentle up-and-down grade through a series of parallel gullies lined with yucca, creosote bushes, silver cholla, ocotillo, beavertail cacti, barrel cacti, and brittlebush. Soon the trail reaches the high point at a rocky ridge overlook. Turn left and walk about 30 yards to the overlook, which contains a monument in honor of William L. Kenyon, a noted desert conservationist and district park superintendent from 1947 to 1959. From here the desert spreads out like the pages of a book. Beyond is a seemingly endless series of *arroyos* (washes) that deposit gravel and silt in deltalike fans, two or more of which are called *bajadas*. These bajadas support a dense mantle of agave, called mescal. On a clear day the Salton Sea can be seen 30 miles to the east.

From the overlook, return to the main trail, turn left, and drop gradually to the highway, which can be seen from this point. Upon reaching the highway, make a right turn and walk 0.2 mile up the highway to the starting point at the Yaqui Pass Primitive Campground.

14 Cactus Loop Trail

A diverse array of cacti are clustered along this nature trail, which is at a higher elevation than others in the park; here you can find wildflowers blooming one or two weeks later than in Borrego Palm Canyon.

See map on page 52.
Start: About 15 miles south of Borrego Springs.
Distance: 1-mile loop.
Approximate hiking time: Less than 1 hour.
Difficulty: Easy.

Trail surface: Dirt trail.
Seasons: October through April.
USGS topo map: Borrego Sink-CA (1:24,000).
Trail contact: Anza-Borrego Desert State Park (see appendix D).

Finding the trailhead: From the park visitor center in Borrego Springs, take Palm Canyon Drive east to Christmas Circle. At the circle, take Borrego Springs Road (S3) south and go 5.6 miles to the Y intersection. Bear right and continue on S3 for 7 miles to Tamarisk Grove Campground, on your left. The signed Cactus Loop Trail trailhead is across from the campground entrance. Park in the shade of the tamarisk trees along the south side of the highway.

The Hike

This short trail begins as a sandy winding path but becomes more rocky as it leads up the canyon. Your self-guided-hike brochure identifies jumping cholla, beavertail cactus, and saltbush. Walking up the canyon instead of driving the desert roads reveals the diversity of desert plant life and its adaptive strategies for desert survival. The nature trail route leads up the wash to the ridge's high point (1,520 feet) then winds gently down the ridge slope to the trailhead on S3. The exit sign is obscured by overgrown brittlebush, but the trail itself is clear.

15 Yaqui Well Nature Trail

The easy trail to Yaqui Well and back features a plethora of cacti and opportunities for birding at the watering hole.

See map on page 52.
Start: About 15 miles south of Borrego Springs.
Distance: 2 miles out and back.
Approximate hiking time: 1 hour.
Difficulty: Easy.

Trail surface: Clear trail.
Seasons: October through April.
USGS topo maps: Tubb Canyon-CA and Borrego Sink-CA (1:24,000).
Trail contact: Anza-Borrego Desert State Park (see appendix D).

Finding the trailhead: From the park visitor center in Borrego Springs, go east 1.9 miles to Christmas Circle. At the circle, turn south on Borrego Springs Road (S3). After 5.6 miles, at the Y intersection, bear right (south) on Yaqui Pass Road (also S3). Continue 7 miles to Tamarisk Grove Campground, which is across the road from Yaqui Well Nature Trail. Park along S3 outside the campground and cross the highway to the trailhead.

The Hike

This nature trail, slightly longer than most of the others in the park, has an informative brochure to accompany you on your walk. The route begins at the highway but quickly angles up a rise on a gentle but rocky trail, and the hiker becomes enveloped in the desert. The nature trail signs are frequent and are clearly situated so each plant is labeled correctly. Jumping cholla are the most numerous, but ironwood and desert mistletoe also appear here.

Approaching the well from the east, the trail becomes sandy and level for the last 0.6 mile. The foliage at the well provides a sharp contrast with the surrounding desert plants. A dense thicket of mesquite crowds around the watery seep. Hardy old mesquite and ironwood trees surround the area. The well is a popular watering spot for local animals, especially birds. Although you can drive to the well via the Yaqui Well Campground road, the walk through the desert makes the existence of this moisture more significant.

16 Wilson Trail

A long east-west trail that follows the old Pinyon Ridge jeep trail (closed to vehicular travel), passing by 4,573-foot Mount Wilson to arrive at a rocky overlook above Borrego Valley. This is one of the longer out-and-back hikes in the park, with sweeping vistas of the central park region.

Start: About 8 miles southwest of Borrego Springs.
Distance: 11 miles out and back.
Approximate hiking time: 5 to 7 hours.
Difficulty: Moderate.

Trail surface: Dirt trail.
Seasons: October through April.
USGS topo map: Tubb Canyon-CA (1:24,000).
Trail contact: Anza-Borrego Desert State Park (see appendix D).

Finding the trailhead: Go 15 miles east of Warner Springs, on Park Route S22 (Montezuma Valley Road); 10.5 miles east of the intersection with S2 or 8 miles southwest of the park visitor center in Borrego Springs, take the Culp Valley Road south. Four-wheel-drive vehicles are recommended on this steep, sandy road. After 0.4 mile stay right at the first road junction. Continue on the main road, ignoring numerous turnouts. The Wilson trailhead is another 2.7 miles up the road, for a total of 3.1 miles from S22, and is marked by a small sign with a turnaround parking area just below a ridge dotted with sage, creosote, and granite boulders.

The Hike

The trail climbs moderately the first 0.6 mile to the ridgetop, opening up panoramic vistas of the Vallecito Mountains to the southeast. It then gradually descends another 0.5 mile to a broad saddle adorned with a heavy mantle of juniper, cholla, and agave. After another 0.4 mile this former jeep trail tops out on a high ridge with an outcrop of sparkling light-colored granite boulders just to the right. This sandy track then levels, climbs, and levels again for another mile. In a few places the trail is somewhat overgrown by vegetation, but all you have to do is look ahead 50 yards or so and you'll easily spot the remnants of the two-track jeep trail.

At this point the trail climbs steeply 0.2 mile, weaving between large boulders, then drops 0.1 mile, followed by a steep 0.2-mile climb to a high side ridge. It then drops slightly and levels out for 1 mile. Soon the ridge is sprinkled with a few piñon pines and cedar adding variety to the mix of high-desert flora.

The old jeep trail appears to end after 5 miles and after climbing gradually to a downed post with a cement base. A more primitive path marked by rock cairns leads steeply up through thick brush for about 0.2 mile. The path tops out in a saddle between the rocky points, including 4,573-foot Mount Wilson, and continues across a broad, open plateau for another 0.3 mile. Here the sandy path disappears as the slope begins to drop eastward.

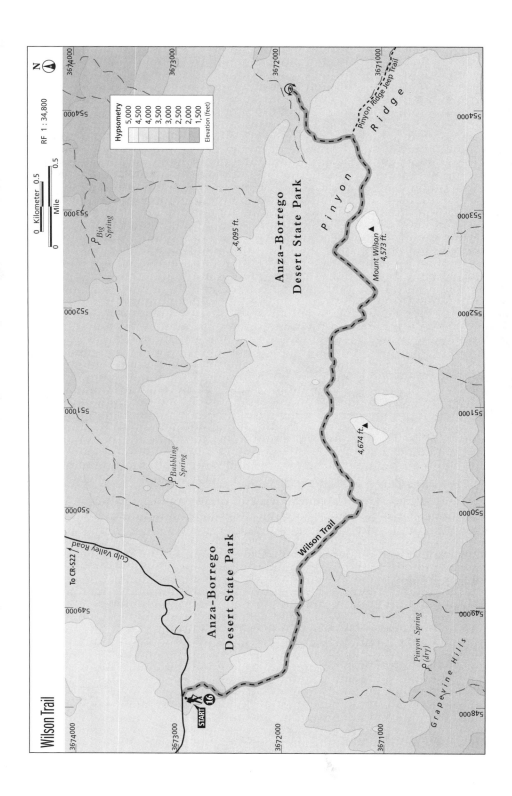

Wilson Trail

RF 1 : 34,800

Hypsometry

5,000
4,500
4,000
3,500
3,000
2,500
2,000
1,500

Elevation (feet)

N

0 Kilometer 0.5
0 Mile 0.5

Anza-Borrego
Desert State Park

Anza-Borrego
Desert State Park

Pinyon Ridge Jeep Trail

Pinyon   R i d g e

Mount Wilson
4,573 ft.

4,674 ft.

4,095 ft.

Wilson Trail

Big
Spring

Bubbling
Spring

Culp Valley Road

To CR-S22

START   16

Pinyon Spring
(dry)

G r a p e v i n e   H i l l s

3674000
3673000
3672000
3671000

3673000
3672000
3671000

548000
549000
550000
551000
552000
553000
554000

548000
549000
550000
551000
552000
553000
554000

The Wilson Trail follows the high ridge near the halfway point.

Before heading back to the trailhead, walk about 100 yards north to the rock-lined lip of the ridge for a stunning view of Borrego Springs, the Salton Sea, and surrounding desert basins and ranges fading far into the distance. This remote stretch of the Grapevine Hills is used extensively by mountain lions, bobcats, and coyotes as evidenced by abundant scat along the trail.

Miles and Directions

- **0.0**   Start at the trailhead.
- **5.0**   The old jeep trail disappears; the primitive dirt trail continues.
- **5.5**   The use trail disappears. Hike north to the overlook.
- **11.0**   Return to the trailhead.

17 California Riding and Hiking Trail: Peña Spring and Culp Valley Overlook

This maintained section of the Riding and Hiking Trail is almost entirely downhill. It goes by Peña Spring, includes the Culp Valley Overlook, then descends to the valley floor and a cross-desert walk to the visitor center in Borrego Springs. Along the way you may enjoy views of Borrego Valley, Coyote Mountain, and the Santa Rosa Mountains.

Start: About 8 miles southwest of Borrego Springs.
Distance: 8.5 miles one way.
Approximate hiking time: 4 to 5 hours.
Difficulty: Strenuous.

Trail surface: Dirt trail except for some overgrown portions of the less-traveled section above Culp Valley Overlook.
Seasons: October through April.
USGS topo map: Tubb Canyon-CA (1:24,000).
Trail contact: Anza-Borrego Desert State Park (see appendix D).

Finding the trailhead: A small sign marks the trailhead 12 miles east of Warner Springs on Park Route S22 (Montezuma Valley Road), 6.8 miles east of Park Route S2. The trailhead is on the north side of the road. This point is 10 miles southwest of the visitor center in Borrego Springs.

The destination point for the car shuttle is the visitor center. Horse parties end their trip at a parking pullout at mile 16 on S22, 1 mile south. Hikers may also prefer this convenient destination since it eliminates a dry 1-mile walk across the valley floor.

The Hike

The California Riding and Hiking Trail spans the varied elevations of Anza-Borrego. Beginning at 4,000 feet in chaparral, it descends through mountain valleys to the desert floor. The transition of vegetative communities is as interesting as the view—and the trip down the ridge offers spectacular vistas.

As you drive to the trailhead, the length and the elevation gain of Montezuma Road may be intimidating. The trail is nowhere near as arduous as the drive up! The trail avoids the rocky ridges you see from the road. Although there is little horse use on the trail due to steepness, neither is this a bighorn-sheep trail.

The early section of trail is the most difficult to find since it is not used often and is overgrown with chaparral. Stay within 50 yards north of the road, and watch for yellow-topped posts hidden by aggressive shrubbery. You can see this peeka-boo trail better by looking ahead about 50 yards. This section is not used frequently, compared with the last 5 miles of the hike, east of Culp Valley. Close to

A large multistemmed cholla stands like a giant candelabra next to the California R & H Trail.

the Montezuma-Borrego Highway (S22), you may pick up traffic noise, but as you wind north of rock outcroppings and ridges, that fades. Soon you are surrounded by wild country.

At the midsection of the hike, the trail goes through Culp Valley, an area formerly used for grazing cattle. Traces of its ranching past are noticeable—such as the stock watering facilities you will spot to your left. Peña Spring, now barely a seep, creates a patch of greenery in the high valley before you climb to the Culp Valley Overlook. This section of the trail is easily accessible to the highway, with a parking area. Frequently visitors take the 0.5-mile hike to enjoy the view. Thus, more signs mark the trail. Apparently more hikers also start the journey here: The trail is more heavily used from this point to the valley below.

Although the Culp Valley Overlook itself is prominently marked with a sign, there are dozens of breathtaking overlooks on the descent to the valley. Don't use up your film on the first one you come to! This 5-mile section will provide many photo opportunities. The trail goes down a series of giant stair steps—sharp descents followed by small landings, each one hosting a cactus display and stunning diversity of

0 Kilometer 1

0 Mile 1

RF 1 : 87,300

N

Indian Head

Borrego Palm Canyon

BORREGO VALLEY

548000mE

552000mE

556000mE

3682000mN

3682000mN

Borrego Springs

SAN YSIDRO MOUNTAIN

Extended Overlook
1,510 ft.

Anza-Borrego Desert State Park

To Borrego Springs

Hellhole Flat

Panorama Outlook

Ode ▲
1,510 ft.

Anza-Borrego Desert State Park

Alternate car shuttle point

Water tanks

Ted ▲
2,369 ft.

S22

Alternate car shuttle point

3678000mN

3678000mN

Hellhole Canyon

Anza Borrego Desert State Park

Chimney ▲ Rock

Peña Spring

Hypsometry

By Jim Spring

START

Montezuma-Borrego Highway

17

S22

Culp Valley

552000mE

556000mE

Hypsometry	
	6,700
	5,700
	4,700
	3,700
	2,700
	1,700
	700
	0
	Elevation (feet)

To Ranchita and CA-79

plants. Between these sandy flat cactus gardens, the trail drops sharply, often via rocky gullies. Even with the town of Borrego Springs spreading out below, you'll have a genuine sense of seclusion; the busy highway to Borrego Springs is beyond the ridge to the south.

Upon reaching the valley floor, you can follow the wide trail to your right to the parking area/trailhead created for horse users. This is a convenient place for a car shuttle. To return to the visitor center complex or the adjacent campground, go straight north from the end of the hillside trail. Trying to find a marked trail on the desert floor is time consuming and unnecessary, since you can see the rooftops of the park buildings immediately to the north. Use the highly visible tree-encircled water tanks as an intermediate guide. The visitor center is 0.3 mile beyond the tanks.

If your driver is late meeting you after your hike, waiting at the visitor center may be a more attractive option than waiting at the parking lot on S22.

Miles and Directions

0.0–0.4 Watch for yellow-topped posts in this overgrown section.

0.4 The trail stops: Head for the saddle on a low ridge.

0.5 Stay left of the wash as the trail skirts the small valley.

0.7 Watch for a primitive stock tank on the hillside (left).

1.2–1.7 You'll see signs at trail intersections at the Culp Valley Overlook area.

1.7–7.5 The trail descends into the valley.

7.5–8.5 There's a 1-mile trailless hike to the visitor center. A marked wash (right) leads to the parking lot for parties on horseback.

18 Panorama Overlook/Extended Overlook

This short but steep climb via a switchback trail up San Ysidro Mountain provides a scenic overlook of Borrego Valley. By continuing higher, you gain an even more expansive view point.

Start: Just west of the campground near the Borrego Springs Visitor Center.
Distance: 2.6 miles out and back.
Approximate hiking time: 3 to 5 hours.
Difficulty: Strenuous.
Trail surface: Rocky trail to overlook; steep rocky use trail to extended overlook.

Seasons: October through April.
USGS topo map: Borrego Palms Canyon-CA (1:24,000).
Trail contact: Anza-Borrego Desert State Park (see appendix D).

Finding the trailhead: From the visitor center at the intersection of Park Route S22 and Palm Canyon Drive in Borrego Springs, follow signs north 0.8 mile to the Borrego Springs Campground. The trail starts near campsite no. 71. A level 1-mile trail from the visitor center northwest to the campground also intersects the Panorama Overlook Trail.

The Hike

From the signed trailhead next to the palm tree at campsite no. 71, take the trail across a flat alluvial fan along the base of the rocky hillside for 0.4 mile to the OVER-LOOK TRAIL sign where the trail begins to switchback up the slope. The clear but steep and rocky trail climbs 240 feet over a distance of 0.3 mile to an open knoll ringed by creosote bushes, offering a wide vista from the eastern foot of San Ysidro Mountain to Borrego Palm Canyon and Borrego Valley.

For an even more expansive view, continue west up the ridge on a use trail, well defined for the first 0.2 mile as it follows the initial level portion of the ridge. The use trail then winds upward through rocks and brush and sometimes all but

Indian Head Mountain glimpsed from the extended Panorama Overlook.

disappears. Simply follow the main crest of the ridge leading toward the distant summit of San Ysidro Mountain. At times the best footing is found along either side of the actual ridgeline.

After another 0.4 mile and 300-foot gain, you'll reach a somewhat level rocky ledge with several flat spots. These make for a wonderful extended overlook—a good place to sit and soak up the majestic desert scenery of canyons, alluvial fans, mountains, valleys, and jagged, exposed ridges. The palm groves of Borrego Palm Canyon are hidden from view, but take time here to scan the slopes for desert bighorn sheep. As with most mountainous use trails, this one is easier to find going down than up.

This extended overlook is a logical turnaround point for a vigorous half-day hike, although it is possible to scramble up the ridge another 4 or 5 miles to the lofty summit of 6,147-foot San Ysidro Peak on the park's western boundary. This would be a very strenuous full-day cross-country climb with more than a vertical mile of gain and loss. Many overly optimistic day hikers have mistakenly spent a cold night on this mountain, usually giving rise to search and rescue operations. Know your limits.

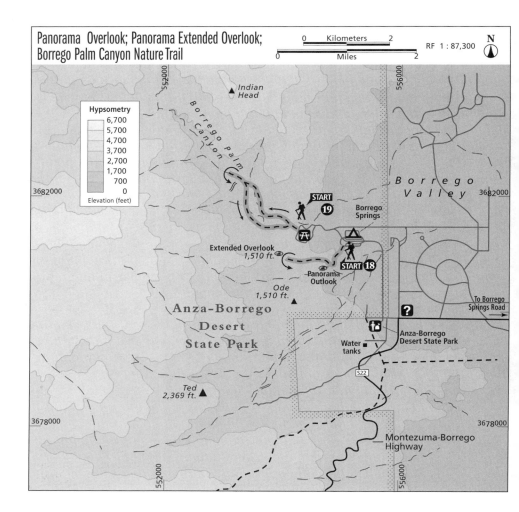

Panorama Overlook; Panorama Extended Overlook; Borrego Palm Canyon Nature Trail

Miles and Directions

0.0 Start at the trailhead at campsite no. 71.

0.4 The switchback trail begins here.

0.7 Reach the Panorama Overlook (1,020 feet).

1.3 End the hike at the extended overlook (1,510 feet).

2.6 Return to the trailhead.

19 Borrego Palm Canyon Nature Trail

What was once a delightful series of palm groves and mountain oases in the park, and the most heavily visited trail, has now become instead an example of the transitory nature of life in the desert. A torrential storm in the mountains above the canyon caused a "one-hundred-year" flash flood in September 2004 and washed away over half the palm trees and most of the trail. Life goes on: The sheep for whom the park is named are sometimes spotted on canyon slopes above the oasis.

See map on page 64.
Start: 0.6 mile north of the visitor center in Borrego Springs.
Distance: 3.5-mile loop.
Approximate hiking time: 1 to 2 hours.
Difficulty: Moderate rock scramble to the oasis and to the canyon overlook.

Trail surface: Washed out; rocky temporary path, flagged and with cairns.
Seasons: October through April.
USGS topo map: Borrego Palm Canyon-CA (1:24,000).
Trail contact: Anza-Borrego Desert State Park (see appendix D).

Finding the trailhead: From the park visitor center in Borrego Springs, go north 1 mile on an access road to Borrego Palm Canyon Campground and Picnic Area. The trail leaves from the northwest end of the picnic area. There is a day-use fee to enter with a motor vehicle.

The Hike

This trail provides a spectacular introduction to the beauty and fragility of the desert. A pond with desert pupfish lies at the start of the trail. Ocotillos abound, as do mesquite, cheesebush, and chuparosa, the "hummingbird plant." Hummingbirds are plentiful, especially in spring. In winter and spring, water flows in the adjacent stream, with small waterfalls. Sharp-eyed hikers can often spot bighorn sheep on the mountain slopes of the canyon, especially in early morning or evening.

Since September 2004 the walk up the trail into the canyon has changed radically. The trail winds through large boulders to what was once one of the largest groves of California fan palms in the country. A short but steeper climb above the oasis leads to an overlook 30 feet above the streambed.

On the way out an alternate route goes along the higher canyon slope to the west, amid a slope of ocotillos. This route also leads back to the parking lot; it is slightly longer (0.5 mile more) and more strenuous (100 feet elevation gain) than the path along the stream. But you also enjoy a loftier view of the canyon mouth below and you get a bigger picture of the devastating flood.

Miles and Directions

0.0 There's a pupfish pond located at the trailhead.

1.5 You'll see the remains of a palm oasis.

1.75 There's an overlook above the oasis.

3.5 Return to the trailhead.

20 Alcoholic Pass

A sweeping vista of the northeastern section of Anza-Borrego is your reward for climbing to Alcoholic Pass.

Start: About 8 miles north of Borrego Springs.
Distance: 3.4 miles out and back.
Approximate hiking time: 2 to 3 hours.
Difficulty: Moderate.
Trail surface: Dirt trail, rocky wash.

Seasons: October through April.
USGS topo maps: Borrego Palm Canyon-CA and Clark Lake-CA (1:24,000).
Trail contact: Anza-Borrego Desert State Park (see appendix D).

Finding the trailhead: From the park visitor center in Borrego Springs, go east on Palm Canyon Drive 1.9 miles to Christmas Circle; continue 0.6 mile past the circle and turn north (left) on DiGiorgio Road. At 5 miles the pavement ends; continue north on Coyote Canyon Road, a rolling, soft dirt road, for 2.6 miles to the trailhead on your right.

The Hike

For centuries Alcoholic Pass has been used by the region's inhabitants to travel from Clark Valley (in the northeast) to Borrego Valley. These use trails were created by countless moccasins before our hiking boots arrived. As you climb to the pass, with its sweeping view, you can develop many theories about the origin of the pass's name.

The hike takes off for the first 0.2 mile up a sandy slope to a trail marker indicating a right turn up a sidehill; the trail follows this ridge up a moderate incline. It becomes progressively rockier as it climbs to the trip register at 1 mile. At that point you have reached a sandy plateau with sweeping views of the San Ysidro Mountains to the west and the Santa Rosa Mountains through the pass to the east.

The winding flat trail continues beyond the register, soon turning upward and becoming more boulder-strewn. At the summit of the pass, it opens into a wide sandy wash sloping northeast down to the plateau above Clark Valley. About 0.6 mile

◄ *Native California fan palm grove at the Borrego Palm Oasis.*

Eastward below Alcoholic Pass toward the Santa Rosa Mountains.

beyond the pass, the wash opens into a high fan, spreading northeastward. This is a good spot to find a shady rock for lunch and/or contemplation before heading back to the trailhead.

Miles and Directions

0.0 From the trailhead, the well-traveled trail heads northeast.

0.2 The trail climbs a ridge.

0.3 The trail steepens sharply.

1.0 The register is located west of the pass itself.

1.1 This pass is a turnaround point. Retrace your steps to the trailhead for the shorter hike option.

1.7 This is the turnaround point for the longer trip option.

3.4 Return to the trailhead.

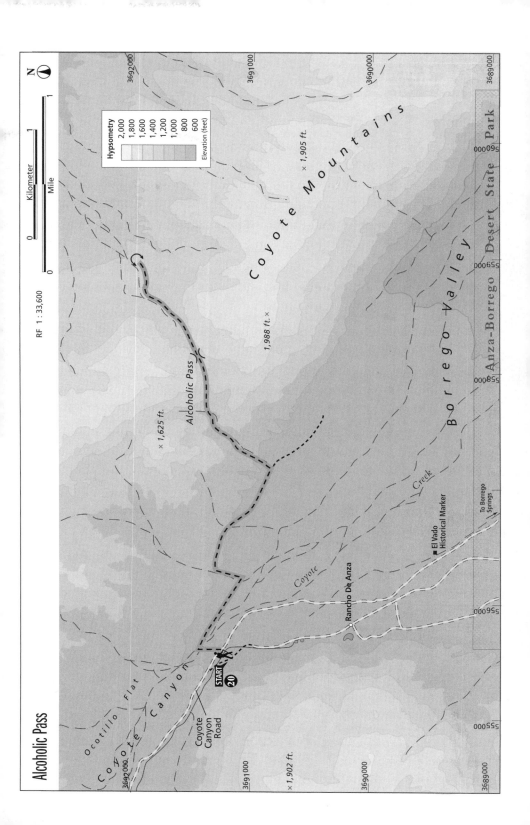

Alcoholic Pass

RF 1 : 33,600

N

Coyote Mountains

Borrego Valley

Anza-Borrego Desert State Park

× 1,905 ft.

1,988 ft. ×

Alcoholic Pass

× 1,625 ft.

Ocotillo Flat

Coyote Canyon

Coyote Canyon Road

START
20

× 1,902 ft.

Coyote Creek

Rancho De Anza

■ El Vado Historical Marker

To Borrego Springs

Hypsometry
2,000
1,800
1,600
1,400
1,200
1,000
800
600
Elevation (feet)

0   Kilometer   1

0   Mile   1

3692000
3691000
3690000
3689000

555000
556000
557000
558000
559000
560000

21 Lower Willows

This soggy, nearly flat hike out and back along Coyote Canyon Creek follows the historic Anza expedition route. Coyote Canyon Road is gated and the canyon is closed to visitors from June 1 to September 30 to protect bighorn-sheep access to water. In winter many birds can be spotted in the lush near-jungle setting of willow thickets, so bring your binoculars.

Start: About 9 miles north of Borrego Springs.
Distance: 4-mile loop.
Approximate hiking time: 2 to 5 hours, depending on distance.
Difficulty: Moderate (due to constant slogging through muck and water).
Trail surface: Dirt path with some rocky and muddy spots; possible stream crossings, so wear old boots.

Seasons: November through May. The trail is cleared each year the week before Thanksgiving; hikers are advised not to use the trail before then as it is generally impenetrable due to overgrown vegetation or erosion from floods.
USGS topo maps: Collins Valley-CA and Borrego Palm Canyon-CA (1:24,000).
Trail contact: Anza-Borrego Desert State Park (see appendix D).

Finding the trailhead: From the park visitor center in Borrego Springs, go east 1.9 miles on Palm Canyon Drive to Christmas Circle; continue east 0.6 mile and turn north (left) onto DiGiorgio Road. Drive north 5 miles until the pavement ends. Continue on unpaved Coyote Canyon Road 5 miles northwest to the Second Crossing (signed). The road is deeply eroded beyond this point, so those with low-clearance vehicles should park here, wade the stream, and walk up Coyote Canyon Road 0.7 mile to the trailhead. The Lower Willows Loop begins on the other side of the stream, about 100 yards past the Third Crossing (signed).

The Hike

The hike up Lower Willows is certain to be a memorable one. In the middle of this arid landscape, the trail follows the stream—along it, across it, in it. The well-signed trail is also used by equestrians since it provides access to Collins Valley and upper Coyote Canyon. The use by horses contributes to the muddy quality of the trail. Posted signs remind hikers that this is a fragile area and it is necessary to stay on the trail, which is often the streambed itself.

For years the Lower Willows streambed was also a roadbed. The Anza expeditions came along this route. The second one, in 1775, came through with a group of 240 settlers and 800 livestock. The water was a welcome relief for the party, but the impact on the riparian zone must have been enormous.

The trail zigzags upstream through dense willow saplings. After this muddy experience, the trail emerges in a wide, dry, sandy wash and the beginning of Middle Willows. At this point, follow the yellow-topped white posts up the bank to the west. On the horizon across Collins Valley, a prominent flat-topped mountain is an

Lower Willows; Indian Canyon; Cougar Canyon; Sheep Canyon

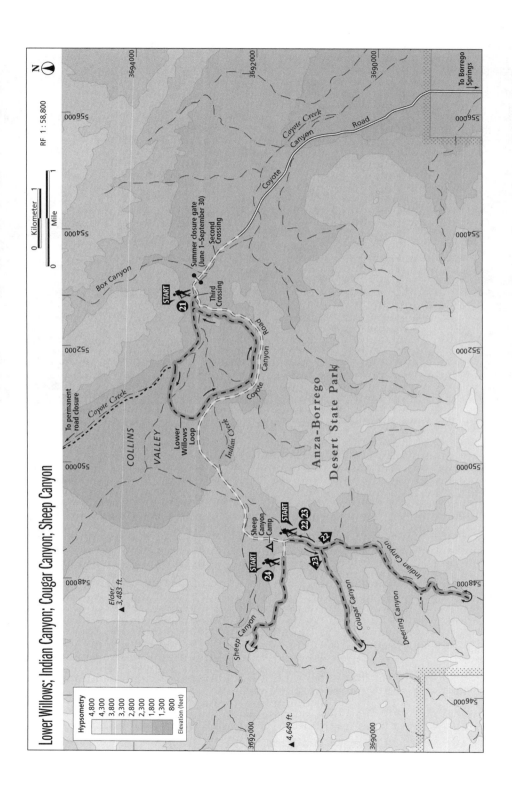

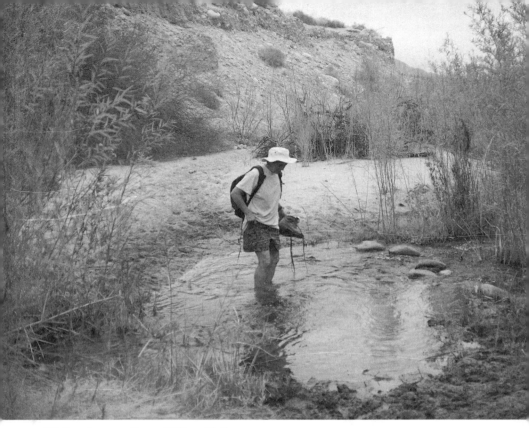

Wading the soggy Lower Willows Trail.

ideal beacon, helping you maintain your westward bearings to Coyote Canyon Road.

Turn left and follow this very rough four-wheel-drive road back to the Lower Willows trailhead. On weekends especially, this section of road is a favorite of the four-wheel-drive crowd. A couple of dicey spots in the canyons challenge even high-clearance vehicles. Be cautious in these spots and give drivers a wide berth.

Note: This section of the park is closed to all visitors from June 1 through September 30 so the bighorn sheep and other species can enjoy the scarce water of Coyote Creek during the hot summer. The gated closure is located right before the Third Crossing.

Miles and Directions

0.0   The trail begins just beyond Third Crossing.

1.0   Emerge from the streambed to a wide wash.

1.1   The trail goes west.

1.9   Turn left on Coyote Canyon Road (dirt road) for the route back to the trailhead.

4.0   Return to the trailhead at Third Crossing.

22 Indian Canyon

This hidden canyon with palm groves and lush vegetation was hit by flooding in 2004. The road to the trailhead has been heavily eroded; contact the park for an update on road conditions before embarking on your outing.

See map on page 71.
Start: About 15 miles northwest of Borrego Springs.
Distance: 4.5 miles out and back if you can drive to the trailhead (11.5 miles if you hike from Third Crossing; 12.5 miles if you hike from Second Crossing).
Approximate hiking time: 3 to 8 hours, depending on how far you can drive.
Difficulty: Strenuous due to eroded trail.

Trail surface: Rocky path, becoming more primitive as you climb.
Seasons: November through April. Coyote Canyon is closed to human visitors from June 1 through September 30 to protect bighorn-sheep access to water sources.
USGS topo map: Borrego Palm Canyon-CA (1:24,000).
Trail contact: Anza-Borrego Desert State Park (see appendix D).

Finding the trailhead: From the visitor center in Borrego Springs, go east 1.9 miles on Palm Canyon Drive to Christmas Circle; continue 0.6 mile beyond the circle to a left turn on DiGiorgio Road. Drive 5 miles to the end of the pavement, then continue north on unpaved Coyote Canyon Road. The first crossing of the stream is not difficult under normal conditions. The Second Crossing may pose a problem for vehicles with low clearance; if so, park there and hike the rest of the way. The distance from the Second Crossing to the Indian Canyon trailhead is approximately 4.6 miles. After the Third Crossing, even high-clearance vehicles may have difficulty. The road beyond that point requires very high clearance, four-wheel drive, and enormous courage. Park near the stream and hike from there.

The hike follows the road, so be careful about traffic, especially on weekends. After you climb the rise to the floor of Collins Valley, you'll see a well-marked section of a horse trail (left) that shortens the trip and avoids road traffic. The actual trailhead is at a parking area 0.1 mile south of the Sheep Canyon road junction where a sign indicates Indian and Cougar Canyons to the south and Sheep Canyon to the west.

The Hike

This hike in Indian Canyon has no convenient road access if your vehicle is not suitable for rough terrain. But this verdant canyon hike is well worth the walk to the trailhead. The stream flow will be reduced in the fall, but the greenery will still be striking.

From the trailhead, the wide trail goes south up the sloping valley floor, surrounded by creosote. When the trail enters the canyon, you may notice damage caused by flooding in 2004. The lush riparian zone was remodeled by the flood. The use trail weaves back and forth across the eroded stream as it goes up the valley. Decades of hiking explorers have created a maze of pathways, which, compounded with the flood damage, make route-finding challenging. The trail becomes faint in

This lone palm tree stands in the Valley of the Thousand Springs in Indian Canyon.

places, but persistent hikers can pick a route by focusing on a distant goal, such as a grove of palm trees.

Heading up the valley through the cobweb of trails, you eventually arrive at a lone palm (0.3 mile from the canyon mouth) at the foot of a slender ridge that marks the confluence of two drainages: Deering Canyon on the west and Indian Canyon on the south. A trail leads to the top of the ridge, from which you gain a panoramic view of this inner valley. Up Deering Canyon, a stair-step palm grove leads up its steep drainage. Sycamores line the more gentle Indian Canyon to the left. Both of these options are worthy of further exploration, although the trail becomes less defined in either direction. Enjoy this remote wilderness before retracing your steps to the trailhead.

Note: If you plan to spend the night in Indian Canyon, remember the park policy regarding camping near water sources. To ensure the nocturnal animals' access to water, it is essential that you camp at least 200 yards from the stream. Remember, too, that all human travel in Coyote Canyon is forbidden from June 1 through September 30; the closure is at the Third Crossing of Coyote Creek.

Miles and Directions

0.0 Start at the Cougar Canyon/Indian Canyon trailhead.

0.5 Continue south at the faded trail signpost where Cougar Canyon goes right.

0.9 The trail hugs the hillside to the right and enters the canyon.

1.8 There's a lone palm at the canyon junction. Deering Canyon is west, while Indian Canyon continues south.

2.25 Continue south into Indian Canyon.

4.5 Turn around and return to the trailhead. (**Note:** It's an 11.5-mile round-trip from Third Crossing and 12.5-mile round-trip from Second Crossing.)

23 Cougar Canyon

If you can drive to the trailhead, Cougar Canyon is a moderate hike up a sloping canyon floor in bighorn-sheep habitat. The trail becomes progressively more primitive as you climb into the canyon.

See map on page 71.
Start: About 15 miles northwest of Borrego Springs.
Distance: 3 miles out and back if you can drive to the trailhead (10 miles if you hike from the Third Crossing of Coyote Creek; 11 miles if you hike from Second Crossing).
Approximate hiking time: 2 hours from canyon mouth.
Difficulty: Moderate from canyon mouth; strenuous for longer hike.

Trail surface: Dirt trail, eroded in places, fading to primitive as you climb.
Seasons: November through April. Coyote Canyon is closed June 1 through September 30 to protect bighorn-sheep access to water sources.
USGS topo map: Borrego Palm Canyon-CA (1:24,000).
Trail contact: Anza-Borrego Desert State Park (see appendix D).

Finding the trailhead: From the Borrego Springs visitor center, go east on Palm Canyon Drive 1.9 miles to Christmas Circle; continue 0.6 mile beyond the circle to left turn on DiGiorgio Road. Drive north on DiGiorgio Road 5 miles until the pavement ends. Continue north 5 miles on Coyote Canyon Road, a primitive but passable route, to the parking area before the Second Crossing (marked with a sign, and also the site of a gauging station). Depending on the water level and clearance of your vehicle, you can also drive to park after the Third Crossing. The road beyond that point requires very high clearance, four-wheel drive, and enormous courage.

The hike from the Second Crossing is about 4.6 miles to the Cougar Canyon/Sheep Canyon junction sign; from the Third Crossing, it is about 4 miles to the junction sign. Follow the jeep road from the crossing, but take the equestrian trail to your left when you reach Collins Valley for a more direct route and to avoid motorized traffic on the road, especially on weekends. From the junction sign, follow the road another 0.1 mile to the Indian Canyon/Cougar Canyon trailhead.

The Hike

This canyon journey is a delightful surprise, not only because of the lengthy hike just to get here, but also because the area's wonders are hidden from view even when you finally arrive at the canyon mouth. Have faith, and keep on hiking.

After Collins Valley and the dry lower reaches of Indian Canyon, the turnoff to Cougar Canyon seems like just another arid desert valley. Then, as you round the bend in the lower reaches of the canyon, your ears may detect the tinkling of a waterfall. Your eyes will be astounded with the lush riparian area. Sandy beaches and inviting pools dot the watercourse down the canyon, all reached by a labyrinth of trails that wind around boulders. Sycamores and palm trees are scattered along the stream bank above rock-lined grottos. Plan on taking time to explore and enjoy this rare water wonderland before your return trip. Some changes to the canyon occurred in the fall-of-2004 flash flood. The canyon floor was scoured in places and some of the trees were swept away. The desert is the scene of dramatic changes!

The stream may be only a trickle in the fall, but the vegetation will still provide a colorful contrast with the rest of Collins Valley. If you plan to camp overnight, remember the park regulations about water sources. Since desert wildlife is largely nocturnal, considerate campers don't obstruct animals' access to water. Camp at least 200 yards away from the stream.

Note: The summer closure of Coyote Canyon, from June 1 through September 30, makes this outing off-limits during that season.

Miles and Directions

0.0   The trail goes south from the Cougar Canyon/Indian Canyon trailhead.

0.5   At the trail junction, a faded sign indicates the Cougar Canyon trail to the right.

1.5   The trail fades as it climbs.

3.0   Retrace your steps to the trailhead. (**Note:** Round-trip from Third Crossing is 10 miles, from Second Crossing 11 miles.)

◀ *The stream in Cougar Canyon brings a swath of greenery to an arid landscape.*

24 Sheep Canyon

A primitive hike through a lush canyon with year-round pools of water, and an optional tough side trip to an idyllic waterfall, Sheep Canyon is a stark contrast to the surrounding desert. You also will see evidence of the 2004 flood that radically altered the landscape.

See map on page 71.
Start: About 15 miles northwest of Borrego Springs.
Distance: 3 miles out and back if you drive to the trailhead (11 miles if you hike from the Second Crossing on Coyote Canyon Road).
Approximate hiking time: 2 hours; 5 hours for longer hike.
Difficulty: Strenuous.
Trail surface: Primitive dirt and rock trail with trailless sections on and above the canyon floor.

Seasons: November through April. The area above Lower Willows, which includes Collins Valley/Sheep Canyon, is closed to human visitors from June 1 through September 30 to protect bighorn-sheep access to water sources.
USGS topo map: Borrego Palm Canyon-CA (1:24,000).
Trail contact: Anza-Borrego Desert State Park (see appendix D).

Finding the trailhead: From the park visitor center in Borrego Springs, drive east 1.9 miles on Palm Canyon Drive to Christmas Circle; continue 0.6 mile beyond the circle and make a left turn on DiGiorgio Road. Drive 5 miles to the end of the pavement, then continue north on unpaved Coyote Canyon Road. The first wash crossing is normally not difficult. The Second Crossing may stop low-clearance vehicles. If stopped, park and continue on foot up the Coyote Canyon Road. The road distance from the Second Crossing to the Sheep Canyon trailhead is approximately 4.6 miles. After the Third Crossing, even four-wheel-drive, high-clearance vehicles may be stopped at the foot of an extremely steep, rocky stretch of the road.

While hiking the road, be on the lookout for four-wheel-drive vehicles, especially on weekends. After climbing to the floor of Collins Valley, veer left on a well-marked horse trail that shortens the distance and avoids vehicular traffic. Upon reaching the signed Cougar Canyon/Sheep Canyon road junction, turn right (northwest) and proceed another 0.25 mile to the official trailhead at the primitive camp near the mouth of Sheep Canyon.

The Hike

Water flows through the rugged confines of Sheep Canyon during most of the year, although the canyon is apt to be dry by the time autumn rolls around. Depending on the season, a bubbling stream flows down steep rocks into deep pools lined by shady grottos. A few palm trees scattered along the brushy cottonwood-sycamore bottom make this twisting gorge a true desert oasis. A primitive on–again/off–again use trail winds up the lower reaches of Sheep Canyon into the North Fork. The "one-hundred-year" flood of 2004 has rearranged the terrain in Sheep Canyon, as well as in the other canyons in the northern part of the park.

Small waterfalls and deep pools are among the surprises in the remote North Fork of Sheep Canyon.

From the primitive camp the rock-lined trail immediately crosses the wash. The trail crosses the stream several times before working up a side ridge at 0.4 mile near the South Fork, which joins the main Sheep Canyon from the left. The South Fork is one of the steepest, roughest canyons in the park and should only be traversed by well-conditioned, experienced rock scramblers. It is possible to take a short but strenuous side trip by entering the South Fork at mile 0.4. The next 0.3 mile consists of gaining 350 feet through heavy brush and over rock slabs to the base of an idyllic 30-foot waterfall overseen by a small palm grove.

After enjoying this sublime setting, double-back to the main canyon and continue up the left side of the North Fork. Shortly, the trail crosses the stream to the right side in a dense mixture of palm and sycamore trees. Within 0.2 mile a huge boulder blocks the trail. Before climbing over the boulder, savor the music of rushing water and the stillness of the deep canyon.

At 0.7 mile the trail drops to several gigantic boulders that form a cavern. Backtrack about 30 yards to a faint path that climbs between the boulders. Maneuver under and around several rock overhangs to follow the most prominent path, which soon crosses over to the left side of the canyon. This is a scenic alcove, with palm trees wedged in a narrow rock chute surrounded by the geologic faulting of tilted rock beds. The trail pitches steeply upward before dropping to the palm grove.

At 1 mile the trail again descends, this time to a lovely pool. Climb the stair-step rock to the left of the pool, soon reaching an overlook above a "weeping" rock where running water fans out across the face of a wall. Continue up the rough, rocky slope to a level shelf where a noticeable trail is again picked up. At 1.2 miles the canyon narrows, with bedded rock rising above two palm trees at 2,150 feet.

At 1.5 miles any resemblance to a trail vanishes near a lovely series of pools nestled beneath tall palms and sycamores. Extremely steep, loose, granitic side slopes demand slow and careful route-finding from this point on. This is a good turnaround point for a 3-mile round-trip sampler of the wild beauty of the North Fork of Sheep Canyon.

Miles and Directions

0.0 The primitive camp trailhead is near the mouth of Sheep Canyon.

0.4 The South Fork enters from the left; continue right up the main North Fork.

1.0 The trail reaches a deep pool just below a "weeping" rock wall.

1.5 The primitive trail disappears, making this a good turnaround point.

3.0 Return to the trailhead. (**Note:** It's an 11-mile round-trip from the Second Crossing, a 10-mile round-trip from the Third Crossing.)

25 Pacific Crest Trail: Table Mountain and Combs Peak

These two out-and-back day hikes take you through colorful canyons and chaparral/woodlands. You can reach some prominent peaks along these remote stretches of the Pacific Crest Trail (PCT).

Start: About 70 miles northwest of Borrego Springs.
Distance: Southern segment, 5 miles out and back to Combs Peak; Northern segment, 5 miles out and back to Table Mountain.
Approximate hiking time: 3 to 5 hours.
Difficulty: Strenuous to Combs Peak; moderate to Table Mountain.

Trail surface: Dirt and rocky trail; short off-trail route-finding climbs to both summits.
Seasons: October through May.
USGS topo map: Bucksnort Mountain-CA (1:24,000).
Trail contact: Anza-Borrego Desert State Park (see appendix D).

Finding the trailhead: To reach the Southern segment, take California Highway 79. About 3.3 miles south of Oak Grove and 10.8 miles north of Warner Springs, turn east on Chihuahua Road. After 6.5 miles the paved road curves right. Continue straight ahead to the end of the pavement and the beginning of the dirt Lost Valley Road. Continue past the biological station gate at 1.7 miles, reaching the park boundary at 3.1 miles. About 2 miles beyond this, the Lost Valley Road intersects the PCT (5.2 miles beyond the pavement). The trail to Combs Peak takes off to the left, heading north.

To find the trailhead for the Northern segment, begin at the fire station in the town of Anza. Drive 1 mile east on California Highway 371, turn right (south) on Kirby Road, then drive 1.1 miles to Wellman Road. (The road names change, but simply follow the paved road). Turn left on Wellman Road and proceed 1 mile to Terwilliger Road. Go right (south) on Terwilliger Road for 3 miles to Coyote Canyon Road, turn left, and continue 1.9 miles to a T intersection. Turn right toward the signed Coyote Canyon dirt road (pavement ends here) and follow the main dirt road 2.1 miles to the UPPER COYOTE CANYON ROAD sign on a hill. Park here and walk about 0.1 mile down rough Coyote Canyon Road to the PCT road crossing. The trail to Table Mountain takes off to the left, heading north.

The Hike

Anza-Borrego contains six long segments of the Pacific Crest Trail (PCT), which are separated from one another by major road crossings or by stretches of the trail that extend outside the park boundary. It is the opinion of the authors that the four park segments of the PCT from Pioneer Mail north to the Lost Valley Road run too close to major roads for quality backcountry hiking or are too long and dry for most destination–oriented day hikers. In contrast, the two remote northern segments presented here are split only by the rough Coyote Canyon Road, offering varied hiking opportunities in a scenic region of higher mountains and deep canyons.

The Pacific Crest Trail meets Lost Valley Road, south of Combs Peak.

The two PCT hikes described below are presented together because they are in close proximity along what is essentially the same stretch of the PCT. With a car shuttle it would be possible to take a 12-mile point-to-point day hike from Lost Valley Road north to Coyote Canyon Road, which is the takeoff point for the out-and-back hike north to Table Mountain.

Southern Segment

The PCT trailhead on the Lost Valley Road is 2 miles east of the park boundary sign. The PCT road crossing is faintly marked on a wooden post, along with a RIVERSIDE COUNTY LINE 6 sign. From the road, hike left (north) on the PCT, which maintains a moderate grade along the eastern slopes of Bucksnort Mountain. After 1.9 miles of climbing along the steep side slopes, the trail comes to a small level saddle at 5,595 feet to the immediate northeast of Combs Peak—the apex of Bucksnort Mountain. Pause among the Coulter pines here for a 180-degree view from lofty San Gorgonio Mountain to the north to the stark crest of the Santa Rosa Mountains and Salton Sea eastward. Coulter pine is also called "big-cone pine," and no wonder. It displays

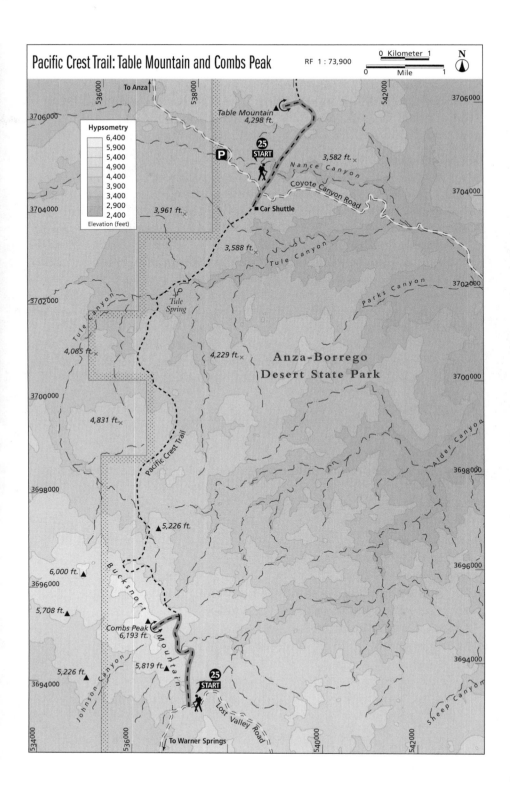

Pacific Crest Trail: Table Mountain and Combs Peak

RF 1 : 73,900

0 Kilometer 1

0 Mile 1

N

536000
538000
542000

To Anza

3706000

Table Mountain
4,298 ft.

3706000

Hypsometry

| 6,400 |
| 5,900 |
| 5,400 |
| 4,900 |
| 4,400 |
| 3,900 |
| 3,400 |
| 2,900 |
| 2,400 |

Elevation (feet)

25 START

P

3,582 ft. ×

Nance Canyon

3704000

Coyote Canyon Road

3704000

3,961 ft. ×

■ Car Shuttle

3,588 ft. ×

Tule Canyon

Parks Canyon

3702000

Tule
Spring

3702000

Tule Canyon

4,065 ft. ×

4,229 ft. ×

**Anza-Borrego
Desert State Park**

3700000

3700000

4,831 ft. ×

Pacific Crest Trail

Alder Canyon

3698000

3698000

▲ 5,226 ft.

3696000

6,000 ft. ▲

Bucksnort

3696000

5,708 ft. ▲

Combs Peak
6,193 ft. ▲

Mountain

Johnson Canyon

5,819 ft. ▲

25 START

3694000

5,226 ft. ▲

3694000

Lost Valley Road

Sheep Canyon

To Warner Springs

534000
536000
540000
542000

the heaviest cones of all pine species on the planet—each cone weighing in at four to five pounds!

To expand the field of view from 180 to 360 degrees, climb southeasterly to the summit of Combs Peak, gaining 600 feet in 0.6 mile. Route-finding through dense brush is required, but the view alone makes the effort worthwhile. Return the way you came to complete this 5-mile round-trip sampler of the PCT.

Northern Segment

From the crest of the hill at the UPPER COYOTE CANYON ROAD sign near the park boundary gate, walk down the rough four-wheel-drive Coyote Canyon Road about 0.1 mile to its intersection with the PCT. This stretch of the PCT is also part of the California Riding and Hiking Trail. Take the trail to the left (north), which is marked by a mountain-lion-warning sign. The trail descends a gully, switchbacks once, then drops to the grassy bottom of colorful Nance Canyon. A gradual grade wraps around a low knoll, then crosses a rugged slope that provides vistas to the east and south of Coyote and other secluded canyons in the wild northern reaches of the park.

The trail continues climbing to a 4,185-foot brush-covered notch on Table Mountain. The actual summit of the broad expanse of the mountain is only a 0.2-mile, 110-foot off-trail climb to the west, less than 0.5 mile south of the north boundary of the park. Most of this 5-mile round-trip route crosses Bureau of Land Management sections of land included within the park's boundaries.

Miles and Directions

Southern segment:
- **0.0** Start at Lost Valley Road (5,050 feet).
- **1.9** Arrive at the saddle northeast of Combs Peak and the beginning of the off-trail climb to Combs Peak.
- **2.5** Reach Combs Peak (6,193 feet).
- **5.0** Return to the trailhead.

Northern segment:
- **0.0** Start at Upper Coyote Canyon Road.
- **0.3** Arrive at Nance Canyon.
- **2.3** Arrive at a 4,185-foot pass east of Table Mountain.
- **2.5** Reach the summit of Table Mountain (4,298 feet).
- **5.0** Return to the trailhead.

Joshua Tree
National Park

S traddling the transition zone between the Mojave and the Colorado Deserts and containing vast regions of enchanting granite rock formations, Joshua Tree National Park is the smallest of the federal parks in Southern California. It's also the closest to the Los Angeles metropolitan area—with the expanding cities of Palm Springs, Palm Desert, and Yucca Valley at its very doorstep. Intensifying pressures on this desert area's wildlands inspired the supporters of the California Desert Protection Act.

Joshua Tree was changed from a national monument to a national park by the 1994 act and was enlarged from 559,995 to 794,000 acres. The act was but one chapter in the legislative history of the Joshua Tree park and its varying size and status. The area was originally set aside as a national monument by President Franklin D. Roosevelt in 1936. Early desert conservationists led by Minerva Hamilton Hoyt had pressed the White House for such protection due to the destructive impact of automobiles and visitors in the 1920s and 1930s and the wholesale removal of Joshua trees and cacti to satisfy urban gardeners, as well as the ravages of mining.

By executive decree, FDR established Joshua Tree National Monument, protecting 825,000 acres from further mining development and placing it under National Park Service administration. In 1950 the pressures of the Cold War and the mining industry caused Congress to remove 289,000 acres from the monument. Again, in 1961 Congress reduced the boundary to permit mining in the monument's perimeter. The 1994 act expanded the new national park to 794,000 acres with additions to the Little San Bernardino Range on the southwest, the Pinto Mountains on the north, the Coxcombs on the east, the Eagle Mountains on the southeast, and the Cottonwoods on the south. Simultaneously the act enlarged the area designated as wilderness in 1976 by 35 percent, to 585,040 acres. Thus 74 percent of the present national park is wilderness.

The new park is undertaking an ambitious management plan in order to both protect its desert lands and provide recreational opportunities for the millions of visitors who arrive annually. A key component of such overall management is a new wilderness management plan where trails, campsites, and area closures are studied

and reviewed with the help of a citizen review committee. Currently there are only six official hiking trails and ten nature trails in the park. The multitude of hiking trails developed as use trails are being studied to determine which should become official trails. Concerns over preserving archaeological and historical sites, managing the recreation demands of bicyclists and rock climbers, and protecting desert habitat and the wildlife that lives here are among the competing factors that need to be evaluated in the park's infancy. Since park rules may change quickly in such an atmosphere, check at the visitor center in Twentynine Palms or Cottonwood for current regulations and guidelines before embarking on a backcountry visit in Joshua Tree National Park.

Natural History

Mountain ranges define the park's boundaries (the Little San Bernardinos, the Cottonwoods, the Eagles and Coxcombs, and the Pinto Mountains) and also dominate its center (the Hexies). The geologic feature that draws visitors, photographers, hikers, and climbers lies in the park's north-central section: the gargantuan monzogranite boulders, domes, and peaks. This ethereal landscape was formed over 180 million years, beginning with the earth's shifting plates and igneous intrusions from the earth's molten core. This activity took place beneath the earth's surface, which was covered by an immense inland sea. Eventually, rising mountain ranges altered climatic conditions, gradually reducing the sea. The former sea floor was forced upward. Lakes and rolling hills, grasslands, and forests developed on the former ocean floor where mastodons, saber-toothed tigers, and other mammals roamed the land before their extinction. The pattern of lifting and eroding began creating Joshua Tree's canyons, rugged mountains, and exposed granite. Thousands of feet of layered sediment, volcanic ash, and metamorphic rock were eroded, producing Joshua Tree's well-known rounded granite topography. Geologic forces continue to modify Joshua Tree with weathering and the constant shifting of the earth's unstable crust.

Plants and Animals

Hiking in Joshua Tree National Park will quickly reveal the contrasts between Colorado Desert and Mojave Desert vegetation. Around the Cottonwood Ranger Station and in the Pinto Basin, creosote, ocotillo, and cholla are the dominant vegetative types in the lower, drier, and hotter Colorado Desert. In the Mojave Desert, ranging from 3,000 to 6,000 feet in elevation and receiving 6 to 8 inches of rainfall per year, there is a virtual explosion of vegetation: piñon-juniper forests on mountain slopes, smoke trees and mesquite with desert mistletoe in the washes, Joshua tree forests on the valley floors with manzanita, catclaw, and brittlebush, and the ever-present creosote bush.

◀ *A Joshua tree attains monumental proportions on*
the Pushawalla Plateau.

Five desert oases are also found in Joshua Tree National Park. These islands of native California fan palms have attracted animal and human visitors for centuries and remain magnets for wildlife- and bird-watchers today.

The preservation of the unique and fragile desert community of plants was one of the leading motivations in the establishment of Joshua Tree National Monument in the 1930s as well as the California Desert Protection Act of 1994. Joshua trees, the enchanting symbol of the park, are slow growers. This member of the agave family takes hundreds of years to reach its mature height of 30 feet. Joshua trees are shallow rooted and thus susceptible to both wind and theft. They are now protected by federal law, as are all plants in the park.

The annual blooming of desert wildflowers occurs primarily from late February through May depending on the weather and elevation. The Joshua Tree National Park wildflower hotline is (760) 767–4684. Several organizations provide flower information for the entire desert area via hotlines: Living Desert, (760) 340–0435; the Mojave Native Plant Society, (702) 648–2177; and the Payne Foundation, (818) 768–3533. The Joshua Tree National Park Association sells an illustrated brochure of wildflowers for $1.25.

Desert animal life here is predominantly nocturnal and usually invisible to the human eye. In Joshua Tree, coyotes are plentiful. Park officials are concerned with this omnivore's habituation to humans and their food, especially around the established campgrounds. Visitors are cautioned not to feed coyotes and to secure their food and garbage to prevent coyote theft. Jackrabbits, kangaroo rats, golden eagles, and yucca night lizards may be spotted going about their business of surviving in the desert. The widely acclaimed desert tortoise, listed as threatened under the Endangered Species Act, also lives here in the Mojave Desert. Among the tortoise's primary enemies (after vehicles) are disease, habitat destruction, illegal collecting, and ravens, whose population has skyrocketed. Hikers lucky enough to see one of these rare turtles should appreciate its presence from afar. All wildlife in the park is protected by federal law. No hunting or collecting is allowed.

The park has a diverse population of birds, many of whom are transients since the area is on a major migration route. For example, even here in the desert, herons and ducks can be seen on Barker Dam Lake on their spring or fall trips. With more than 250 species on the checklist, birding in Joshua Tree National Park is exciting. The National Park Association has published a birder's checklist with information on each species, available for 50 cents.

Human History

Ten thousand years ago, early humans found conditions in the Pinto Basin, with its verdant meadows and slow river, ideal for their hunting-and-gathering, seminomadic lifestyle. Little is known of postglacial Pinto Man, however, since he traveled light and left only spear points and traces of habitation sites.

Serrano, Chemehuevi, and Cahuilla groups of Native Americans from the Great Basin and Colorado River to the east occupied the Joshua Tree area in small bands at the time of the European arrival in the 1700s. Their nomadic lives centered on the oases. They used a wide variety of desert plants as food and medicine. The Cottonwood Spring Nature Trail provides interesting information on these materials and Cahuilla use of desert products. These early groups hunted with bow and arrow and created pottery. They left behind petroglyphs, pictographs, and *morteros* at various sites in the park. All archaeological sites are protected by federal law: Do not remove or deface any artifacts. Please leave them for future generations to enjoy.

American interest in this desert region began with miners in the 1860s. The intense search for and development of mineral resources was to continue for the following century. Due to abnormally wet winters in the 1880s, ranchers soon followed to build watering tanks and establish cattle herds on the sparse grasslands of Joshua Tree's higher valleys. Mining excitement continued, with numerous booms and consequent busts, but ranching faded as a profitable lifestyle when more normal precipitation returned in the early 1900s. Most of the barriers built to hold water, called tanks, have been erased as sand and sediment have filled in the reservoirs behind the crude dams. Barker Dam Lake is one exception; the others are vanishing into the desert. The Keys Ranch is a reminder of the ranching heyday in the desert. On the other hand, conspicuous mine sites, mills, mining equipment, and prospectors' dwellings are ubiquitous here. All mine shafts are considered dangerous and should be avoided by visitors. The vast majority have not been secured and are hazardous.

Regulations

With the recent expansion and upgrade to national park status, the park administration is evaluating policies and programs to meet the dual goal of preservation and recreation. Check at the visitor center for updated regulations before embarking on your hike.

The entrance fee for Joshua Tree National Park is currently $15.00 for a seven-day pass or $5.00 for seven days if you walk in. A $50.00 National Park Pass entitles you to unlimited park entrance at any national park for one year. Fee stations are located at all major entrances.

All nine campgrounds in the park are open year-round, six of them on a first-come, first-served basis. From backcountry registration boards, camping is permitted at least 1 mile from a road and 500 feet from any trail. Large sections of the park have been designated day-use-only areas in order to protect access to water for desert wildlife, especially bighorn sheep. These Special Resource Protection Zones are currently in the Wonderland of Rocks/Queen Mountain/Fortynine Palms Canyon region in the north; northwest of Keys View in the central region; around the Pushwalla Plateau in the south; in a portion of the Coxcomb Mountains on the eastern end; and near Lost Palm Oasis in the southeast. If your plans include backcountry camping, be sure to check at a ranger station for the current day-use-only boundaries, some of which may be changed as a result of backcountry plan revisions and wildlife requirements.

Gathering of firewood or of any vegetation is forbidden throughout the park. Ground fires are allowed only in established fire rings in the campgrounds.

Backcountry campers must begin their trips at one of twelve backcountry trail boards. Overnight parking is allowed only at these locations, since cars may not be left overnight elsewhere on the park roads. Campers must register at these boards before their trips. It is also suggested that day hikers register, for safety as well as for the park's statistical use.

Bicycles, like all vehicles, must remain on designated roads. To accommodate greater bike use, the park contemplates providing additional biking opportunities in the expansion areas of former BLM lands on the southern side of the Little San Bernardino and Cottonwood Mountains.

Dogs and other pets must remain within 100 yards of roads and campgrounds, and must be leashed at all times. As is the case of all the desert parks, it is strongly recommended that all pets, especially dogs, be left at home. They are not adapted for the desert; the indigenous animal population does not appreciate them either.

The presence of private inholdings is a challenge for park administration. Boundaries are generally posted. Hikers must respect private property in their travels by closing gates and staying off private land when posted.

With the management of Joshua Tree in transition, it is wise to stop at the visitor center or a ranger station to get updated regulations and information on park policies. The visitor centers in Twentynine Palms, Blackrock Canyon, and at the Cottonwood entrance have excellent maps, brochures, and books, as well as knowledgeable staffs. Call or check the park's Web site for hours. Information on weather and road conditions is also essential for successful hiking in Joshua Tree National Park.

How and When to Get There

Joshua Tree National Park is bounded on the south by Interstate 10. The Cottonwood entrance to the park is 65 miles west of Blythe and 52 miles east of Palm Springs. California Highway 62 (Twentynine Palms Highway) curves along the park's northern boundary. There are two entrances on the north: the West Entrance south of the town of Joshua Tree and the North Entrance south of Twentynine Palms. The latter is the location of the park's main visitor center.

For air travel, the closest airport is at Palm Springs. Other commercial air facilities are in Riverside and Los Angeles, 100 and 150 miles west of the park respectively.

Daytime temperatures at Joshua Tree average around one hundred degrees during June, July, August, and September. Comfortable hiking weather predominates during the rest of the year, although it can get toasty as early as May. July and August frequently bring brief thunderstorms; rain also occurs in December and January. Weather charts are not reliable, however. In February we experienced rain, snow, *and* hot weather, so desert hikers need to be prepared for a variety of climatic conditions.

The rocky trail climbs steeply to the Hexahedron Mine.

Joshua Tree National Park Hikes at a Glance

Hike (Number)	Distance	Difficulty*	Features	Page
Arch Rock Nature Trail (43)	0.3 mile	E	geology	145
Barker Dam Nature Trail Loop (57)	1.1 miles	E	historic site, archaeology	178
Black Rock Loop Trail (62)	10.5 miles	S	vista	195
Boy Scout Trail/Willow Hole (59)	12.0 miles	M	wash, boulders	182
California R & H Trail:				
Covington Flat to Keys View (61)	15.0 miles	M/S	highest peak	191
Keys View to Park Route 11 (42)	11.0 miles	M	vista	141
Cap Rock Nature Trail (47)	0.4 mile	E	nature trail	155
Cholla Cactus Garden				
Nature Trail (35)	0.25 mile	E	nature trail	120
Conejo Well/Eagle				
Mountains (30)	12.0 miles	M	historic site	104
Contact Mine (51)	3.4 miles	S	mine site	164
Cottonwood Spring/				
Moorten's Mill Site (27)	1.0 mile	E	oasis, mill site	98
Cottonwood Spring				
Nature Trail (29)	1.2 miles	E	nature trail	103
Coxcomb Mountains (31)	7.0 miles	M	vista	107
Crown Prince Lookout (45)	3.0 miles	E	vista	151
Desert Queen Mine				
and Wash (49)	4.0 miles	E/M	mine sites	158
Fortynine Palms Oasis (52)	3.0 miles	M	oasis	166
Golden Bee Mine (34)	4.0 miles	S	mine site	118
Hexahedron Mine (37)	8.4 miles	M	mine site	125
Hidden Valley Nature Trail (58)	1.0 mile	E	nature trail	180
High View Nature Trail (63)	1.3 miles	M	nature trail	198
Indian Cove Nature Trail (54)	0.6 mile	E	nature trail	172
Keys View Loop/				
Inspiration Peak (40)	1.75 miles	E/M	vista	134
Lost Horse Mine Loop (41)	7.8 miles	S	mine site, vista	137
Lost Palms Oasis (26)	7.6 miles	M	oasis	95
Lucky Boy Vista (48)	2.5 miles	E	vista	156
Mastodon Peak Loop (28)	3.0 miles	E/M	mine, mill sites	101
Pine City (50)	3.4 miles	E	mine site	160
Pine City/Canyon (50)	6.5 miles	E/M	canyon	160
Pleasant Valley to El Dorado Mine/				
Pinto Basin (36)	7.7 miles	M	mine site	122
Porcupine Wash/				
Ruby Lee Mill Site (32)	7.9 miles	M	wash, mill site	111

Porcupine Wash to				
Monument Mountain (33)	14.0 miles	S	wash, peak	115
Pushawalla Plateau/Canyon (39)	10.2 miles	S	vista, canyon	130
Quail Wash to				
West Entrance Wash (60)	8.2 miles	M	vista	187
Johnny Lang Canyon (60)	14.2 miles	S	historic sites	189
Ryan Mountain (46)	3.0 miles	S	vista	152
Sand Dunes (38)	2.5 miles	E	sand dunes	128
Skull Rock Nature Trail (44)	1.7 miles	E	nature trail	148
Sneakeye Spring (53)	1.0 mile	S	canyon	169
Wall Street Mill (55)	2.0 miles	E	mill site	173
Wonderland Wash (56)	2.0 miles	E	boulders	176

*E=easy, M=moderate, S=strenuous

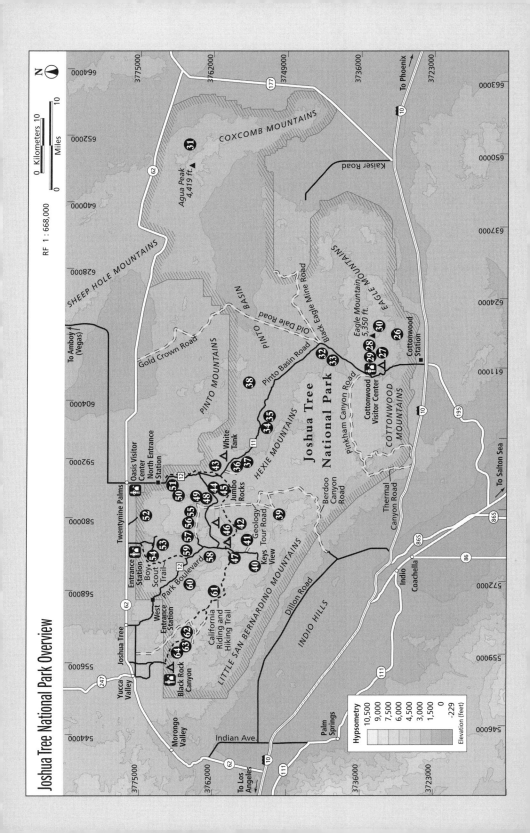

Joshua Tree National Park Overview

RF 1 : 668,000

N

0 Kilometers 10
0 Miles 10

Joshua Tree National Park

Hypsometry
10,500
9,000
7,500
6,000
4,500
3,000
1,500
0
-229
Elevation (feet)

SHEEP HOLE MOUNTAINS

COXCOMB MOUNTAINS

Agua Peak
4,419 ft. ▲ 51

PINTO MOUNTAINS

PINTO BASIN

Gold Crown Road

Old Dale Road

Pinto Basin Road

Black Eagle Mine Road

Kaiser Road

To Amboy
(Vegas)

Twentynine Palms

Oasis Visitor Center
North Entrance Station

White Tank

Jumbo Rocks

Geology Tour Road

Keys View

HEXIE MOUNTAINS

Joshua Tree
National Park

Pinkham Canyon Road

Berdoo Canyon Road

EAGLE MOUNTAINS

Eagle Mountain
5,350 ft. ▲

Cottonwood Visitor Center

Cottonwood Station

COTTONWOOD MOUNTAINS

Thermal Canyon Road

To Salton Sea

Entrance Station

Boy Scout Trail

Park Boulevard

West Entrance Station

California Riding and Hiking Trail

LITTLE SAN BERNARDINO MOUNTAINS

Dillon Road

INDIO HILLS

Black Rock Canyon

Joshua Tree

Yucca Valley

Morongo Valley

Indian Ave.

Palm Springs

To Los Angeles

Indio

Coachella

To Phoenix

26 Lost Palms Oasis

Right at the southern edge of the park is an oasis with the largest group of California fan palms in Joshua Tree National Park. Take this moderate out-and-back hike to an overlook, then continue down to the oasis, and go even farther down Lost Palms Canyon if you're up for it.

Start: 42 miles southeast of Twentynine Palms and 1.2 miles southeast of Cottonwood Visitor Center.
Distance: 7.6 miles out and back.
Approximate hiking time: 4 to 6 hours.
Difficulty: Moderate.

Trail surface: Dirt path.
Seasons: October through April.
USGS topo map: Cottonwood Spring-CA (1:24,000).
Trail contact: Joshua Tree National Park (see appendix D).

Finding the trailhead: From California Highway 62 in Twentynine Palms, take Utah Trail south 4 miles to the North Entrance of the park; continue south on Park Route 12 4.8 miles to the Pinto Y intersection. Turn left onto Park Route 11 and go 32 miles to the Cottonwood Visitor Center. Turn left and drive 1.2 miles to the Cottonwood Spring parking area.

From the south, take the Cottonwood Canyon exit from Interstate 10, 24 miles east of Indio. Go north 8 miles to the Cottonwood Visitor Center. Turn right and go 1.2 miles to the Cottonwood Spring parking area.

The Hike

This is a dry, high hike with no protection from sun and wind. It is a heavily signed route, with arrows at every bend and every wash crossing, and even mileage posts.

The trail follows the up-and-down topography of the ridge-and-wash terrain. At each ridge, one hopes to spot the oasis ahead, particularly if it is a hot and sunny day. Not until the final overlook will such hopes be realized. And after crossing numerous ridges, descending rocky paths to narrow canyons, and winding up to more ridges, it is a welcome site!

This is the largest group of California fan palms in Joshua Tree National Park, and they are majestic. The oasis is a day-use-only area to protect bighorn-sheep access to water; you may be lucky enough to spot one of the elusive animals on the rocky slopes above the oasis.

A rocky path leads 0.3 mile from the overlook to the oasis. Large boulders, intermittent streams, willow thickets, and sandy beaches make this a delightful spot in which to pause before your return trip.

Miles and Directions

0.0 The trail begins above the oasis at Cottonwood Spring. The well-marked trail goes up a wash and over a ridge. Continue straight to the oasis.

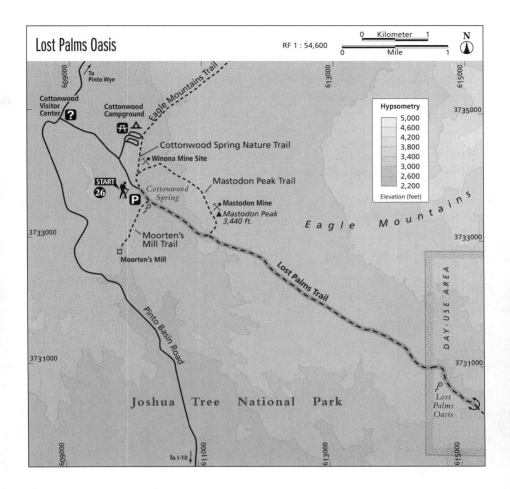

Lost Palms Oasis

RF 1 : 54,600

0   Kilometer   1

0   Mile   1

N

To
Pinto Wye

Cottonwood
Visitor
Center

Cottonwood
Campground

Eagle Mountains Trail

Cottonwood Spring Nature Trail

Winona Mine Site

START
26

Cottonwood
Spring

Mastodon Peak Trail

Mastodon Mine

Mastodon Peak
3,440 ft.

Moorten's
Mill Trail

Moorten's Mill

Pinto Basin Road

Lost Palms Trail

E a g l e   M o u n t a i n s

Hypsometry

5,000
4,600
4,200
3,800
3,400
3,000
2,600
2,200
Elevation (feet)

D A Y - U S E   A R E A

Joshua   Tree   National   Park

Lost
Palms
Oasis

To I-10

3.5   View the palm oasis from the canyon overlook.

3.8   Reach the floor of the oasis.

7.6   Return to the trailhead.

Option: The more energetic hiker may like to continue about another mile down the canyon through the willows and around the pools, along an intermittent rusty pipe that was used to channel water to a mining site far to the south. The trail, such as it is, becomes more challenging, with larger boulders to contend with, but at the end you'll reach another set of palm trees—the Victory Palms. When your rock-scrambling is satisfied, it is time to return to the oasis, and retrace your steps to the spring.

◀ *Looking south from Lost Palms Oasis toward Victory Palms and Chiriaco Summit.*

27 Cottonwood Spring/Moorten's Mill Site

A short hike down Cottonwood Wash allows you to enjoy a lush spring, an arid desert wash, and a historic mining site—truly a cross section of the variety of Joshua Tree National Park.

Start: 42 miles southeast of Twentynine Palms and 1.2 miles southeast of Cottonwood Visitor Center.
Distance: 1 mile out and back.
Approximate hiking time: Less than 1 hour.
Difficulty: Easy.

Trail surface: Sandy wash.
Seasons: October through April.
USGS topo map: Cottonwood Spring-CA (1:24,000).
Trail contact: Joshua Tree National Park (see appendix D).

The road ramp at Little Chilcoot Pass, built by miners in the 1800s, enabled freight wagons to bypass the rock waterfall in Cottonwood Canyon.

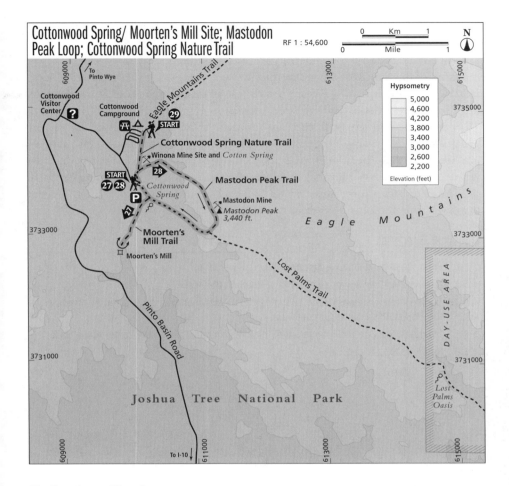

Cottonwood Spring/ Moorten's Mill Site; Mastodon Peak Loop; Cottonwood Spring Nature Trail

RF 1 : 54,600

Finding the trailhead: From Twentynine Palms, take Utah Trail south 4 miles from California Highway 62 to the North Entrance of the park. Continue south on Park Route 12 for 4.8 miles to the left turn on Park Route 11 at the Pinto Y intersection (signed for Cottonwood Spring). Drive south 32 miles to the Cottonwood Campground and Visitor Center. Turn left and drive 1.2 miles to the parking area. The oasis is down the ramp to the southeast; you can see the palm trees from the parking lot.

From the south, take Interstate 10 24 miles east of Indio to the Cottonwood Canyon exit; turn north and continue 8 miles to the Cottonwood Campground and Visitor Center. Turn right and drive 1.2 miles to the parking area.

The Hike

Cottonwood Spring is a lovely patch of greenery in an otherwise arid landscape. The cottonwoods are natives. The palms appeared around 1920, probably by seeds transported by the birds. The sight is satisfying, and obviously the birds enjoy the location.

The hike down the wash provides a display of a wash plant community in the Colorado Desert. Mesquite and smoke trees are dominant.

The ramp around the boulders in the wash will be quite a surprise. The determination of the miners of the last century to use this route for their vehicles is noteworthy. The ramp is massive; yet even with it in place, the trek up or down the wash must have been arduous with a loaded wagon.

Seeing the mill site will cure any thought of romanticizing the life of the prospector in these parts. Although the wash is lovely for its solitude and silence, living here must have been grim. "Cactus" Slim Moorten was here for less than ten years. All that remains of his mill are pieces of rusty equipment and rusting car parts.

The hike back up the wash brings you back to the oasis, which looks greener than ever after a sojourn into drier country.

Miles and Directions

0.0   From the parking lot, take the ramp down to the oasis.

0.1   After enjoying the spring area, continue south in the wash.

0.25 Boulders block the easy wash; to the right is a section of road constructed by miners in the 1880s. This is Little Chilcoot Pass.

0.5   Moorten's Mill Site is the turnaround point. There's a trailpost in the center of the wash.

1.0   Return to the trailhead.

28 Mastodon Peak Loop

A loop hike, the Mastodon route winds by a historic mining site and takes you to the top of the monzogranite mound that resembles a prehistoric elephant for those with an imagination. On the return leg, you can enjoy the greenery at Cottonwood Spring.

See map on page 99.
Start: 42 miles southeast of Twentynine Palms and 1.2 miles southeast of Cottonwood Visitor Center.
Distance: 3-mile loop.
Approximate hiking time: 1.5 to 3 hours.
Difficulty: Easy; moderate if the peak is included. The peak requires some scrambling but provides excellent views.
Trail surface: Dirt path.
Seasons: October through April.
USGS topo map: Cottonwood Spring-CA (1:24,000).
Trail contact: Joshua Tree National Park (see appendix D).

Finding the trailhead: From California Highway 62 in Twentynine Palms, take Utah Trail south 4 miles to the North Entrance of the park; continue on Park Route 12 for 4.8 miles to the Pinto Y intersection. Turn left onto Park Route 11 and go south 32 miles to Cottonwood Visitor Center. Turn left and go 1.2 miles to the oasis.

From the south, take the Cottonwood Canyon exit from Interstate 10, 24 miles east of Indio; go north 8 miles to Cottonwood Visitor Center, then right (east) 1.2 miles to the Cottonwood Spring parking lot. Walk west from the parking lot, back up the road 0.1 mile to beginning of the nature trail on your right. Walk up the nature trail 0.3 mile to the junction with the Mastodon Peak route. From the Cottonwood Campground, the trail begins 0.2 mile from campsite no. 13A on loop A, via the nature trail segment, which begins at the campground and meets at the same junction.

The Hike

This trail takes you by two historic sites and a lofty overlook of the southern region of the park. Either approach to the trail includes the nature trail. The view of the old gold mill and the mine is in direct contrast with the Indians' use of the riches of the desert; the latter left no ruins or scars on the environment.

The trail is clearly marked with signposts and a rock-lined path. The lower section of the hike is up a sandy wash to the Winona mill site. Building foundations and other remnants are all that remain of the mill that refined the gold from the Mastodon mine in the 1920s. The exotic plant specimens at adjacent Cotton Spring were planted by the Hulsey family, who owned the mill and mine.

The trail winds up the hill above the mill to the mine, which was operated by George Hulsey between 1919 and 1932, when it was abandoned. Carefully thread your way up by the sign above the mine and through the mine ruins (in direct

From this vantage point—and if you squint—the mound of granite does resemble a mastodon.

contradiction of park warnings to stay clear of old mines) to a trailpost and arrow pointing east. A major freeway-style sign indicates your options and the various distances to the spring, the oasis, and the peak from this point.

The climb to the peak (0.1 mile) is on an unsigned trail, although the well-used path is easy to discern, and cairns appear at critical spots. The use trail goes to the right of a boulder pile, across a slab of granite, and winds around to the northeast side of the peak to the summit, on the opposite side from the mine site. Minor boulder scrambling is necessary. The view is well worth the effort.

After the peak the trail resumes its zigzag rocky path through the canyon, well signed with arrows. It is on this portion of the trail that you can see clearly the elephant likeness in the peak behind you. About 0.4 mile after the peak is the intersection with the Lost Palms Trail. Turn right for the walk down the winding trail to Cottonwood Spring and the parking lot. Turn left for the longer hike to Lost Palms Oasis (6.3 miles round-trip from this junction and back to the parking lot).

Miles and Directions

0.0–0.2 Take the nature trail from the parking area.

0.5   At the junction with Mastodon Peak Trail, turn right and immediately encounter the Winona mill ruins and Cotton Spring.

1.5   The trail continues above the Mastodon Mine.

1.6   At this junction, turn left to the peak (0.1 mile round-trip).

2.0   At the junction with the Lost Palms Trail, turn right to return to the parking area.

2.6   At Cottonwood Spring, continue up the ramp to the parking area.

3.0   Return to the trailhead.

29 Cottonwood Spring Nature Trail

This easy out-and-back nature trail identifies the desert plants and provides information about their use by Native Americans.

See map on page 99.
Start: 42 miles southeast of Twentynine Palms and 1.2 miles southeast of the Cottonwood Visitor Center.
Distance: 1.2 miles out and back.
Approximate hiking time: 1 hour or less.
Difficulty: Easy.

Trail surface: Dirt path.
Seasons: October through April.
USGS topo map: Cottonwood Spring-CA (1:24,000).
Trail contact: Joshua Tree National Park (see appendix D).

Finding the trailhead: From California Highway 62 in Twentynine Palms, take Utah Trail south 4 miles to the North Entrance; continue south on Park Route 12 for 4.8 miles to the Pinto Y intersection. Turn left onto Park Route 11 and go 32 miles to Cottonwood Visitor Center. Turn left and go 1.2 miles to the Cottonwood Spring parking area. Walk 0.1 mile west along the road to the nature trail on your right. The trail also begins at the eastern ends of loops A and B in the campground and goes to Cottonwood Spring. If you're not camping there, however, it is not possible to park at the campground.

From the south, take the Cottonwood Canyon exit from Interstate 10, 24 miles east of Indio, and drive north 8 miles to the Cottonwood Visitor Center. Turn right and go 1.2 miles to the parking area.

The Hike

The broad clear trail leads up a wash from the road near the spring, eventually winding up to a low ridge leading to the campground. This is one of the most informative nature trails in the park. The signs are legible, placed with the appropriate plants, and highly educational.

The information on this nature trail identifies the plants common to this region of the Colorado (Sonoran) Desert. The unique focus of the signs is on the Cahuilla Indians' use of the plants for food, medicine, and household goods. A Cahuilla elder provided the information. The detailed explanations of the processes used by the original inhabitants create genuine admiration for their sophistication. Several of the plants originally developed by the Indians are now grown and marketed commercially, such as creosote tea and jojoba.

If you choose to continue on to the Mastodon Peak Trail, that intersection is halfway down the nature trail from its northern end. Or you can walk back down to the parking lot, reviewing the new information you have learned.

30 Conejo Well/Eagle Mountains

A long but gently graded walk across the open Colorado Desert takes you through a gap in the remote Eagle Mountains to the remains of a historic well site. This is a long outing, suitable only for those with skills in cross-country navigation.

Start: 42 miles southeast of Twentynine Palms and 1.2 miles southeast of Cottonwood Visitor Center.
Distance: 12 miles out and back.
Approximate hiking time: 5 to 7 hours.
Difficulty: Moderate.
Trail surface: Dirt path, sandy wash.

Seasons: October through April.
USGS topo maps: Porcupine Wash-CA; Conejo Well-CA; and Cottonwood Spring-CA (1:24,000).
Trail contact: Joshua Tree National Park (see appendix D).

Finding the trailhead: From California Highway 62 in Twentynine Palms, take Utah Trail south 4 miles to the park's North Entrance; continue south on Park Route 12 for 4.8 miles to the Pinto Y intersection. Bear left onto Park Route 11 and drive 32 miles south to Cottonwood Visitor Center. Turn left and go 1.2 miles to the campground. The trail begins at campsite no. 17 on the B loop.

From the south, take the Cottonwood Canyon exit north from Interstate 10, 24 miles east of Indio; go north 8 miles to Cottonwood Visitor Center. Turn right and go 1.2 miles to the Cottonwood Spring parking area.

The Hike

The clear, well-defined trail is actually a closed four-wheel-drive mining road. It takes off in a northeasterly direction from the Cottonwood Campground. The first 100 yards pass a series of planted shrubs. The Eagle Mountains rise to the southeast above an alluvial fan coated with cholla, creosote, and yucca. The trail continues up a sandy wash marked every so often by rock cairns. At 0.5 mile the wash splits; stay left. The old two-track is plainly visible for the most part, continuing in a nearly straight line.

Looking northeast from the Eagle Mountain Trail at mile 2.

At 2 miles the trail cuts north and crosses a large rock-walled wash. For the next 0.5 mile, it crosses several side washes and small ridges. At this point it is heading northeast toward a broad sloping pass through the north end of the Eagle Mountains. For a strenuous side climb to 5,350-foot Eagle Peak, leave the trail at around mile 3 for a good approach. Look for a broad ridge leading to the south for a route to this apex of the Eagle Mountain Range.

At mile 3 California juniper become more prevalent along with denser clumps of yucca. The trail tops the broad pass at 3,440 feet then follows a wide wash through a gap in the Eagle Mountains, with Eagle Peak rising ruggedly to the south. The junction to the Conejo Well site takes off to the right (south) at 5.3 miles in a garden of cholla. This junction is easy to miss, but it is marked by a rock cairn.

The Conejo Well trail takes off at a 45-degree angle to the right up the left side of a swale in a patch of brittlebush. It heads south toward a rugged canyon on the north side of Eagle Mountain. After another 0.5 mile, it enters the mouth of a narrow rocky canyon distinguished by columns of red rock jutting upward to the slopes of Eagle Mountain. The old mining road climbs another 0.2 mile to the well site,

Conejo Well/Eagle Mountains

RF 1 : 43,800

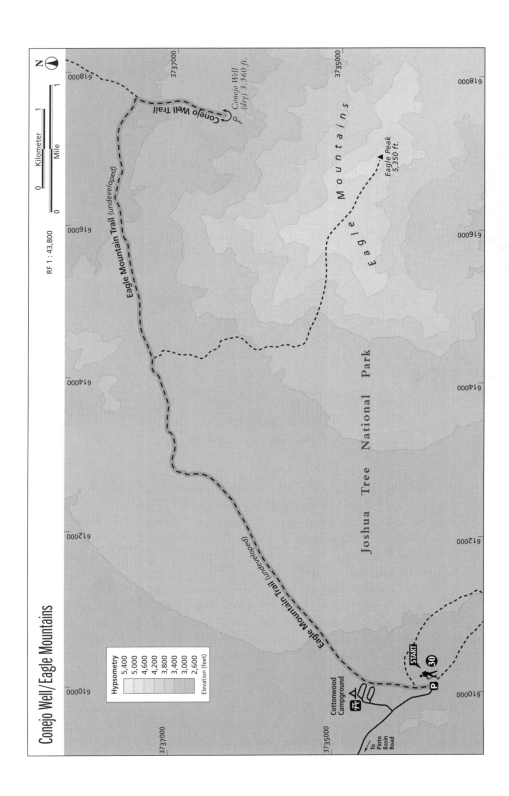

Hypsometry

5,400
5,000
4,600
4,200
3,800
3,400
3,000
2,600

Elevation (feet)

Cottonwood Campground

To Pinto Basin Road

START

P

30

Eagle Mountain Trail (undeveloped)

Joshua Tree National Park

Eagle Mountains

Eagle Peak 5,350 ft.

Eagle Mountain Trail (undeveloped)

Conejo Well Trail

Conejo Well (dry) 3,360 ft.

N

0   Kilometer   1

0   Mile   1

where only a few rusted pipes and cans are found. Depending on the light, a shallow cave appears to overlook the well site 0.3 mile upslope. In fact, the dark opening is merely a shallow rock overhang. Retrace your route to complete this 12-mile round-trip exploration of remote Colorado Desert country.

This hike is considered a cross-country route of travel by the park. It should be undertaken only by hikers with navigation skills.

Miles and Directions

0.0 The path gradually climbs from the trailhead.

3.0 The trail begins a gentle ascent to the high point of 3,440 feet. A possible cross-country route to Eagle Peak leads to the south.

4.5 The trail crosses a prominent northeast-southwest trending wash.

5.3 At the junction with the trail to Conejo Well, turn right (south).

6.0 Arrive at the Conejo Well site.

12.0 Return to the trailhead.

31 Coxcomb Mountains

The Coxcombs lie in the wildest and most remote corner of the park. Here you can achieve a profound feeling of solitude, with hidden basins, expansive vistas, and jagged jumbles of granite in every direction. Not a hike for the novice, this outing requires advanced skills in cross-country navigation.

Start: About 45 miles east of Twentynine Palms.

Distance: 7 miles out and back.

Approximate hiking time: 3 to 5 hours.

Difficulty: Moderate for the suggested route; peak climbing in this region is strenuous.

Trail surface: Sandy washes with moderate bouldering at the mouth of the canyon.

Seasons: October through May.

USGS topo maps: Cadiz Valley SW-CA and Cadiz Valley SE-CA (1:24,000).

Trail contact: Joshua Tree National Park (see appendix D).

Finding the trailhead: From Twentynine Palms, at the traffic light junction of Twentynine Palms and Adobe Road, drive east on California Highway 62 (Twentynine Palms Highway) 41.9 miles to an unsigned sandy dirt road, which is also 1.9 miles east of a parking turnout. This is a difficult road to find, so watch carefully. Turn right (south) and drive 4.5 miles southeasterly to the end of the road at the canyon mouth. Four-wheel drive is recommended due to the soft-sand road surface. It is advisable to stop 0.5 mile before the end of the road and park to the right on firm ground above the wash. The final 0.5 mile is in a deep sandy wash, and there is no place to park outside of the wash at the canyon entrance.

The Hike

The Coxcombs are likely the most rugged and perpendicular mountains in Joshua Tree National Park, in its wildest and least-visited northeast corner. Their relative isolation alone, far from any services, makes their exploration a true wilderness experience. The recommended starting point for this hike provides the easiest access into the Coxcombs. It is also the only road access from the north; the southern access point is at Pinto Wells.

The mouth of the canyon is blocked by huge boulders, a somewhat formidable beginning to this otherwise moderate hike. Begin by taking a use trail to the right up and around the first set of boulders. The remaining boulders are easy to scramble over and around for the next 0.25 mile to where the sandy wash opens up and provides easy walking. The open wash also provides magnificent views of the rugged Coxcombs, especially to the right (south-southwest), with their great slanting blocks and vertical columns of reddish rock.

At 0.5 mile the wash splits; stay to the left and continue southeast up the smaller of the two washes. At 0.8 mile the first low pass is reached. Continue to the southeast on a faint use trail, which drops down a series of small ridges and gullies toward the large wash seen far in the distance. Cathedral-like rock spires tower overhead. At 1 mile the confines of a rocky wash are reached. At 1.4 miles the wash widens, joined by another wash from the right, with spectacular vistas back to the northwest. Continue down another 0.3 mile to where the main wash turns sharply to the left (north). This canyon wash is worth exploring as a side trip if time permits. It leads north to northeast another 1.5 miles to a canyon entrance that opens to a broad alluvial fan on the north side of the mountains.

Return to the junction at mile 1.7. The side wash entering from the left (southeast) is the route to the Inner Valley. Hike southeasterly up this winding but widening wash. At 2.1 miles a wash enters from the right; continue to the left up the main wash. Soon the country opens up into the lower end of the Inner Valley—a vast plateaulike expanse of open desert ringed by jagged spires, mounds, and formations of rocks—white to red and in every conceivable shape. The wash bends around to the right and heads southwest up the broad alluvial fan of the upper reaches of the valley. The fan/wash rises gradually for another mile to a prominent pass at mile 3.5 (3,090 feet), which serves as a panoramic overlook of the vast desert of Pinto Basin to the south. Hold on to your hat: This is also a natural wind tunnel.

Retrace your route to complete this 7-mile round-trip. If you're planning to stay overnight, find a sheltered campsite in the upper valley near the overlook or in the lower east end of the valley outside the day-use area that includes much of this route—the limit is meant to protect wildlife, including rare desert bighorns. There

◀ *Looking down the bouldery Coxcomb Canyon at mile 0.3.*

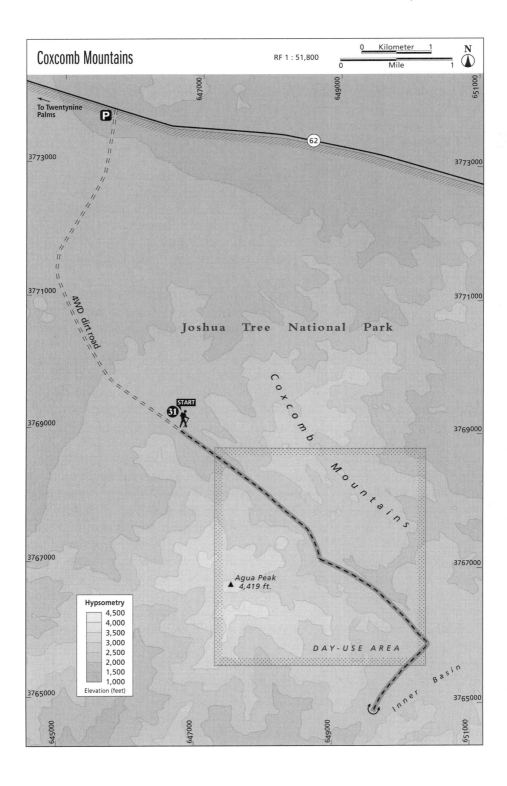

Coxcomb Mountains

RF 1 : 51,800

N

To Twentynine Palms

P

62

3773000

3773000

647000

649000

651000

4WD dirt road

3771000

3771000

Joshua Tree National Park

C o x c o m b

START
31

3769000

3769000

M o u n t a i n s

3767000

3767000

Agua Peak
▲ 4,419 ft.

Hypsometry

Elevation (feet)
4,500
4,000
3,500
3,000
2,500
2,000
1,500
1,000

DAY-USE AREA

Inner Basin

3765000

3765000

645000

647000

649000

651000

are many tantalizing opportunities for boulder scrambling and canyoneering on all sides of the Inner Valley, particularly into some of the larger side canyons bordering the east side of the valley near the overlook. Overnight backpackers would need to carry at least two gallons of water per person per day.

This hike should be undertaken only by hikers skilled in cross-country navigation.

Miles and Directions

0.0 Begin at the mouth of the canyon (2,640 feet).

0.0–0.3 You have to scramble over some boulders before arriving at a sandy wash.

0.8 Arrive at a low pass (2,970 feet).

1.7 A side wash enters from the southeast; continue up this wash.

2.5 Arrive at the Inner Valley.

3.5 Arrive at the Pinto Basin Overlook (3,090 feet).

7.0 Return to the trailhead.

32 Porcupine Wash/Ruby Lee Mill Site

This is a loop hike, requiring competence in cross-country navigation since it is not on a park-maintained trail. You have the opportunity of finding a historic mining site as well as petroglyphs on the route.

Start: About 30 miles southeast of Twentynine Palms and 8 miles north of Cottonwood Visitor Center.
Distance: 7.9-mile loop.
Approximate hiking time: 4 to 5 hours.
Difficulty: Moderate.

Trail surface: Dirt path, sandy wash.
Seasons: October through April.
USGS topo map: Porcupine Wash-CA (1:24,000).
Trail contact: Joshua Tree National Park (see appendix D).

Finding the trailhead: From California Highway 62 in Twentynine Palms, take Utah Trail south 4 miles to the North Entrance; continue on Park Route 12 for 4.8 miles to the Pinto Y intersection. Bear left onto Park Route 11 and go 21.3 miles south to the Porcupine Wash Backcountry Board, on your right.

From the south, take the Cottonwood Canyon exit from Interstate 10, 24 miles east of Indio. Go north 8 miles to the Cottonwood Entrance. Continue north 8.9 miles to the Porcupine Wash Backcountry Board, on your left.

The Hike

With topo map in hand, you will enjoy this moderate hike. Although the directions make it sound extremely complex, this is a very straightforward hike. The trail is fairly visible; moreover, the ridge to the east and the Hexie Mountains to the south

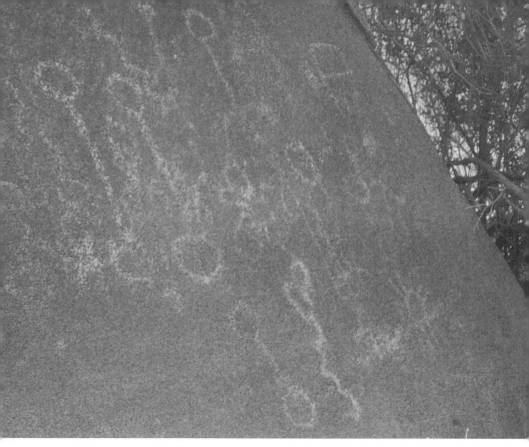

Petroglyphs on granite boulder in Porcupine Wash.

are permanent markers, so you won't lose your bearings. The granite formations here are imaginative. Porcupine Wash is especially artistic with its smoke trees and water-sculpted boulders. The small S-curve canyon midway down the wash displays the power of water in this arid environment.

The variety of desert topography and vegetation is especially striking. The boulder-strewn sloping alluvial fan on the first half of the hike displays the vegetation typical of the Colorado Desert. Cholla cactus and creosote dominate the landscape. Curving through the foothills of the Hexie Range and dropping to the wash, you enter a new habitat—an active wash. The scouring action of flash flooding promotes the growth of smoke trees. The seeds require the grinding sands of floods to remove their protective covering in order to germinate, so instead of finding a water-swept wasteland, you find a smoke-tree paradise in the wash.

Porcupine Wash demonstrates a variety of wash architecture. Broad and narrow areas both exist, depending on the resistance of rock walls along the sides. The wash is wide at the junction with the Ruby Lee trail, but 2 miles farther east it becomes

Porcupine Wash/Ruby Lee Mill Site; Porcupine Wash to Monument Mountain

RF 1 : 38,300

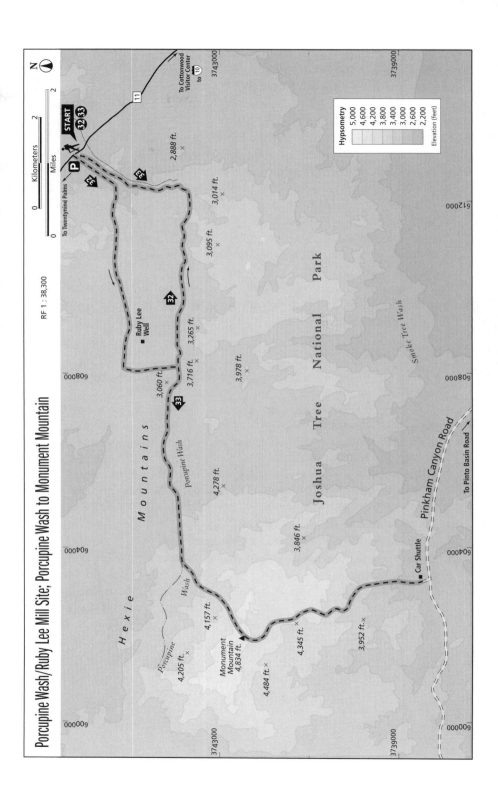

a slot canyon with narrow S-curves between the 200-foot-high walls. This narrow section lasts almost 0.5 mile before the wash opens again.

The mill site dates from the mid-1930s. The mill's career must have been quite brief, judging from its size. Not much is left. This area of Joshua Tree was not productive for mining.

A petroglyph site is located near the mouth of the wash. The rock face upon which the signs are engraved is turned to the east. Clearly these messages are intended for travelers approaching the entrance of the wash, en route toward Monument Mountain, visible directly to the west. Their meaning, however, remains a mystery. As is the case with all archaeological and historic artifacts, these are protected by federal law. Leave them untouched for others to enjoy.

Emerging from the wash, bear left along the foot of the ridge. By heading north you will shortly see the parking area and backcountry board to the northeast, guiding you back to your car.

This is not a maintained trail or route. It is quite washed out and invisible in places, and is considered cross-country travel by the park, for which hikers need a higher level of route-finding skills.

Miles and Directions

0.0–0.2 At the Porcupine Wash Backcountry Board, follow the jeep trail to the borrow pit southwest of the parking area.

0.2 Angle northwest across the alluvial fan. The trail heads toward a low notch at the far end of the ridge to the west.

1.5 At the broad high point (2,750 feet) marked with a cairn, the trail winds between granite boulders, with periodic cairns.

2.8 The wash narrows and the trail cuts between two boulder piles. Look for the small Ruby Lee Mill site, marked only with tailings, a stone foundation, the usual debris, and a small sign etched on a boulder.

3.0 The trail bears south. Cairns mark the route.

3.4 The trail drops to Porcupine Wash. Follow the wash left (east).

6.1 Beyond the canyon, bear left. Look for petroglyphs.

7.9 Return to the parking area.

33 Porcupine Wash to Monument Mountain

This outing is a strenuous point-to-point day hike to the highest peak in the Hexie Range, Monument Mountain (4,834 feet). You can savor sweeping views of the desert in every direction. It can also be done as an out-and-back hike to the peak.

See map on page 113.
Start: About 30 miles southeast of Twentynine Palms; 8 miles north of Cottonwood Visitor Center.
Distance: 14 miles one way (with car shuttle).
Approximate hiking time: 4 to 6 hours out and back to peak, or 6 to 7 hours for the shuttle hike.

Difficulty: Strenuous, with some moderately difficult boulder scrambling.
Trail surface: Clear wash use trail for 7.5 miles followed by 5.5 miles cross-country.
Seasons: October through April.
USGS topo maps: Porcupine Wash-CA and Washington Wash-CA (1:24,000).
Trail contact: Joshua Tree National Park (see appendix D).

Finding the trailhead: From California Highway 62 in Twentynine Palms, take Utah Trail south 4 miles to the North Entrance; continue on Park Route 12 for 4.8 miles to the Pinto Y intersection. Bear left onto Park Route 11 and go 21.3 miles south to the Porcupine Wash Backcountry Board, on your right.

From the south, take the Cottonwood Canyon exit north from Interstate 10, 24 miles east of Indio. Go north 8 miles to the Cottonwood Visitor Center, then continue north 8.9 miles to the Porcupine Wash Backcountry Board, on your left.

For a car shuttle: On Park Route 11, drive 8.9 miles south of the Porcupine Wash Backcountry Board to the Cottonwood Visitor Center. Turn right (north) on the four-wheel drive *only* Pinkham Canyon Road directly across the highway from the visitor center and drive 5.2 miles to the dirt road turnout on your right. Park here for the point-to-point pickup or the round-trip climb to Monument Mountain.

The Hike

This hike requires skills in backcountry navigation. The route is not maintained by the park. From the backcountry board, head almost due south past the borrow pit, staying close to a line of boulders to your right. Within 0.5 mile Porcupine Wash becomes well defined. After about 1.5 miles the wash bends gradually to the right in a westerly direction. Another mile will bring you into a canyon with a series of S curves. The grade is gentle, and the open wash allows for easy going.

At 4.5 miles the remains of the old Ruby Lee Mill road come into view as it meets Porcupine Wash from the north (right). Continue up the wash through a low canyon and into a broad basin, distinguished by increasingly dense yucca. The wash itself is lined with creosote bushes and smoke trees. As the basin opens up, the distinctive cone summit of Monument Peak can be seen on the skyline to the southwest.

Jumbled rocks near the site of the Ruby Lee Mill.

Continue hiking up Porcupine Wash, passing a series of striking white rock columns at 5.2 miles. After another 0.1 mile the first large gully enters the main wash from the left. At 5.5 miles the remnants of the old overgrown four-wheel-drive road are visible on the right side of the canyon, but the wash offers easier walking. At 5.6 miles Monument Mountain can be seen to the southwest.

At 5.9 miles a second major side canyon enters from the left. Stay to the right on a bearing toward Monument Mountain. The valley widens here with an increasing density of yucca.

At 7 miles the peak drops below the ridge to the south. Continue up the wash another 0.5 mile before cutting cross-country southward toward the first line of high ridges. The country is open with scattered catclaw, creosote, and yucca. Up on the ridge at about 3,950 feet, the summit will present itself—as well as a suitable route around a series of deep canyons leading to the north ridge. This ridge requires more rock scrambling than other possible routes to the east, but the approach is more direct with fewer ups and downs. Upon reaching the summit, look for the peak register to learn of the experiences of previous climbers. More important, enjoy the spellbinding view with desert basins and ranges stretching as far as the eye can see.

To continue on a point-to-point route to Smoke Tree Wash on the Pinkham Canyon Road, take the southeast ridge for the shortest and easiest way down. The ridges and swales on the south side of the mountain are strewn with rugged outcrops of volcanic rock ribs that resemble backbones of dinosaurs. There is some up and down and a bit of route-finding on this serpentine ridge, but avoid the temptation to drop off of it for a "shortcut." This prominent southeast ridge offers the best and most enjoyable means of covering 3 miles and losing 1,600 feet to Smoke Tree Wash. After descending the foot of the ridge, hike about 1 mile across the flat to the road and your waiting shuttle vehicle. This point can also be the start and end of a cross-country climb (6 miles out and back) to Monument Mountain.

Miles and Directions

0.0–0.2 From the Porcupine Wash Backcountry Board, head south past the borrow pit.

0.2–1.5 Continue south up Porcupine Wash.

1.5–2.5 The wash trail winds up a series of S-curves in a canyon.

2.5–4.5 Continue up the wash.

4.5 The Ruby Lee jeep trail enters the wash from the right (north).

4.5–7.5 Continue up the wash into a broad basin.

7.5 Leave the wash for the cross-country route to the Monument summit.

10.0 Reach the summit of Monument Mountain.

14.0 Arrive at Pinkham Canyon Road (one-way hike).

Option: For an out-and-back trip, the route up to Monument Peak can be retraced back to the Porcupine Wash Backcountry Board, making for a long 20-mile day trip or a more reasonable overnight backpack with a night spent near Porcupine Wash if sufficient water is carried.

34 Golden Bee Mine

This is a fairly strenuous outing due to the rocky climb to the mine site. Once you get there you'll enjoy a magnificent view of the valley and surrounding mountain ranges.

Start: 18.6 miles south of Twentynine Palms.
Distance: 4 miles out and back.
Approximate hiking time: 2 to 4 hours.
Difficulty: Strenuous.
Trail surface: Dirt path, rocky wash, rocky trail.

Seasons: October through April.
USGS topo map: Fried Liver Wash-CA (1:24,000).
Trail contact: Joshua Tree National Park (see appendix D).

The lofty vantage point of the Golden Bee Mine provides a stunning vista of Pinto Basin.

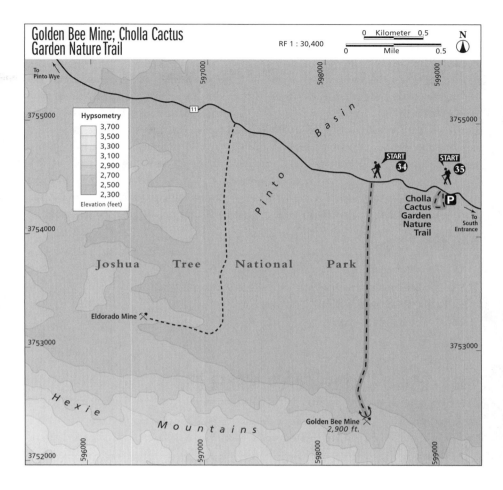

Golden Bee Mine; Cholla Cactus Garden Nature Trail

RF 1 : 30,400

Finding the trailhead: From the park visitor center in Twentynine Palms, go south on Utah Trail 8.2 miles to the Pinto Y intersection. Bear left onto Park Route 11 and drive to milepost 10 just before the Cholla Cactus Garden Nature Trail. The trailhead is on the southeast side of PR 11, 0.25 mile northwest of the Cholla trail, where the old road is blocked off. This trailhead is 20 miles north of the Cottonwood Visitor Center and 18 miles south of the Oasis Visitor Center in Twentynine Palms.

The park has plans for an interpretive wayside, which would allow for parking at the trailhead. Until then, your vehicle should be left at the nearest turnout, about 1 mile northwest on PR 11.

The Hike

The trail starts out on the south side of PR 11 next to a 25–mph–speed–limit sign and heads south between two small volcanic cones. For the first 1.3 miles, the trail remains fairly level and is generally easy to follow. It crosses several washes marked by rock cairns. If you become temporarily lost, head toward the highest point on the southern horizon. In so doing, you'll eventually cross the trail when it becomes more distinct on the alluvial fan.

At 1.3 miles the trail crosses a wash and begins a steep 0.7-mile ascent to the mine. This extremely steep, rocky trail is washed out in a couple of places but well defined as a hiking route. From below, the uppermost mine site is hidden from view, but it sits in a notch in the left-hand (south) canyon. This 1930s mine contains a considerable amount of debris: metal, timbers, rusted pipe, rock walls, mine adits, tanks, and cable. Please do not disturb or remove any of these historic artifacts.

The mine is located near the top of a pass that drops southward into Fried Liver Wash. It provides a spectacular view to the north, particularly in the evening as the setting sun lights up Pinto Basin beneath the imposing mass of the Pinto Range.

Miles and Directions

0.0 The unsigned trailhead is on PR 11.
1.3 The trail crosses a wash and begins a steep climb to the mine.
2.0 Arrive at Golden Bee Mine (2,900 feet).
4.0 Return to the trailhead.

35 Cholla Cactus Garden Nature Trail

Here's an unusually dense stand of the distinctive "jumping" cholla cactus. The nature trail lies on the lower edge of the transition from Mojave Desert to Colorado Desert.

See map on page 119.
Start: 19 miles south of Twentynine Palms and 20 miles north of the Cottonwood Visitor Center.
Distance: 0.25-mile loop.
Approximate hiking time: Less than 30 minutes.

Difficulty: Easy.
Trail surface: Dirt path.
Seasons: October through April.
USGS topo map: Fried Liver Wash-CA (1:24,000).
Trail contact: Joshua Tree National Park (see appendix D).

Finding the trailhead: From California Highway 62 in Twentynine Palms, take Utah Trail south 4 miles to the North Entrance of the park; continue on Park Route 12 south 4.8 miles to the Pinto Y intersection. Turn left onto Park Route 11. The Cholla Cactus Garden parking area is on the right near mile marker 10, 6.3 miles south of the intersection.

The Hike

This massive array of cholla, a common species of the Colorado (Sonoran) Desert, is impressive even when it is not in bloom. From mid- to late February to mid-March,

A dense stand of cholla cactus on the nature trail above Pinto Basin marks the northern end of the Colorado (Sonoran) Desert.

there is intense bee activity at the garden. Those with sensitivity or phobias about bees should avoid visiting during the pollination season.

This is a self-guided trail with brochures explaining the numbers posted on the trail. But even without a pamphlet for interpretation, the density of the cholla, which extend well beyond the fenced edge of the garden, is impressive.

The views of the Hexie Mountains, the Pinto Range, and the Pinto Basin contribute to making the Cholla Cactus Garden a spectacular spot on the edge of this southern desert region.

36 Pleasant Valley to El Dorado Mine/Pinto Basin

This is a mostly downhill point-to-point hike, with opportunities for side trips to two mine sites, the Hexahedron and the El Dorado. The route begins in Pleasant Valley, crosses a low pass in the Hexie Mountains, and ends up in the Pinto Basin. Due to its trailless nature, this hike should only be undertaken by those skilled in cross-country desert navigation.

Start: About 19 miles south of Twentynine Palms.
Distance: 7.7 miles one way.
Approximate hiking time: 3 to 5 hours.
Difficulty: Moderate.
Trail surface: Rocky dirt path, sandy wash.

Seasons: October through May.
USGS topo maps: Malapai Hill-CA and Fried Liver Wash-CA (1:24,000).
Trail contact: Joshua Tree National Park (see appendix D).

Finding the trailhead: From the park visitor center in Twentynine Palms, go south on Utah Trail 8.2 miles to the Pinto Y intersection. Stay to the right on Park Route 12 and drive another 5.1 miles to Geology Tour Road (signed SQUAW TANK at the junction). (From the other direction, this turnoff is 15.1 miles southeast of the town of Joshua Tree.) Turn left (south) on Geology Tour Road (washboard dirt) and drive 7.1 miles to the Pleasant Valley Backcountry Board, on the left side of Geology Tour Road in the one-way loop section in Pleasant Valley.

   For a car shuttle: At the Pinto Y intersection bear left on Park Route 11. Drive south to the pullout on the right just northwest of milepost 8.

The Hike

This interesting point-to-point excursion of nearly 8 miles starts in Pleasant Valley along the upper Fried Liver Wash and the southern base of the Hexie Mountains, ending up in the northwestern edge of the vast Pinto Basin. The trip presents an opportunity to explore the sizable El Dorado Mine site. The hike should only be done by those skilled in backcountry navigation.

   The hike begins in a dry lake bed, which can be clearly delineated by walking up the sidehill to the north 100 feet or so before returning to the trail. At 0.3 mile a left-hand turn heads toward the hills. Stay to the right on the main traveled trail heading east.

   Within another 0.2 mile Joshua trees are first seen along the trail. At 1.5 miles the trail passes by an old wooden post with no sign. Soon the trail and Fried Liver Wash become one and the same. At 2.5 miles a fence crosses the wash next to a hillside to the left. Turn left (north) and follow the fence line for about 0.2 mile to an old iron gatepost. Follow the trail leading uphill to the right. After another 0.1 mile you'll come to a trail junction in a flat; take the right-hand fork, which continues east in a small valley lined with Joshua trees. For a side trip, take the left-hand fork to the Hexahedron Mine.

Pleasant Valley to El Dorado Mine/Pinto Basin

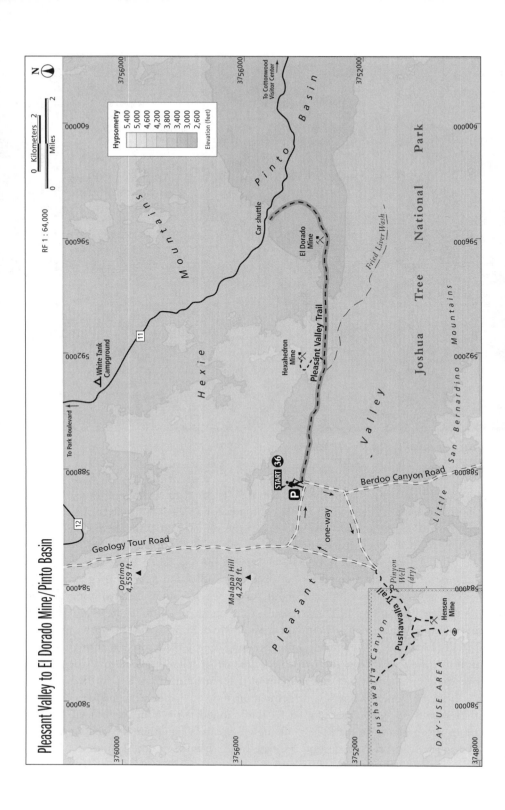

RF 1 : 64,000

Hypsometry

Elevation (feet)
5,400
5,000
4,600
4,200
3,800
3,400
3,000
2,600

White Tank Campground

To Park Boulevard

Geology Tour Road

Optimo 4,559 ft.

Malapai Hill 4,228 ft.

START 36

P

one-way

Berdoo Canyon Road

Pinyon Well (dry)

Pushawalla Canyon

Pushawalla Trail

DAY-USE AREA

Hensen Mine

Pleasant Valley

Hexie Mountains

Hexahedron Mine

Pleasant Valley Trail

El Dorado Mine

Car shuttle

Pinto Basin

To Cottonwood Visitor Center

Fried Liver Wash

Little San Bernardino Mountains

Joshua Tree National Park

The remains of the El Dorado Mine (elevation 2,650 feet).

At 3.8 miles the trail drops into a rough, rocky ravine, climbing out of it after another 0.1 mile. The gradual ascent continues for another 0.2 mile to a 3,170-foot pass overlooking the Pinto Basin to the east. After another 0.1 mile the trail all but disappears in the rock-strewn gully. Follow the wash down.

After 0.2 mile a small mine adit appears on the left, one of countless such holes in these hills. At this point the wash becomes sandier and easier to negotiate. Here and there a rusty water pipe sticks out. As the wash drops, the canyon opens up to ever-expanding views of Pinto Basin. After another 0.6 mile the wash widens, becoming more braided and difficult to walk down. At 5.7 miles the wash trail passes the El Dorado Mine. A single leaning building on the right looks as though a good puff of wind would blow it down. The huge piles of tailings give moot evidence that this mine produced the largest number of different minerals of any in the park.

If the El Dorado Mine is your destination and you've not arranged for a car shuttle, return the way you came for an 11.4 mile round-trip—a full day indeed. To continue the point-to-point hike, walk down the wash another 0.5 mile, gradually curving left (northward) around the base of the hill. Keep going another 1.5 miles north to northwest to an old mining road below the Tripples (Silver Bell) Mine, which leads to the parking area immediately northwest of milepost 8 on PR 11.

Miles and Directions

0.0 Start at the Pleasant Valley Backcountry Board.

0.3 The trail splits—stay right.

2.5 Where the fence crosses the wash, turn left (north).

2.8 Stay right at the trail junction with the Hexahedron Mine trail.

4.1 The trail tops a pass at 3,170 feet.

5.7 Arrive at the El Dorado Mine (2,650 feet).

7.7 Reach the end point of the hike at PR 11.

37 Hexahedron Mine

After a 3-mile hike down Fried Liver Wash, the mining-history enthusiast will enjoy exploring what remains of this old mine site. Even the nonhistorian will be thrilled by the view from the lofty aerie in the Hexie Mountains.

Start: 19 miles south of Twentynine Palms.
Distance: 8.4 miles out and back.
Approximate hiking time: 3 to 5 hours.
Difficulty: Moderately strenuous.
Trail surface: Rocky dirt path, sandy wash.

Seasons: October through May.
USGS topo map: Malapai Hill-CA (1:24,000).
Trail contact: Joshua Tree National Park (see appendix D).

Finding the trailhead: From the park visitor center in Twentynine Palms, go south on Utah Trail 8.2 miles to the Pinto Y intersection. Stay to the right on Park Route 12 for 5.1 miles to Geology Tour Road, which begins 15.1 miles southeast of the town of Joshua Tree. Turn left (south) on Geology Tour Road, which is signed SQUAW TANK at the turnoff. The Pleasant Valley Backcountry Board/trailhead is on the left after 7.1 miles.

The Hike

From the Pleasant Valley Backcountry Board, this trail heads east in Pleasant Valley, along the foot of the Hexie Mountains across a dry lake bed. The rough-hewn Hexie Mountains rise to the immediate north. At 0.3 mile the trail splits; keep to the right. Old mine diggings can be seen on the hillside to the north. Soon the stark openness of the dry lake bed is moderated by a few Joshua trees near the trail.

At 1.5 miles the trail passes a wooden post with no sign. The trail then enters the head of Fried Liver Wash, dropping very gradually to the southeast. A fence crosses

Hexahedron Mine shaft.

the wash at 2.5 miles. Take a left here and follow the fence north for about 0.2 mile to an old iron gatepost where a trail continues uphill to the right. Follow the trail another 0.1 mile onto a flat containing a trail junction. At this point the trail leading up to the mine can be clearly seen on the hillside to the north. Turn left and climb the rough, rocky trail another 1.4 miles to the Hexahedron Mine.

A roofless stone house stands guard near the mine adit, offering magnificent vistas of monzogranite quartz mounds northward. The main adit lies a short distance beyond, at the end of the trail. Retrace your route to complete this 8.4-mile round-trip. On the way back down, you'll be able to clearly see the outline of the dry lake bed.

For those staying overnight, there are good campsites near the upper reaches of Fried Liver Wash.

Miles and Directions

0.0 Start at the Pleasant Valley Backcountry Board (3,250 feet).

0.3 The trail splits—stay to the right (east).

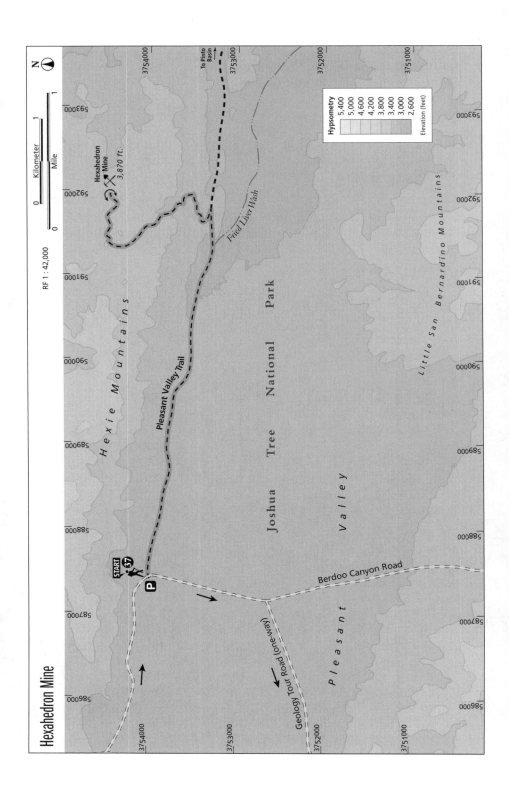

Hexahedron Mine

RF 1 : 42,000

N

Kilometer

Mile

Hypsometry

5,400
5,000
4,600
4,200
3,800
3,400
3,000
2,600

Elevation (feet)

Hexie Mountains

Hexahedron
Mine
3,870 ft.

To Pinto
Basin

Fried Liver Wash

Pleasant Valley Trail

Joshua   Tree   National   Park

Valley

Little San Bernardino Mountains

START
37

P

Berdoo Canyon Road

Geology Tour Road (one-way)

Pleasant

2.5	Go north at the Fried Liver Wash fence crossing.
2.8	At the trail junction, take the trail on the left.
3.8	This is the high point of the trail (3,890 feet).
4.2	Arrive at Hexahedron Mine (3,870 feet).
8.4	Return to the trailhead.

38 Sand Dunes

Although the name is misleading (these are really hills, not dunes), this flat hike into the Pinto Basin gives you a sense of the wind's power to alter terrain in the desert.

Humble sand hills with the Pinto Mountains rising in the background.

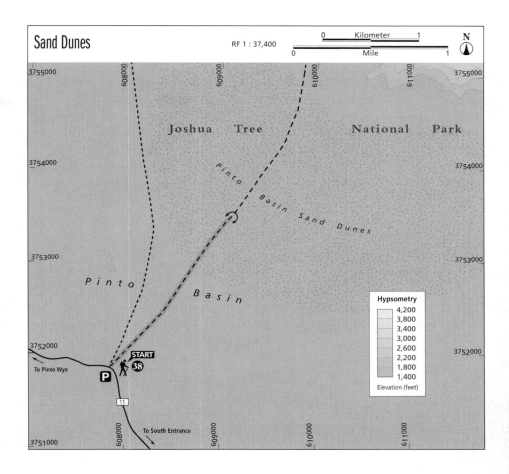

Start: 13.5 miles north of Cottonwood Visitor Center.

Distance: 2.5 miles out and back.

Approximate hiking time: 1 to 3 hours.

Difficulty: Easy.

Trail surface: Dirt route.

Seasons: January through April.

USGS topo map: Pinto Mountain-CA (1:24,000).

Trail contact: Joshua Tree National Park (see appendix D).

Finding the trailhead: The route takes off from the Turkey Flats Backcountry Board, which is on the east side of Park Route 11, 16.2 miles south of the Pinto Y intersection and 13.5 miles north of the Cottonwood Visitor Center.

The Hike

From the Turkey Flats Backcountry Board, head northeast on a line toward the high point on the distant horizon, 3,983-foot Pinto Mountain. The sand dunes can be seen about a mile away as a low-lying dark ridge or mound. Actually, these are not true sand dunes. The blowing sand collects on the face of a low gravel ridge, thus giving the appearance of a dune.

Begin by heading 0.2 mile up a large wash, which leads to a sand bowl. Continue northeasterly for another mile across a creosote-brittlebush flat to the sand dunes. This is a delightful place to visit during winter and, especially, spring, when primrose and other wildflowers are in bloom. Spend some quiet time here, wandering along this windswept uplift of sand, reflecting on how the ever-present desert winds have both created and kept in place these dunes over thousands of years.

To return, simply walk toward the highest point to the southwest, which is the crest of the Hexie Mountains, and you'll soon end up back at the backcountry board on PR 11.

39 Pushawalla Plateau/Canyon

This is an adventuresome day trip to the Pushawalla Plateau in the Little San Bernardino Mountains. Along the way you will enjoy seeing remnants of the mining era, hidden canyons, and expansive vistas to the Salton Sea and beyond. It's not a trip for those unskilled at backcountry navigation in the desert.

Start: About 27.5 miles south of Twentynine Palms.
Distance: 10.2 miles out and back.
Approximate hiking time: 5 to 7 hours for the long trip; 3 to 5 for the hike to the pass.
Difficulty: Strenuous.

Trail surface: Rocky wash, rocky trail, cross-country route.
Seasons: October through May.
USGS topo map: Malapai Hill-CA (1:24,000).
Trail contact: Joshua Tree National Park (see appendix D).

Finding the trailhead: From the park visitor center in Twentynine Palms, go south on Utah Trail 8.2 miles to the Pinto Y intersection. Stay to the right on Park Route 12 and drive another 5.1 miles to the signed Geology Tour Road (four-wheel drive recommended). (From the other direction, the turnoff is 15.1 miles southeast of the town of Joshua Tree.) Turn left (south) on Geology Tour Road (four-wheel drive recommended). The unsigned trailhead is 10.2 miles south next to the 15km post. Park at the Pinyon Well parking area and begin the hike up the wash.

The Hike

This is an interesting hike with several side excursions into a remote and lightly used region of the park. All of the variations are out and back. They include going up "Pinyon Well" canyon to Pushawalla Pass, side-tripping up to Pushawalla Plateau, and dropping into the upper stretches of Pushawalla Canyon. These hikes are suggested only for those with skills in backcountry navigation, as the trails are not maintained.

The wash widens just below Pushawalla Pass at 2.3 miles.

The trail starts up a wash near the mouth of the Pinyon Well canyon, which drains east from Pushawalla Pass. The country is characterized by scattered juniper and Joshua trees, punctuated with spires of columnar rocks overlooking the canyon. The wash forks at 0.3 mile; stay to the right.

At 0.8 mile the canyon narrows just below the remains of a water trough and concrete foundations at Pinyon Well. A mine shaft is fenced off for public safety. At 1 mile (3,880 feet) a rock slide blocks the canyon; cut left on a use trail that quickly leads back to the wash. Look here for the remnants of the original asphalt roadway built by the miners.

At 1.2 miles the canyon again forks; stay left up the main wash. At 1.6 miles a piñon–juniper wash dotted with Joshua trees enters from the left (south) at 4,140 feet. For an expansive view of the canyon, take a 0.2-mile walk up the open wash to where heavy brush makes further hiking difficult.

At 1.9 miles the wash forks with the trail to Pushawalla Pass continuing to the left. At 2.2 miles the wash is again blocked by a rock slide, which can be avoided by taking the use trail to the left. At 2.4 miles (4,400 feet) the wash again forks; the smaller wash to the right is the route to Pushawalla Pass. Turn around here for a total out-and-back hike of 5.6 miles.

For a 0.6-mile side trip to some historic mining ruins (shown on the topo map), head up the left-hand wash at mile 2.4. After about 0.1 mile, climb toward the right-hand canyon on the right side of the draw. Soon you'll see the largely overgrown mining road up ahead. Follow it another 0.2 mile to the two roofless rock houses sitting just above a wet spring. Retrace your steps back to the right-hand fork, which climbs up the wash another 0.4 mile to 4,660-foot Pushawalla Pass at the head of Pushawalla Canyon. The pass is marked by an iron-post gate. Hold onto your hat, for the pass is truly a classic high-desert wind funnel, decorated by piñon-juniper and live oak. If the pass is your goal, backtrack to complete your 6.2-mile round-trip.

Pushawalla Plateau

An old mining trail takes off to the south uphill about 50 yards east of Pushawalla Pass; several rock cairns mark the spot. The trail is quite steep in places but easy to follow. At 0.8 mile the trail passes by mining remains, including a rock foundation (5,120 feet). This is potentially a hazardous area because of unsecured vertical mine shafts nearby. The trail begins to fade here, but simply continue straight, angling upward to the left another 0.2 mile to the 5,200-foot crest of the Pushawalla Plateau ridge. Joshua trees and rock mounds characterize the landscape. Savor the spectacular views southward to the Salton Sea and in every direction in these remote Little San Bernardino Mountains. Seldom-visited ridges and canyons radiate below, and there is always the wind to keep you company.

Pushawalla Canyon

If time and energy permit, drop into the head of Pushawalla Canyon, where Joshua trees grow out of the wide, sandy bottom. To get there from the pass, walk around the right side of the iron gate and descend the trail on the left side of the gully to the broad wash. The canyon deepens as it drops, thereby enriching its sense of solitude. You'll lose 400 feet in the first 0.5 mile, so gauge your time accordingly for the return leg of this out-and-back adventure.

Miles and Directions

- **0.0** Start at the Pinyon Well trailhead.
- **0.8** Arrive at the Pinyon Well site.
- **1.2** Where the canyon forks, stay left up the main wash.
- **2.4–3.0** Take the left-hand fork for a side trip to the Henson Well Mill site.
- **3.4** Arrive at Pushawalla Pass.
- **4.4** Arrive at Pushawalla Plateau.
- **5.4–6.4** A side trip down Pushawalla Canyon can be taken.
- **10.2** Return to the Pinyon Well trailhead.

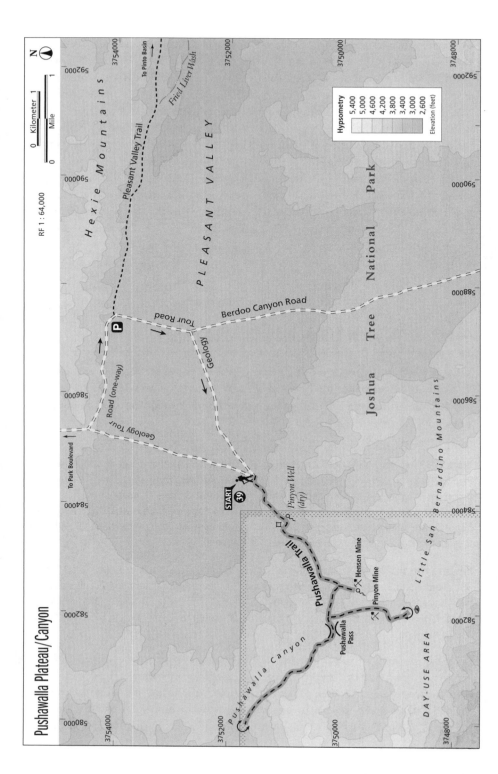

Pushawalla Plateau/Canyon

RF 1 : 64,000

N

0 Kilometer 1

0 Mile 1

Hypsometry

	5,400
	5,000
	4,600
	4,200
	3,800
	3,400
	3,000
	2,600

Elevation (feet)

Hexie Mountains

To Pinto Basin

Fried Liver Wash

Pleasant Valley Trail

PLEASANT VALLEY

Geology Tour Road

Berdoo Canyon Road

P

Joshua   Tree   National   Park

Geology Tour Road (one-way)

To Park Boulevard

Little San Bernardino Mountains

START

Pinyon Well (dry)

Pushawalla Trail

Hensen Mine

Pinyon Mine

Pushawalla Canyon

Pushawalla Pass

DAY-USE AREA

592000
590000
588000
586000
584000
582000
580000

3754000
3752000
3750000
3748000

Options: An overnight trip is not recommended here because the day-use area extends several more miles down Pushawalla Canyon—and because a point-to-point hike all the way down Pushawalla Canyon to the Dillon Road would require an inordinately long car shuttle. However, if distance and shuttle time are not obstacles, this long point-to-point route is an adventurous option. At this writing there is no end-of-the-road parking area at Pushawalla Canyon Road, which ends at the park boundary. However, the National Park Service does have plans to put in a backcountry board and parking area at this location.

Also for the adventurous hiker, the Pushawalla Canyon–Blue Cut loop provides a long 15-mile day trip or more moderate overnighter with a backpack camp in lower Pushawalla or upper Blue Cut Canyon outside of the day-use area. The basic route involves descending Pushawalla Canyon about 3.5 miles below the pass, turning right up Blue Cut Canyon for about 2 miles to the pass, then dropping eastward into Pleasant Valley for the return trip to the Pinyon Well trailhead on Geology Tour Road.

40 Keys View Loop/Inspiration Peak

What a view! From either the loop or the peak, you can see forever on a clear day. With the usual air pollution, however, you see a lot less. On the loop you can also pick up information on the geology of Joshua Tree National Park and the increase of air pollution in the desert basins.

Start: 23.3 miles southwest of Twentynine Palms.
Distance: 1.75 miles with loop and out and back to peak.
Approximate hiking time: Less than 30 minutes for the loop; an hour or so for the peak.

Difficulty: Easy; moderate for peak hike.
Trail surface: Dirt path.
Seasons: October through June.
USGS topo map: Keys View-CA (1:24,000).
Trail contact: Joshua Tree National Park (see appendix D).

Finding the trailhead: From California Highway 62 in the town of Joshua Tree, take Park Boulevard south 1 mile to where it becomes Quail Springs Road; continue 4.3 miles to the West Entrance of the park. Follow Park Route 12 for 11.2 miles to Keys View Road (Park Route 13), which continues to the right (south). Turn south on Keys View; go 5.8 miles to the end of the road.

The Hikes

This clear, paved, barrier-free path to Keys View Loop is the highest trail in the park accessible by a paved road. You can count on a brisk breeze, so bring your windbreaker. The view point is on the crest of the Little San Bernardino Mountains. As

From Inspiration Peak (5,550 feet) looking north to the Wonderland of Rocks.

such, it provides an expansive view of the Coachella Valley and the San Bernardino Range to the west. Unfortunately, the view is all too often obscured by pollution from the Los Angeles Basin. Information boards contrasting smog levels give the viewer a good idea of how air pollution affects visibility at differing distances. The smog also endangers the biological integrity of the park itself.

The park has plans for exhibits at Keys View that will discuss earthquakes and point out landmarks. Until then your park map will help orient you to the view.

A short side trip to Inspiration Peak makes a nice addition for those who like to get even higher. A hiker symbol marks the trailhead on the right (north) side of the parking area at Keys View. The somewhat steep, rocky trail is well worn and in good condition. Nearly 400 feet are gained to a false summit in the first 0.5 mile.

Look carefully for the trail continuing to the right. It drops 100 feet into a saddle and then climbs around the left side, gaining 120 feet in the next 0.25 mile. Keys View sits far below to the south, as do the Coachella Valley and prominent peaks of the higher San Bernardino Range. The added perspective gained on the steep canyons and high ridges makes this steep, short climb more than worthwhile.

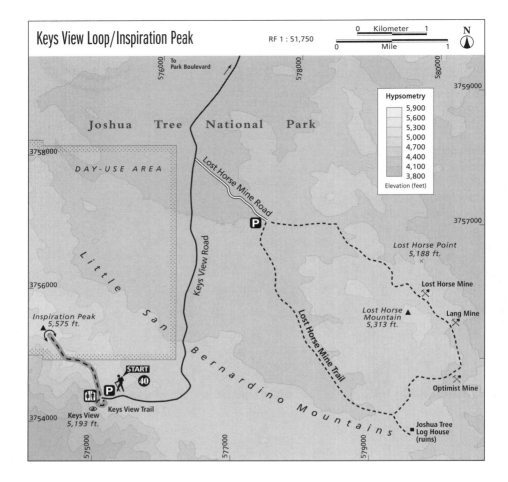

An easily followed use trail continues another 0.1 mile northwest along the main crest until it reaches a mound of large boulders. The Inspiration Peak hike can be extended by scrambling over the rocks and dropping into another saddle containing a small storage shed. Climbing cross-country up the ridgeline to the next high point offers even broader views of the park stretching west and north to the Wonderland of Rocks.

From Inspiration Peak, double-back 0.75 mile on the trail leading back down to the Keys View parking area.

41 Lost Horse Mine Loop

This loop trip includes two mines, a mountain, unusual ruins of a Joshua tree cabin, and expansive vistas of the Wonderland of Rocks, Malapai Hill, and Pleasant Valley. Only those skilled at backcountry desert navigation should undertake the full loop.

Start: 23 miles southwest of Twentynine Palms.
Distance: 7.8-mile loop.
Approximate hiking time: 5 to 6 hours.
Difficulty: Strenuous.

Trail surface: Mostly dirt trail.
Seasons: October through May.
USGS topo map: Keys View-CA (1:24,000).
Trail contact: Joshua Tree National Park (see appendix D).

Finding the trailhead: Drive south on Keys View Road, which begins 18 miles southeast of the town of Joshua Tree via Park Boulevard and Quail Springs Road, or 20 miles southwest of the Oasis Visitor Center at Twentynine Palms by way of Park Route 12. Continue south on Keys View Road for 2.6 miles to the signed Lost Horse Mine Road. Turn left (southeast) and drive to the Lost Horse Mine parking area/trailhead, which is at the end of this 1.1-mile dirt road.

The Hike

This multifaceted hike offers something for every hiking enthusiast: a moderate climb to a large mining complex then a more strenuous trail for those wishing to experience a bit of adventurous route-finding. There are also side trips to several high panoramic points. The loop trip—follow it clockwise—is recommended only for those skilled in backcountry navigation; others may want to turn around at the Lost Horse Mine for a moderate out and back of four to five hours' duration.

The clear and wide but somewhat rocky trail climbs moderately for 1 mile across high desert swales of juniper, yucca, a few stunted Joshua trees, and nolina (commonly called bear grass), a member of the agave family often mistaken for yucca because of its long spearlike leaves. At 2 miles the trail reaches the lower end of the Lost Horse Mine. This is the largest, essentially intact, historic mining site in the park, and you could easily spend several hours here observing rock buildings, mine shafts, a large wooden stamp mill, and a winch above the mill that was used to lower miners and equipment into the mine. The largest mine shaft, some 500 feet deep, is covered. However, other smaller ones remain unsecured on the hillsides, so exercise caution when wandering around this site.

This was one of the most profitable mines in the park. A German miner named Frank Diebold made the first strike. He was later bought out by prospector Johnny Lang, who happened onto the strike in 1893 while searching for a lost horse. He and his partners began developing the mine two years later. Their process involved crushing ore at the mill, then mixing it with quicksilver (mercury), which bonded

The remains of an early-day Joshua tree log house.

with the gold so that it could be separated from the ore rock. After visiting the mine, you can double-back the way you came for a moderate 4-mile round-trip.

For a bird's-eye view of the Lost Horse Mine and its surroundings, hike north 0.2 mile on the trail that climbs above the fenced-off stamp mill. A 0.1-mile use trail continues up to Lost Horse Point (5,188 feet), which affords a magnificent panorama of surrounding basins and peaks, including the Wonderland of Rocks to the north. From here you can see a trail running southeast to a pass. Using care on the loose rocks, drop down this trail and walk 0.2 mile to the pass to climb 5,313-foot Lost Horse Mountain. From the pass, climb southwest 0.3 mile up the ridge, gaining 200 feet, to the long ridgetop that forms the summit of the mountain. There is a faint use trail that is easier seen coming down than going up, but climbing is easy on or off the use trail.

To continue the loop drop back to the pass and continue dropping steeply to the southeast on a rough and rocky trail 0.4 mile to the unsecured Lang Mine. The trail ends here; continue on a well-defined trail that contours another 0.2 mile on the

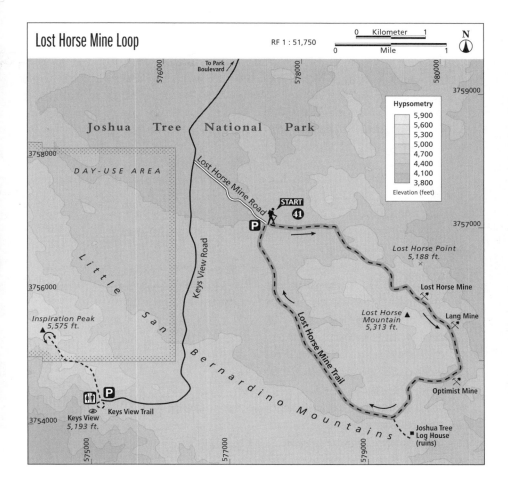

Joshua   Tree   National   Park

DAY-USE AREA

Hypsometry

	5,900
	5,600
	5,300
	5,000
	4,700
	4,400
	4,100
	3,800

Elevation (feet)

To Park
Boulevard

Lost Horse Mine Road

START
41

Lost Horse Point
5,188 ft.

Lost Horse Mine

Lost Horse
Mountain
5,313 ft.

Lang Mine

Optimist Mine

Lost Horse Mine Trail

Keys View Road

Little   San   Bernardino   Mountains

Inspiration Peak
5,575 ft.

Keys View Trail

Keys View
5,193 ft.

Joshua Tree
Log House
(ruins)

hillside to a small flat spot marked by a large cairn. This is the end of the trail and the start of the short cross-country segment. Instead of dropping any farther, angle sharply upward and to the right (southwest) to the closest ridge, wrapping around the small hill to the right for about 0.1 mile. From here the stone chimney, tailings, and trail of the Optimist Mine can be seen downhill and across the gully to the south.

Drop down to the chimney in 0.1 mile and pick up the easy-to-follow trail, which winds uphill and to the right. The trail travels westward in and around several small hills and gullies 0.4 mile to a wooden post with the number 8. After another 0.4 mile the trail drops into a wide wash at about mile 4.4 in the loop trip.

Take an interesting short side trip to a Joshua tree log house by hiking up the wash to the first fork at 0.2 mile. Continue southeast on the left-hand fork another 0.2 mile to the cabin ruins, which are on the left side of the wash along with the faint remnants of an old mining road. This structure stands as a rustic reminder of why Joshua trees are so scarce in this heavily prospected mining district.

Return to the junction and continue northwest down either the trail or the wash, both of which end up on the Lost Horse Mine Road about 100 yards below the parking area. The trail provides firmer walking but at times disappears in the wash. When in doubt simply follow the wash—eventually you'll pick up the trail on one of its several crossings. The wash is bounded by low-lying ridges with the valley opening up to vistas of distant mountains to the northwest. Joshua trees become larger and more abundant on this return leg of the loop as the distance increases from the mining sites. Upon reaching the Lost Horse Mine Road, turn right and walk the remaining short distance to the parking area/trailhead.

Note: Those wishing to backpack and camp overnight on the loop route must start at the Juniper Flats Backcountry Board, 1.5 miles north of the turnoff to the Lost Horse Mine trail, 0.25 mile east of the parking area, thereby adding 3.5 miles to the loop. There are several good campsites near the junction of the trail and wash near mile 4 of the loop.

Miles and Directions

0.0 Begin at the Lost Horse Mine parking area/trailhead.

2.0 Arrive at Lost Horse Mine.

2.2 Arrive at Lost Horse Point.

2.4 Arrive at a pass southeast of the mine.

2.7 Reach Lost Horse Mountain (5,313 feet).

3.4 Arrive at Lang Mine.

3.6 Reach the end of the trail/beginning of the cross-country leg.

3.8 Arrive at Optimist Mine.

4.5 The trail enters and follows a wash.

4.9 You'll see the ruins of a Joshua tree log house.

7.8 This is the end of the loop.

42 California Riding and Hiking Trail: Keys View Road to Park Route 11

Here you'll find solitude in a busy region of the park, as well as sweeping vistas of Juniper Flats and the Pinto Basin. Two sections of the California Riding and Hiking Trail, largely downhill over a broad trail, can be hiked as a single unit of 11 miles as a point-to-point day hike, or broken into 6.5- and 4.4-mile one-way units.

Start: 15 miles southwest of Twentynine Palms.
Distance: 11.1 miles one way, with car shuttle.
Approximate hiking time: 4 to 6 hours.
Difficulty: Moderate.
Trail surface: Dirt path.

Seasons: October through April.
USGS topo maps: Keys View-CA and Malapai Hill-CA (1:24,000).
Trail contact: Joshua Tree National Park (see appendix D).

Finding the trailhead: From California Highway 62 in Twentynine Palms, take Utah Trail south 4 miles to the North Entrance of the park; continue on Park Route 12 for 15.8 miles to the Keys View Road left turn, which is at the Cap Rock Nature Trail. Turn left (southwest) on Keys View and continue 1.1 miles to the Juniper Flats Backcountry Board on your right. The trail itself crosses Keys View Road just to the north of the board parking area. A spur trail leads you to the main trail.

    For a car shuttle: For a partial trip, your pickup point is on Geology Tour Road, 10.2 miles down PR 12 from the North Entrance, on your left; the backcountry board and parking area are south on Geology Tour Road, 1.4 miles, on your right. For the longer hike, the pickup spot is on Park Route 11 near the Arch Rock Nature Trail and White Tank Campground. From the North Entrance go south on PR 12 for 4.8 miles to the Pinto Y junction; turn left on PR 11 and go south 2.3 miles to the Twin Tank Backcountry Board, on your right.

The Hike

Whether done as one long hike or two short hikes, these outings provide an excellent tour of the central area of Joshua Tree National Park. The California Riding and Hiking Trail is largely sandy. These sections feature a fairly broad pathway; the final 4.4 miles are on a trail as wide as a city sidewalk. In spite of its title, there is minimal horse usage. We never saw a hoofprint on our hike.

    The trail is well marked with arrowed signposts, and even features mile markers (mile 1 is on the slightly used portion starting near the North Entrance), so you always know where you are. Except for a gradual 250-foot rise in the first portion after Ryan Campground, the trail is nearly all downhill. This, combined with the easy footing, makes it possible to stroll along enjoying the scenery.

    And the scenery is superb! From Keys View you cross the interior valley south of Ryan Mountain. Although you are not in a remote corner of the park, there is

The California R&H Trail near the White Tank Campground provides sweeping vistas of the Pinto Basin and Range to the east.

a definite sense of total solitude. Hiking through the valley and on down the ridge into Pleasant Valley, you'll enjoy a wide field of vision, unlike the wash and canyon hikes elsewhere in the park. The Little San Bernardinos rise to the right, and the Pinto Mountains loom larger in the distance to the east. The distinctive peaks of Ryan Mountain, Malapai Hill, the Hexie Range, and Crown Prince Lookout punctuate your trip.

The final section of the hike is the easiest portion of the Riding and Hiking Trail in the park. Many hikers park at either end and do it as an easy out and back, avoiding the hassle of the car shuttle. West to east, of course, the downhill slope is advantageous. And what a vista there is as you descend gradually toward the Pinto Basin stretching before you into the hazy distance. With only a bit of imagination, you can envision the early Pinto Basin inhabitants enjoying life around the lake that once lay in the grassy valley between the mountains. With a net loss of elevation of nearly 600 feet, the 4.4-mile section also gives you a relaxed opportunity to notice vegetation changes as you descend from the Mojave to the Colorado (Sonoran) Desert. The

California Riding and Hiking Trail: Keys View Road to Park Route 11

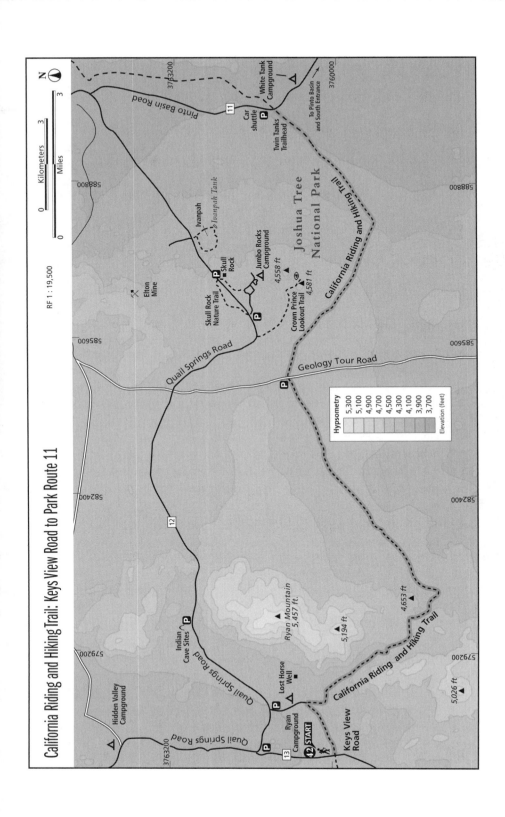

Joshua trees are numerous and large at your 4,500-foot commencement at Geology Tour Road. Gradually, they become more sparse and quite small, until they are nearly nonexistent. Instead, creosote dominates, and cholla cacti increase. By the end of the hike, you are in a new botanical environment.

If you have more time and energy, the Twin Tanks monzogranite region is immediately west of the backcountry board on PR 11. You can see the hulking granite formations to the north of the trail as you approach the board. These looming forms are quite a bit larger than they appear, for they are hiding in a ravine, crouching below the horizon. A 1-mile hike west of the board will take you to this fanciful granite playground with curiously eroded caves, tunnels, and sculptures.

Note: In Joshua Tree the backcountry boards are not located exactly on the California Riding and Hiking Trail. In each case, the trail crosses the road slightly to the north or to the south of the board itself. The board structures are large enough for you to spot them above the desert vegetation, and feeder trails will lead you to or from the boards at the beginning and end of your hikes.

Miles and Directions

0.0–0.7 From the Juniper Flats Backcountry Board, the trail leads northeast toward Ryan Campground, then turns east.

1.5 Arrive at a saddle pass, the high point of the hike (4,540 feet).

2.5 The mine site is below the trail to the right. Fifty yards farther the trail goes right through prospectors' ruins.

6.5 Cross Geology Tour Road.

10.9 Arrive at PR 11.

11.1 The board and parking area are 0.2 mile north for an 11.1-mile one-way hike.

43 Arch Rock Nature Trail

This short nature walk features geology lessons, which are illustrated by the striking white granite formations that surround you. There's also an opportunity for a side trip to an old cattle tank that continues to provide a patch of greenery in the desert.

Start: 8.5 miles south of Twentynine Palms.
Distance: 0.3-mile loop.
Approximate hiking time: 30 minutes to 1 hour.
Difficulty: Easy nature trail.

Trail surface: Dirt path.
Seasons: October through April.
USGS topo map: Malapai Hill-CA (1:24,000).
Trail contact: Joshua Tree National Park (see appendix D).

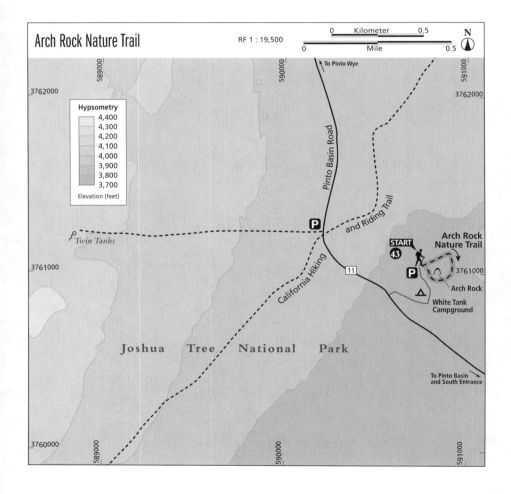

Arch Rock Nature Trail

RF 1 : 19,500

Hypsometry

4,400
4,300
4,200
4,100
4,000
3,900
3,800
3,700

Elevation (feet)

To Pinto Wye

Pinto Basin Road

and Riding Trail

Twin Tanks

California Hiking

START
43

Arch Rock
Nature Trail

P

Arch Rock

White Tank
Campground

Joshua Tree National Park

To Pinto Basin
and South Entrance

Finding the trailhead: From California Highway 62 in Twentynine Palms, take Utah Trail south 4 miles to the North Entrance of the park; continue south on Park Route 12 for 4.8 miles to the Pinto Y intersection. Turn left at the Y onto Park Route 11 and go 2.8 miles to the White Tank Campground, on your left. Turn into the campground and follow the inconspicuous nature-trail sign to the trailhead, on the left immediately after the campground information board.

The Hike

The focus of this nature trail is on the unique geology of the fascinating rock formations that abound in this area of the park. Informational signs present a sophisticated series of geology lessons, far beyond the simplistic rock identification that usually occurs on such a trail. The trail itself is an adventure in geology as it winds through imaginative boulders to the famed Arch Rock.

A side trip from this rock through the slot to the northeast leads to the site of an old cattle tank, which is no longer holding water but has created a habitat for birds and other desert creatures.

The geology lesson covers the formation of igneous rock, the origins of White Tank granite, erosion, selective erosion, dikes, and faults. The remainder of your visit in the park will be greatly enhanced by this knowledge. For example, 1 mile west of White Tank Campground are the Twin Tanks. Like Arch Rock, these granite formations are gracefully sculpted by the forces of weather and are inviting to explore. Twin Tanks also has two partially buried old tank sites.

The granite arch on the Arch Rock Nature Trail.

44 Skull Rock Nature Trail

This easy nature trail, located at the Jumbo Rocks Campground, winds through the fanciful rock formations that make this region of the park so distinctive.

Start: 12 miles south of Twentynine Palms.
Distance: 1.7-mile loop.
Approximate hiking time: 1 to 2 hours.
Difficulty: Easy.
Trail surface: Dirt path.

Seasons: October through April.
USGS topo map: Malapai Hill-CA (1:24,000).
Trail contact: Joshua Tree National Park (see appendix D).

This eroded monzogranite boulder gives Skull Rock Nature Trail its morbid name.

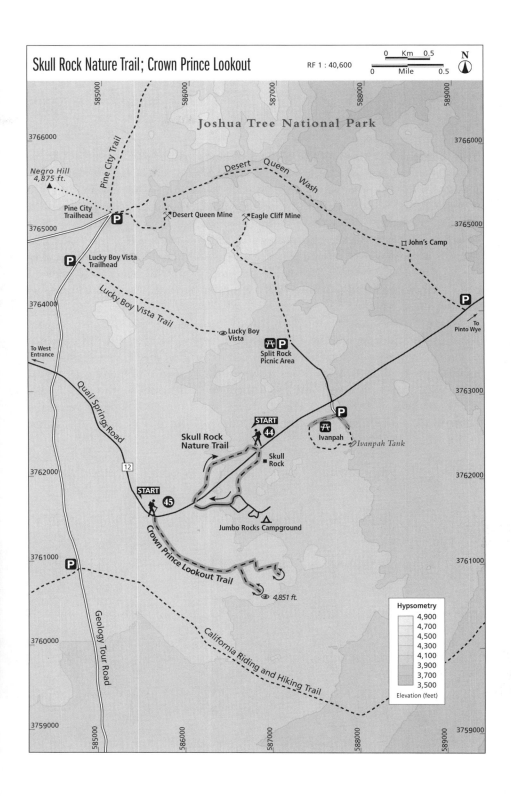

Skull Rock Nature Trail; Crown Prince Lookout

RF 1 : 40,600

0   Km   0.5
0   Mile   0.5

N

Joshua Tree National Park

Pine City Trail

3766000

Negro Hill
4,875 ft.

Pine City
Trailhead   **P**

Desert Queen Mine

Eagle Cliff Mine

Desert   Queen   Wash

John's Camp

3765000

P   Lucky Boy Vista
Trailhead

Lucky Boy Vista Trail

3764000

Lucky Boy
Vista

Split Rock
Picnic Area

P

To
Pinto Wye

To West
Entrance

Quail Springs Road

3763000

P

12

START
44

Skull Rock
Nature Trail

Ivanpah

Ivanpah Tank

Skull
Rock

3762000

START
45

Jumbo Rocks Campground

Crown Prince Lookout Trail

3761000

P

Geology Tour Road

4,851 ft.

California Riding and Hiking Trail

3760000

Hypsometry

4,900
4,700
4,500
4,300
4,100
3,900
3,700
3,500

Elevation (feet)

3759000

Finding the trailhead: From California Highway 62 in Twentynine Palms, take Utah Trail south 4 miles to the North Entrance of the park; continue on Park Route 12 for 4.8 miles to the Pinto Y intersection. Bear right, still on PR 12, and continue 3.8 miles to the signed Skull Rock Nature Trail trailhead.

The Hike

This loop trail is divided by PR 12. The northern half of the loop begins at the Skull Rock sign on the highway and goes northward; at 0.7 mile it ends at the Jumbo Rocks Campground entrance. To pick up the rest of the trail from there, it is necessary to walk down through the campground (0.5 mile) to the end of loop E to get to the other half. This northern half of the loop has not recently been renovated by the park. Several signs are so weathered they are illegible. The trail is haphazardly marked with rocks and is not always clear. Although the eroded boulders are a spectacular sight, the information provided is not thematic. Basic geology, plant identification, and desert survival tips are intermixed. The park has plans to improve the signage.

Across the road, on the southern half of the loop, the signs are recent, more plentiful, and more instructive. They focus on desert diversity and the interconnectedness of the plants and animals that make this region their home. The famous, much-photographed Skull Rock sits at the entrance (or exit) of the southern loop, immediately adjacent to the road. From there, the trail winds southward 0.5 mile to the southern end of Jumbo Rocks Campground on the E loop. Hike up the campground road to pick up the northern loop opposite the campground entrance on PR 12.

45 Crown Prince Lookout

Named for its role as a World War II lookout, this high point above the desert floor still provides a vantage point for hikers, with views of Queen Valley, from Pushawalla Plateau to Queen Mountain, Twin Tanks, Arch Rock, and the Pinto Range.

See map on page 149.
Start: 12 miles south of Twentynine Palms.
Distance: 3 miles out and back.
Approximate hiking time: 2 to 3 hours.
Difficulty: Easy.

Trail surface: Sandy trail.
Seasons: October through April.
USGS topo map: Malapai Hill-CA (1:24,000).
Trail contact: Joshua Tree National Park (see appendix D).

The trail to Crown Prince Lookout leads clearly to the overlook jutting above the plateau in the distance.

Finding the trailhead: From California Highway 62 in Twentynine Palms, take Utah Trail south 4 miles to the North Entrance of the park; continue south on Park Route 12 for 4.8 miles to the Pinto Y intersection. Bear right and continue on PR 12 another 3.7 miles to Jumbo Rocks Campground. Park in the visitor lot at the entrance, or along the north side of the road, and walk west along the road shoulder 0.25 mile to the trailhead at the sharp curve in the road west of the campground. The trail is marked by six huge stones placed there to block vehicle access on this former jeep route. The trailhead is unsigned.

The Hike

This easy hike follows a well-defined old jeep track up a broad sandy ridge. At 1.3 miles the trail splits at a Y. To the right the trail heads for a huge boulder pile; do not be intimidated, for the trail curves around to an adjacent promontory and does not climb the peak. From the vista point, you can see the valleys to the east and the vast White Tank granite formations that lie between here and the Pinto Mountains. For the adventuresome hiker, wend your way to the top of Crown Prince to see the remains of the World War II observation post, the lookout for which the outing is named. It's an interesting historical aspect of the hike.

Back at the Y, the trail now on the right is also a gentle 0.2-mile track. It ends in a broad, sandy turnaround. A footpath continues to the right of a more modest boulder pile and ends at an old mine site.

The walk back to PR 12 is entirely downhill.

46 Ryan Mountain

Unlike most other peaks in the park, Ryan Mountain is located right by a paved road, so there's no long warm-up before the climb begins. When you reach the summit, you'll be rewarded with a panoramic view of the park.

Start: About 20 miles southwest of Twentynine Palms.
Distance: 3 miles out and back.
Approximate hiking time: 4 to 5 hours.
Difficulty: Strenuous.
Trail surface: Dirt and rock path.

Seasons: October through May.
USGS topo maps: Indian Cove-CA and Keys View-CA (1:24,000).
Trail contact: Joshua Tree National Park (see appendix D).

Finding the trailhead: From California Highway 62 in Joshua Tree, drive south on Park Boulevard for 1 mile. It changes to Quail Springs Road; continue 4 miles to the West Entrance of the park. Follow Park Route 12 for 12.5 miles to Ryan Mountain Trailhead, on your right (south). The signed parking area is 2.1 miles east of the junction with Keys View Road.

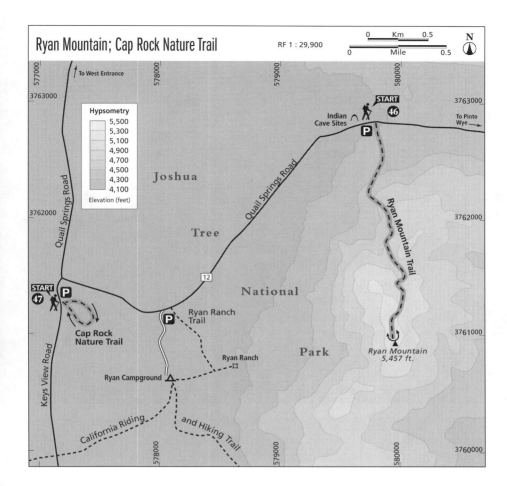

Ryan Mountain; Cap Rock Nature Trail

RF 1 : 29,900

0   Km   0.5

0   Mile   0.5

N

To West Entrance

Hypsometry

5,500
5,300
5,100
4,900
4,700
4,500
4,300
4,100

Elevation (feet)

Joshua

Tree

National

Park

START
46

Indian
Cave Sites

To Pinto
Wye

Ryan Mountain Trail

Ryan Mountain
5,457 ft.

START
47

Cap Rock
Nature Trail

Quail Springs Road

Keys View Road

Quail Springs Road

12

Ryan Ranch
Trail

Ryan Ranch

Ryan Campground

California Riding

and Hiking Trail

3763000

3762000

3761000

3760000

577000

578000

579000

580000

The Hike

The trail leaves from the parking area through a massive boulder gate of White Tank granite sculpted by selective erosion. This well-signed official park trail is quite a display of rock workmanship. Steeper portions of the trail feature stair-steps artfully constructed from plentiful native rocks, so it's easy walking up and there's no skidding going down. The trail winds around the hill by the trailhead and takes a relatively gentle slope to the peak.

If you have spent several days walking nature trails, visiting mine sites, and hiking canyon washes, this peak climb provides a welcome aerial view of where you've been in the central portion of the park. On your return, don't miss the Indian Cave sites at the western end of the parking area. A sign indicates their location. The fire-stained rock shelters provide a reminder of the centuries of use that this land has seen from human visitors.

The granite boulders of Wonderland of Rocks stretch off to the north from Ryan Mountain.

Miles and Directions

0.0 Start at the trailhead.

0.1 Huge boulders frame the trail.

0.4 The trail begins a steep climb.

1.5 Reach the summit of Ryan Mountain.

3.0 Return to the trailhead.

47 Cap Rock Nature Trail

Here's a loop trip around a spectacular monzogranite formation on a hard-surfaced barrier-free path. Signs along the trail provide information about desert plants.

See map on page 153.
Start: 22 miles southwest of Twentynine Palms.
Distance: 0.4-mile loop.
Approximate hiking time: Less than 30 minutes.

Difficulty: Easy.
Trail surface: Hard surface, barrier-free.
Seasons: October through May.
USGS topo map: Keys View-CA (1:24,000).
Trail contact: Joshua Tree National Park (see appendix D).

Cap Rock, with its sporty visor, is a popular spot for rock climbers.

Finding the trailhead: From California Highway 62 in Joshua Tree, take the Park Boulevard exit south 1 mile, to where it turns into Quail Springs Road, and continue 4 miles to the West Entrance of the park. Continue on Park Route 12 for 15 miles to the right turn on Keys View Road. The Cap Rock parking area is on the left (east) side of road 0.1 mile from the intersection.

The Hike

This easy nature trail is paved and designed to accommodate wheelchairs. Numerous informational signs dot your route. The focus of the information is on the desert plants that grow around these fascinating quartz monzonite boulder piles. Cap Rock itself is nearby; frequent use by rock climbers makes this an interesting scene.

48 Lucky Boy Vista

This outing provides a vista of the Split Rock region of the park. The trail also takes you to the remains of the Elton Mine.

Start: 16 miles south of Twentynine Palms.
Distance: 2.5 miles out and back.
Approximate hiking time: 2 to 3 hours.
Difficulty: Easy.
Trail surface: Sandy trail.

Seasons: October through April.
USGS topo map: Queen Mountain-CA (1:24,000).
Trail contact: Joshua Tree National Park (see appendix D).

Finding the trailhead: From California Highway 62 in Twentynine Palms, take Utah Trail south 4 miles to the North Entrance of the park; continue on Park Route 12 for 4.8 miles to the Pinto Y intersection. Bear right and stay on PR 12 another 5.2 miles to the dirt road on your right (directly opposite Desert Queen Mine Road, which goes south). Turn north on the dirt road and go 0.8 mile to a gated road going east. Park there.

The Hike

This relatively flat hike to the Elton Mine site is on a broad sandy jeep track, which is in better shape than the Desert Queen Mine Road you took to get here. The trail climbs gradually above a yucca and piñon boulder garden to the north. At 1 mile there is a gate; continue around it. Shortly afterward you will see the fenced-off mine shafts on your right. Just beyond the mine on a lofty plateau is a magnificent overlook of the Split Rock region of the park. For a short hike, this outing provides you with an opportunity for desert solitude, a great view, and a historic site.

The reverse view on the trip back to the car is equally spacious.

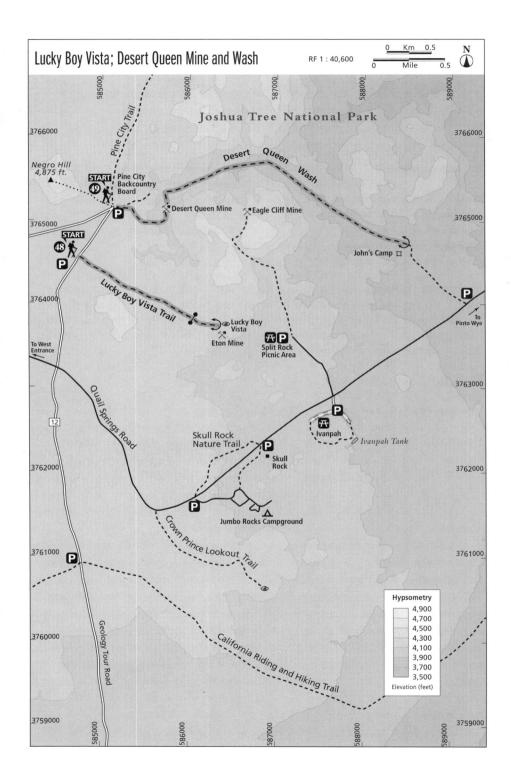

Lucky Boy Vista; Desert Queen Mine and Wash

RF 1 : 40,600

0 — Km — 0.5
0 — Mile — 0.5

N

Joshua Tree National Park

Negro Hill
4,875 ft.

Pine City Trail

START
49

Pine City
Backcountry
Board

Desert Queen Wash

Desert Queen Mine

Eagle Cliff Mine

John's Camp

START
48

Lucky Boy Vista Trail

Lucky Boy
Vista

Eton Mine

Split Rock
Picnic Area

To West
Entrance

To
Pinto Wye

Quail Springs Road

12

Skull Rock
Nature Trail

Skull
Rock

Ivanpah

Ivanpah Tank

Jumbo Rocks Campground

Crown Prince Lookout Trail

Geology Tour Road

California Riding and Hiking Trail

Hypsometry

4,900
4,700
4,500
4,300
4,100
3,900
3,700
3,500

Elevation (feet)

49 Desert Queen Mine and Wash

The view of the Desert Queen Mine, the largest and longest-running mine in the park, from the overlook near the trailhead will tantalize you to explore farther down the wash, where traces of additional mines and miner settlements are located.

See map on page 157.
Start: 15 miles south of Twentynine Palms.
Distance: 4 miles out and back.
Approximate hiking time: 1 to 5 hours, depending on distance.
Difficulty: Easy (to overlook); moderate (to mine site and on down the wash).

Trail surface: Sandy trail.
Seasons: October through April.
USGS topo map: Queen Mountain-CA (1:24,000).
Trail contact: Joshua Tree National Park (see appendix D).

Finding the trailhead: From the visitor center in Twentynine Palms continue south on Utah Trail 8.2 miles to the Pinto Y intersection. Stay to the right on Park Route 12 and drive 5.2 miles to a right turn on a dirt road immediately opposite the signed Desert Queen Mine Road, which heads south. Turn north on the one-lane dirt road and drive 1.4 miles to its end at the Pine City Backcountry Board and parking area.

The Hike

This trip covers a variety of mine sites, from the most prosperous in the area (Desert Queen) to those that obviously were not successful. The Desert Queen was in operation from 1895 to 1961 and was one of the most productive gold mines in the Southern California desert. The magnitude of the Desert Queen operation is not evident from the gaping holes in the mountainside but from the massive tailings that drip like blood down the mountain into the wash below. The debris left around the site—which continues to appear miles down the wash—is also evidence of the environmental repercussions of the industrial use of the desert.

The experience of hiking down the wash erases the sight of the damage to the mountainside. The huge boulders that rise above and periodically in front of you, blocking your way, are reminders of the forces of nature that are still in operation. The vegetation of the wash is profuse and diverse. Mesquite, creosote, and smoke trees line the wash, sometimes even blocking your passage. The intermittent power of rushing water scours the wash, but these durable plants enjoy this location.

Mining sites farther down the wash represent the other end of the economic spectrum from the Desert Queen. Unlike the Keys operation, the other sites are small. The artifacts found around the miners' dwellings indicate a grim existence for these workers. This was primitive living. The size of the tailings shows that the excavations were not extensive. These mining projects did not last long.

Walking back up the wash after visiting John's Camp, you can revel in the beau-

Remains of a miner's bungalow at the Desert Queen Mine site.

ties of the canyon. Then, turning the last corner, you encounter the mining equipment left in the wash by the Desert Queen. Two distinct worlds are preserved by Joshua Tree National Park; we can learn much by being aware of both of them.

Miles and Directions

0.0 From the trailhead, the broad trail goes east. Disregard the cable barricade, which was put there to deter vehicles, not hikers.

0.3 At the old stone ruins of a miner's dwelling, the rocky road winds down to the wash below.

0.6 Overlook. Climb to the mines, then return to the wash.

1.3 Huge boulders block the wash. Take the crude trail on the bank to the right (west) to get around these obstacles.

1.5 Where the wash widens, the old prospector site is on the low shelf to your right.

1.8 Another boulder tumble blocks the narrow wash. Follow the cairns and the game trail to the left.

2.0 At the silvery "anthill" above the wash on the left bank, bear right to the John's Camp site on the low bank on the right.

4.0 Return to the trailhead by walking back up the wash.

50 Pine City/Canyon

The short option on this hike takes you to a picturesque former mining camp. The longer, more adventurous outing heads on down the colorful canyon, with several steep rock pitches requiring some scrambling near the North Entrance, where your car shuttle awaits you.

Start: 15 miles south of Twentynine Palms.
Distance: 6.5 miles one way.
Approximate hiking time: 2 to 4 hours for short hike; 5 to 7 for longer one.
Difficulty: Easy (Pine City); strenuous (Pine City Canyon).

Trail surface: Clear trail to Pine City; cross-country on mostly clear washes down Pine City Canyon.
Seasons: October through May.
USGS topo map: Queen Mountain-CA (1:24,000).
Trail contact: Joshua Tree National Park (see appendix D).

Finding the trailhead: From the visitor center in Twentynine Palms, continue south on Utah Trail 8.2 miles to the Pinto Y intersection. Stay to the right on Park Route 12 for 5.1 miles to the unsigned dirt road on your right (directly opposite Desert Queen Mine Road, which goes south). Turn right (north) on the dirt road and drive 1.4 miles to the end of the road at the Pine City Backcountry Board.

For car shuttle: Park at the North Entrance introduction board, 0.5 mile south of the North Entrance on the west side of PR 12. The North Entrance is 4 miles south of Twentynine Palms.

The Hike

Except for a few mine shafts grated over for public safety, all that remains of Pine City is the wind rustling through the pines. Still, the short and easy walk to the Pine City site provides ample opportunities for exploration and for savoring its bouldery beauty. The trail maintains an even grade across a high Mojave Desert plateau covered with Joshua trees.

At mile 1.1 an obscure trail leads to the right for 0.3 mile to a picture-perfect pocket of monzoquartz granite ringed with piñon pines. The main trail to Pine City continues left. At 1.6 miles another trail takes off to the right, dropping 100 feet in 0.2 mile to the dry Pine Spring. The spring lies just above the narrow notch of a steep, boulder-strewn canyon. This pleasant spot is well suited for a picnic or for just plain relaxing. Bighorn sheep rely on the cool shelter of this place when people aren't there.

Note: To avoid disturbance of sheep and other wildlife, the Pine City/Pine Spring/upper Pine Canyon area is within a much larger day-use area. Camping is

Looking down lower Pine City Canyon.

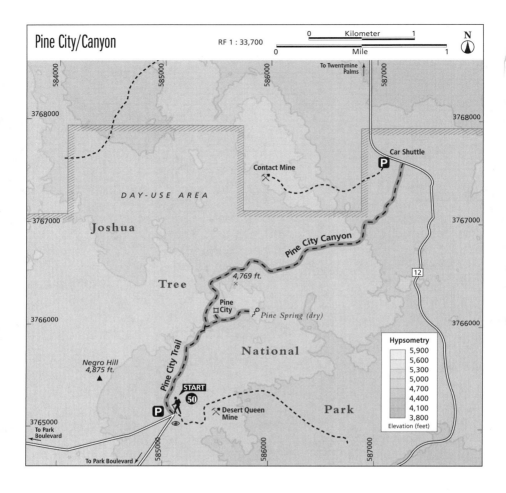

RF 1 : 33,700

0   Kilometer   1

0   Mile   1

N

To Twentynine Palms

Car Shuttle

Contact Mine

DAY-USE AREA

Joshua

Pine City Canyon

4,769 ft.

Tree

Pine City

Pine Spring (dry)

12

3766000

National

Negro Hill 4,875 ft.

Pine City Trail

START

50

Desert Queen Mine

Park

Hypsometry

Elevation (feet)
5,900
5,600
5,300
5,000
4,700
4,400
4,100
3,800

To Park Boulevard

To Park Boulevard

currently allowed south of Pine City in accordance with park regulations. Check at the visitor center in case these boundaries are altered.

From the Pine Spring turnoff, continue left another 0.1 mile to the Pine City site, which is immediately east of the trail in a wide, sandy flat next to a huge round boulder sitting atop a rock platform. You could easily spend several hours poking around the myriad side canyons and interesting rock formations that surround the Pine City site. The site contains at least one grated mine shaft and at least one more that is unsecured, so caution is called for. Return the way you came to complete this level 3.4-mile out-and-back hike.

To continue a point-to-point trip down Pine City Canyon, stay left on the trail for another 0.5 mile northeast of the Pine City site, to where it ends on a ridge next to a small hill. Drop into the broad saddle southwest of the 4,769-foot hill shown on the topographic map. If time and energy permit, this hill provides an easy walkup for a stunning view in all directions. From the saddle, drop down the steep gully to the main Pine City Canyon wash. A few rock cairns mark the way.

The upper reaches of Pine City Canyon are spectacular, lined with great columns of gray and red rock. The canyon drops steeply, requiring boulder hopping and, at times, the use of "all fours" to negotiate the steep but stable rocks. For out-and-back hikers wishing to sample a bit of this steep-walled canyon, hike a mile or so down to about the 4,000-foot level to a good turnaround point. This upper stretch harbors the deepest and most dramatic section of the canyon. Below 4,000 feet the canyon narrows and steepens with several more difficult rock sections requiring skill and agility with both hands and feet. Here the canyon is trending east to northeast and is dropping about 500 feet per mile. Multicolored bands of rippled rock—purple, red, yellow—grace the floor of this canyon lined with barrel cacti.

At 3,350 feet the country begins to open up. Although high ridges are nearby, the wash leaves the deeper canyon. This is also where the transition from the high Mojave Desert to the lower Colorado Desert becomes apparent, where cholla cacti dot the open desert. The last 2 miles involve easy walking down a broad wash to PR 12, a mellow time to relax and reflect upon the rugged splendor of Pine City Canyon. The wash meets the highway about 0.2 mile south of the parking area/introduction board, which is 0.5 mile south of the North Entrance.

Miles and Directions

0.0 Start at the Pine City Backcountry Board/trailhead.

1.1 Continue left at the trail junction with the right-hand trail leading to an old mine site.

1.6 Continue left at the right-hand trail to Pine Spring.

1.7 Arrive at the Pine City site. Turn around here to return to the trailhead.

2.2 The trail ends on a ridge above Pine City Canyon.

2.3 The use trail drops to Pine City Canyon.

6.5 The Pine City Canyon wash meets PR 12.

51 Contact Mine

Just inside the North Entrance to the park lies this historic gold-and-silver mine. It's a steep rocky trail to the mine site, but you will be rewarded with a splendid view, as well as the opportunity to get a feel for life as a desert miner.

Start: 4.5 miles south of Twentynine Palms.
Distance: 3.4 miles out and back.
Approximate hiking time: 3 to 5 hours.
Difficulty: Strenuous.
Trail surface: Rocky path.

Seasons: October through April.
USGS topo map: Queen Mountain-CA (1:24,000).
Trail contact: Joshua Tree National Park (see appendix D).

The Contact Mine sits on the hillside above the trail.

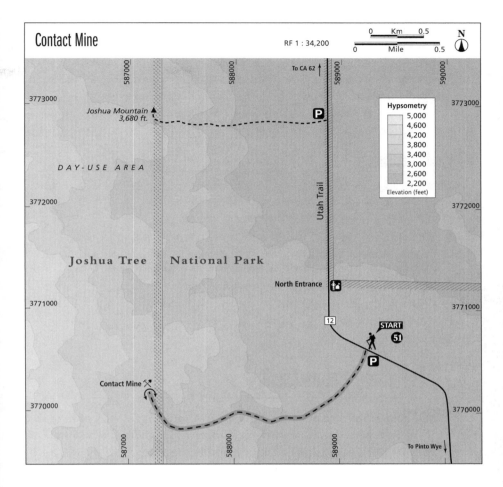

Finding the trailhead: From California Highway 62 in Twentynine Palms, take Utah Trail south 4 miles to the North Entrance of the park; continue on Park Route 12 for 0.5 mile to the trailhead on the right (west), at the park-entrance information board and parking area.

The Hike

The old mining trail that takes you to the Contact Mine is as impressive in its engineering as the mine itself. The old road cuts through solid rock, avoids gullies with remarkable rock foundations, and cuts across the sides of steep hills. The hiking path has become very rocky due to erosion, but the workmanship of the original road builders is still evident.

The hiker is exposed to the elements along the entire trail. Pick a cool day to enjoy this one!

The rising trail provides stunning views into the Pinto Mountains to the east, as well as into the craggy chain of peaks running from Twentynine Palms southward.

At each bend in the trail, as it winds around another rocky ridge, you expect to see the mine. Not until 1.6 miles are you rewarded with the sight of the mine above on the hillside. At this point are side trails developed by the miners to handle two-way traffic. Count on spending additional time at the mine to prowl around the buildings and other artifacts, but beware of unsecured and hazardous mine shafts.

The hike back down reinforces one's awe with the work involved with developing the Contact Mine in the early 1900s.

Miles and Directions:

0.0–0.2 From the board, follow the old jeep trail southwest and left of the huge boulders that stand apart from the other disorganized piles of granite.

0.2 At the wash, take the trail on top of the dike on the right.

0.4 At the dike's end, bear right, with the wash on a faint trail around a boulder pile.

0.45 There's a rising road ramp, dating from mining days, on the left across the wash. Take this ramp up from the wash and follow the road to the mine. Cairns mark the trail.

1.6 The mine site becomes visible on the mountainside above.

1.7 Arrive at the day-use-only mine site.

3.4 Return to the trailhead.

52 Fortynine Palms Oasis

This 3-mile round-trip hike rewards the energetic hiker with a display of fan palms and a lush willow thicket, a favorite habitat for birds and bighorn sheep. Visitors are asked to stay on the trail to minimize damage to the vegetation.

Start: 6 miles west of Twentynine Palms and 11 miles east of Joshua Tree.
Distance: 3 miles out and back.
Approximate hiking time: 2 to 4 hours.
Difficulty: Moderate.
Trail surface: Rocky path.

Seasons: October through April.
USGS topo map: Queen Mountain-CA (1:24,000).
Trail contact: Joshua Tree National Park (see appendix D).

Finding the trailhead: From California Highway 62, 11.2 miles east of Park Boulevard in Joshua Tree, take Fortynine Palms Canyon Road south to the end (2 miles). From Twentynine Palms, take CA 62 for 5.5 miles west of Twentynine Palms to the Fortynine Palms Canyon Road exit, then south 2 miles to the road's end at a parking area.

The Hike

This is a clear but rocky trail to the Fortynine Palms Oasis. From the parking lot, it climbs to its highest point in the first half of the trip; from this elevation you have a

The towering palms of Fortynine Palms Oasis.

view of Twentynine Palms, and shortly later, as the trail curves to the right, you have your first glimpse of the palms 0.75 mile ahead, down in a rocky gorge. The descent to the oasis traverses dry, rocky terrain; even the desert shrubs are dwarfed by the harsh conditions. Miniature barrel cacti dot the slopes. The windy, dry hills above make the oasis even more striking.

At Fortynine Palms the huge old palms tower above a dense willow thicket that provides a congenial habitat for numerous desert birds. Hummingbirds are frequent visitors. The canyon is also a mecca for desert bighorn sheep. In this idyllic setting, the palm trees have a bizarre appearance. Their fire-scarred trunks bear tragic witness to the destructive urges of knife-wielding visitors who have tattooed the trunks with initials, signs, and names. The sight of these assaults on the palms is incongruous in such a setting, and highly disturbing.

Hikers should stay on the trail to avoid trampling young vegetation at the oasis. The multitude of use trails are damaging rare plants and endangering the next generation of palm trees.

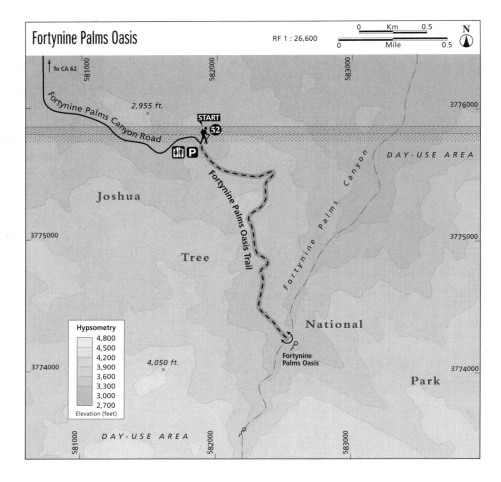

Fortynine Palms Oasis

RF 1 : 26,600

For the adventuresome and energetic explorer, the canyon beyond the oasis (to the right) can be explored as far as time and interest permit. The use trail is intermittent, and the boulders are challenging, but the curving canyon is inviting. After your exploration, the hike back to the parking lot provides sweeping views of the desert below.

Note: Day use only is permitted in this area to protect bighorn-sheep access to the water supply.

Miles and Directions

0.0 From the parking area, hike up the trail on the slope south of the roadway.

0.3 The trail makes a sharp turn to the right; continue climbing.

0.5 Climb to the top of the ridge, where you'll have your first view of the oasis.

1.0 Cross the wash and continue downhill.

1.5 Arrive at the oasis, and explore the valley beyond if desired.

3.0 Return to the trailhead.

53 Sneakeye Spring

The climb to the dry spring involves scrambling over and around elephantine boulders, which clog the steep canyon. This is a hike for the hardy, with the reward of visiting a high hidden valley.

Start: 10 miles west of Twentynine Palms.
Distance: 1 mile out and back.
Approximate hiking time: 2 to 3 hours.
Difficulty: Strenuous, with boulder scrambling.
Trail surface: Dirt path to cross-country boulder route in canyon.

Seasons: October through April.
USGS topo map: Indian Cove-CA (1:24,000).
Trail contact: Joshua Tree National Park (see appendix D).

Finding the trailhead: From California Highway 62, 9.8 miles east of Park Boulevard in Joshua Tree, take Indian Cove Road south 3 miles to the campground. Bear right at the Y intersection and follow signs for the hiking trail parking area.

From Twentynine Palms, take CA 62 for 7 miles west of the Utah Trail junction to Indian Cove Road. Go south on Indian Cove 3 miles to the campground entrance. Bear right and follow signs to the hiking trail parking area.

The Hike

This short but challenging hike takes you from a busy region of the park to an isolated high valley with pockets of greenery and oak trees, although the spring no longer is in evidence. This is a journey to an untrammeled wilderness. Due to its difficult entrance through the boulder-filled gorge, this hike appeals only to the adventuresome audience.

The first portion of the hike is deceptively easy. Curving around the monzogranite, the trail is clear and level. Only when you arrive at the wash will you perceive the difficulties that lie ahead. Careful climbing through the boulders is a pleasure due to their grainy surface. The greater hazard is the rapacious catclaw springing up wherever there is any earth available.

The high valley you reach on the northern edge of the Wonderland of Rocks has several side canyons to explore and mature oak trees for shade and relaxation. There is no water, in spite of the name of the hike; be sure to bring plenty with you.

Descending through the boulders can be as tricky as climbing them. The 1-mile distance of the hike is misleading because such boulder travel is very time-consuming.

Miles and Directions

0.0 From the parking area, follow the trail southwest around large boulders.

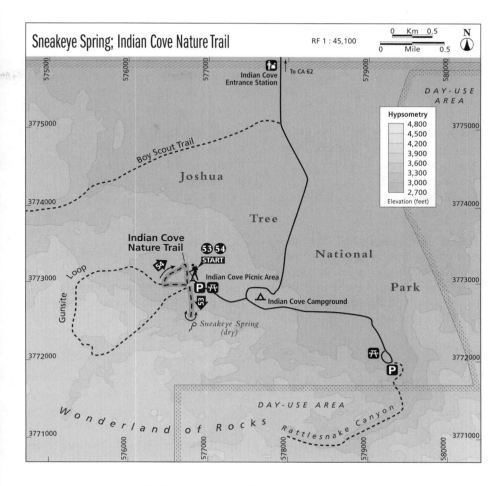

Sneakeye Spring; Indian Cove Nature Trail

RF 1 : 45,100

0.2 Drop into the wash. The easiest ascent of the canyon is via the sandy hill to the west (on the left).

0.3 At the top of the sandy slope, begin climbing over the elephantine boulders into the canyon.

0.5 There are several branches of canyon to explore from here.

1.0 Return to the parking area.

◄ *The rocky draw, filled with granite boulders, makes the Sneakeye Spring hike challenging.*

54 Indian Cove Nature Trail

Situated on the northern edge of the Wonderland of Rocks, this short nature trail at the Indian Cove Campground features information about desert-wash vegetation.

See map on page 171.
Start: 12 miles east of Joshua Tree and 10 miles west of Twentynine Palms.
Distance: 0.6-mile loop.
Approximate hiking time: Less than an hour.
Difficulty: Easy.

Trail surface: Sandy wash.
Seasons: October through April.
USGS topo map: Indian Cove-CA (1:24,000).
Trail contact: Joshua Tree National Park (see appendix D).

Finding the trailhead: From California Highway 62, 9.8 miles east of Park Boulevard in Joshua Tree, take Indian Cove Road south 3 miles to the campground. Bear right at the Y intersection and follow the signs for the nature trail parking area.

From the east, take CA 62 for 7 miles west of the Utah Trail intersection in Twentynine Palms; take Indian Cove Road south 3 miles to the campground and follow signs to the parking lot for the nature trail.

The Hike

This self-guided nature trail is one of the more difficult such paths to follow due to scarcity of arrows, trail indicators, and informational signs. It begins just west of the parking area then travels across an alluvial fan and down into a broad wash. A short 0.2 mile later, it exits the wash and returns to the parking area.

The information provided ranges from background on Paleo-Indians to desert plant and animal identification to physical geology. There is no thematic common denominator.

It's easy to miss the path's exit from the wash. Watch for the desert senna identification sign on your right immediately after the paperbag bush sign. That's your signal to bear right out of the wash to pick up the trail back to the parking area.

55 Wall Street Mill

With a pretentious name to attract the big investors from the east, this site will be of interest to the mining historian. Artifacts of the ranching past are also plentiful near the Keys homestead. The adjacent Wonderland of Rocks provides contrast with these defunct desert enterprises.

Start: 20 miles southeast of the town of Joshua Tree.
Distance: 2 miles out and back.
Approximate hiking time: 2 to 4 hours.
Difficulty: Easy.

Trail surface: Dirt path.
Seasons: October through April.
USGS topo map: Indian Cove-CA (1:24,000).
Trail contact: Joshua Tree National Park (see appendix D).

Finding the trailhead: From California Highway 62 in Joshua Tree, take the Park Boulevard exit and go 1 mile south to where it becomes Quail Springs Road; continue on Quail Springs Road 4 miles to the park's West Entrance. Follow Park Route 12 for 8.7 miles to Hidden Valley Campground/Barker Dam Road. Turn left (east) into the campground. Bear right immediately after the entrance and follow the paved road 1.6 miles to the Barker Dam Road and parking area.

The Hike

From the common trailhead, follow the park sign to the right for the Wall Street Mill. This level hike displays the desert's power of preservation. Rusty old trucks still have their tires. Antique cars sit peacefully beneath oak trees. The mill, protected by the National Register of Historic Places due to its local technological and mechanical uniqueness, still stands with its machinery intact, albeit a tad rusty. A barbed-wire fence also protects the mill from visitors. Nearby are hulks of vehicles and other artifacts of life in the desert seventy or so years ago. A park sign at the mill explains its workings, with an excellent drawing—actually a blueprint of its original design in the 1920s. This is a fun voyage of discovery, even for those who might not be machinery buffs.

The ranch house to the left of the trail and the windmill at mile 0.5 are remnants of the ranching era in the Queen Valley. The Keys family has been involved in both ranching and mining for the past century.

The Wall Street Mill was part of the Keys's industrial complex. Built by Bill Keys to process the ore from the Desert Queen Mine, it was in operation for only a few years before falling into disuse. One reason for its short life span is that Bill Keys had a run-in with Worth Bagley, his neighbor, over the use of the road to the mill. The painted rock at 0.7 mile marks the spot of the final altercation and of Bagley's death. Convicted of murder, Keys spent five years in prison but was later exonerated. Apparently he had shot Bagley in self-defense.

The rusty remains of the Wall Street Mill sit atop the hill adjacent to the majestic Wonderland of Rocks.

The trail shares its trailhead with the Wonderland Wash hike. The proximity of the mill and the mounds of monzogranite provide appropriate contrast between the reign of man and of nature in this wild country.

Return to the parking area by the same dirt path.

Miles and Directions

0.0 From the Barker Dam parking area, take the Wall Street Mill trail to the east.

0.2 At the former parking area for the mill and Wonderland Wash, continue east.

0.3 Turn right at the fork. The ruins of a pink adobe house are 200 yards to your left.

0.4 Two paths come together: If you were tempted to visit the ruins, this is where you will rejoin the mill route.

0.5 With the windmill and debris on your right, continue north, parallel to Wonderland Wash.

0.7 Observe the modern petroglyph commemorating the death of Worth Bagley, for which Bill Keys served time in San Quentin.

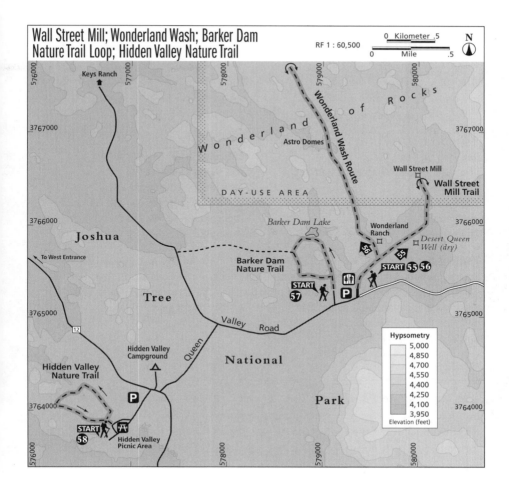

Wall Street Mill; Wonderland Wash; Barker Dam Nature Trail Loop; Hidden Valley Nature Trail

RF 1 : 60,500

0 Kilometer .5

0 Mile .5

N

Keys Ranch

3767000

Wonderland Wash Route

W o n d e r l a n d   o f   R o c k s

Astro Domes

DAY-USE AREA

Wall Street Mill

Wall Street Mill Trail

3767000

3766000

Barker Dam Lake

Joshua

To West Entrance

Barker Dam Nature Trail

Wonderland Ranch

Desert Queen Well (dry)

56

55

START 55 56

3766000

START 57

Tree

3765000

Valley Road

Queen

Hidden Valley Campground

National

3765000

12

Hidden Valley Nature Trail

Park

3764000

P

START 58

Hidden Valley Picnic Area

3764000

Hypsometry

	5,000
	4,850
	4,700
	4,550
	4,400
	4,250
	4,100
	3,950

Elevation (feet)

1.0 Arrive at the mill site. After exploring the various artifacts, return to the trailhead via the same route.

2.0 Arrive at the trailhead.

56 Wonderland Wash

This flat, easy hike leads into the Wonderland of Rocks, a fantasyland of monzo-granite sculptures and mounds. You will probably have lots of company, for this is a favorite location for Joshua Tree rock climbers.

See map on page 175.
Start: 20 miles southeast of the town of Joshua Tree.
Distance: 2 miles out and back (longer for exploration).
Approximate hiking time: 1 to 3 hours.

Difficulty: Easy.
Trail surface: Sandy path.
Seasons: October through April.
USGS topo map: Indian Cove-CA (1:24,000).
Trail contact: Joshua Tree National Park (see appendix D).

Finding the trailhead: From California Highway 62 in the town of Joshua Tree, take Park Boulevard south 1 mile to where it becomes Quail Springs Road. Continue on Quail Springs Road 4 miles to the West Entrance of the park. Continue southeast on Park Route 12 for 8.7 miles to the Hidden Valley Campground. Turn left into the campground and take the immediate right turn (signed to Barker Dam). Follow this paved road 1.6 miles to the first road on your left, which goes to the parking area.

The Hike

The use trail into Wonderland Wash is easy to follow due to the footsteps of the hundreds of rock climbers who enjoy these acres of White Tank granite. From the parking area, follow the signed trail to the east to the first fork, and bear left toward the ruins of a pink house, which you can see from the fork. Head for the house, then follow the beaten path to the left into the nearby shallow wash, only about 50 feet from the house site. The narrow wash is easy to follow, with periodic pathways weaving from bank to bank as you follow it northward into the Wonderland.

Plentiful oak and prickly pear, as well as the remnants of a dam in the wash, are other attractions of this hike—but the primary focus is on the huge rock formations that stretch in all directions. This is an enchanted world of whimsically eroded granite mounds. Well into the wash (1 mile from the trailhead) are the formations known as the Astro Domes to rock climbers who enjoy scaling their massive surfaces. The voices of climbers usually can be heard echoing from various points among the boulders, and their silhouettes may startle you when they appear hundreds of feet above atop these obelisks.

The trip back down the wash to the trailhead will be equally interesting, since the rock formations look different from the new angle.

The trail up Wonderland Wash winds through myriad granite boulders of all sizes.

Miles and Directions

0.0 From the parking area, take the signed trail heading east. At the first fork, bear left to the ruins of a pink adobe ranch house.

0.5 Cut by the house and enter the wash to your left, following the beaten use trail.

0.6 Continue winding north in the wash, between awesome rock formations.

1.0 The huge domes of monzogranite are the Astro Domes.

2.0 Return to the parking area.

57 Barker Dam Nature Trail Loop

A 1-mile loop, this trail has something to appeal to every hiker: spectacular geology, the only lake in the park, a rich array of petroglyphs, artifacts of the ranching era, and information about desert plant life and its uses by Native Americans.

See map on page 175.
Start: 20 miles southeast of the town of Joshua Tree.
Distance: 1.1-mile loop.
Approximate hiking time: 1 to 2 hours.
Difficulty: Easy.

Trail surface: Sandy path.
Seasons: October through April.
USGS topo map: Indian Cove-CA (1:24,000).
Trail contact: Joshua Tree National Park (see appendix D).

Finding the trailhead: From California Highway 62 in Joshua Tree, take Park Boulevard south 1 mile to where it turns into Quail Springs Road; continue on Quail Springs Road 4 miles to the West Entrance of the park. Follow Park Route 12 for 8.7 miles to the Hidden Valley Campground and Barker Dam turnoff to the left (east); bear right at the paved road immediately after entering the campground and drive 1.6 miles to the Barker Dam Road parking lot.

The Hike

This highly informative nature trail is a step back in time, both in terms of prehistory and with respect to the futile, short-lived attempts to raise cattle back in the early 1900s. Barker Dam was built by ranchers Barker and Shay in a natural rock catch basin to store water for cattle. In 1949–1950 the dam was raised by Bill Keys, owner of the Desert Queen Mine and the nearby Keys Ranch, then a private inholding. When filled to capacity by seasonal rains, the lake behind the dam encompasses twenty acres. Because it is surrounded by a magnificent rock ring of monzonite granite, it looks almost as though it is nestled in a high Sierra cirque at 11,000 feet. Today, the lake is used by bighorn sheep and many other species of wildlife, including shorebirds and migratory waterfowl—some of the last creatures one would expect to find in the desert!

The trail is clear and sandy, winding through a couple of tight places in the rocks, reaching Barker Dam at 0.4 mile. Notable plant species en route include Turbinella oak, adapted to the high Mojave Desert above 4,000 feet, and nolina, a yucca look-alike that provided food for the Cahuilla Indians, who baked it like molasses.

Bill Keys built innovative stone watering basins, designed to prevent spillage of the precious desert water, below the dam.

From Barker Dam Lake the trail heads west and south through a series of intimate little alcovelike valleys containing rock-lined gardens of Joshua trees, cholla, and yucca. At 0.8 mile the trail comes to a signed path leading 100 feet right to a large

Barker Dam was built at a narrow spot in the canyon.

panel of petroglyphs, which are etchings in stone made by early Native Americans. The petroglyphs are on the face of a large rock amphitheater/overhang. Sadly, a movie crew painted the carvings so that they would show up better on film. The rock faces just to the southeast of these vandalized petroglyphs contain undamaged petroglyphs, which are largely concealed by dense brush. This early encampment of immeasurable value includes rock mortars used for the grinding of nuts and seeds along with petroglyphs of a scorpion, a man with long fingers, women in dresses, who were likely early settlers, and other figures better left to your imagination. Vegetation is being re-established along this cliff wall, so please be careful to avoid trampling the new plantings and other vegetation.

The loop continues another 0.3 mile back to the parking area/trailhead.

Miles and Directions

0.0   Start from the Barker Dam parking area.

0.4   Arrive at Barker Dam Lake.

0.8   Take the signed path that leads to a large panel of petroglyphs.

1.1   The loop ends back at the parking lot.

58 Hidden Valley Nature Trail

Ringed by mounds of monzogranite boulders, this is truly a hidden valley. The nature trail winds around the valley, with signs about local history and desert ecology. You may be distracted, however, by the sight of the rock climbers scrambling and swinging overhead.

See map on page 175.
Start: 14 miles southeast of the town of Joshua Tree.
Distance: 1-mile loop.
Approximate hiking time: 1 to 2 hours.
Difficulty: Easy.

Trail surface: Sandy path.
Seasons: October through April.
USGS topo map: Indian Cove-CA (1:24,000).
Trail contact: Joshua Tree National Park (see appendix D).

Finding the trailhead: From California Highway 62 at Joshua Tree, take Park Boulevard south 1 mile to where it becomes Quail Springs Road. Continue on Quail Springs Road 4 miles to the West Entrance of the park; stay on the same road (now Park Route 12) 8.7 miles to the Hidden Valley Nature Trail and Picnic Area on your right. After you turn off the main road, follow the paved road to the right less than 0.1 mile to the parking area.

The Hike

The trail from the parking area winds upward through the boulders to Hidden Valley.

The monzogranite boulders of Hidden Valley attract rock climbers.

This part of the trail consists of old asphalt, so following it is easy. The rest of the journey is unpaved but clearly marked with signs, arrows, or fallen logs. There is some low-intensity rock walking.

Many possible pathways diverge in all directions within the valley. Most are created by the numerous adventuresome rock climbers who are attracted to the massive blocks of granite that create the valley walls. It is likely that you will hear and see them on your hike.

New signs along the nature trail emphasize natural history, sustainability in the desert, and human activities. The abnormally high rainfall (10 inches per year) of the late nineteenth century led to the development of cattle ranches here. The McHaney Gang allegedly used Hidden Valley as a base camp for their large rustling operation in the Southwest until they turned their energies to gold mining. They began developing the Desert Queen Mine in 1895. It was eventually taken over by Bill Keys, who became quite the desert magnate—a successful rancher and miner until his death in 1969.

The advent of the automobile in the 1920s brought new visitors aplenty to the desert, seriously endangering the fragile environment. In the 1930s Minerva Hamilton

Hoyt led efforts to protect the region, resulting finally in Franklin D. Roosevelt's 1936 declaration of Joshua Tree National Monument. In 1950 the boundary of the monument was sizably reduced in order to permit extensive mining. The larger area was restored with the California Desert Protection Act of 1994.

Note: This is a day-use area; no camping is permitted.

59 Boy Scout Trail/Willow Hole

This hike skirts along the western edge of the Wonderland of Rocks, with an out-and-back trip to Willow Hole, deep within the Wonderland, ending at Indian Cove Road.

Start: 11.4 miles southeast of the town of Joshua Tree.
Distance: 12 miles one way.
Approximate hiking time: 6 to 10 hours.
Difficulty: Moderate (for south to north downhill); strenuous (from north to south uphill).

Trail surface: Clear trail/wash with a steep but good trail segment between miles 4 and 5.
Seasons: October through April (Boy Scout Trail); October through May (Willow Hole).
USGS topo map: Indian Cove-CA (1:24,000).
Trail contact: Joshua Tree National Park (see appendix D).

Finding the trailhead: From California Highway 62 at Joshua Tree, take Park Boulevard south 1 mile to where it becomes Quail Springs Road; follow it another 4 miles to the West Entrance of the park. Continue 6.9 miles to the Keys West Backcountry Board, which is the starting trailhead, on the left (north) side of the highway.

    Car shuttle: From CA 62, 9.8 miles east of Park Boulevard, take Indian Cove Road south 1.6 miles to the Indian Cove Backcountry Board on your right (west side of the road).

The Hike

The Boy Scout Trail provides access to several high-quality hikes within and adjacent to the Wonderland of Rocks. The most complete and enjoyable choice is to hike mostly downhill from the Keys West Backcountry Board to the Indian Cove Backcountry Board, taking in an excursion deep into the fascinating Wonderland of Rocks at Willow Hole. This 12-mile journey on foot samples much of the diversity of this amazing landscape. If a car shuttle is out of the question, an excellent second choice is to hike 6.6 miles out and back to Willow Hole. This trip shares the first 1.3 miles of the Boy Scout Trail from the Keys West Backcountry Board.

    The popular, well-signed Boy Scout Trail climbs gradually along the west side of the Wonderland of Rocks through a picturesque Joshua tree forest sprinkled with yucca and cholla cacti, gaining only 90 feet in the first 1.3 miles. The trail offers gorgeous views of the San Bernardino Mountains to the southwest, and the nearby

The path is fairly level near the south end of the Boy Scout Trail.

mounds of monzonite quartz add a real sense of majesty to this high Mojave Desert country. The right side (east) of the entire Boy Scout Trail is open to day use only so that desert wildlife can visit water sources undisturbed. Backpackers can camp on the west side as long as they are at least 500 feet from the trail. Also, be advised that there is no public access to the Keys Ranch inholding, which is just east of the Boy Scout Trail during the first 0.5 mile.

The following two legs of the hike are described from the trail junction at 1.3 miles. The right-hand trail leads to Willow Hole and is signed DAY USE ONLY. The left fork is the Boy Scout Trail and is signed HORSE AND FOOT TRAIL and INDIAN COVE 7 MILES.

Willow Hole

The clear, sandy trail maintains a fairly constant but gradual downhill grade in a northeasterly direction, winding through impressive columns and pillars of White Tank granite. At 2.5 miles the trail enters and follows a sandy wash. At 2.7 miles a wash enters from the right; continue left down the wider wash. At 3 miles another wash joins from the right, which makes for a tempting side trip into a secluded little valley. A large boulder blocks the wash 0.2 mile up, which is a good turnaround point; or you can continue up a bit farther by lifting yourself up and through the narrow rock notch to the clear wash beyond. Double-back to the Willow Hole wash. At 3.1 miles the wash widens into a huge circular bowl surrounded by majestic cliffs. Willow Hole comes into view at 3.3 miles with its dense tangle of large willow trees creating a moist microenvironment that holds seasonal pools of water. To get to the other side of the grove, bend down and walk through the center of Willow Hole on an overgrown use trail or take a well-worn use trail around the right side. Either way the view from the east end of Willow Hole is very worthwhile, especially down the wash toward Rattlesnake Canyon. Retrace your route 2 miles back to the trail junction, now at 5.3 miles total. At about 3.9 miles on the way back, it is possible to take the wrong wash in a narrow, rocky area. In general, stay right on the more traveled wash.

Boy Scout Trail

From the trail junction at 5.3 miles, take the right-hand fork, which is signed HORSE AND FOOT TRAIL and INDIAN COVE 7 MILES. For the next 2 miles, the trail stays fairly level in a high Joshua tree plateau with yucca/rock gardens galore. After climbing at mile 7, the trail gradually drops along rocky side gullies but remains clear and easy to follow. At about 7.5 miles until the end, the trail is occasionally marked with steel pipe with two white stripes on top along with a few wooden posts. At 7.6 miles the trail drops into and follows a clear wash to mile 8, where a cement water trough and constructed rock wall are found in the wash.

At 8.2 miles the trail leaves the wash, making a sharp turn to the left (west). This turn is easy to miss, so watch for a steel-pipe trail marker behind a piñon pine to the left. This is also where the wash narrows and drops steeply into an extremely rugged canyon. This constructed portion of the trail is narrow and rocky but in good condition. It drops and then climbs to mile 8.6, where a good view opens up to the canyon far below. The trail then switchbacks steeply down to a wash at mile 9; following the wash for another mile. The wash is easy walking but is bound by extremely steep rocky slopes and cliff rock near mile 10.

At mile 10 a steel pipe on the right marks the departure of the trail from the wash, where it then crosses over into the main wash, following it to mile 10.5. At mile 10.5 a well-marked trail climbs out of the wash to the right and cuts across 1.5 miles of open desert alluvial fan vegetated with creosote, yucca, cholla cacti, and Mormon tea. Most impressive are the recurring mounds of granite sprinkled like great dollops of frozen yogurt across the desert. At mile 12 the trail ends at the Indian Cove Backcountry Board.

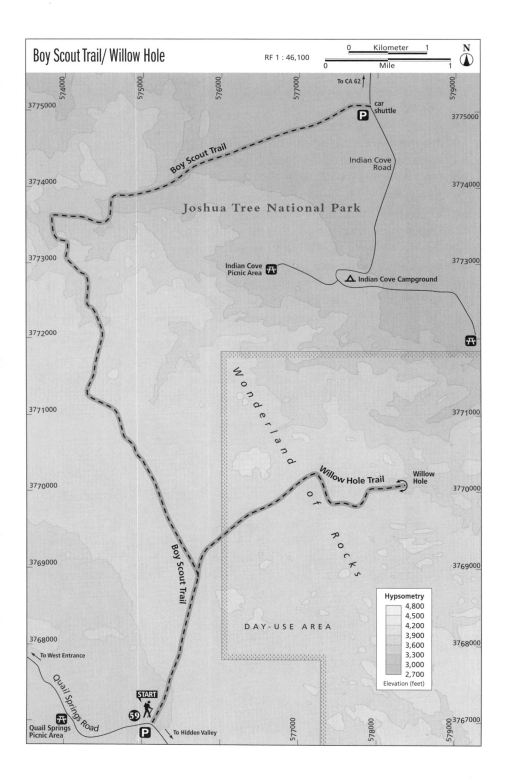

Boy Scout Trail/ Willow Hole

RF 1 : 46,100

0   Kilometer   1

0   Mile   1

N

To CA 62

car shuttle

Indian Cove Road

Boy Scout Trail

Joshua Tree National Park

Indian Cove Picnic Area

Indian Cove Campground

Wonderland of Rocks

Willow Hole Trail

Willow Hole

Boy Scout Trail

DAY-USE AREA

To West Entrance

Quail Springs Road

Quail Springs Picnic Area

START

59

P

To Hidden Valley

Hypsometry

Elevation (feet)
4,800
4,500
4,200
3,900
3,600
3,300
3,000
2,700

574000
575000
576000
577000
579000
577000
578000
579000

3775000
3774000
3773000
3772000
3771000
3770000
3769000
3768000
3767000

Miles and Directions

0.0   Start from the Keys West Backcountry Board.

1.3   Arrive at the Boy Scout Trail/Willow Hole Trail junction. Follow the right-hand trail to Willow Hole.

2.5   The trail enters and follows a wash.

3.3   Arrive at Willow Hole. Retrace your steps back to the junction.

5.3   Reach the junction. Take the Boy Scout Trail to the right.

7.0   This is the high point of the trail at 4,250 feet.

7.6   The trail drops into and follows a wash.

8.0   A cement water trough and constructed rock wall are found in the wash.

8.2   The trail makes a sharp left turn out of the wash.

8.6   The rocky trail climbs to 4,070 feet for a panoramic view.

8.9   The trail drops into the wash and follows it for 1 mile.

10.0   Here the trail crosses over into a side gully, dropping to the main wash.

10.5   The trail leaves the canyon and cuts across open desert.

12.0   The trail ends at the Indian Cove Backcountry Board, where you pick up your car shuttle.

Options: For a three- to five-hour out-and-back hike, hike the 6.6 miles to Willow Hole. When you return to the trail junction at mile 5.3, take the left-hand trail back to the Keys West Backcountry Board. Another option is to skip Willow Hole and hike 8 miles directly to Indian Cove.

60 Quail Wash to West Entrance Wash

This point-to-point trip requires a car shuttle, but it is well worth the inconvenience. Along the way you will see dense stands of Joshua trees, historic cabin ruins, and a mine, and you'll have expansive views of Quail Mountain and several scenic side canyons to explore.

Start: 10 miles southeast of the town of Joshua Tree.
Distance: 8.2 miles one way (with car shuttle).
Approximate hiking time: 6 to 8 hours.
Difficulty: Moderate.
Trail surface: Dirt trail, sandy washes.

Seasons: October through May.
USGS topo maps: Joshua Tree South-CA and Indian Cove-CA (1:24,000).
Trail contact: Joshua Tree National Park (see appendix D).

Finding the trailhead: From California Highway 62 in the town of Joshua Tree, take Park Boulevard south 1 mile to where it becomes Quail Springs Road; continue 4 miles to the West Entrance. Continue 6.1 miles on Park Route 12 to Quail Springs Picnic Area on your right.

　　Car shuttle: 1.2 miles inside of the West Entrance on PR 12 is a pullout on the north side of the road near the wash exit of the trail. The exit point of the hike is 1 mile south of the West Entrance on PR 12.

The Hike

This hike requires skills in backcountry navigation. The trail starts out through an open Joshua tree desert ringed by a distant horizon of jagged peaks dotted with mounds of granite. The clear, sandy trail leads west-northwest and is easy to follow. At 0.6 mile it crosses the wash and continues on the left side, providing much firmer walking than the wash.

　　The trail angles closer to the rocky hillside on the left (south) and intersects the Johnny Lang Canyon trail at mile 2. This is the first major canyon to the south and makes for a strenuous but exciting option (see below). For this hike, continue west on the main trail after passing Johnny Lang Canyon. At mile 3 the trail passes by the second major canyon to the south, which leads up toward the highest point in the park: 5,813-foot Quail Mountain. At 3.2 miles several steel posts mark a fence line across the wash. The trail begins to leave the open desert, dropping into a wide gap through the mountains. At mile 4 the trail dips to the southwest and crosses the Smith Water Canyon Wash at 4.5 miles. Joshua trees are especially thick in this area. If time permits, this is an interesting place to explore, both in lower Smith Water Canyon and south toward the Quail Springs site shown on the topo map.

　　At 5 miles the trail/wash enters a recent burned-over area with fire-blackened Joshua trees dominating the landscape to the south. For the next 1.5 miles, the trail weaves in and out of the wash. For the most part the wash is easier to find and follow

than the trail. At 6.5 miles the trail joins the wash at a National Park Service boundary fence in another burn area. At 6.7 miles the trail reaches a rock-cable boundary fence, which is signed NPS BOUNDARY US. Do not cross the fence onto the adjacent private property. Instead, turn right and follow the fence on a well-defined use trail eastward. Soon the trail disappears in West Entrance Wash. Continue up the wide sandy wash for about a mile. Look for a side wash angling left (northeast) next to a distinctive rock mound on the left. Head up this wash, where you'll come to a rock ledge dropoff within 0.1 mile. Climb up the ledge and continue up the wash another 0.4 mile to PR 12. At this point you've walked a good distance, so let's hope your shuttle will be waiting for you. If not, at least you're only a mile south of the West Entrance.

Miles and Directions

0.0 Start at the Quail Springs Picnic Area.

2.0 Arrive at the junction with the trail heading south up Johnny Lang Canyon. Stay to the right.

3.0 The trail passes the second major valley to the south, which leads toward Quail Mountain (5,813 feet).

4.5 The trail passes the mouth of Smith Water Canyon.

5.0 The trail enters a fire area.

6.7 The trail reaches the north boundary of the park; turn right (west) up West Entrance Wash.

7.7 Leave the West Entrance Wash and head northeast up a side wash.

8.2 Arrive at PR 12, 1 mile south of the West Entrance.

Option: This 6-mile out and back up Johnny Lang Canyon to the Lang Mine adds two to three hours to the Quail Wash hike. It's a strenuous side trip. The Lang Canyon trail intersects the Quail Springs Trail at mile 2. This is the first major canyon to the south. This trail is easy to miss, but it takes off from the main trail at a forty-five-degree angle heading southwest from near the foot of the ridge. The Johnny Lang Canyon trail passes just to the left of a small hill 0.2 mile up. It then crosses a wash at 0.3 mile, angling southwest to the base of the hill. It turns south for another mile to the Lang cabin site, staying on the right side of this wide lower valley all the way to the cabin ruins. If in doubt, follow the main Johnny Lang wash.

The remnants of the cabin, such as they are, are located on a bench about 50 feet to the right of the wash at 3,980 feet. All that remains are part of a rock foundation and piles of rusted cans and metal. A fairly well-defined use trail takes off from the cabin site. From here it is possible to see a large dark-topped hill (Point 4549 on the topo map) about 1 mile south; this is on the route leading up to the mine.

◀ *The open shaft at the Johnny Lang Mine.*

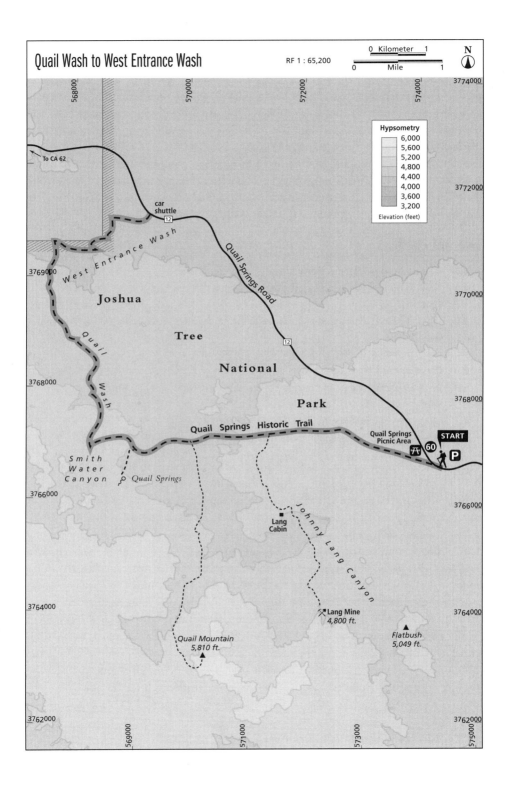

Quail Wash to West Entrance Wash

RF 1 : 65,200

Hypsometry

6,000
5,600
5,200
4,800
4,400
4,000
3,600
3,200

Elevation (feet)

0 Kilometer 1

0 Mile 1

N

568000
570000
572000
574000

3774000

To CA 62

car shuttle

12

West Entrance Wash

Quail Springs Road

12

Joshua

Tree

National

Park

Quail Wash

Quail Springs Historic Trail

Quail Springs Picnic Area

START

P

60

3772000

3769000

3770000

3768000

3768000

Smith Water Canyon

Quail Springs

3766000

3766000

Lang Cabin

Johnny Lang Canyon

3764000

Lang Mine 4,800 ft.

Flatbush 5,049 ft.

Quail Mountain 5,810 ft.

3764000

3762000

3762000

569000
571000
573000
575000

The use trail crosses the wash several times during the next 0.6 mile before coming to a manzanita flat just before a gully on the right. Cross the gully and head to the right up the ridge (south) toward the dark-topped hill (which has a knob and saddle to its left). On the backside of the hill, you'll intersect the rocky remains of an overgrown road that leads south into a gully below the mine. From this point you can see the mine tailings to the south, high on the hillside just below a prominent rock outcropping. Drop into the gully, then ascend the ridge southward, gaining 300 feet in the remaining 0.25 mile to the unsecured mine shaft. At 700 feet above the canyon, the mine entrance and platform is certainly a room with a view. Retrace your route for the 3-mile descent back to Quail Wash.

61 California Riding and Hiking Trail: Covington Flat to Keys View, Quail Mountain

On this trip lies the park's highest peak. It's a point-to-point hike, requiring a car shuttle, along a well-marked trail. The outing to the peak is a strenuous cross-country scramble, rewarded with outstanding views of the region.

Start: 12 miles south of the town of Joshua Tree.
Distance: 15 miles one way.
Approximate hiking time: 7 to 11 hours.
Difficulty: Moderate (R & H Trail); strenuous (Quail Mountain).
Trail surface: Dirt path; short cross-country section to peak.

Seasons: October through May.
USGS topo maps: Joshua Tree South-CA; East Deception Canyon-CA; and Keys View-CA (1:24,000).
Trail contact: Joshua Tree National Park (see appendix D).

Finding the trailhead: From California Highway 62 and Park Boulevard in the town of Joshua Tree, go east on CA 62 for 3.4 miles to La Contenta. Turn right (south) on La Contenta and go 2.9 miles to Covington Flat Road. La Contenta is paved for only a mile; thereafter it is a washboardy narrow dirt road but suitable for passenger vehicles. Turn right at the BACKCOUNTRY TRAILHEAD sign and take a cut-over 1.9 miles to Upper Covington Flat Road. Turn left, again following signs to the Upper Covington Backcountry Board, on Upper Covington Flat Road and go 2 miles southeast to the board and parking area. The trail leaves from behind the board.

If covering the continuous length of the California Riding and Hiking Trail is not your goal, this segment of the trail can also be accessed by continuing on the Lower Covington Flat Road to the dead end at the picnic area. The trail from the picnic area joins this trail after the first mile.

Car shuttle: From CA 62 in Joshua Tree, take Park Boulevard south 1 mile to where it becomes Quail Springs Road, which you take for 4 miles to the West Entrance. Continue 10 miles on Park Route 12 to the intersection with Keys View Road (Park Route 13). Bear right on

Polly Cunningham pauses at the 6-foot cairn on the windswept top of Quail Mountain.

Keys View and drive 1 mile to the Juniper Flats Backcountry Board, near where the California Riding and Hiking Trail crosses Keys View Road.

The Hike

Neither wide nor well-pruned, this section of the California Riding and Hiking Trail is evidently not heavily traveled, although it is frequently signed with arrows and mileposts. This is definitely a long-pants excursion, or your legs will suffer on both the basic trail and the side trip to Quail Mountain.

Evidence of wildlife is considerably more plentiful on the first 5 miles of the trail from Covington Flat—deer, sheep, rabbits, rodents, coyotes—than elsewhere on the trail. Unlike the Riding and Hiking Trail segment out of the Black Rock Campground, this section shows no signs of use by horses. The first 5 miles are also highly enjoyable as you climb up and down over a series of descending ridges. The crest of each ridge provides a "Wow!" reaction as the panoramas of the park open before you. Even without climbing Quail Mountain, this section of the Riding and Hiking Trail provides sweeping vistas of the Little San Bernardino Range to the south,

California Riding and Hiking Trail: Covington Flat to Keys View, Quail Mountain

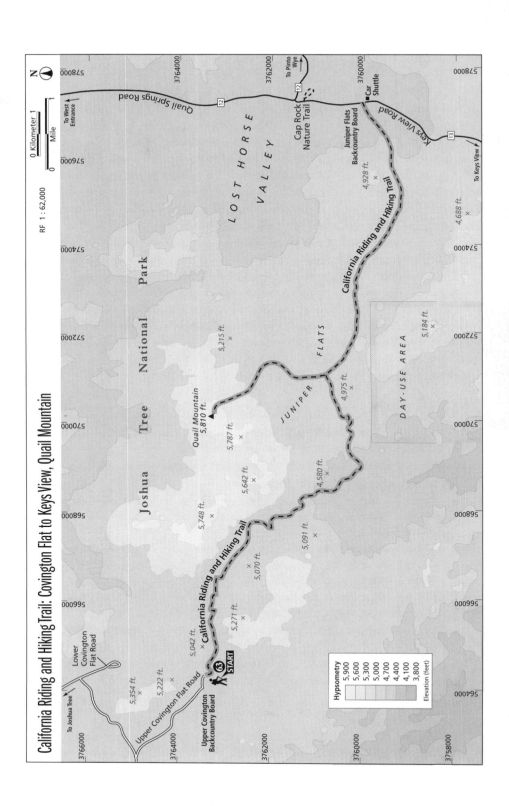

RF 1 : 62,000

N

0 Kilometer 1

0 Mile 1

Hypsometry

5,900
5,600
5,300
5,000
4,700
4,400
4,100
3,800

Elevation (feet)

To Joshua Tree

Lower Covington Flat Road

Upper Covington Flat Road

5,354 ft.

5,222 ft.

Upper Covington Backcountry Board

START 63

California Riding and Hiking Trail

5,042 ft.

5,271 ft.

5,070 ft.

5,091 ft.

5,748 ft.

5,642 ft.

5,787 ft.

Quail Mountain 5,810 ft.

5,215 ft.

JUNIPER FLATS

4,580 ft.

4,975 ft.

DAY-USE AREA

5,184 ft.

Joshua Tree National Park

LOST HORSE VALLEY

Quail Springs Road

To West Entrance

To Pinto Wye

12

12

Cap Rock Nature Trail

Juniper Flats Backcountry Board

4,928 ft.

California Riding and Hiking Trail

Car Shuttle

Keys View Road

13

To Keys View

4,688 ft.

578000
576000
574000
572000
570000
568000
566000
564000

3766000
3764000
3762000
3760000
3758000
3764000
3762000
3760000

the Pinto Range to the east, and the various pinnacles in the central section of the park.

The climb to Quail Mountain is easy to plan from this south approach since the peak is visible from your takeoff point at milepost 23 on the Riding and Hiking Trail and most of the way after that as well. The approach up the wash is challenging, but it is better than trying the southeast ridge. The downfall of piñon limbs that makes the wash/ravine so difficult is the result of a 1978 burn on the mountain.

As you climb to the naked summit, you will be stunned by the dimensions of the cairn. It is a tower of well-placed rocks at least 5 feet high. From a distance, the mountain looks exactly like the bird for which it was named. The views from Quail Mountain are spectacular. The entire park spreads out in every direction. After enjoying the windy view, return via your route to the spur road and the Riding and Hiking Trail. The points you picked on your way up should help you locate the trail.

The last 5 miles down the Riding and Hiking Trail after the peak ascent are not anticlimactic. The overwhelming natural wonders of Joshua Tree are ever-present. The Wonderland of Rocks grows immense as you get farther into Juniper Flats. The White Tank formations of Ryan Mountain also become more massive as you approach Keys View Road. This hike represents the pinnacle of a Joshua Tree experience for both the ascent to the highest peak in the park and the journey through its wild heartland.

Miles and Directions

0.0–1.5 From the parking area, the well-marked trail goes over a ridge and along a hillside piñon-juniper forest. The largest Joshua tree is in 0.1 mile.

1.7 Bear right at the intersection with the spur trail from Covington Picnic Area at milepost 28.

2.0–3.5 The trail goes over a series of ridges.

5.0 Milepost 23, nearly hidden by a large juniper on your right, is the start point for a side trip to Quail Mountain. The road appears to be a flat wash lacking telltale wheel tracks. Turn left.

5.5 The road ends. Head northeast toward Quail Mountain. Look back and select distinctive features in the landscape to help you locate your return route. Cross through the prickly shrubbery toward a fire break that cuts over the northeast ridge.

6.1 You'll see two lower ridges and a wash—turn left and follow the wash toward the mountain. Note your location so you can exit here on your return trip.

6.4 Bear right at the fork in the wash after a rock outcropping of contorted striped strata on the left (west) side. (Cairns and footprints help.)

6.8 The wash becomes narrow, rocky, and littered with downed trees, but stay in the ravine.

7.1 Emerge from the ravine, which has finally petered out; scramble up to the ridge to the right.

7.5 A huge cairn marks the summit. Return the way you came.

10.0 Resume the trip to Keys View Road.

15.0 Arrive at the backcountry board, to the right of the trail.

62 Black Rock Loop Trail: Eureka Peak and Back via California Riding and Hiking Trail

From the backcountry board just south of the subdivisions of Yucca Valley, you can embark on a long hike to the highest summit in this section of the park. The route up is woodsy and primitive. On the loop trail down from the peak, it is not unusual to encounter equestrian traffic—and the horses have the right of way.

Start: 3 miles south of Yucca Valley.
Distance: 10.5-mile loop.
Approximate hiking time: 4 to 6 hours.
Difficulty: Strenuous.
Trail surface: Sandy wash and trail; road.

Seasons: October through May.
USGS topo maps: Yucca Valley South-CA and Joshua Tree South-CA (1:24,000).
Trail contact: Joshua Tree National Park (see appendix D).

Finding the trailhead: From California Highway 62 in Yucca Valley, turn south on Avalon Avenue. Go 0.7 mile to where it becomes Palomar Drive. Continue south on Palomar Drive for 2.3 miles to the left turn onto Joshua Tree Lane. Take Joshua Tree Lane for 1 mile to the dead end at San Marino Avenue, where you turn right. Continue on San Marino for 0.3 mile to its dead end at Black Rock Road. Turn left on Black Rock to the park entrance. The backcountry board, which looks unlike all other backcountry boards in Joshua Tree National Park (this one is simply a bulletin board), is on your left, within only 50 yards of the campground entrance. Park there. The trailhead is immediately east of the board area.

The Hike

As the mileage log below indicates, this is a very well-marked trail, both up Eureka Peak and down the California Riding & Hiking Trail return trip. In spite of that, there is a sense of wilderness excitement, since the hike to the peak gets out of the wash and into mountain canyons and ravines. Even with the intermittent signs, you can feel like an explorer.

The view from the peak is magnificent. The San Bernardinos, with their mantle of snow in winter and early spring, rise in the western distance. The park's ranges stretch away to the south and east. Although there is a road and parking area immediately downhill from the peak, it does not appear to be heavily used due to its distance from CA 62.

The return journey down the R & H track is the most heavily horse-used portion of this trail through the park. Elsewhere there is no trace of horse traffic. Here, trail signposts are almost unnecessary—just follow the hoofprints. Nevertheless, numerous arrow posts mark your way. There are, however, no mile markers as there are on the other sections. While signs on the higher section are nonexistent, the lower end of the trail sports painted, stenciled, and planted signposts verifying your location.

Descending the California R & H Trail from Eureka Peak.

For a day trip close to populated Yucca Valley, this is the ideal outing. The exertion of the hike to the peak contrasts nicely with the relaxed stroll back down the wash via the Riding and Hiking Trail. The focus on wild mountains on the way up also contrasts with the views of the subdivisions of Yucca Valley on the way down.

Note: The Black Rock Canyon area has numerous hiking trails. A diagrammatic map is posted at the trailhead, or you can get one at the ranger station. These trails are signed. During the hike you will encounter numerous signposts. Most of these were put into place by volunteer equestrians. These are being replaced with etched metal signs by the park trail crew.

Miles and Directions

Note: The park plans to replace many of these signs.

0.0   From the trailhead, go east toward a nearby wash. The first 2-mile section of the Eureka Peak Trail coincides with the California Riding and Hiking Trail (Calif. R & H).

1.5   Ignore the junction with "FT." Stay left on the R & H over the saddle to the upper valley.

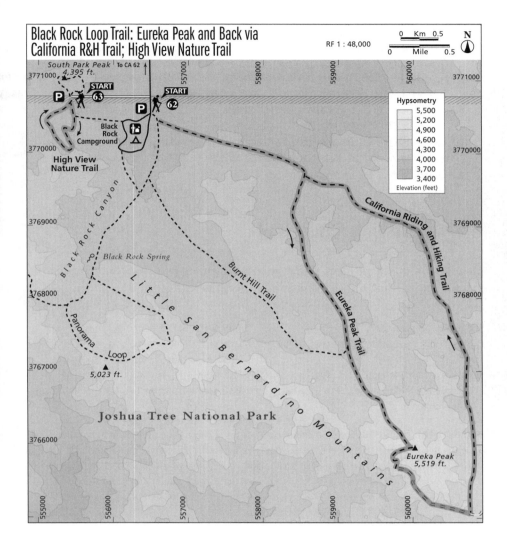

Black Rock Loop Trail: Eureka Peak and Back via California R&H Trail; High View Nature Trail

RF 1 : 48,000

0   Km   0.5

0   Mile   0.5

N

South Park Peak   To CA 62
4,395 ft.

START
P 63

START
P 62

Black Rock Campground

High View Nature Trail

Hypsometry
5,500
5,200
4,900
4,600
4,300
4,000
3,700
3,400
Elevation (feet)

California Riding and Hiking Trail

Black Rock Canyon

Black Rock Spring

Burnt Hill Trail

Eureka Peak Trail

Little San Bernardino Mountains

Panorama Loop

5,023 ft.

Joshua Tree National Park

Eureka Peak
5,519 ft.

2.0   A junction clearly signposted EP marks the Eureka Peak Trail. Turn up the wash.

2.3   Disregard the junction with "SL." Continue in the well-traveled main wash as it climbs and narrows.

3.8   A comforting EP arrow is posted in the wash. Continue straight up the wash.

4.0   At the BF/EP signpost, follow the EP arrow to the right.

4.3   The EP/BH marker confirms you're on the correct trail as it becomes a twisting footpath up the ravine to the peak.

4.9   At the mountain ridge, turn left to the summit (0.1 mile), right to the parking area and Covington Road, which you'll take down to meet the Calif. R & H Trail for the hike back to Black Rock Campground.

5.2   At the parking area, turn left and take the road downhill to the R & H Trail.

5.7   Find the R & H Trail on your left in a valley before Covington Road begins climbing. A large brown and white sign is 30 yards off the road; what you will probably notice first is the house-shaped backcountry-regulations sign, which is only 10 yards off the road under a huge Joshua tree. Head north down the sloping wash.

8.5   Back at the original fork where you met the Eureka Peak Trail, continue on the R & H Trail back to the campground.

10.3   Watch for the left turn where the trail returns to the backcountry board and the wash (and the horse traffic); continue north. You can see the campground from here.

10.5   Arrive back at the backcountry board.

63   High View Nature Trail

Just west of the Black Rock Campground, this outing provides a lofty view of surrounding peaks and the sprawl nearby in Yucca Valley.

See map on page 197.
Start: 5 miles southeast of the town of Yucca Valley.
Distance: 1.3-mile loop.
Approximate hiking time: 0.5 to 2 hours.
Difficulty: Moderate.

Trail surface: Dirt path.
Seasons: October through May.
USGS topo map: Yucca Valley South-CA (1:24,000).
Trail contact: Joshua Tree National Park (see appendix D).

Finding the trailhead: From California Highway 62 in Yucca Valley, turn south on Avalon Avenue and drive 0.7 mile to where it becomes Palomar Drive. Continue on Palomar 2.3 miles to the left turn on Joshua Tree Lane. Take Joshua Tree Lane 1 mile to the T intersection at San Marino Avenue. Turn right and go 0.3 mile to Black Rock Road. Turn left on Black Rock and drive south 0.5 mile to the park entrance. Immediately before the entrance, turn right (west) onto a dirt road and go west 0.8 mile to the parking area.

The Hike

This nature trail travels to the top of a hill, providing a view over the Yucca Valley and the eastern end of the park. There is a register at the summit, as well as a bench. The trail follows a relatively gentle route as it climbs 320 feet. Numbered sites line the trail; the brochures are available at the Black Rock Ranger Station in the adjacent campground.

If you're staying at the campground, a hilly but far more scenic route exists that connects the campground with the nature trail. It leaves from the top of the loop above the ranger station and enters the nature trail loop in its first section. Although it is clearly marked, this alternate route from the campground has an aura of wilderness. We spotted two coyotes hunting for rabbits in the middle of the afternoon on our loop hike from the campground.

Option: Heading north out of the parking area is a 0.8-mile loop trail to the top of South Park Peak. This gentle ascent lies outside of Joshua Tree National Park. It is part of the Yucca Valley Parks District.

Mojave National Preserve

B ig and empty" aptly describes Mojave National Preserve, which, at 1.6 million acres, makes up 10 percent of the entire Mojave Desert region in its eastern end. The dry landscape we see now is the product of a wetter past, with ancient sedimentary rocks from what was once an ocean floor preserved by the stark aridity of today's climate. The preserve is a varied mix of jagged peaks, colorful serpentine canyons, booming sand dunes, volcanic cinder cones, dry lake beds, historic mines, rock art by Paleo-Indians, and vast expanses framed by the largest concentration of Joshua trees in the world.

In 1976 Congress established the California Desert Conservation Area, directing the Bureau of Land Management (BLM) to come up with a management plan for the half of this twenty-five-million-acre region that is in the public domain. As a result, BLM set up the 1.5-million-acre East Mojave National Scenic Area in 1980. Unfortunately, the East Mojave continued to be impacted by indiscriminate off-road vehicle use, mining, overgrazing, and wanton vandalism. Greater protection was called for, but the wheels of politics sometimes turn slowly. In 1986 U.S. senator Alan Cranston of California first introduced the California Desert Protection Act, but passage took the same amount of time required for the 1964 Wilderness Act—eight long years! The act transferred the East Mojave from the BLM to the National Park Service and upgraded the designation from administrative "scenic area" to statutory "preserve."

"Preserve" rather than park status for Mojave means the continuation of preexisting hunting in accordance with state regulations. Mojave National Preserve is the only National Park Service unit in the California desert where hunting is permitted. As an added safety precaution, hikers should wear hunter's orange or other bright colors when hiking in the preserve during the fall hunting season. Other "grandfathered" uses include mining preexisting claims and cattle grazing. The OX Cattle Company (a major grazing permittee) is a colorful remnant of the Old West, with origins traceable to 1888. The historic OX Ranch headquarters in the Lanfair Valley has been sold to the National Park Service. Indeed, livestock grazing seems marginal at best in this sparsely vegetated land. Of the more than a dozen original grazing allotments in the preserve, all but one have been retired.

Geologic Signatures on the Landscape

When visiting the preserve, one can look in any direction and be reminded of Mojave's geologic past—a land molded by earthquakes, fault lines, sinking valleys, and rising mountains formed by the tearing apart of the earth's crust. Domes, cinder cones, and lava beds tell the tale of volcanic eruptions of monumental proportions. The Mojave Desert was uplifted around 140 million years ago by pressure from plates of the earth's crust grinding against one another. Seventy million years of erosion reduced an astounding 20,000 to 25,000 feet of sedimentary rock to gently sloping terrain. The mountain ranges of Mojave were uplifted along rows of faults about thirty million years ago as continental plates collided. During a wetter time, about eighteen million years ago, Mojave resembled African savannahs with large herds of grazing animals.

As recently as 15,000 years ago, the Mojave River flowed aboveground into the now-gone Lake Manly in Death Valley. After the last ice age, roughly 10,000 years ago, the climate became much drier. This is partly because the Mojave Desert sits in the rain shadow of the lofty Sierra Nevada and other ranges to the south and west. Cinder cone activity dates back 7.6 million years to 8,000 years ago, but lava flows took place as recently as 800 to 1,000 years ago just west of Cima Dome—a huge 1,500-foot-high symmetrical mound of ancient granite exposed by erosion.

Life in the Desert

Elevations in the preserve range from around 800 feet to the nearly 8,000-foot summit of Clark Mountain, supporting a corresponding diversity of plants and animals. The most common shrub at lower elevations, the creosote bush is a perfectly adapted desert survivor with narrow, resinous leaves that prevent water loss. As the older stems in the plant's center die, a cloned ring of new stems is formed that can live for hundreds of years. Creosote bushes are able to completely tap surrounding soil moisture, which effectively keeps away competing vegetation. Above 3,000 feet the dark gray bark of the intricately branched blackbrush gives the land a dark, somber look. Joshua trees are prevalent here on well-drained gravel plains. These members of the yucca family are usually the largest plants in their landscape. Their branches seem to lift upward like the arms of the biblical prophet Joshua—hence the name given by early Mormon settlers. Spanish bayonet and the larger Mojave yucca are also common in this mid-elevational range. Piñon-juniper woodlands occur at still higher elevations, in such exposed places as the rocky slopes of the rugged New York and Providence Mountains.

◄ *A climber pauses for a look at the view from Table Mountain.*

The old OX Ranch was recently acquired by the National Park Service.

Mojave National Preserve is home to a seldom-seen but rich array of fauna—mammals, birds, insects, and reptiles, all of which are adapted to lack of water and intense heat. Coyotes are abundant, although you will not see and hear as many in the ranching country of East Mojave as you would in Death Valley or Joshua Tree. The abundance of rodents and rabbits can be determined as easily by looking up as down: Raptors are commonly seen riding the air currents, seeking their prey. Several small bands of desert bighorn sheep keep a sharp eye out for the predatory mountain lion in secluded mountains and canyons. One of the more distinguished denizens is the threatened desert tortoise. Protection of tortoise habitat was one of the most compelling arguments for passage of the California Desert Protection Act, so much so that someone placed a tortoise on President Clinton's desk when he signed the bill into law on October 31, 1994.

Human History

Paleo-Indians likely lived and hunted in the Mojave region around the end of the last ice age, 10,000 to 14,000 years ago. As the climate became drier, these people made greater use of seeds, nuts, and roots for food. The more recent native peoples of the Mojave included the Chemehuevi, who were the southernmost band of Piutes. The harshness of the land kept this population of hunter-gatherers small. The petroglyphs we see today throughout Mojave are largely the product of more ancient peoples who predated the Chemehuevi. A good example of this artistry is found near Piute Creek along the Mojave Trail. Archaeologists believe that some of the rock art comprises tribal clan markings of territory or trails.

The Mojave Trail was a route for both early Native American trading and European travel into the region. In 1776 a Spanish priest named Francisco Garces became the first European to visit what is now the Mojave National Preserve. Following the Mojave Trail, Garces and his tribal guides traveled past Piute Creek, the New York and Providence Mountains, and Kelso Dunes. The first American to traverse the Mojave was the renowned trapper Jeddediah Smith. Smith made the difficult journey in 1826 and then again a year later in a much shorter time by traveling at night to escape the scorching 120-degree summer heat. The route was again followed in 1857 by Edward Beale, who laid out a wagon road along the Mojave Trail. Beale achieved notoriety by using camels as pack stock. After the road was completed, the camels were turned loose in the desert and eventually died off. During the 1860s primitive army outposts were built along the road about a day's travel apart. These outposts, such as the one at Piute Creek, were abandoned in 1868 when the overland mail route was rerouted away from the Mojave Road.

Miners swarmed into the region in the 1870s, leaving countless prospect adits, tunnels, and shafts, but the mines didn't boom until the railroad arrived in 1883. Ten years later a 30-mile short-line railroad from Goffs north to the New York Mountains replaced the Mojave Road as a freight route. The railroad served both mining and a developing cattle industry, which somehow survives to this day. Homesteaders came into the East Mojave around 1910 during a series of wet years, but most had left by 1925 after the normal dry weather resumed.

Park Regulations and Facilities

The Mojave National Preserve is one of the newest, largest, least developed, and least regulated of all of the units in the National Park System. Sensitive and respectful visitor use will go a long way toward keeping regulations to a minimum, which is a goal of the National Park Service in the preserve. Mojave National Preserve is one of the few units in the National Park System without an entrance fee. However, the National Park Service is likely to institute a fee in 2008. Check with a Mojave National Preserve office or the Web site (www.nps.gov/moja) for details.

Nearly half of the preserve, some 700,000 acres, is designated wilderness in twenty-two separate units. Some of the boundaries near roads and washes have been posted. Please respect the wilderness by doing everything possible to lessen the impact of your visit. The desert is at once both rugged and fragile. No off-road

vehicular travel is allowed, so please keep vehicles on designated routes. As with the other parks, vehicles must be street legal. Heavy rains during the winter and spring of 2005 adversely impacted most preserve roads. Thus, four-wheel drive is recommended for all unmaintained dirt roads, which provide the only vehicular access for many of the hikes.

At this time the National Park Service is continuing the long tradition of open-desert camping in the preserve. Car camping is allowed at backcountry sites with existing fire rings next to secondary roads. If you're camping beyond the road, backcountry permits are not required. The only requirements are to camp at least 0.25 mile from any water source to avoid disturbing wildlife, and to set up camp off the trail a minimum of 0.5 mile from any road or developed area. Please follow zero-impact practices and carry out all trash.

There are only seven developed trails in the preserve. A 2-mile (one-way) trail to Teutonia Peak on Cima Dome takes off from a signed trailhead on the Cima Road south of Interstate 15. An 8-mile (one-way) trail between Hole-in-the-Wall and Mid Hills Campgrounds can be reached from either campground. The Lake Tuendae Nature Trail is a 0.25-mile round-trip from the Zzyzx parking area on the west end of the preserve. The Rings Trail is a short but challenging 30-minute out-and-back descent into Banshee Canyon using metal rings bolted into the rock. A short nature trail with signs identifying desert plants connects the Hole-in-the-Wall Campground to the Hole-in-the-Wall Information Center. Quail Basin and Kelso Dunes are also developed trails.

There are two developed fee campgrounds in the preserve and one in the state recreation area. The Hole-in-the-Wall (HITW) Campground (thirty-five sites) and adjacent Information Center are 18 miles north of Interstate 40 on Black Canyon Road. The Mid Hills Campground (twenty-six sites) is 25 miles north of I–40, 2 miles off Black Canyon Road. The Providence Mountains Campground (six sites) is 17 miles northwest of I–40 at the end of Essex Road. All three are open year-round on a first-come, first-served basis. Fire pits are provided, but if you want a fire, bring wood with you; collecting or cutting wood in the desert is not allowed. Water, vault-toilets, trash containers, and picnic tables are available year-round at the two park campgrounds. The HITW Campground also has a dump station. The Black Canyon Equestrian and Group Campground is located across the road from the HITW Information Center and Campground. Reservations are accepted for group camps only and are required; call HITW at (760) 928–2572. The HITW Information Center offers seasonal visitor programs and has public telephones. Educational materials are available at HITW and the Kelso Depot Information Center. There are no services in the preserve—no stores, gas, or motels—so bring everything you need. As always when traveling in the desert, bring plenty of water.

◀ *North of mile 1 on the Hole-in-the-Wall to Mid Hills hike.*

Mojave National Preserve

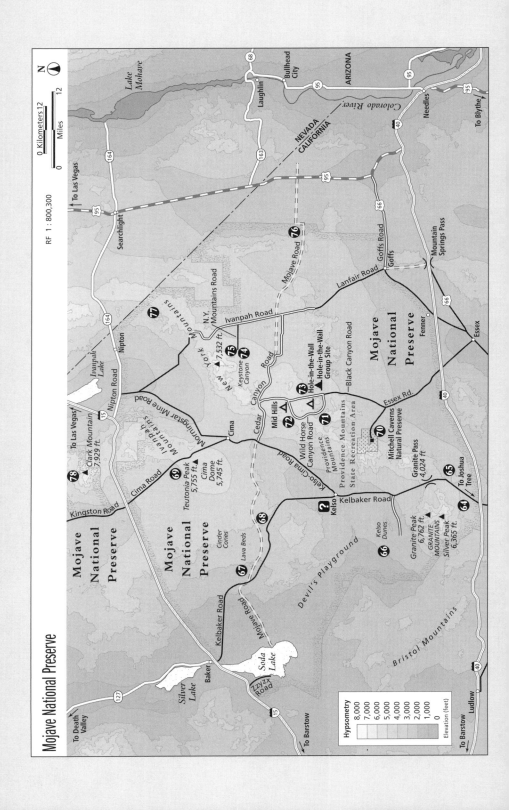

RF 1 : 800,300

0 Kilometers 12
0 Miles 12

N

The park service has recently refurbished the historic Kelso Depot in the heart of the preserve to its original 1924 condition. It is now a beautiful visitor information and education center and a major attraction in its own right. This facility, known as the Kelso Depot Information Center, opened officially in December 2005 and is an excellent starting point for exploring Mojave National Preserve.

It may be tempting to feed wildlife but remember that "a fed animal is a dead animal." Wild creatures must remain wild if they are to survive. All elements of the environment—plants, cultural and historical artifacts, rocks—are protected so that they can be enjoyed by others. Pets must be confined or kept on a short leash but may join you anywhere in the preserve. Better yet, leave them at home so that both they and you can have a better time. Although legal hunting is allowed in season, target shooting is not.

The exterior boundaries of the preserve contain a large amount of private inholdings. It is important to obey NO TRESPASSING signs, close gates, and, in general, respect private property.

Providence Mountains State Recreation Area

In 1956 the State of California acquired the Mitchell Caverns from the Mitchell family. Subsequent land transfers from the BLM have increased the park to its present 5,900 acres along the rugged eastern slopes of the Providence Mountains, encompassed within the south-central portion of the preserve. To safeguard wildlife, only day use is allowed outside the campground. The Mitchell Caverns are the only limestone caves in the California park system and can only be visited with a guided ranger tour. The 1.5-mile hike/tour takes one-and-a-half to two hours and is offered one to three times a day depending on season and day of the week. There is one short nature trail near the visitor center/campground, plus a longer trail to Crystal Spring that leads to the edge of the backcountry, high in the Providence Mountains (see Hike 70).

How and When to Get There

The "lonesome triangle" of the Mojave National Preserve is bounded on the north by Interstate 15 and on the south by I–40. These two interstate highways join in Barstow, about 50 miles west of the preserve. The paved Kelbaker Road crosses the preserve from Baker south to I–40, halfway between Barstow and Needles. The paved Kelso-Cima Road takes off from Kelso Depot and heads north to I–15. The National Park Service has restored the historic Kelso Depot to mint condition. This grand old building and its grounds are a must-see attraction between hikes. Several shorter paved roads and improved dirt roads access major mountain ranges and points of interest. The closest major commercial airport is 50 miles northeast of the preserve at Las Vegas. There are no motels or service stations in the preserve and very few close by. Don't drive into the preserve without plenty of gas, food, area maps, and water. Services are available in surrounding communities, such as Needles on the east, Barstow on the west, and Baker to the north on I–15. Cell phone service is unreliable.

Rifle deer season is mid–October to early November, with quail season continuing until the end of January.

From the standpoint of hiking comfort, October through May is generally the best season to visit the preserve. Summer daytime temperatures typically exceed one hundred degrees. Depending on winter and early-spring rains, wildflowers burst forth in a splash of color from March through May.

We continue to recommend USGS maps as the best and most detailed maps available for the Mojave area, however, they are not sold at the Mojave National Preserve Visitor Centers. Order USGS maps by calling (888) ASK–USGS or online at www.usgs.gov/pubprod/.

Mojave National Preserve Hikes at a Glance

Hike (Number)	Distance	Difficulty*	Features	Page
Caruthers Canyon (74)	3.0 miles	M	canyon, mine site	242
Castle Peaks (77)	6.6 miles	M	spires, vista	253
Clark Mountain/				
North Canyon (78)	4.4 miles	M	mountain canyon	256
Clark Mountain summit	10.0 miles	S	vista, peak	259
Crystal Spring Overlook (70)	2.2 miles	M	spring, vista	228
Eagle Rocks (72)	2.0 miles	E/M	boulders, vista	236
Fort Piute/Piute Gorge (76)	7.0 miles	M/S	historic site, archaeology, gorge	249
Hole-in-the-Wall to Mid Hills (71)	8.4 miles	M/S	vistas	231
Kelso Dunes (66)	3.0 miles	M/S	dunes, vista	216
Keystone Canyon (75)	3.8 miles	M	canyon, flora	245
Lava Tube (68)	1.5 miles	E	cave, cinder cones	222
North Lava Bed Wash (67)	2 miles	E	geology, archaeology	219
Quail Spring Basin (65)	5.9 miles	M	boulders, vistas	214
Silver Peak (64)	9.6 miles	S	vista, peak	211
Table Top Mountain Loop (73)	7.0 miles	S	vista, peak	238
Teutonia Peak/Cima Dome (69)	4.0 miles	M	vista	225

*E=easy, M=moderate, S=strenuous

64 Silver Peak

Silver Peak provides a spectacular view of south-central Mojave. The vista from the 6,365-foot mountaintop in the Granite Mountains is a panorama of the desert landscape. In addition to being part of Mojave National Preserve, the Granite Mountains also have special recognition as a nature preserve. Tread lightly.

Start: About 45 miles southeast of Baker.
Distance: 9.6 miles out and back.
Approximate hiking time: 6 to 8 hours.
Difficulty: Strenuous.
Trail surface: Dirt two-track; use trail to summit.

Seasons: October through June.
USGS topo map: Bighorn Basin-CA (1:24,000).
Trail contact: Kelso Depot Information Center (see appendix D).

Finding the trailhead: From Interstate 40, 77.5 miles east of Barstow and 64 miles west of Needles, take the Kelbaker Road exit north into the preserve. At 10.1 miles north of the freeway exit, take the unmarked dirt road on the left (west) of Kelbaker. There is another dirt road almost opposite this one going east on the other side of Kelbaker. Four-wheel drive is recommended for this dirt road that leads west 1.8 miles to a small plateau, where a wilderness boundary post marks the end of motorized use. Park there. This spot is also an excellent car campsite.

The Hike

From the parking area, you can see the highest point on the western horizon, Silver Peak, your destination. The view from that point is magnificent, but the journey to get there is no less spectacular. Please keep in mind that some of the land here is owned by the Granite Mountains Research Center, which is conducting long-term research. Do not disturb any study plots or remove flagging in the area. The trail is deteriorating and provides challenging but enjoyable hiking. Turnout promontories provide respite from the steep ascent, plus panoramic views. There may be evidence of wild burros in the valley.

The trail ends at 4.6 miles, at an elevation of 6,075 feet. Even if you do not go on to the summit, there's a great view from here. To reach the summit of Silver Peak, follow the trail as it winds around the mountain and climbs 300 feet in its final 0.2-mile climb—it is quite strenuous. Your efforts are rewarded when you reach the rocky summit, especially if it is a clear day.

The change in altitude on this hike results in a wide variety of desert plants, from the creosote-sage scrub at the parking area and throughout the lower valley to increasing cholla and eventually to piñon-juniper woodlands. Any hiker will also certainly notice the desert's ability to erase the evidence of past uses; the trail upon which you travel is a prime example. The remnants of cattle ranching are scattered around and are deteriorating rapidly. This is a wilderness area that has earned that label.

The journey back the way you came is excellent for its scenery, too, looking out

A hiker enjoys the view eastward from the slopes of Silver Peak.

at the southern extension of the Providence Mountain range. In the valley below you will see the entire trail as it goes nearly straight east to the parking area. Once you reach the alluvial fan and then the canyon floor, the trail surface becomes very gentle. We completed this leg of the hike in the dark (with the help of a half-moon), and, except for the catclaw, it was easy going.

Miles and Directions

0.0 Take any of the three dirt two-tracks (all banned to vehicles) off the plateau; they converge in the wash below. Head west toward the Granite Mountains up Cottonwood Wash.

0.2 Pass through 12-foot gate posts and come to a fork. Take the fainter (right) trail.

3.0 The trail enters the canyon, framed by huge boulders. Plow through the Mormon tea as you continue to follow the trail.

3.2 Continue to hike straight up the slight shelf, looking at the trail 50 yards ahead/above.

4.6 At trail's end, the use trail to Silver Peak is marked by cairns.

4.8 Follow the trail as it winds around the mountain in its final 0.2-mile climb to the summit.

9.6 Make your descent, then retrace your route back to the trailhead.

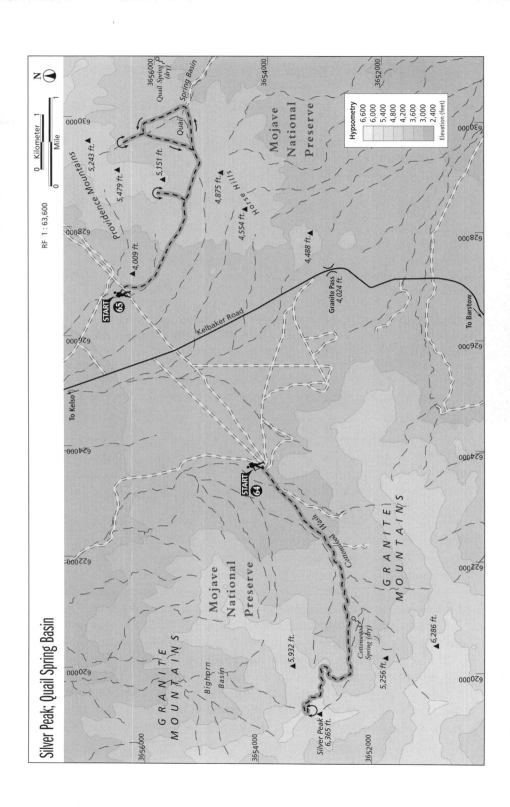

Silver Peak; Quail Spring Basin

RF 1 : 63,600

N

0   Kilometer   1

0   Mile   1

Hypsometry

6,600
6,000
5,400
4,800
4,200
3,600
3,000
2,400

Elevation (feet)

Providence Mountains

5,243 ft. ▲

5,479 ft. ▲

5,151 ft. ▲

4,875 ft. ▲

4,554 ft. ▲

Horse Hills

4,488 ft. ▲

Quail Spring (dry)

Spring Basin

Quail

Mojave
National
Preserve

4,009 ft. ▲

START
G5

Kelbaker Road

To Kelso

Granite Pass
4,024 ft.

To Barstow

START
G4

Cottonwood Wash

GRANITE
MOUNTAINS

6,286 ft. ▲

Cottonwood
Spring (dry)

5,256 ft. ▲

Silver Peak ▲
6,365 ft.

5,932 ft. ▲

Bighorn
Basin

GRANITE
MOUNTAINS

Mojave
National
Preserve

3656000

3654000

3652000

620000

622000

624000

626000

628000

630000

3656000

3654000

3652000

65 Quail Spring Basin

This basin hike is an easy lollipop loop with two side trips around granite formations with opportunities for climbing boulders and peaks. Immense monzogranite boulder mounds dot the route. You'll enjoy the views of the Granite Mountains and the Kelso Dunes.

See map on page 213.
Start: About 45 miles southeast of Baker.
Distance: 5.9-mile lollipop (side trips of 0.5 mile and 0.6 mile; additional distance for investigating the granite mounds).
Approximate hiking time: 3 to 4 hours.
Difficulty: Moderate.

Trail surface: Dirt path.
Seasons: October through May.
USGS topo map: Van Winkle Spring-CA (1:24,000).
Trail contact: Kelso Depot Information Center (see appendix D).

Finding the trailhead: From Interstate 40, 77.5 miles east of Barstow and 64 miles west of Needles, take the Kelbaker Road exit north into the preserve. About 10 miles from the freeway exit, there is a dirt road on your right (east). There is another dirt road almost immediately across Kelbaker heading west at this spot. Four-wheel drive is recommended for this dirt road, which winds to the east 0.9 mile to the wilderness boundary post on the right. This marks the end of vehicular use. The parking area has been improved and the trailhead is signed.

The Hike

This hike in the south end of the Providence Mountains takes you on a gentle slope up from the valley floor, enabling you to see the panorama of this central Mojave region without climbing a mountain. The view of the Kelso Dunes, the Granite Range, and the Providence Mountains makes the first 2 miles of the hike (and the last 2) most spectacular. Closer at hand, the first section of the hike travels through brittlebush and creosote bushes, with mounds of monzogranite piled in fantastic shapes as a backdrop to the east. These are soaring boulders in a cathedral-like setting, and vertical columnar granite reaches hundreds of feet over you. In addition to their size, the boulders have been eroded into imaginative shapes, producing holes and caverns as well as cartoon representations of mice, skulls, and faces.

The peaks of these granite mountains look impressive as you hike up the rise from the parking area, but the loftiest one is in the back row and can be viewed (and climbed, if you wish) from the eastern valley. Plenty of other bouldering activity exists for those who are not enticed by the peak. These large dollops of granite ice cream have a superb gritty yet firm surface for scrambling.

From the trailhead, the trail rises gently on the alluvial fan. A fork at 1.5 miles provides an opportunity to explore granite boulders by turning left on a short dead end. Return to the main trail and continue over the high point on the ridge (4,350 feet) and drop to the fork at mile 2, where the return loop comes back on the left. Continue east into Quail Spring Basin. At mile 2.5 a basalt outcropping on your left marks the wash/trail where you turn and begin to climb northwest toward the notch in the Providence Range. As you continue to the junction at mile 3.4, the lofty granite spires become more awesome. At the junction, a side trip to the right takes you up a rocky gorge. For the very ambitious hiker, this would be the route to the loftiest peak (5,479 feet) above the basin. Your return to the trailhead follows the trail to the left back to the major intersection at mile 2. Magnificent vistas and fascinating rock formations are numerous throughout your trek with or without side trips.

Miles and Directions

0.0 Climb the gentle alluvial fan from the trailhead.

1.5 At the fork explore to the left, then follow the right-hand trail.

1.9 Cross the low pass over the ridge.

2.0 At the fork the left trail is the return loop. Take the right trail.

2.5 At the basalt outcropping, go left up the wash/trail.

3.4 At the high point of the loop hike, turn right for access to the peak, left to meet the main trail.

3.9 Intersect the main trail and turn right.

5.9 Complete the loop hike back at the trailhead.

66 Kelso Dunes

This trailless romp through a sand dunes ecosystem to a dune summit is a unique experience for your visit to Mojave. The golden sand dunes contrast dramatically with the surrounding rocky mountains and desert.

Start: About 40 miles southeast of Baker.
Distance: 3 miles out and back.
Approximate hiking time: 2 hours.
Difficulty: Moderate; strenuous to the top of the dunes.

Trail surface: Sand. No trail. Line-of-sight cross-country sand dune route.
Seasons: October through April.
USGS topo map: Kelso-CA (1:24,000).
Trail contact: Kelso Depot Information Center (see appendix D).

Finding the trailhead: From Interstate 40, 77.5 miles east of Barstow and 64 miles west of Needles, take Kelbaker Road north 15.3 miles to signed Kelso Dunes Road on your left. Drive west 3 miles on the improved dirt road to the second parking area where there is a vault toilet and exhibits on desert ecology and wildlife. The trail to the dunes is directly behind these.

The Hike

The Kelso Dunes were created by 10,000 to 20,000 years of unrelenting winds, sending the sand of the Mojave River delta into these ever-changing formations. This landform (created by wind) is actively moving, but only back and forth due to the contrary wind pattern. At times these dunes "sing" or "boom," something that only 10 percent of the world's dunes can do.

The mountain ranges nearby represent violent volcanic activity. The dunes contrast sharply with the surrounding topography by their softly rounded shapes and their rosy glow. The fine sand consists of rose quartz, feldspar, and magnetite. The quartz gives it the rosy color. The magnetite produces a black-stripe effect on the windswept ridges of the dunes.

Not an arid wasteland, the dunes are home to more than one hundred species of plants and many animals. The tracks of the latter—kangaroo rats, sidewinders, kit foxes, and scorpions, among others—are visible along your hike. The dunes are also home to the Kelso Jerusalem cricket, which exists nowhere else.

Follow the hiker-established foot trail as best as possible as you go northwest to the most westerly dune. The hike to the base of this hill is moderate, rising only 250 feet in 1 mile. For an ascent of the dune—a strenuous 0.5-mile climb—hike to the saddle east of the tall dune, and then hike westerly up the ridge to its apex (3,000 feet). From this lofty spot, you can enjoy spectacular views of the Devil's Playground

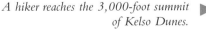

A hiker reaches the 3,000-foot summit of Kelso Dunes.

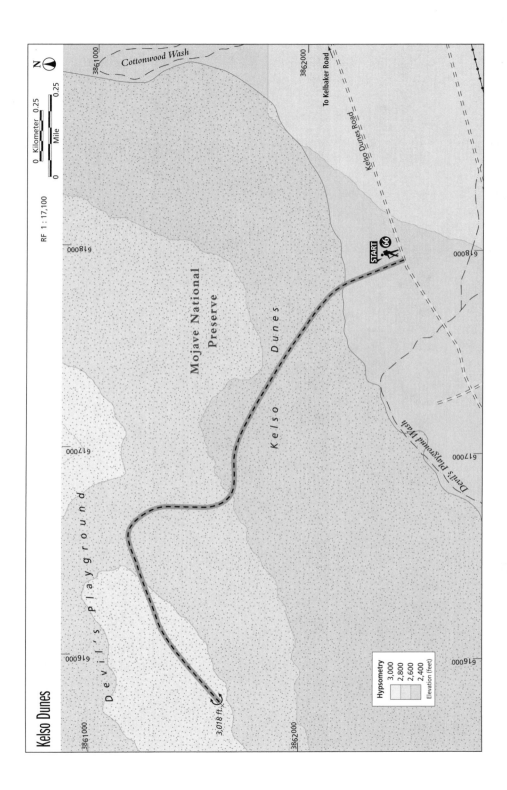

Kelso Dunes

RF 1 : 17,100

Cottonwood Wash

Mojave National Preserve

Devil's Playground

Kelso   Dunes

3,018 ft.

START 66

To Kelbaker Road

Kelso Dunes Road

Devil's Playground Wash

Hypsometry
3,000
2,800
2,600
2,400
Elevation (feet)

0   Kilometer   0.25
0   Mile   0.25

N

to the north and the Providence Range to the east. The dimensions of the Kelso Dunes are impressive and are best seen in all their vastness from this high spot.

Hiking back, try to retrace your steps in order to minimize damage to the fragile dune environment.

67 North Lava Bed Wash

This outing in the lava beds gets you up close to these interesting igneous rock formations. In addition to geology, this hike provides a glimpse of both the history and prehistory of the region in that the profile of the lava beds abuts a narrow turn of the historic Mojave Road.

Start: About 14 miles southeast of Baker.
Distance: About a 2-mile lollipop or out and back.
Approximate hiking time: 1 to 2 hours.
Difficulty: Easy.
Trail surface: Rocky dirt path, clear wash, lava rock, primitive burro trail; cross-country segment for the loop.

Seasons: October through April.
USGS topo map: Indian Spring-CA (1:24,000).
Trail contact: Kelso Depot Information Center (see appendix D).

Finding the trailhead: From Baker on Interstate 15, drive south on Kelbaker Road for 14.1 miles to the first major wash on the left (east), which is the trailhead. This point is also 22.4 miles northwest of Kelso on Kelbaker Road and 0.4 mile north of the only gap in these lava hills. The trailhead is unsigned, but there is a large place to park just off the east side of the highway, adjacent to a prominent outcropping of lava rock.

The Hike

Start by climbing up toward the large outcrop of lava above and to the right of the trailhead. About 30 feet up and just below the lava wall, you'll pick up a faint trail, partly overgrown, that parallels the cliff face for about 0.5 mile. The slow but usable trail provides a good introduction to volcanic geology along this northern edge of the vast lava-bed region of the northwestern Mojave National Preserve. Especially interesting is the cutaway lava cliff face, which exposes the profile of the rock along with a colorful display of red, green, and gray lichens on the lava formations. The historic Mojave Road makes a sharp turn at this point. The Mojave Road was first used by Native Americans and later developed by the military to encourage settlement in the region.

There is a surprising array of desert plants in this austere lunarscape. You'll see barrel cacti, desert holly, bursage, yucca, creosote, chicory, beavertail, and various

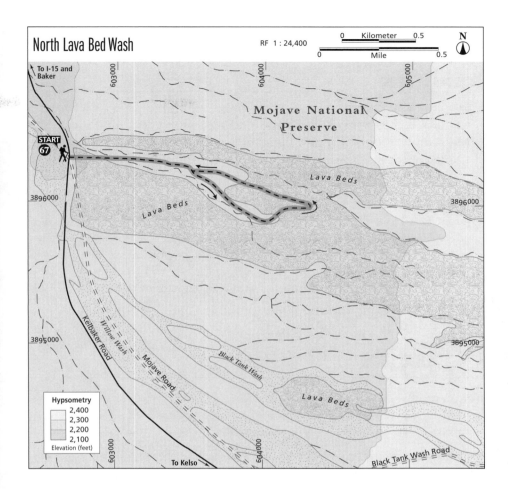

North Lava Bed Wash

RF 1 : 24,400

Mojave National Preserve

Lava Beds

Lava Beds

Lava Beds

START 67

To I-15 and Baker

3896000

3896000

3895000

3895000

Kelbaker Road

Willow Wash

Mojave Road

Black Tank Wash

Black Tank Wash Road

To Kelso

Hypsometry
2,400
2,300
2,200
2,100
Elevation (feet)

cholla cacti to name only a few. You may also see chuckwalla, rattlesnakes, horned lizards, kangaroo rats, black-throated sparrows, and desert tortoise.

At 0.5 mile the cliff trail ends at a jumbled lava talus slope. To add more variety to this overland route, climb up to the plateau to the immediate right (south), which you can also do at the beginning of the hike. Make a circle cross-country of a mile or more into the interior of the lava flow. You can gradually angle around back into the main wash. Depending on where you rejoin the wash, you may come across a distinctive turnaround point for the hike. The wash opens up into a wide sandy oval encircled by smooth, gray stone and dark, deeply eroded lava. A side wash narrows up and to the right, but the main wash lies above a 20-foot dry gray stone/lava rock waterfall that can be easily climbed. From the dry fall the mostly clear wash can be

◀ *Looking east along a vertical lava cliff wall above the wash.*

easily followed for about 0.6 mile back down to the trailhead to complete this brief lava-beds exploration.

Miles and Directions

0.0 Begin at the trailhead.

0.1 Climb up to the right to a primitive trail just below the lava rock cliff.

0.5 At the end of the cliff trail, climb (right) onto the adjacent plateau/ridge.

1.4 Hike along the ridge cross-country; drop to the left (north) back to the wash, and hike 0.6 mile back down the wash to complete the loop.

2.0 Return to the trailhead.

Option: *Lava Flow*—This hike begins and ends in Black Tank Wash, about 1.5 miles south of North Lava Bed Wash on Kelbaker Road. The unsigned trailhead contains a large parking area just to the east of Kelbaker Road near the intersection of Black Tank Wash and the historic Mojave Road. Climb the lava wall on either side of the wash and wander across the lava flow into its fascinating interior, making a loop back to the trailhead.

68 Lava Tube

This short hike to—and down into—a unique volcanic cavelike formation can be extended to the reddish-black moonscape of nearby cinder cones.

Start: About 25 miles southeast of Baker.
Distance: 1.5 miles out and back.
Approximate hiking time: 1 to 2 hours.
Difficulty: Easy.
Trail surface: Dirt use trail to tubes; rocky cross-country route to cones.

Seasons: November through April.
USGS topo map: Indian Spring-CA (1:24,000).
Trail contact: Kelso Depot Information Center (see appendix D).

Finding the trailhead: From Baker on Interstate 15, drive south on Kelbaker Road for 19.9 miles and turn left (north) onto the unsigned Aikens Mine Road. Continue north for 4.8 miles to the first junction. Turn left and drive about 0.2 mile to a corral with a large area for parking. From Kelso in the south, drive north on Kelbaker Road, 14 miles to Aikens Mine Road. Depending on road conditions, four-wheel drive may be advisable because of areas of deep sand.

The Hike

Follow an old road for about 0.25 mile north and then watch on the right for the narrow trail to the lava tube entrance. A narrow steel ladder allows for a careful descent of some 20 feet to the floor of a main cavern chamber. The ladder is not

Park interpreter James Woolsey descends into a lava tube.

maintained, so enter cautiously at your own risk. The lava tube was formed when an ancient volcano erupted, causing a rapid flow of lava. The outer flow took longer to cool than the inner flow, forming this cavelike opening in the earth. Bring a headlamp or flashlight and be prepared for an area with a low ceiling that requires stoop walking or hands-and-knees crawling to access the larger cave. You may see bats as well as ropy strands of pahoehoe lava on the cave walls. If you explore the tubes during the hot months, you'll love this dark, cool respite from the scorching sun. Watch for snakes near the entrance.

After climbing out of the lava tube, you may want to stretch your legs to the nearest of thirty-two cinder cones that dot this 25,600-acre portion of the preserve, which has been designated a National Natural Landmark. The cones have been dated back some ten million years and are made up of what may be the densest rock on the planet. An easy 1 mile or so of walking from the tubes will get you up and back from the closest cone to the north. The modest rise in elevation to the top of the cone provides an excellent overview of this amazing, eerie landscape.

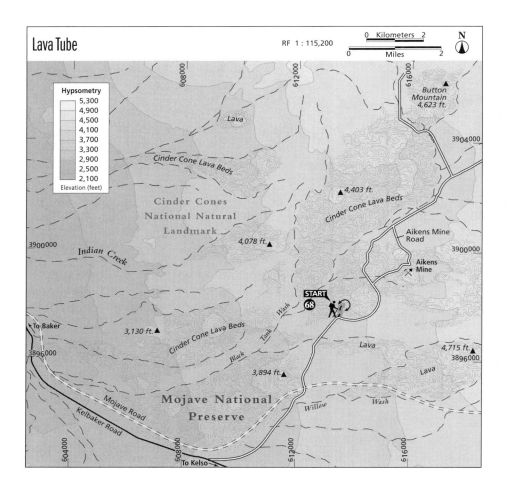

Lava Tube

RF 1 : 115,200

Hypsometry
5,300
4,900
4,500
4,100
3,700
3,300
2,900
2,500
2,100
Elevation (feet)

Lava

Cinder Cone Lava Beds

Cinder Cones
National Natural
Landmark

Indian Creek

3900000

4,078 ft.▲

3,130 ft.▲

Cinder Cone Lava Beds

To Baker

3896000

Black

Tank

Wash

3,894 ft.▲

Mojave Road

Kelbaker Road

**Mojave National
Preserve**

Willow

Wash

To Kelso

604000

608000

612000

616000

▲ Button
Mountain
4,623 ft.

3904000

4,403 ft.▲

Cinder Cone Lava Beds

Aikens Mine
Road

3900000

Aikens
Mine

START
68

Lava

4,715 ft.▲

3896000

Lava

Options: *Aikens Mine*—From the trailhead, return to the main dirt road. Drive north on Aikens Mine Road a few more miles to the closed Aikens Mine, which once excavated lava for home and yard decoration. Although it's an eyesore, the mine does allow you to peer into the inside of a cinder cone.

Willow Wash—This dry willow-lined streambed lies just off Aikens Mine Road. It offers cinder cone vistas and a glimpse into prehistoric times with evidence of early human habitation.

69 Teutonia Peak/Cima Dome

This short but steep out and back on one of only seven maintained trails in the Mojave National Preserve, within the wilderness boundary, ends at a rocky point. From here you look out at an extensive Joshua tree forest. The surrounding volcanic geology is interspersed with mounds of white monzonite. The expansive scenic vistas stretch into the hazy desert infinity.

Start: About 35 miles northeast of Baker.
Distance: 4 miles out and back.
Approximate hiking time: 2 to 3 hours.
Difficulty: Moderate.
Trail surface: Dirt path with rocks on peak section.

Seasons: October through June.
USGS topo map: Cima Dome-CA (1:24,000).
Trail contact: Kelso Depot Information Center (see appendix D).

Finding the trailhead: From Interstate 15, 25 miles northeast of Baker, take the Cima Road exit to the paved Cima Road. Continue southeasterly on Cima Road for 11.2 miles, reaching the signed trailhead parking area with an interpretive sign, on the west side of the road 0.1 mile north of Sunrise Rock. Coming from the south on Kelso-Cima Road, the trailhead is 6.7 miles north of Cima Junction.

The Hike

The Teutonia Peak Trail is one of only seven maintained trails in the entire 1.6-million-acre Mojave National Preserve. The well-signed trailhead contains an informative wildlife/woodland vegetation exhibit. Here you'll learn a bit about the ladder-back woodpecker, Scott's oriole, desert night lizard, night snake, and yucca moth, which pollinates the Joshua tree. The evergreen Joshua tree is not a tree at all but, rather, a striking member of the yucca family. The trail was extensively rehabilitated in 2003 and is now much improved.

For the first 0.5 mile, the sandy, clear trail climbs gently through this vast Joshua tree forest to the first gate, crosses a trail, and continues southwest. At 0.9 mile the trail reaches some old mine tailings and open shafts, the largest of which has been fenced off for public safety. Here the trail changes to a narrower path before coming to a gate and crossing another trail at 1 mile. At 1.1 miles the base of the northwest summit ridge of Teutonia Peak is reached at 5,220 feet. The trail is rocky but in good condition as it ascends a slope of prickly pear, yucca, juniper, and stunted Joshua trees. The final 0.5 mile climbs steeply on a series of rock steps. At 2 miles the trail ends in a notch between two large mounds of monzonite granite, just below the bouldery cliff summit of 5,755-foot Teutonia Peak.

Don't attempt the difficult summit unless you are an experienced rock climber. Instead, spend some time exploring the endless nooks and pockets surrounding the

Teutonia Peak to the southwest.

peak. Teutonia Peak is actually an extensive complex of granite outcroppings, boulders, and huge mounds of monzonite. Walk out on the fairly level ridge to the east to gain an excellent overall perspective of the peak complex and much of the preserve to the north and east. Stunted Joshua trees mix with juniper all the way to this lofty 5,640-foot level.

The end-of-the-trail notch provides a magnificent view southwestward of Cima Dome, which gradually rises 1,500 feet above the surrounding desert to an elevation almost equal to that of Teutonia Peak. The dome is a huge symmetrical hump of monzonite formed when a core of molten rock cooled and hardened deep beneath the surface of the earth. It has since been uncovered by millions of years of erosion, resulting in the unusual landscape we see today. Cima Dome is adorned by the densest Joshua tree forest in the world. These trees are a different, more spindly variety than those found to the south in Joshua Tree National Park.

After you've soaked up the view and enjoyed a bit of exploration around the peak, double-back on the trail to the trailhead to complete this diverse 4-mile round-trip hike/climb.

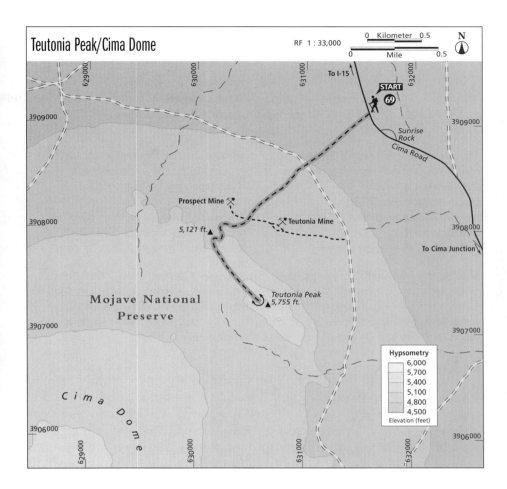

Teutonia Peak/Cima Dome

RF 1 : 33,000

Hypsometry
6,000
5,700
5,400
5,100
4,800
4,500
Elevation (feet)

To I-15

START
69

Sunrise
Rock

Cima Road

Prospect Mine

5,121 ft.

Teutonia Mine

To Cima Junction

Mojave National
Preserve

Teutonia Peak
5,755 ft.

Cima Dome

Miles and Directions

0.0 Start at the signed Teutonia Peak trailhead.

0.5 Arrive at the first gate.

0.9 Observe mine shafts and tailings.

1.0 Arrive at the second gate.

1.1 The trail starts up the northwest summit ridge.

2.0 Take in the view from the notch in the rocks, just below the summit.

4.0 Return to the trailhead.

70 Crystal Spring Overlook

This short but steep canyon hike leads to a mountain spring high in the Providence Mountains. Here you'll enjoy towering columns of volcanic rock, sweeping vistas, and a chance to view birds, desert bighorn sheep, and other wildlife.

Start: About 60 miles west of Needles, surrounded by the south-central region of the Mojave National Preserve.
Distance: 2.2 miles out and back.
Approximate hiking time: 1 to 2 hours.
Difficulty: Moderate.
Trail surface: Steep rocky path.

Seasons: October through May (or November through March to avoid rattlesnakes).
USGS topo map: Fountain Peak-CA (1:24,000).
Trail contact: Providence Mountains State Recreation Area and Mitchell Caverns Natural Preserve (see appendix D).

Finding the trailhead: From Interstate 40, take the Essex Road exit, which is 44 miles west of Needles and 100 miles east of Barstow. Drive north on the well-signed, paved Essex Road for 16 miles to the recreation area, visitor center, and campground at the end of the road. The signed trailhead to Crystal Spring is next to the picturesque stone visitor center, which was the residence of Jack and Ida Mitchell from the 1930s through the mid-1950s.

The Hike

The short but steep Crystal Spring trail provides a wonderful introduction to the power and spellbinding beauty of a high desert canyon on the dramatic east slope of the perpendicular Providence peaks. Although steep and rocky in places, the trail is easy to follow to its end, but be careful of catclaw and other spiny vegetation that can snag you along the way. As you climb you'll see the gently graded Mary Beal Nature Trail below and across the canyon.

Within only 0.2 mile the trappings of civilization seem far away with the continuing gain in distance and elevation. The rugged canyon contains an interesting mix of both limestone and volcanic rock, with the reddish volcanic extrusion known as rhyolite being most striking. The rock platform supporting the pipeline Mitchell built to water his resort in the 1930s is still visible across the canyon. The steep rocky hillsides and gullies are densely covered with prickly pear, barrel and cholla cacti, as well as piñon pine and Mojave sagebrush.

With the increase in elevation, there is an increasing sense of entering a relatively lush microenvironment. For the first 0.7 mile, the trail climbs on the left side of the ravine then crosses over to the right side. The trail continues steeply for the next 0.3 mile until coming to the end of the trail at 4,920 feet, just below the spring. To reach

The Crystal Spring trail winds through a
cactus garden at mile 0.3.

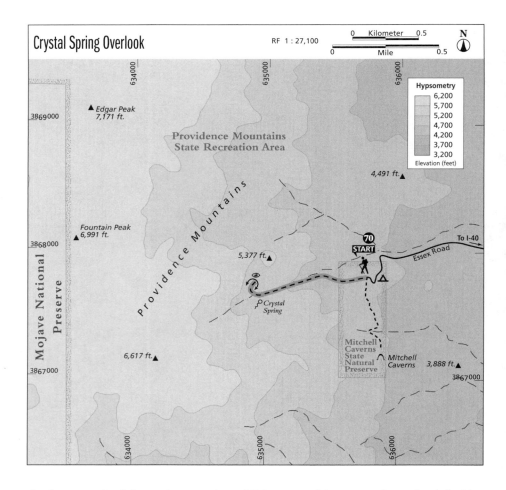

RF 1 : 27,100

0   Kilometer   0.5

0   Mile   0.5

N

Hypsometry

	6,200
	5,700
	5,200
	4,700
	4,200
	3,700
	3,200

Elevation (feet)

▲ Edgar Peak
7,171 ft.

Providence Mountains
State Recreation Area

4,491 ft.▲

Fountain Peak
▲ 6,991 ft.

Providence Mountains

5,377 ft.▲

To I-40

START

Essex Road

Crystal
Spring

Mojave National
Preserve

6,617 ft.▲

Mitchell
Caverns
State
Natural
Preserve

Mitchell
Caverns

3,888 ft.▲

the lower end of the spring, continue hiking up a faint use trail on the left side, which climbs and then quickly drops to the grottolike opening of the brush-lined spring. Cross over and climb the opposite slope to an overlook at 1.1 miles.

This 4,960-foot-high viewpoint, next to a jagged column of red rhyolite, is a great place to pause and soak up the view. On a clear day the Hualapai Mountains in Arizona are visible, 105 miles east. More than 300 square miles of the Clipper Valley can be seen, along with the low ridgeline of the ancient Colton Hills basalt, which at 1.8 billion years old is as old as the deepest layer of rock exposed in the Grand Canyon. Take time to feel the power of this secluded canyon but remember that the spring is used by bighorn sheep and other wildlife, so disturbance must be kept to a minimum.

The extremely thick growth of willow and other shrubbery at and above the spring inhibits farther travel directly up the canyon. To complete this 2.2-mile out-and-back hike, retrace your route back to the visitor center.

Miles and Directions

0.0 Begin at the Crystal Spring trailhead (4,300 feet).

0.2 The trail steepens.

0.6 The trail levels out.

0.7 The trail crosses a gully and climbs steeply to the end.

1.0 The trail ends at Crystal Spring (4,920 feet).

1.1 Arrive at the overlook (4,960 feet).

2.2 Return to the trailhead.

Options: From the overlook, it is possible to continue climbing on a strenuous cross-country route to the top of 6,991-foot Fountain Peak or 7,171-foot Edgar Peak along the high crest of the Providence Range. Both summits are six- to ten-hour round-trips and require an early start, good conditioning, and lots of experience in negotiating steep terrain with loose rock. From the overlook, the recommended route heads toward a saddle to the immediate north, then southwest up a prominent ridge for 1.5 miles, and finally angles north another mile to Fountain Peak. Edgar Peak rises another extremely rugged mile to the north.

71 Hole-in-the-Wall to Mid Hills

A hike on one of only seven maintained trails in the preserve leads you across rolling terrain with a deep volcanic canyon and high desert vistas of volcanic plugs, granite mounds, and distant mountains.

Start: About 65 miles northwest of Needles.

Distance: 8.4 miles one way.

Approximate hiking time: 4 to 6 hours.

Difficulty: Strenuous if hiked uphill south to north; moderate if hiked downhill from north to south.

Trail surface: Dirt trail and rocky wash.

Seasons: November through May.

USGS topo map: Columbia Mtn-CA (1:24,000).

Trail contact: Hole-in-the-Wall Information Center (see appendix D).

Finding the trailhead: From Needles, drive 44 miles west on Interstate 40 to the Essex Road exit. Travel 10 miles northwest on Essex Road, then turn right on Black Canyon Road. Drive another 10 miles to Wild Horse Canyon Road. Turn left and continue another mile to the trailhead parking area on the right. For a more secure parking location, you may wish to park at the visitor center and start the hike at the Rings Trail. You may also begin or end the hike at the northernmost point, off Wildhorse Canyon Road across from the Mid Hills Campground.

Looking up into the mouth of Banshee Canyon.

The Hike

Although more difficult, a south-to-north route on this trail, mostly uphill, is recommended for several reasons. First, if you leave during the morning—which you should certainly do given the length of the hike—you'll have the sun at your back rather than in your face, a definite plus during the warmer months. Second, by climbing up into the higher desert, you can better appreciate subtle changes in vegetation and geology in this varied land. But perhaps the best reason is that you will better enjoy the fantastic volcanic geology of Banshee Canyon by dropping into it when fresh early in the day, rather than the other way around. That said, most visitors still prefer to hike downhill from Mid Hills to Hole-in-the-Wall. If you elect to go with the flow, gravity that is, simply reverse the following hike description.

When you get to the "Rings" trailhead at the picnic area, be sure to walk left a short distance to the overlook, protected by a guardrail high above a narrow, pocketed canyon. One of many "holes" can be seen high in a volcanic wall to the south. Some fifteen million years ago, volcanic eruptions spilled layer upon layer of lava and ash here. The mesas seen in this area are isolated remnants of these lava flows. The many holes in the rock are the product of uneven cooling, made larger by erosion. It's a wonderland of caverns, ledges, and openings. The reddish color on the dark gray volcanic rock is caused by oxidation. Wind and moisture continue to mold this unusual landscape.

From the trailhead, the descent into spectacular Banshee Canyon is steep and potentially hazardous. Two sets of steel ring handholds are attached to pins in the rock. Although the rings add an element of safety, great care must be exercised when making the descent. The volcanic walls of the canyon are deeply pocked by erosion. Within 0.2 mile the 215-foot drop to the canyon floor has been achieved. Be on the lookout for snakes in the narrow "Rings" area.

Numerous temptations for side climbing and exploration present themselves. When you're ready, continue down another 0.1 mile to the canyon mouth from where Barber Butte rises impressively to the north. Follow the signed trail across a wash. At 0.5 mile the trail intersects the wash. Bear right and follow a cholla- and yucca-lined wash surrounded by distant mesas. Look back to the sheer cliff walls of the canyon you've just descended.

At 1 mile the trail reaches a signed junction. The Wild Horse Canyon trailhead is 0.25 mile south, and the trail to Mid Hills heads north. Turn right at this junction toward the Mid Hills Campground and continue up a ridge toward a gap in the mesas. Here the trail makes a gradual ascent of an alluvial fan. A wall of dark volcanic rock parallels the trail to the right.

At 1.7 miles a low pass is reached. Dropping down another 0.1 mile, the trail crosses a gate signed 6.2 MILES TO MID HILLS. The mileages on the signs are wrong as often as not. A deep lava canyon wash winds to the left. The steep, rocky trail drops to the wash, where a trail sign points up the wash to the right. A trail junction appears at 2.2 miles; stay right. Striking white cliffs of volcanic ash topped with a dark volcanic crown rise majestically to the left. Another trail junction is met at 2.4 miles; again follow the sign and veer to the right. At 2.5 miles the signed trail leaves the wash and turns left (north), leaving the sweeping mesas to the south. For the next mile, the trail follows a wash and then climbs up a sandy ridge in high, open desert where white, granite boulders begin to dot the landscape.

About one-third of the way up the trail, evidence appears of the Hackberry fire caused by lightning in June 2005. More than 70,000 acres were affected. Although lightning fires are a natural part of ecosystems, it will take many years for the piñon-juniper woodland to recover fully.

At 4.3 miles the trail crosses a dirt road that leads to the tailings of the abandoned Gold Valley Mine, where a working windmill provides water for cattle. For a side trip to the mine/windmill site, turn right at this junction and follow the road southeasterly for 0.5 mile.

Continuing north toward Mid Hills, the trail soon passes through a gate signed 3.8 MILES TO MID HILLS, intersecting another trail. For the next 0.5 mile, the trail climbs

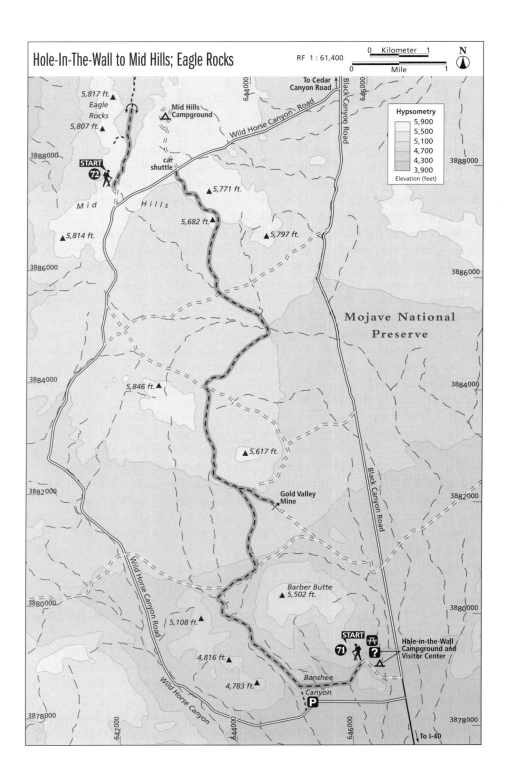

Hole-In-The-Wall to Mid Hills; Eagle Rocks

RF 1 : 61,400

0   Kilometer   1

0   Mile   1

N

5,817 ft.
Eagle
Rocks
5,807 ft. ▲

Mid Hills
Campground

To Cedar
Canyon Road

Wild Horse Canyon Road

Black Canyon Road

646000

Hypsometry

	5,900
	5,500
	5,100
	4,700
	4,300
	3,900

Elevation (feet)

3888000

START
72

car
shuttle

▲ 5,771 ft.

3888000

M i d   H i l l s

5,682 ft. ▲

▲ 5,797 ft.

▲ 5,814 ft.

3886000

3886000

Mojave National
Preserve

▲ 5,846 ft.

3884000

3884000

▲ 5,617 ft.

3882000

Gold Valley
Mine

3882000

Black Canyon Road

Wild Horse Canyon Road

Barber Butte
▲ 5,502 ft.

3880000

5,108 ft. ▲

3880000

START
71

Hole-in-the-Wall
Campground and
Visitor Center

4,816 ft. ▲

4,783 ft. ▲

Banshee

Canyon

Wild Horse Canyon

P

3878000

3878000

642000

644000

646000

To I-40

a small pass from where, at 5,350 feet, a vast juniper–sage plateau opens up ahead with small, pointed peaks and mesas adorning the landscape. At 5 miles the trail crosses another fence, signed MID HILLS 3.1 MILES. Take the signed trail to the right.

For the next 0.7 mile, the trail descends a sandy gully then curves around to the left (north) and begins climbing. At 5.9 miles a FOLLOW WASH sign points up the wash as it again turns left. The only confusing point in this otherwise well-signed hike is encountered at mile 6.2 where a FOLLOW WASH sign points up the wash to the Mid Hills Campground and a signed trail leaves the gravelly wash to the right. Take the trail to the right. The FOLLOW WASH sign indicates a short loop return route for hikers starting at the Mid Hill Trailhead.

At 6.8 miles the trail passes a gate signed 1.2 MILES TO MID HILLS. The steadily climbing trail reaches a spring/seep. It then drops into a narrow gully and climbs steeply to the high point of 5,600 feet at 8 miles. The end-of-the-trail windmill can be seen from here. A gradual drop over the final 0.4 mile concludes this point-to-point traverse from Banshee Canyon to the Mid Hills in the middle of Mojave.

Miles and Directions

0.0 Start at the "Rings" trailhead at the Hole-in-the-Wall Picnic Area.

0.2 The steep descent to the canyon floor ends here.

0.3 Arrive at the mouth of Banshee Canyon.

1.0 At the signed trail junction with Wild Horse Canyon Trail, turn right toward the Mid Hills Campground.

2.2 Stay right at the trail junction.

2.4 Veer right at this trail junction.

2.5 The signed trail leaves the wash and turns left (north).

4.3 The trail crosses the Gold Valley Mine road; continue straight (north) and through a gate signed 3.8 MILES TO MID HILLS.

5.0 The trail crosses a fence signed MID HILLS 3.1 MILES.

5.9 At the FOLLOW WASH sign, turn left and proceed up the wash.

6.2 The signed trail leaves the wash to the right. A FOLLOW WASH sign points up the wash to the left to the Mid Hills Campground.

6.8 Arrive at a fence/gate signed 1.2 MILES TO MID HILLS.

8.0 Reach the high point at 5,600 feet.

8.4 Arrive at the signed endpoint at the Mid Hills trailhead next to the windmill.

72 Eagle Rocks

This is an easy stroll to a unique formation of monzogranite boulders.

See map on page 234.
Start: About 70 miles northwest of Needles.
Distance: 2 miles out and back (plus extra mileage for exploring the boulders and the valley between the piles).
Approximate hiking time: 1 to 2 hours.
Difficulty: Easy to the boulders; moderate for exploring boulder piles.
Trail surface: Dirt path with some rocks.
Seasons: November through May.
USGS topo maps: Columbia Mtn.-CA and Mid Hills-CA (1:24,000).
Trail contact: Hole-in-the-Wall Information Center (see appendix D).

Finding the trailhead: From Needles, drive 44 miles west on Interstate 40 to the Essex Road exit. Travel 10 miles northwest on Essex Road, then turn right on Black Canyon Road and continue for 10 more miles, passing Wild Horse Canyon Road. Continue north on Black Canyon Road another 5 miles and turn left onto the upper end of Wild Horse Canyon Road. Drive 2.8 miles to the first dirt road on your right after the Mid Hills Campground turnoff. Turn onto this unmarked dirt road, which occurs at the first sharp southward bend in Wild Horse Canyon. Drive 0.2 mile on the dirt road to a junction; park here if you don't have a four-wheel drive. Bear right and drive 0.1 mile to the wilderness boundary post at the end of the road on your right. Park at a wide spot on the road; the signed trail is your trail.

The Hike

The Eagle Rocks tower above the Mid Hills and are prominent beacons along the entire Kelso–Cima Road. These lumpy granite formations stand out in sharp contrast with the angular mountains in this central Mojave region. They beckon the curious hiker from afar but, oddly enough, disappear from sight as you approach the trailhead, obscured by the surrounding hills.

The hike heads downhill on a gentle, sandy trail, gradually mixing with a small wash, until the junction at 0.5 mile. It is not until 0.6 mile that the Eagle Rocks gradually appear. And what a surprise they are!

Much like the monzogranite of Joshua Tree National Park, these hulking boulders have rounded contours, immense size, and fantastic shapes. The powerful boulders tower 350 feet above the base of each pile. There are even Joshua trees on the hillsides near the boulder piles. This form of igneous rock is, upon closer inspection, quite chunky, resembling conglomerate with rectangular pieces of quartz imbedded in the surface. It provides great traction for adventuresome rock scramblers. Advanced rock-climbing skills are mandatory for the larger boulders, but novices can enjoy exploring the perimeter of the mounds.

The small valley between the two dominant boulder piles is an enchanting nook of wilderness to explore. A use trail leads 0.7 mile down the narrow valley,

Spires of Eagle Rocks' granite rise above the Mid Hills of Mojave National Preserve.

following a small wash. The canyon protects large piñon pines and live oaks from the strong winds that dwarf these species in more exposed locations nearby.

As you walk back along the trail to the parking area, you'll again be surprised at how quickly these granite obelisks disappear from view. Yet, as you travel around the preserve, you'll notice their prominence on the horizon.

Miles and Directions

0.0 Start at the trailhead, posted with a wilderness boundary marker at the dirt road.

0.5 At the junction with another trail, turn left uphill.

0.7 At the Y junction, either way is 0.1 mile to the granite fields; both are dead ends.

0.8 The trail dead-ends at the boulder fields. There's a faint use trail down the valley between the boulder piles.

2.0 Return to the trailhead.

73 Table Top Mountain Loop

This cross-country hike gets you on top of a distinctive, steep-sided butte in the heart of Mojave National Preserve. It can be done as either an out-and-back or loop hike. The ascent of the isolated flat-topped mesa provides a view of monzonite boulder formations and a 360-degree panorama of almost all of the preserve.

Start: About 70 miles northwest of Needles or 65 miles southeast of Baker.
Distance: 7-mile loop or out and back.
Approximate hiking time: 4 to 5 hours.
Difficulty: Strenuous.
Trail surface: Dirt trail and rocky wash, but most of route is cross-country.

Seasons: September through May.
USGS topo maps: Columbia Mountain-CA and Woods Mountains-CA (1:24,000).
Trail contact: Hole-in-the-Wall Information Center (see appendix D).

Finding the trailhead: From Baker, drive east on Interstate 15; take the Cima exit and head south on Cima Road for 28.5 miles to Cima Junction. Turn right (south) on Kelso-Cima Road and continue for 4.9 miles to Cedar Canyon Road; turn left (east) on Cedar Canyon Road and drive 6.4 miles to Black Canyon Road; turn right (south) on Black Canyon Road and drive 6.4 miles to the unsigned trailhead, which is on the east side immediately north of a cattle guard. Pull off on the east side of the road and park in a large turnaround camping area. The trail begins on an old dirt road on the northeast edge of the parking area.

From Needles drive 42 miles west on Interstate 40 and turn north onto Essex Road. After 10 miles turn north onto Black Canyon Road. Continue north 13.6 miles to the unsigned trailhead, which is on the right (east) side of the road just past a cattle guard. Park as described above.

Check on road conditions for Cedar Canyon and Black Canyon Roads, especially after rain or snow.

The Hike

There are a variety of approaches to Table Top Mountain, ranging from moderate to strenuous, but the final ascent to the summit is strenuous regardless of which route you choose. Table Top Mountain is bound by a private subdivision in Round Valley to the immediate north, posted against trespass. The park has purchased much of Gold Valley, but the 160-acre core, where there are homes, is privately owned. One of the advantages of this suggested route is that it takes place entirely on public land. The somewhat long 3.5-mile (one-way) approach traverses a variety of terrain with constantly changing views.

Begin by heading east up a draw on a clear trail that provides an easy start to an otherwise strenuous hike. Continue walking slightly downhill on the trail as it passes through a gate/fence at 0.3 mile. At 0.6 mile make a sharp left turn at a junction. The trail climbs up a wash next to an old broken waterline for another

Approaching the steep ascent of Table Top Mountain.

0.5 mile to a windmill/water tank used for watering cattle. An abandoned mine entrance and remnants of a mining road can be seen on the hillside to the left. A huge rock outcropping rises to the right, serving as a good landmark for the return trip along the base of the ridge. For point of reference, the windmill is the takeoff point for both the more difficult ridge-route loop and the base of the ridge out-and-back trip.

For the ridge route, proceed to the right along a fence, cross it, and climb northeast to the summit ridge behind and to the left of the previously mentioned large rock outcropping. To avoid trespassing on private land, keep to the right (south) side of the ridge. At 1.4 miles you'll likely end up close to a large rock cairn. From here climb straight up the ridge toward a prominent piñon pine on the horizon. At 1.7 miles and 5,700 feet, the ridge becomes very rocky but remains fairly level on a southeasterly line toward the flat-topped mountain. The ridge then drops to around 5,600 feet close to the wilderness boundary. For the next 0.4 mile, the going is difficult, requiring boulder scrambling, bushwhacking, and edging around sharp-spined yucca and other cacti. In general, skirt to the right of cliff faces and huge granite boulders.

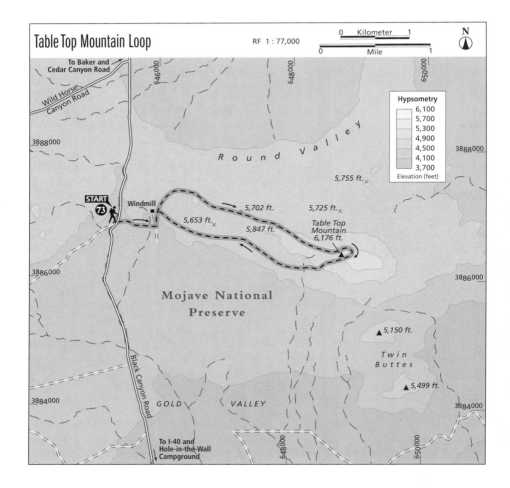

RF 1 : 77,000

0 Kilometer 1

0 Mile 1

N

To Baker and
Cedar Canyon Road

Wild Horse
Canyon Road

3888000

R o u n d   V a l l e y

Hypsometry

| | 6,100 |
| 5,700 |
| 5,300 |
| 4,900 |
| 4,500 |
| 4,100 |
| 3,700 |

Elevation (feet)

3888000

5,755 ft.×

START
73

Windmill

5,702 ft.

5,725 ft.×

5,653 ft.×

5,847 ft.

Table Top
Mountain
6,176 ft.

3886000

3886000

**Mojave National
Preserve**

▲ 5,150 ft.

*T w i n
B u t t e s*

Black Canyon Road

▲ 5,499 ft.

3884000

GOLD   VALLEY

3884000

To I-40 and
Hole-in-the-Wall
Campground

At 2.8 miles the route becomes considerably easier with cow paths and side washes gradually climbing for 0.4 mile to the striking 5,810-foot western base of Table Top Mountain. The mountain is capped by sheer cliffs of dark lava atop a ring of white granite. The final 0.3-mile climb to the 6,176-foot summit is steep with loose rocks, but the route is direct and straightforward. Once you arrive at the base of the cliffs, the top is equally accessible by going either to the right or left and then up through a break in the cliffs. However, the route to the left (north) is somewhat faster.

On top, look for the peak register placed there in April 1983 by the Desert Peaks Chapter of the Sierra Club. The large plateau is well vegetated with sage, Mormon tea, rabbitbrush, and juniper. By all means walk along the rim for a chance to see raptors in the cliffs as well as ever-changing vistas. Table Top Mountain is strategically located between the jagged peaks of the Providence Mountains to the southwest and the rugged New York Mountains and Castle Peaks to the north.

Symmetrical Cima Dome fills the northwest horizon. Virtually all of the vast preserve can be seen from this central volcanic laccolith (plug).

For the return journey, ease your way down a break in the cliffs just west of the summit, proceeding cautiously on the steep, loose rock. After losing about 250 feet in 0.3 mile at the base of the steepest slope of the mountain, angle to the right (west) along a juniper–clad ridge. Continue dropping for another 0.4 mile to 5,600 feet in a wide upper wash encircled by piñon–juniper and boulders. At 0.9 mile the route crosses a bouldery draw: Drop to the left for another 0.4 mile to a flat bench at 5,300 feet.

For those going up on this route, look for a distinctive duck-head–shaped rock upslope and to your left.

At 1.6 miles cross a barbed-wire fence and angle northwesterly near the hillside on the right. At 2 miles the route passes just below the high pillar of rocks seen earlier from the windmill site. The windmill is visible straight ahead to the northwest. Continuing westward you'll soon intersect the trail. Go left and walk down to the trail junction, then turn right for the final 0.6 mile to the trailhead, thereby completing this exhilarating loop in Mojave's heartland.

Miles and Directions

0.0 From the trailhead, the trail heads east up a draw (5,180 feet).

0.3 Pass through a gate/fence.

0.6 Make a sharp left turn (north) at the junction.

1.1 The windmill/water tank marks the beginning of the cross-country route, with two options: Go north up the ridge of Table Top Mountain or hike along the base of the ridge.

Ridge Route:

1.4 Climb northeast to the summit ridge, keeping to the right side of the ridge to avoid private land.

1.7 Hike southeast along the ridge.

2.3 Skirt to the right below the cliff rocks.

3.2 Arrive at the base of Table Top Mountain.

3.5 Reach the summit (6,176 feet).

7.0 Return to the trailhead.

Base of Ridge Route:

1.9 Cross a barbed-wire fence.

2.2 Look upslope and left for a large duck-head-shaped granite rock. This is a good place to begin climbing toward Table Top Mountain.

3.2 Arrive at the southwest base of the mountain.

3.5 Reach the summit (6,176 feet).

7.0 Return to the trailhead.

74 Caruthers Canyon

Granite boulders and spires and an old mine site are tucked away up in Caruthers Canyon in the New York Mountains.

Start: About 65 miles northwest of Needles.
Distance: 3 miles out and back.
Approximate hiking time: 1 to 2 hours.
Difficulty: Moderate.
Trail surface: Rocky path.

Seasons: November through May.
USGS topo maps: Ivanpah-CA and Pinto Valley-CA (1:24,000).
Trail contact: Hole-in-the-Wall Information Center (see appendix D).

Finding the trailhead: From Needles, drive 45 miles west on Interstate 40 to the Essex Road exit. The Lanfair Road from Goffs is a shorter but far less traveled and maintained route. Travel another 10 miles northwest on Essex Road, then turn right on Black Canyon Road and continue another 10 miles to Wild Horse Canyon Road. Turn left for 1 mile and stop at the Hole-in-the-Wall Information Center to check on current road conditions. Then continue north on Black Canyon Road for another 10 miles to Cedar Canyon Road. Turn right and drive 15 miles to the Ivanpah/Lanfair intersection. Turn left (north) on Ivanpah Road and drive 5.7 miles to New York Mountain Road (signed). The turn is in a cattle feedlot for the OX Ranch and occurs right before a cattle guard. Drive 5.9 miles on New York Mountain Road and turn right onto an unmarked but well-traveled road into Caruthers Canyon. Continue north, disregarding a junction at 1.2 miles. At 1.8 miles locate a suitable place to leave your vehicle in the wide area before descending to the wash. The road from the wash at that point becomes progressively more impassable; the road instead becomes the hiking trail.

The Hike

The lush canyon bottom here is framed by spires of golden granite. A diverse plant community flourishes in Caruthers Canyon due to high elevation and plentiful water. There is also evidence of animal life, although, as in most desert habitats, it remains invisible during the day. Animal footprints around standing pools of water indicate their presence. If water is in Caruthers during your visit, please be considerate of the canyon's permanent residents and don't use the stream as a thoroughfare or play area. Desert water is too precious for such disrespect.

Your route is the old mine road to the Giant Ledge Mine. Like most roads of this kind, it exhibits remarkable engineering but is very rough. It is astonishing that it could be used by mine vehicles, especially ones loaded with ore. In the past decades it has deteriorated. It becomes increasingly rocky as you climb at 0.7 mile. Although the road is legally open since it is not in wilderness, nature is taking care of things and reclaiming it from the four-wheel-drive crowd with well-placed rock slides and fallen boulders. For a hiker, it also means slow going.

Numerous backcountry campsites dot the lower canyon. Some are tidy, but others show evidence of years of Bureau of Land Management's laissez-faire manage-

Granite mounds and spires rise within Caruthers Canyon in the New York Mountains.

ment, with scattered debris—broken glass, car parts, cans, bottles. The campsite on the spur at 0.2 mile is highly developed, with a cement table, barbecue, and fire ring. This is the work of an industrious camper!

The boulders of the canyon are certainly the most noteworthy focus of this trip. Fantastic balancing acts are everywhere. Twenty-ton boulders are frozen in a pirouette on 30-foot spires. Above the canyon on the eastern horizon is a hole-in-the-boulder that may grow to an arch eventually. The colors of the granite are as fascinating as the shapes. The central 300-foot granite mound has a golden tone, looking like a mound of petrified butterscotch. Your route curves around this formation, rising to the mine in the canyon above.

The mine site is a grotesque scar in this beautiful canyon. Massive tailing piles slump right into the creek bed below the mine. The hillside itself is pockmarked with gaping mouths of defunct mines. Be cautious near these, and do not go into them; often old mine shafts are unstable. The only equipment that remains is the chute used to deliver ore into the vehicles that carried it down the tricky mine road. The mine site provides a striking contrast with the natural beauty that surrounds it.

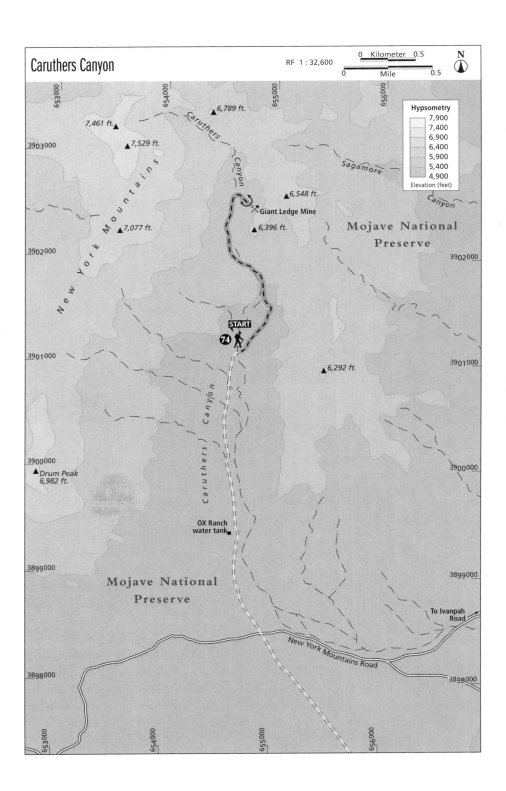

Caruthers Canyon

RF 1 : 32,600

N

Hypsometry

7,900
7,400
6,900
6,400
5,900
5,400
4,900
Elevation (feet)

653000   654000   655000   656000

3903000

7,461 ft.

7,529 ft.

6,789 ft.

Caruthers

Canyon

New York Mountains

7,077 ft.

6,548 ft.

Giant Ledge Mine

6,396 ft.

Sagamore

Canyon

Mojave National
Preserve

3902000

START

74

3901000

6,292 ft.

Caruthers Canyon

3900000

Drum Peak
6,982 ft.

OX Ranch
water tank

3899000

Mojave National
Preserve

To Ivanpah
Road

New York Mountains Road

3898000

After carefully looking around the mine site, return down the canyon to your vehicle at the mouth.

Miles and Directions

0.0 The trail begins at a wide wash.

0.2 Turn left at the fork. If you do explore to the right, you will find a well-appointed camp-site.

0.8–0.9 Cross the wash, where there is often water in winter and spring.

1.5 Arrive at Giant Ledge Mine.

3.0 Return to the trailhead.

75 Keystone Canyon

This remote canyon in the rugged New York Mountains is bound by scenic granite towers and chaparral woodland that leads up to a historic mine.

Start: About 70 miles east of Baker and 77 miles northwest of Needles.

Distance: 3.8 miles out and back (with side-trip options ranging from a 0.5-mile out and back to an additional 4-mile out-and-back peak climb).

Approximate hiking time: 2 to 3 hours; additional 3 to 4 hours for peak.

Difficulty: Moderate for hike; strenuous for peak climb.

Trail surface: Rocky dirt two-track; off-trail to summit.

Seasons: October through May.

USGS topo map: Ivanpah-CA (1:24,000).

Trail contact: Kelso Depot Information Center (see appendix D).

Finding the trailhead: From Interstate 15, take the California Highway 164 exit and drive 3.6 miles east to Ivanpah Road. Turn right (south) and drive about 12 miles to Ivanpah, where the paved road changes to dirt. After another 6 miles turn right onto a rough unsigned road, for which four-wheel drive is recommended. Take another immediate right, passing the defunct Lecy Well. Stay to the right after 1 mile, then to the right on the main road. The unsigned trailhead/parking area is about 1.9 miles from Ivanpah Road, just before the road crosses the wash. This spot is a good campsite if you're planning to stay the night.

The Hike

Keystone is one of the premier canyons in the wild and rugged New York Mountains. Here you will find some of the most fascinating flora in the Mojave Desert—from chaparral brush fields to piñon–juniper and turbinella oak to lonely pockets of white fir clinging to windswept ridges. The New York Mountains host an amazing array of plants—some 300 species have been identified.

Granite spires tower above Keystone Canyon in the New York Mountains.

From the trailhead/parking area, the old two-track trail crosses the wash a few times before intersecting a mine road at 0.5 mile. Continue to the right up the main fork of the canyon, where you'll quickly pass Live Oak Canyon on your right. The view is striking, with granite spires punctuating the far horizon. On up the main canyon, an old rusty water pipe marks a trail on your left that leads 0.25 mile uphill to Keystone Spring. After hiking the old deteriorating two-track 1.9 miles, you'll have made the 1,000-foot climb from the trailhead to an old abandoned copper mine. Scattered boards and slag heaps tell the tale of shattered hopes from a mine that produced mostly dreams. Retrace your route to complete your exploration of this scenic gateway to New York Peak.

Miles and Directions

0.0 From the unsigned trailhead/parking area, the road crosses a wash.

0.5 At the junction with the mine road, continue to the right.

0.75 At the junction with Live Oak Canyon, continue to the left.

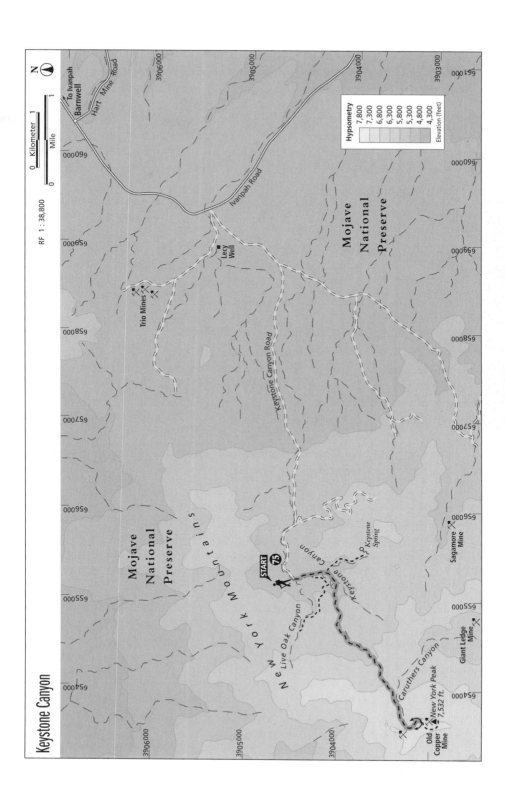

Keystone Canyon

RF 1 : 38,800

N

0 Kilometer 1

0 Mile 1

Hypsometry

7,800
7,300
6,800
6,300
5,800
5,300
4,800
4,300

Elevation (feet)

To Ivanpah
Barnwell

Hart Mine Road

Ivanpah Road

Lecy
Well

Trio Mines

**Mojave
National
Preserve**

Keystone Canyon Road

**Mojave
National
Preserve**

New York Mountains

START 75

Live Oak Canyon

Keystone Canyon

Keystone Spring

Sagamore
Mine

Caruthers Canyon

New York Peak
7,532 ft.

Old
Copper
Mine

Giant Ledge
Mine

3906000
3905000
3904000
3903000

651000
652000
654000
655000
656000
657000
658000
659000
660000
661000

1.1 At the junction with the Keystone Spring trail, continue to the right.

1.9 The hike ends at the old copper mine. Retrace the trail to the trailhead.

3.8 Arrive back at the trailhead.

Options: Options off this main trail include a shorter excursion up *Keystone Canyon* to a grassy waterhole. This desert oasis is nestled in a steep, brushy north-facing draw up Live Oak Canyon from the main Keystone Canyon. Also, don't miss the easy 0.5-mile round-trip to Keystone Spring by way of an old mining trail that takes off 1.1 miles up the main-facing draw at 6,020-foot elevation.

Stone ruins—After the first mile on Keystone Canyon Road, take the first right-hand fork and continue another 0.5 mile; park next to a campsite. From here, take a short 0.5-mile round-trip hike up a small unnamed canyon just north of Keystone Canyon, bounded by hills dotted with piñon-juniper, cholla, and sage. You'll quickly come to picturesque stone walls, perhaps built by early cowboys.

A far more strenuous hike is an ascent of 7,532-foot-high *New York Peak,* the apex of the New York Mountains, climbing from the end of the Keystone Canyon hike at the old copper mine. This steep, challenging off-trail climb is only for experienced, well-conditioned hikers with route-finding ability. Be prepared for loose rocks and cliff faces that force an up-and-down route that is mostly parallel to the west ridge above the canyon. After gaining the north summit ridge to the peak, work your way south along the boulder-strewn divide to a rounded knob (7445 BM), just west of the rock columns that form the highest point in the range. Rock-climbing skills are needed to reach the actual top, especially during winter and early spring when snow in the cracks and fissures makes climbing both dangerous and difficult. From this lofty vantage point, you'll see the entire northeast quarter of the preserve—from radiating canyons to distant basins and ranges.

76 Fort Piute/Piute Gorge

This loop hike takes you to the only year-round stream in the East Mojave Desert. It retraces the route of early pioneers. Along the way, you visit the ruins of an army fort, view petroglyphs, and return via a dramatic gorge through the Piute Hills.

Start: About 74 miles northwest of Needles.
Distance: 7-mile loop.
Approximate hiking time: 3 to 4 hours.
Difficulty: Moderate to fort; strenuous return via gorge.
Trail surface: Dirt path, at times rocky; rocky wash.

Seasons: October through May.
USGS topo maps: Signal Hill-CA and Homer Mountain-CA (1:24,000).
Trail contact: Hole-in-the-Wall Information Center (see appendix D).

Finding the trailhead: From Needles, drive 37 miles west on Interstate 40 to the Fenner/Essex exit. (Call ahead for road conditions.) Continue 10 miles northeast to Goffs and turn left onto Lanfair Road. Drive another 16 miles north to the Cedar Canyon/Ivanpah/Lanfair Road junction. Make a right turn almost immediately onto a dirt road on your right with a small white PT&T sign. Head straight for a concrete building. Follow this road straight east for 3.9 miles, disregarding all other roads at intersections. At 3.9 miles turn right on an AT&T cable route and continue east to the Piute Hills. At 10.3 miles from the Ivanpah turnoff, turn left onto a marginal dirt road just before reaching a cattle guard. Proceed north for 0.5 mile and park in a wide turnaround marked with several rock cairns. The trail is the road that leaves this parking area and goes east to the ridge of the Piutes.

The Hike

Due to a human-caused fire in autumn 2004, Fort Piute, Piute Creek, and Piute Gorge were closed to visitors for one year to allow streamside vegetation to recover. The area has now reopened.

The Fort Piute/Piute Gorge hike is the perfect journey for the hiking party or the individual with diverse interests. It has petroglyphs for the archaeologist, an original Mojave Road segment for the emigrant historian, an old army fort for the military specialist, and a spectacular mile-long gorge for the geology enthusiast. The combination of all these aspects also makes it exciting for the generic adventurer.

The distance from the main road intersection at Cedar Canyon and the Ivanpah/Lanfair Road to the trailhead should not intimidate you. But these dirt roads were heavily rutted by winter 2005 rains. While it's virtually a straight shot 10.3 miles east to the Piute Hills from the intersection, a four-wheel-drive vehicle is necessary. Call for road conditions.

The counterclockwise loop, as described here, begins at the south trailhead. In doing the hike in this direction, you are walking down the Mojave Road (labeled

Old Government Road on the topo map) and not up, the way the emigrants did (unless you omit the gorge trip and return this way). While historically the eastward direction is incorrect, the Mojave Road would be an exercise in boredom after the magnificence of the Piute Gorge. This way the experiential height of the trip occurs on the trip out through the gorge—and the gorge is twice as impressive coming up from its lower eastern end.

The section of the hike (0.0 to 2.1 miles) on the Mojave Road is certain to create respect for the gutsy pioneers who used this thoroughfare. Built and guarded by the U.S. Army pursuant to our nineteenth-century policy to populate the West as quickly as possible, the Mojave Road followed an old Native American track. Be sure to pause at the saddle (0.2 mile from the trailhead), where the track is now closed to wheeled vehicles. Turn and look west. It is easy to relive the mixed feelings the emigrants must have had after struggling to reach this point, seeing the Mojave Desert stretching to the western horizon.

Hike on east down the Mojave Road. This segment rising from Fort Piute was known as one of the most arduous of the entire journey. As you will shortly discover, the volcanic rocks do not make a smooth road surface. Wagons without springs or shocks had a difficult time, as did the folks who had to walk along behind the Conestogas.

Where the road finally reaches the Piute stream are several petroglyph sites. Do not touch or deface them—leave them for others to enjoy.

When you reach the stream (2.1 miles), you'll revel in the lush vegetation, the watercress, and the sound of a gurgling brook. A considerate hiker does not use a riparian zone for a trail. Such use devastates vegetation and degrades the streambed. This resource is too precious for the desert residents to risk such destruction. Please use the trail high on the north bank instead. There's a more panoramic view from this high trail anyway.

Downstream 0.5 mile the ruins of Fort Piute are impressive for their remoteness. All that remain are the stone foundation of the blockhouse and a stone corral. Duty here must have been grim. The vista out over the Great Basin is endless. The emigrants traveling by this point had survived an incredible journey.

Heading back westward from the fort along the same high north-bank trail, the focus shifts to the mountain looming above. From this low point of the hike (2,700 feet), the Piute Hills look a lot more impressive than they do from the west, where they're a low line of hills—nothing in comparison to the Providence and New York ranges. Your trip through the gorge will change this perception forever. Traveling above the canyon and above Piute Spring gives you an eagle's view of the depth of the gorge 300 feet below. The descent into the gorge is neither arduous nor dangerous if you take the prescribed route (see mileage log). Be sure to stay up high until you nearly reach the mountainside and then travel down the side gorge, entering from the north just as the Piute wash disappears into the mountain.

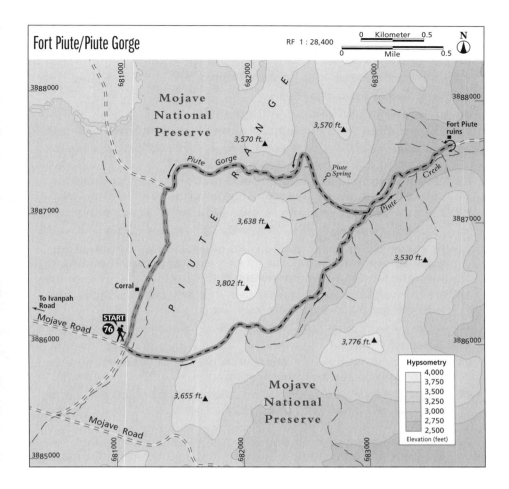

RF 1 : 28,400

0   Kilometer   0.5

0   Mile   0.5

N

Mojave
National
Preserve

3888000

3888000

681000

682000

683000

R A N G E

3,570 ft.

Fort Piute
ruins

3,570 ft.

Piute Gorge

Piute
Spring

Creek

Piute

3887000

3887000

3,638 ft.

P I U T E

3,530 ft.

Corral

3,802 ft.

3,776 ft.

3886000

3886000

To Ivanpah
Road

Mojave Road

START
76

Hypsometry

4,000
3,750
3,500
3,250
3,000
2,750
2,500
Elevation (feet)

Mojave
National
Preserve

3,655 ft.

3885000

Mojave Road

681000

682000

683000

The trip through the heart of the mountain range is a geologist's delight. The display of volcanic rock types, faulting and folding, and erosion is the most dynamic in the Mojave National Preserve. The peaks tower 600 feet above the sandy gorge floor. In places the gorge is no more than 10 feet wide. There are a few segments where stepping up a dry waterfall is necessary, but there is no boulder scrambling.

Like Alice in Wonderland, you emerge from the west entrance into a totally alien landscape. "Where am I?" is your first thought. The Mojave desert floor is 300 feet above the gorge exit, so the deeply eroded cliffs and mesas that greet you are unexpected. The well-cairned trail to the left, 0.1 mile from the gorge mouth, takes you back up to the familiar Mojave landscape, 1 mile north of where you started.

Whether your interests are Native Americans, emigrants, army recruits, or geology, this loop hike is sure to inspire you. It is definitely worth the long drive to the eastern edge of the preserve since it is unlike any other hike in the region.

Miles and Directions

0.0 Head east on the trail, which winds north along a fence.

0.2 Go through the gate and up the rocky trail to the ridge.

0.5 Reach the peak of the saddle (Piute Hill).

0.5–1.1 Hike down the Mojave Road.

1.1 Erosion has taken out the roadbed. Notice that the road drops into a wash to your right.

2.0 After the bend in the wash, at the reddish orange rocks, the road leads out of the wash to the left. This area has numerous petroglyphs. Be respectful.

2.1 At the streambed, cross and go upstream for 10 yards to cross in the willows and pick up the trail high on the north bank heading east. Do not use the streambed as a trail.

2.6 After reaching the fort ruins, turn around. Return on the north-bank trail to the intersection.

3.1 Continue west on the high bank trail. A large cutaway mountain is your beacon.

3.8 The trail seems to end at a crumbling precipice where you see the wash below turning and disappearing into the gorge. On the hill above you to the right are numerous cairns marking the trail. Climb and continue northwestward.

4.0 At the T intersection directly opposite the mouth of the gorge, take the well-cairned trail to the left, zigzagging down to a feeder canyon from the north.

4.2 Continue down the canyon to the main gorge/wash. Several dry falls require scrambling.

4.3–5.5 Hike up the gorge.

5.6 At the gorge exit, notice the cairn in the wash and others on your left marking the trail up from the canyon to the plateau above.

6.0 The trail comes over a crest to a parking area. Unless you have a driver to move your car for you, turn left and walk south on the dirt road that parallels the hills, by a cattle stockade, to the starting point.

7.0 Arrive back at the original parking area.

77 Castle Peaks

The volcanic turrets and spires of the Castle Peaks form a dramatic backdrop for unlimited exploration, adjacent to a rambling hiking corridor that penetrates deep into the remote northeast corner of the preserve.

Start: About 84 miles northwest of Needles.
Distance: 6.6 miles out and back (plus another 2 miles off-trail to the Castle Peak spires).
Approximate hiking time: 3 to 6 hours.
Difficulty: Moderate.

Trail surface: Sandy two-track trail and wash.
Seasons: October through May.
USGS topo map: Castle Peaks-CA (1:24,000).
Trail contact: Hole-in-the-Wall Information Center (see appendix D).

Finding the trailhead: From Needles, drive 37 miles west on Interstate 40 to the Fenner/Essex exit, then head northeast for 10 miles to Goffs. Turn left onto Lanfair/Ivanpah Road and drive 29 miles north to the junction with Hart Road (Barnwell historic site) and turn right (east). (Call for dirt road conditions.) If driving from the north from Interstate 15, take the California Highway 164 exit and drive 3.6 miles east to Ivanpah Road. Turn right (south) and drive about 12 miles to Ivanpah, where the paved road changes to dirt, then about 7 more miles to Barnwell. Turn left onto Hart Road. After driving 4.8 miles continue left (straight) for another 0.9 mile and turn left (north) onto the unsigned Castle Peak Road.

Drive another 2.8 miles to the end of the road near the signed wilderness boundary. Four-wheel drive is recommended for this rough road, and in particular the last mile requires a high-clearance vehicle. There is a large parking area and good campsite located about 100 yards before the end of the road. On the drive near the dam, watch for coveys of Gambel's quail.

The Hike

The aptly named Castle Peaks mark the northeast extension of that steep range of granite and limestone known as the New York Mountains. These jagged peaks are a cluster of dark red and brown spires streaked with white and are made up of volcanic andesite.

From the end-of-the-road wilderness boundary, follow an old grazing road that is gradually being reclaimed by the wilderness. The trail reaches a low divide at 1.3 miles, from which the views of the Castle Peaks continue to improve as you hike northward. This is classic high desert country with a varied mix of Joshua trees, Mojave yucca, and buckhorn cholla. The trail climbs a bit more to a saddle next to a distinctive granite dome on the left. The old roadbed ends abruptly just below the pass. Stay to the right and follow a wide sandy wash downhill. After another 0.5 mile the wash widens with a steeper gradient, bound by a surprisingly dense forest of Joshua trees. At this point several side washes have converged into the main wash. The lower wash is easy walking, bounded by occasional low walls of volcanic cliff rock with distant dark spires jutting up in every direction.

At 3.3 miles the trail ends at a stock tank and rustic old corrals—a picturesque

The Castle Peaks as seen from the trail.

remnant of the Old West. This is in one of the many recently retired grazing allotments in the preserve. The range already shows signs of recovery. For this varied 6.6-mile out and back, turn here and retrace your route to the trailhead. On the way back and close to the corrals, a two-track goes to the left. Keep to the right up the main wash. Stay to the right two more times as the wash splits en route to the saddle. At this point you'll pick up the old grazing road that leads back to the trailhead.

Miles and Directions

0.0 Start at the trailhead/wilderness boundary.

1.3 A two-track trail reaches the low divide.

1.6 At the high point the two-track trail ends. Follow the wash to the right.

2.7 Reach a confluence of side washes.

3.3 The corrals mark the end of the trail. Retrace your route to the trailhead.

6.6 Arrive back at the trailhead.

Options: *Castle Peaks Exploration*—After reaching the first rise at around mile 1.3, cross a fence and hike cross-country about 0.5 mile to the base of the highest spire.

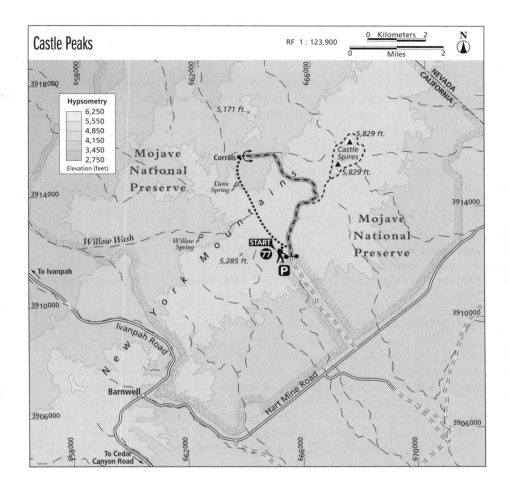

Castle Peaks

RF 1 : 123,900

0 Kilometers 2

0 Miles 2

N

Hypsometry

	6,250
	5,550
	4,850
	4,150
	3,450
	2,750

Elevation (feet)

3918000

658000

662000

666000

670000

NEVADA
CALIFORNIA

5,171 ft.

5,829 ft.

Castle
Spires

5,829 ft.

Mojave
National
Preserve

Corrals

Dove
Spring

3914000

3914000

Mojave
National
Preserve

Willow Wash

Willow
Spring

START

77

P

5,285 ft.

To Ivanpah

3910000

3910000

Ivanpah Road

New York Mountains

Barnwell

3906000

3906000

To Cedar
Canyon Road

Hart Mine Road

As you wander around the foot of the sheer walls, you'll find notches to climb up into for spectacular views framed by a wonderland of dark volcanic columns, pillars, spires, and turrets. Slopes are dotted with juniper, yucca, and scattered Joshua trees. Southward, the Lanfair Valley is ringed by distant mountain ranges stretching across the eastern flank of the preserve. This mile-high basin is home to a magnificent Joshua tree forest as well as a rich history of railroads, homesteads, and cattle ranches. You might spot golden eagles and other raptors as well as mule deer that find refuge in this rugged terrain. Plan on a pleasant 2- to 3-mile round-trip ramble to and around the base of the spires. With a roadside camp near the end of the road, you could spend a couple of interesting days exploring the Castle Peaks.

Dove Spring—From the corrals, an alternate but more strenuous return route would be to follow a side draw southwest for about 0.8 mile to Dove Spring. From there an experienced off-trail hiker can travel southeasterly up and down side ridges, winding around columns and pillars, eventually intersecting the lower end of the trail close to the trailhead.

78 Clark Mountain/North Canyon

At 7,929 feet Clark Mountain is the rooftop of the preserve. It is also an isolated enclave that is cut off from the main preserve by Interstate 15. Its elevation and isolation combine to make it the preserve's most distinctive landmark for many miles in every direction.

Start: About 43 miles northeast of Baker and 51 miles north of Kelso Depot.
Distance: 4.4 miles out and back (plus optional 5 to 6 miles out and back to the summit).
Approximate hiking time: 3 hours (optional 8 to 10 hours to and from peak).
Difficulty: Moderate in canyon; strenuous to peak.

Trail surface: Dirt and gravelly two-track for first 2 miles; steep, rocky, brushy bushwhack beyond.
Seasons: November through June for canyon hike; April through June for peak.
USGS topo map: Clark Mountain-CA (1:24,000).
Trail contact: Kelso Depot Information Center (see appendix D).

Finding the trailhead: From I-15, about 27 miles east of Baker, take the Cima Road/Excelsior Mine Road exit, turn left and drive north on the paved Excelsior Mine (Kingston) Road 7.7 miles to the graded Powerline Road. Turn right (east) and drive about 6 miles to a rougher road. Turn right (south) and drive about 2 miles to another dirt road that runs east-west along the north side of Clark Mountain. Continue left (east) for about 0.5 mile and park next to an old mining road at the lower end of the North Canyon valley. Four-wheel drive is recommended for the latter part of this route. The old road is blocked by the berm of the main road and by a wilderness boundary sign. There are no trailhead signs, so find a wide spot for parking. You can also access this spot from the east by driving west from the I-15 Yates Well exit, 5 miles south of Primm on the state line. But be warned. The steep, rocky, four-wheel-drive Colosseum Gorge Road is not for the faint of heart.

The Hike

From your jumping-off point near the wide valley mouth of Clark Mountain's north canyon, you'll have a panoramic view of the rugged north-face rim and amphitheater of the nearly 8,000-foot-high massif. This huge mountain, cut off from the rest of the preserve by I-15, has a long history of human use, including mining since the late nineteenth century. The most recent mining activity on the mountain slopes involved exploration for turquoise and copper during the 1990s. Today Clark Mountain is "rewilding," thanks to wilderness designation and sensitive nonmotorized use by the public.

Begin by hiking the two-track trail toward the walls of the upper North Canyon. The higher canyon is defined by a V-shaped notch below the formidable cliff rim of Clark Mountain. Despite its lofty elevation and north aspect, this is a

Clark Mountain is to the southwest when viewed from the east ridge.

waterless canyon, so carry plenty of water to drink. The two-track weaves up and through an alluvial fan dotted with piñon-juniper and agave. Ash-filled pits have been found on Clark Mountain where early natives roasted agave for food. Cheme-huevi, Piute, and Mojave Indians lived here over the millennia, as evidenced by pet-roglyphs and rock shelters.

At 0.9 mile a side canyon enters from the right; continue left. At mile 1.6 the canyon narrows dramatically, with soaring volcanic cliffs pocketed with cave open-ings. Watch for bighorn sheep and mule deer. You might also see feral burros, a non-native nuisance that might scold you with a loud bray just for being there. At 2 miles a massive wall forces the canyon sharply to the right. At this point the old roadbed ends and the narrow passageway becomes rough, rocky, and brushy. Look to the right for a faint game trail that climbs straight up to join a distinct path. The path drops to the canyon floor only to be blocked by a chokestone at mile 2.2. A series of steep chasms feed into the canyon here, making further up-canyon travel difficult to impossible. Retrace your route to complete this challenging exploration of the North Canyon.

Clark Mountain/North Canyon

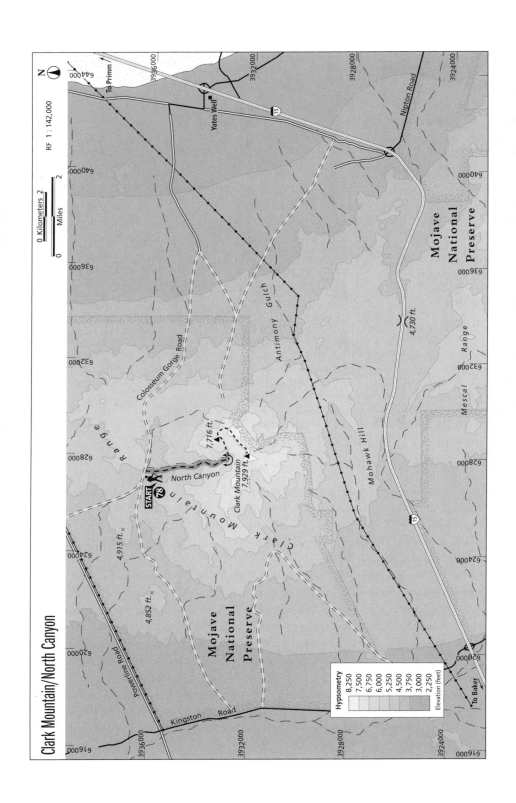

RF 1 : 142,000

0 Kilometers 2

0 Miles 2

Hypsometry

8,250
7,500
6,750
6,000
5,250
4,500
3,750
3,000
2,250

Elevation (feet)

To Primm

Yates Well

Nipton Road

Mojave National Preserve

Antimony Gulch

Colosseum Gorge Road

7,716 ft.

North Canyon

Clark Mountain 7,929 ft.

START 78

Clark Mountain Range

4,915 ft. ×

4,852 ft. ×

Mojave National Preserve

Powerline Road

Kingston Road

Mohawk Hill

Mescal Range

4,730 ft.

To Baker

Miles and Directions

0.0 Begin the hike from the wilderness boundary near the mouth of the canyon.

0.9 Where the canyon enters from the right, continue left.

1.6 The canyon narrows.

2.0 Reach the end of the old canyon roadbed.

2.2 Where the chokestone blocks the canyon, retrace your route to the trailhead.

4.4 Arrive back at the wilderness boundary.

Option: *Clark Mountain Northeast Ridge/Summit*—The peak can be climbed from this point by experienced, well-conditioned backcountry hikers. At the chokestone you've already gained 1,300 vertical feet from the trailhead, with a strenuous 1,700 feet remaining to the summit.

Begin the rock scramble by climbing straight up the left slope. You'll soon intersect a ridge that becomes more distinct as you gain elevation. The footing is loose, but handholds are solid, so long as they are carefully tested. Avoid cliffs by scrambling around slopes that are steep but usually well protected by vegetation. After about two hours of steady climbing, you'll reach a rocky point shown on the topo map as 2,352 meters (7,716 feet). From there you'll have an eagle's view of the entire north basin, rimmed by cliffs. On a clear day you'll see snowcapped Telescope Peak in Death Valley, along with numerous desert ranges far into Nevada's Great Basin.

From this rocky outcrop you can visualize a good cross-country route to the peak, which is still nearly 2 miles to the south. Drop to the nearby saddle and work up the steep side slope to the main northeast divide, and then onto the first false summit. Upon gaining the crest, the actual summit is an easy walk. Along the way you'll see stands of stately white fir gracing the higher ridges and north slopes.

The best way back down to the canyon bottom is the way you came up. Because of steep, unstable footing, the descent will take as long as the ascent. That's okay. Take your time to avoid injury. As you descend, look for feeder ridges and clear avenues to the right in order to bypass a particularly cliffy ridge that is higher and to the south. When at last you reach the canyon bottom, the gentle 2 miles back to the trailhead will seem like a cakewalk.

Death Valley National Park

D eath Valley's intimidating name is said to have originated in 1849 when an anonymous member of the forty-niners, after nearly dying while seeking a shortcut to the newly discovered California goldfields, turned around at the final view and exclaimed, "Good-bye, Death Valley!" Now it's our turn to say hello to one of the world's most imposing and contrasting landscapes. The extremes of Death Valley, from soaring snowcapped peaks to North America's hottest, driest, and lowest desert, command respect and entice discovery.

In 1933 President Herbert Hoover proclaimed Death Valley a national monument, a status less protective than that of national park because of mining conflicts. The monument was expanded in 1937 when President Franklin Roosevelt added the 300,000-acre Nevada triangle. In 1952 President Truman added forty acres of Devil's Hole in Nevada to protect a rare variety of desert pupfish. With mining a major issue in Death Valley, the 1976 Mining in Parks Act is of special significance. This law began phasing out mining in the monument by closing Death Valley to the filing of new claims. The number of old claims has since decreased from 50,000 to fewer than 150, with only one active mine remaining.

The status of the monument was further elevated in 1984 when the United Nations recognized Death Valley as part of the Mojave and Colorado International Biosphere Reserve. Finally, on October 31, 1994, Death Valley received long overdue national park classification when President Bill Clinton signed the California Desert Protection Act into law. The 2-million-acre national monument became a more than 3.3-million-acre national park, with 95 percent of the park designated wilderness. In so doing, Death Valley became the nation's largest national park outside Alaska.

A Long and Complex Geologic Past

The land of extremes that is Death Valley is best dramatized when afternoon shadows from 11,049-foot Telescope Peak are cast across the Badwater Basin, 282 feet below sea level. Combine this amazing vertical relief with recent volcanic craters,

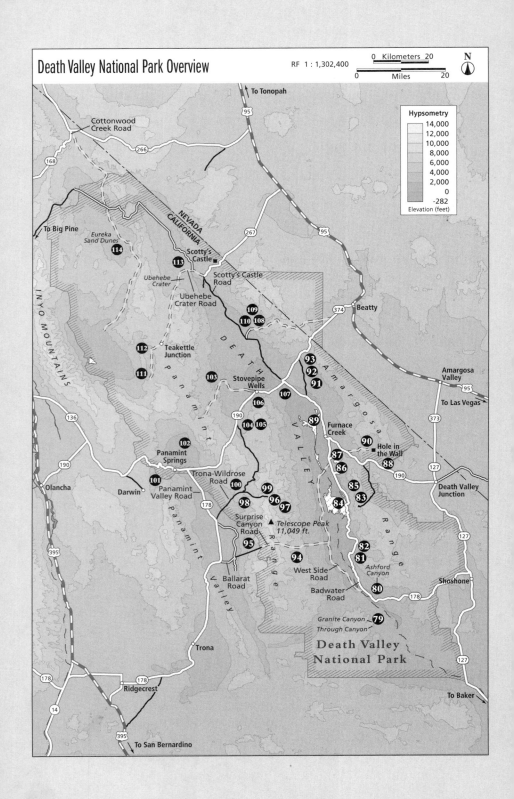

Death Valley National Park Overview

RF 1 : 1,302,400

0 Kilometers 20

0 Miles 20

N

Hypsometry

14,000
12,000
10,000
8,000
6,000
4,000
2,000
0
-282
Elevation (feet)

To Tonopah

Cottonwood
Creek Road

NEVADA
CALIFORNIA

To Big Pine

Eureka
Sand Dunes

Scotty's
Castle

Scotty's Castle
Road

Ubehebe
Crater

Ubehebe
Crater Road

Beatty

INYO MOUNTAINS

Teakettle
Junction

DEATH

Amargosa
Valley

To Las Vegas

Stovepipe
Wells

Panamint

Furnace
Creek

Hole in
the Wall

VALLEY

Panamint
Springs

Trona-Wildrose
Road

Death Valley
Junction

Olancha

Darwin

Panamint
Valley Road

Surprise
Canyon
Road

Telescope Peak
11,049 ft.

Amargosa

Range

Shoshone

Ballarat
Road

West Side
Road

Badwater
Road

Ashford
Canyon

Range

Panamint

Valley

Trona

Granite Canyon
Through Canyon

**Death Valley
National Park**

Ridgecrest

To Baker

To San Bernardino

towering sand dunes, and flood-scoured canyons and you begin to appreciate a long and complicated geologic history.

Death Valley is at the western and youngest edge of the Basin and Range Province (the Great Basin). As such, its relatively youthful topography is extreme, with mountains still growing and basins still sinking. The oldest rocks date back 1.8 billion years but have been too severely changed to be reliably interpreted for geologic history.

Rocks a mere half billion years old are more predictable. The Funeral and Panamint Mountains are made up of these weathered limestones and sandstones. The rocks point to a warm, shallow sea from around 570 million to 250 million years ago. The sea left layers of sediment and a myriad of marine fossils. Between 1933 and 1994 researchers discovered 500 species of fossil plants and animals within the monument. Now that the boundaries have been expanded by 50 percent, the new park may prove to be the most fossil-rich national park in the United States and perhaps in the world.

Death Valley is next to the boundary of two interconnected plates in the earth's crust. When the plates moved slowly in relation to each other, compression folded and fractured the brittle crust. This caused the land surface to push up and the sea to gradually recede west. Most of this faulting took place from 250 million to 70 million years ago. Active mountain building then alternated with inactive periods of mountain-reducing erosion.

Volcanic activity prevailed from seventy million to three million years ago. Mountain building stretched and weakened the earth's crust, forming weak spots through which molten material could erupt. This volcanic activity moved westward from Nevada, producing a chain of volcanoes east of the park from Furnace Creek southeast to Shoshone. Eruptions of cinder and ash account for the flamboyant colors of borate mineral deposits at Artist's Palette.

Around three million years ago, the floor of Death Valley began to form. Compression was replaced by a pulling apart of the earth's crust, causing large blocks of land to slowly slide past one another along faults. These extensional forces formed parallel north-south trending valleys and mountain ranges. The salt flats of Badwater Basin and the Panamint Range make up one block that is rotating to the east. The valley floor, known as a half-graben, continues to slip down along the fault at the foot of the Black Mountains. This dropping is evident in recently exposed fault scarps near Badwater. Meanwhile, erosion continues with flash floods carrying rocks, sand, and gravel from surrounding hillsides to alluvial fans that spread like gigantic funnels from every canyon mouth. More than 9,000 feet of sediments and salts lie beneath the half-graben floor at Badwater.

Climate has also been a major force in these ongoing changes. During the last major continental ice age, the bottom of Death Valley was covered by a system of huge lakes. As the climate warmed, the lakes disappeared—about 10,000 years ago.

Death Valley serves as a backdrop for the remains of the miner's cabin at Keane Wonder Spring.

A much smaller lake system formed 2,000 years ago during a cold period. This water then evaporated, leaving behind today's salt deposits.

The Ubehebe Craters in the northern end of the park tell the tale of recent volcanic activity of several thousand years ago. The craters were formed by violent steam explosions caused when molten material mixed with groundwater. Erosion, earthquakes, and subsidence continue to reshape the surface of one of North America's most dramatic and ever-changing landscapes.

A Tapestry of Life: Don't Let the Name Fool You

More than 1,000 plant species thrive in the incredibly wide range of elevations and habitats found within the park—from dry alkali flats below sea level to the subalpine crests of the highest Panamint summits. These species include nineteen endemics found *only* within the boundaries of the park, such as telescope bedstraw, Panamint monkey flower, and Eureka Dunes evening primrose. Another twenty-three species have the majority of their range within the park, such as magnificent lupine and

Death Valley sage. No fewer than thirteen species of cactus grow within the park. Ironically, this driest of deserts is home to more species of marsh grass than cactus.

Spring wildflowers are a pageant worth waiting for. The white of desert-star, red of Indian paintbrush, pink of desert five-spot, yellow of desert gold, and blue of Arizona lupine are what dreams are made of. But as with everything, there are good years and bad years. A spectacular year for the showy plants of these desert annuals depends on well-spaced rainfall throughout winter and early spring, enough warming sun, and few drying winds. The premier blooming periods in the park are usually late February to mid-April in the lower elevations of valley floors and alluvial fans, early April to early May for midslopes up to 4,000 feet, and late April to early June above 4,000 feet in the Panamints and other mountain ranges.

Death Valley is home to at least fifty-one species of mammals, thirty-six species of reptiles, five species of amphibians, and six species of fishes. Some of the animals, such as desert bighorn sheep, live near springs in inaccessible mountains and canyons. The nocturnal kit fox is common in most of Death Valley. Coyotes may be seen from the salt flats up to the highest mountain plateaus. Some species have been introduced, such as the burro was in the 1880s. The reptile list includes the threatened desert tortoise and the mostly nocturnal Mojave sidewinder rattlesnake. Five species of desert pupfish live in the park, four of which are endemic to Death Valley. These endemics are the Saratoga pupfish, Salt Creek pupfish, threatened Cottonball Marsh pupfish, and the endangered Devil's Hole pupfish. These tiny members of the killfish family vary from 1 to 2.5 inches long. They lived in ancient freshwater lakes during the last ice age. As the climate became drier, the pupfish became isolated in widely separated warm springs and creeks, gradually adapting to higher temperatures and increased salinity.

Human History

Death Valley has been the site of at least four Native American cultures, beginning about 10,000 years ago with a group of hunter-gatherers known as "the Nevares Spring people." Game was abundant during this wetter period. As the climate became drier, they were replaced by the Mesquite Flat people about 4,000 years later. Then the Saratoga Spring people arrived about 2,000 years ago when the hot, dry desert was similar to today's conditions. These people were skilled hunters who created large, intricate stone patterns in the valley. Nomadic desert Shoshone moved into the valley about 1,000 years ago. Like many people today, they camped near water sources in the valley during winter, then headed up into the cooler mountains during summer to escape searing heat.

The first non-native people to enter the valley were two groups of emigrants on their way to the California goldfields in 1849. From the 1880s to early 1900s, mining was sporadic in the region. Lack of suitable transportation limited mining to only the highest-grade ore. Perhaps the best-known but shortest-lived mine was the Harmony

Borax Works, active from 1883 to 1888. It was most famous for its twenty-mule wagons and the *Death Valley Days* radio and television programs. W. T. Coleman built the wagons that hauled the processed mineral 165 miles across the desert to the railroad at Mojave. Gold and silver mining picked up in the early 1900s with such large-scale ventures as the Keane Wonder Mine, but then came the Panic of 1907. Profitable large-scale hardrock mining in Death Valley ended around 1915. During World War II talc was mined here until markets made mining unprofitable. In 1989 these talc-mining claims were bought by the Conservation Foundation and donated to the National Park Service in 1992.

Weather

This land of extremes doesn't end with topography, vertical relief, and a Noah's ark of wildlife. Recorded temperatures range from a sizzling 134 degrees to a freezing low of 15 degrees. The valley experiences an average annual temperature of 76 pleasant degrees—somewhat deceiving given the summer averages at well above 100 degrees. Temperatures will be 3 to 5 degrees cooler along with increased precipitation for every 1,000-foot vertical increase in elevation. One balmy July day in 1972, with the air temperature at 128 degrees, a ground temperature of 201 degrees was measured at Furnace Creek. With no protective shade, any attempt to hike the salt flats in these conditions could be a terminal experience. For hiking comfort, November to April is hard to beat. Average highs are in the 60- to 90-degree range on the valley floor, cooling considerably at higher elevations. The loftiest mountaintops are often snow-covered from November to May.

Precipitation figures can be misleading, as an annual average of less than 2 inches of rain falls in Death Valley. The mountain ranges can catch torrential winter downpours, causing flash flooding, road closures, and trail washouts. To check on current road and trail conditions, consult the Death Valley Web site (www.nps.gov/deva) before heading to the desert.

Rules to Enjoy the Park

At this time overnight backcountry hikers and campers are not required to obtain a permit, which is unusual for a "big name" national park. This may change, so always check the park's Web site or the visitor center for the latest regulations. However, filling out a backcountry registration form is recommended for backpackers. These forms are available at the Furnace Creek Visitor Center or at any ranger station.

Limited open-desert car camping is allowed at Death Valley, a sprawling park with more than three million acres of wilderness and 600-plus miles of dirt roads. The basic rule is that backcountry camping is permitted 2 miles beyond any paved

◄ *Dante's View provides a spectacular panorama of Badwater 6,000 feet below, with the snow-capped 11,049-foot Telescope Peak in the distance.*

road, day-use-only area, or developed area. Car campers must use preexisting campsites and park next to the roadway to reduce impact and to avoid violating the wilderness boundary, which, in most cases, closely parallels the road. A high-clearance vehicle is usually needed to travel 2 or more miles from pavement on a dirt road that is open for camping. Camping is not allowed on day-use-only roads, including the Titus Canyon Road, West Side Road, Wildrose Road, and Racetrack Road from Teakettle Junction to Homestake Dry Camp. Camping is also prohibited at three historic mining areas, including the Ubehebe Lead Mine. Actually, the safe thing to do is to avoid camping at any mining area. Backcountry camping is not allowed on the valley floor from 2 miles north of Stovepipe Wells south to Ashford Mill.

Overnight group size is limited to fifteen people and no more than six vehicles. Campsites in the backcountry must be at least 200 yards from any water source to avoid disturbing wildlife in these fragile and limited sites. In view of the recent park and wilderness designations at Death Valley, it is important to obtain a copy of the latest backcountry regulations at the Furnace Creek Visitor Center or nearest ranger station.

Off-road vehicle use is prohibited, not only because the land away from roads is wilderness and closed to motorized use, but also because the desert is fragile and painfully slow to recover from damage. Bicycles are permitted on all paved and open dirt roads but are not allowed on trails, off roads, or in park wilderness. Campfires are only allowed in fire pits at developed campgrounds. If you want a fire, bring wood in from outside; gathering the scarce wood here is unlawful. Remember that the park is a museum of undisturbed nature, so removal of any rocks, wood, plants, animals, or historic artifacts is prohibited.

No matter how pitiful the begging coyote may appear, do not feed wildlife. To do so causes them to depend on unnatural food sources, which is tantamount to a death sentence. Speaking of animals, leave your pets at home if at all possible. They must be restrained at all times and are not allowed off roads, on trails, or in park wilderness. Of course, any type of weapon is strictly prohibited in the park.

Campgrounds, Services, Fees

Nine developed National Park Service campgrounds with more than 1,500 sites are well distributed in the central to north-central region of the park. Four of these are free, one of which, Wildrose, is open year-round, weather permitting. The Wildrose Campground is reached by way of the rough Wildrose Canyon Road. The other three higher-elevation campgrounds, Emigrant, Thorndike, and Mahogany Flat, are open spring to fall depending on weather conditions. Of the five fee campgrounds, Furnace Creek and Mesquite Spring are open all year. Texas Spring, Sunset, and Stovepipe Wells are at or below sea level and are open October to April.

The main visitor center and Death Valley Natural History Association (DVNHA) is located at Furnace Creek, with other visitor centers at Beatty, Nevada, and Scotty's Castle. Scotty's Castle Visitor Center and Museum is open every day all year from 8:30 A.M. to 5:00 P.M. The main visitor center and museum at Furnace Creek is open from 8:00 A.M. to 5:00 P.M. These hours are subject to change, so check at the park upon your arrival. The National Park Service has prepared an excellent series of free handouts on such topics as geology, mining history, plants, wildflowers, wildlife, special points of interest, and more. During the high season of November through April, rangers and naturalists present evening talks and guided nature walks.

The two park entrance stations are located at Furnace Creek and Grapevine, which is 3.5 miles from Scotty's Castle. The entrance fee is $20 per vehicle and is good for seven days. A Death Valley National Park annual pass is also available for $40. A $50 Golden Eagle Pass provides unlimited admission to the entire National Park System nationwide and is good for one year. U.S. citizens sixty-two and older can purchased a one-time Golden Age Pass for $10, which allows unlimited entry to all National Park System areas. Golden Age Pass holders also receive a 50 percent discount on campground fees.

Food, supplies, and gas can be purchased at Furnace Creek Ranch and Stovepipe Wells. Fuel can also be bought at Scotty's Castle. Distances in the sprawling park are vast, so be sure to travel with plenty of gas, water, food, and other necessary supplies.

The few trails in the park that are formally maintained are described in some of the recommended hikes that follow. Use trails in drainages may largely disappear after a flash flood. Many of the trailless routes follow natural corridors, such as deep canyons. In the desert, hiking use is generally light with vast distances between trailheads, which, in turn, lead to routes without directional signs. Lack of hiker conveniences found in other, more heavily visited parks and wilderness is more than made up for by solitude, and by the spirit of adventure that awaits those willing to explore this magnificent park on foot.

How to Get There

Primary road access to the park from the south is via California Highway 127 from Interstate 15 at Baker. California Highway 178 leads west into the park from CA 127 near Shoshone. California Highway 190 heads west into the park from CA 127 at Death Valley Junction. On the west side, CA 178 takes off from U.S. Highway 395 and enters the park by way of Panamint Valley. CA 190 takes off to the east from US 395 at Olancha, entering the park just west of Panamint Springs. The network of roads within the park run the gamut, from all-weather pavement to a series of rocky washboard ruts that can loosen every bolt and try the patience of the most determined motorist. The closest large commercial airport is at Las Vegas, about 135 miles southeast of Furnace Creek.

Death Valley National Park Hikes at a Glance

Hike and Hike Number	Distance	Difficulty*	Features	Page
Ashford Canyon/Mine (80)	3.0 miles	M	mine site	274
Badwater (84)	1.0 mile	E	salt flats	286
Dante's View (83)	1.0 mile	E	vista	283
Darwin Falls (101)	3.0 miles	S	stream, fall, vista	333
Desolation Canyon (86)	5.2 miles	M	canyon/vista	290
Eureka Dunes (114)	3.0 miles	M	sand dunes	375
Fall Canyon (109)	16.0 miles	S	dry fall, canyon	359
Golden Canyon/ Gower Gulch Loop (87)	6.5 miles	M	scenery, geology	293
Grotto Canyon (105)	4.0 miles	E	canyon	348
Harmony Borax Works (89)	1.0 mile	E	historic site, salt flats (option)	298
Hummingbird Spring (98)	3.0 miles	M	historic site, vista	327
Hungry Bill's Ranch/ Johnson Canyon (94)	3.8 miles	S	historic site, vista	312
Keane Wonder Mine (91)	4.0 miles	S	mill and mine site	304
Keane Wonder Spring (92)	2.0 miles	E	spring, mine site	307
Little Bridge Canyon (106)	7.0 miles	S	canyon	350
Marble Canyon (103)	9.6 miles	M	canyon, archaeology	340
Monarch Canyon/Mine (93)	3.0 miles	E	dry fall, mill site	309
Mosaic Canyon (104)	3.6 miles	M	canyon	344
Natural Bridge (85)	2.0 miles	E	geology, canyon	288
Nemo Canyon (100)	3.6 miles	M	canyon	331
Panamint Dunes (102)	9.0 miles	M	sand dunes	336
Pyramid Canyon (88)	4.0 miles	M	canyon, geology	297
Red Wall Canyon (110)	7.0 miles	M	canyon	362
Salt Creek Interpretive Trail (107)	0.5 mile	E	nature trail	353
Sidewinder Canyon (81)	4.6 miles	M	canyon	276
South Fork Hanaupah Canyon (97)	6.0 miles	M	mine site, scenery	324
Surprise Canyon/Panamint City (95)	13.0 miles	S	stream, canyon, mine/townsite	316
Telescope Peak (96)	14.0 miles	S	vista	320
Through-Granite Canyons (79)	15.0 miles	S	remoteness, scenery	271
Titus Canyon Narrows (108)	4.2 miles	E	canyon	356
Klare Spring	12.0 miles	S	canyon, spring	358
Ubehebe/Little Hebe Craters (113)	1.5 miles	E	volcanic craters	372
Ubehebe Lead Mine/ Corridor Canyon (112)	6.0 miles	M	mine site/canyon	369
Ubehebe Peak (111)	6.2 miles	S	vista	365
Upper Hole-in-the-Wall (90)	11.0 miles	S	canyon, geology	300
Wildrose Peak (99)	8.4 miles	S	vista	329
Willow Canyon (82)	5.0 miles	M	canyon	280

*E=easy, M=moderate, S=strenuous

79 Through-Granite Canyons

A long, challenging canyon loop in the wild, lightly visited Owlshead Mountains, these canyons take you to a remote desert range in the southern end of the park.

Start: About 54 miles south of Furnace Creek.
Distance: 15-mile lollipop.
Approximate hiking time: 8 to 10 hours.
Difficulty: Strenuous.
Trail surface: Off-trail sandy washes, gravelly fans, and canyons with short rocky sections.

Seasons: November through March.
USGS topo maps: Confidence Hills East-CA and Confidence Hills West-CA (1:24,000).
Trail contact: Furnace Creek Visitor Center & Museum (see appendix D).

Finding the trailhead: From Ashford Junction on Badwater Road (California Highway 178), 26 miles southwest of Shoshone and 48 miles south of Furnace Creek, drive south on the wide gravel Harry Wade Road. After about 5.9 slow miles, look for a wide parking spot alongside the bermed roadway, which will be next to Confidence Wash and about 1 mile before the Confidence Mill site. Driving Harry Wade Road from the south is not recommended because it is four-wheel drive at best and impassable during flooding.

The Hike

Upon reaching the jumping-off point for this lengthy desert trek, you'll have driven through a section of Death Valley known as "the Narrows." The brown Confidence Hills to the immediate west are an eroded scarp of the southern Death Valley fault. It was once believed that the adventurous Harry Wade family used the road as an escape route from Death Valley in 1850.

From your parking spot, you can see the prominent rounded hill beyond the Confidence Hills that forms the southern gateway to Through Canyon. A higher range of mountains rises beyond. Begin by hiking southwesterly toward the trailing southern edge of the Confidence Hills. Soon you'll cross the broad, gravelly creosote plain of the normally dry Amargosa River. Skirt around the hills to the lower wash of Granite Canyon. Hike up the wide, high-walled wash to the forks of the wash at about 2 miles. Cross the wash and continue to hike southwesterly toward Through Canyon, reaching the mouth at about 4.3 miles. To the immediate south is the prominent rounded hill that you could see from the trailhead. Look back, to the east, for varied views of fans, buttes, and the jagged teeth of volcanic peaks.

Hillsides bordering the wash are a jumble of volcanic rock with granitic bedrock. In the spring you might see flowering buttercups and the tiny blue flowers of chia along with desert holly, smoke trees, creosote and saltbush, to name only a few. You'll follow the trails of feral burros for the next couple of miles, with color-banded shades of red, white, and brown rock overhead. The valley splits about 2.3 miles above the mouth; keep to the right. Another mile brings you to a broad upper

Looking down the upper reaches of Through Canyon.

basin. The main wash curves left to the horizon. Angle to the right (north) for the crossover to Granite Canyon. Continue right as the valley steepens, reaching a saddle between the two canyons at 7.8 miles.

The route follows a short side canyon down to the floor of Granite Canyon, guarded by great spires and rock columns. From here turn left for a short 0.5-mile round-trip exploration of the narrow upper reaches of Granite Canyon. You'll quickly come to an 8-foot dry fall that can be readily climbed. But the next chokestone, only 50 yards beyond, is more difficult. This is a good turnaround point for the hike back down Granite Canyon. Granite Canyon is steeper and more bouldery than Through Canyon but can be easily negotiated on a mostly sandy wash. After another mile the canyon widens to a valley. Low granite walls on the left side lead up to a colorful red chasm. Overall, Granite is a wonderful contrast to Through Canyon, especially in the upper end, where moderate bouldering and narrow canyons are true delights. Along the way you'll see broken quartz monzonite that is unlike most other places in the park.

After exiting the wide mouth of Granite Canyon at 11 miles, continue down the wash toward the southern edge of the Confidence Hills. When you reach the base

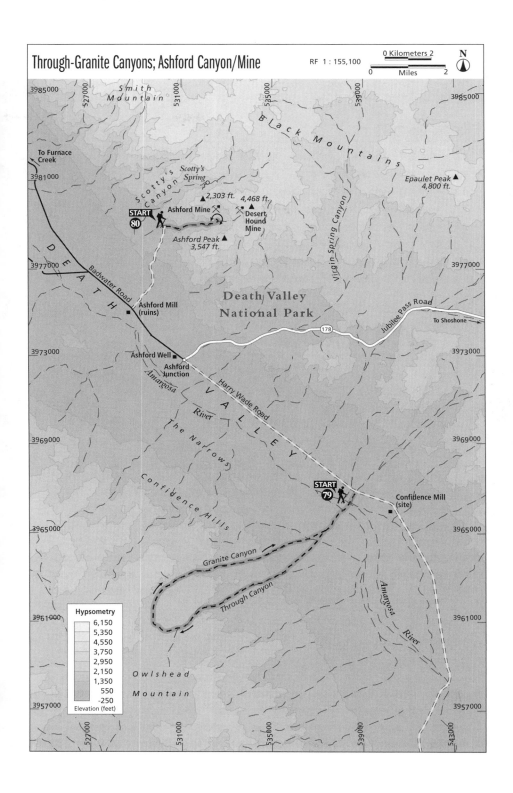

Through-Granite Canyons; Ashford Canyon/Mine

RF 1 : 155,100

0 Kilometers 2

0 Miles 2

N

Smith Mountain

527000 531000 535000 539000

3985000

B l a c k   M o u n t a i n s

To Furnace Creek

3981000

Scotty's Canyon

Scotty's Spring

▲ 2,303 ft.   4,468 ft.
              ▲

START 80 Ashford Mine ✕   ◦ Desert Hound Mine

Ashford Peak ▲
3,547 ft.

Epaulet Peak ▲
4,800 ft.

Virgin Spring Canyon

3977000

Badwater Road

Ashford Mill
(ruins) ■

Death Valley National Park

Jubilee Pass Road

To Shoshone →

178

3973000

Ashford Well ■

Ashford Junction

Amargosa

Harry Wade Road

River

V A L L E Y

3969000

The Narrows

Confidence Hills

START 79

Confidence Mill
(site) ■

3965000

Granite Canyon

Through Canyon

Amargosa

River

3961000

Hypsometry	
	6,150
	5,350
	4,550
	3,750
	2,950
	2,150
	1,350
	550
	-250

Elevation (feet)

Owlshead
Mountain

3957000

527000 531000 535000 539000 543000

3985000
3981000
3977000
3973000
3969000
3965000
3961000
3957000

D E A T H

of these brown hills in the serpentine steep-walled wash, you'll intersect the stem of this "lollipop" loop. Roughly retrace the first 2 miles of the route in a northeasterly direction back to Confidence Wash, thereby completing this adventuresome 15-mile exploration.

Miles and Directions

0.0   Start at the parking area at Confidence Wash on Harry Wade Road.

2.0   Arrive at the southern edge of the Confidence Hills.

4.3   Arrive at the mouth of Through Canyon.

7.4   Angle right (north) to the Granite-Through Canyon divide.

7.8   Arrive at the divide between the Granite and Through Canyons.

11.0   Arrive at the mouth of Granite Canyon.

13.0   Arrive again at the southern edge of the Confidence Hills.

15.0   Return to the parking area at Confidence Wash on Harry Wade Road.

80 Ashford Canyon/Mine

An extensive mine site with several intact buildings lies up a remote and narrow canyon. The rocky mining road has become a hiking trail, leading to the historic early-twentieth-century mine site.

See map on page 273.
Start: About 45 miles south of Furnace Creek.
Distance: 3 miles out and back.
Approximate hiking time: 2 to 3 hours.
Difficulty: Moderate.
Trail surface: Rocky trail.

Seasons: October through April.
USGS topo map: Shore Line Butte-CA (1:24,000).
Trail contact: Furnace Creek Visitor Center & Museum (see appendix D).

Finding the trailhead: From California Highway 127, 1.7 miles north of Shoshone, turn left (west) on California Highway 178 (East Side Badwater Road/Jubilee Pass Road), which leads to the park boundary. After entering the park, drive 25.1 miles to the signed Ashford Mill Road on the left, 1.9 miles north of Ashford Junction and 26.9 miles south of Badwater. Turn right (east) onto the unsigned Ashford Canyon Road leading northeast directly across from the Ashford Mill site. If coming from the north, drive 44.5 miles south of Furnace Creek on Badwater Road to Ashford Canyon Road on the left. Follow this four-wheel-drive road for 3 miles to the mouth of Ashford Canyon. Park and hike from here.

The Hike

The Ashford (Golden Treasure) Mine was discovered in 1907 and was sold a few years later to supply gold ore to the Ashford Mill. The early years were probably its

Ashford Mine buildings 1.6 miles up Ashford Canyon are surrounded by high, rugged peaks.

most productive, since the mine sold for more money than it ultimately yielded. The inefficiency of the mill was at least partly to blame.

From the mouth of the canyon, the old mining trail climbs steeply up the left side of the deep, narrow Ashford Canyon. Rock slides and erosion are gradually erasing any sign of the trail as nature reclaims the land. But there is still enough evidence of rock construction and built-up roadbeds to make this route fairly easy to follow.

After dropping into the canyon bottom, the road crosses the wash several times. Several steep sections of slanted rock are avoided as the trail pitches right or left. Huge round mine timbers and scattered diggings are found about halfway up. At 1.3 miles the road crosses the wash and contours to the left around the slope, climbs slightly, and then drops to the mining camp.

The buildings are still somewhat intact, containing some of the furniture and appliances used by the miners. Although they made no effort to clean up their trash, one has to marvel at the incredible determination and optimism the miners must have had to carve such an extensive operation out of such difficult terrain. The miners sure had a view in this southern stretch of the Black Mountains, with Ashford

Peak soaring to the south and the rugged canyon below opening to the Owlshead and Panamint Mountains westward. Retrace your route to complete this 3-mile round-trip exploration of some of Death Valley's mining history.

Miles and Directions

0.0 Start at the trailhead at the mouth of Ashford Canyon.

0.3 Climb out of the wash (right), bypassing a dry fall/rock slide.

0.5 The trail follows the wash up a rough, rocky surface.

1.3 The trail crosses the wash and climbs the slope to the left.

1.5 Arrive at Ashford (Golden Treasure) Mine.

3.0 Return to the trailhead by the same route.

Options: Other nearby mining sites include the Desert Hound Mine high on the mountaintop a mile to the northeast, and Scotty's Canyon, which is the next canyon to the north a couple of miles. With the aid of a topo map, a 4-mile round-trip hike to Scotty's Canyon is well worth exploring. The canyon has perennial water from a spring.

81 Sidewinder Canyon

This steep, rugged canyon opens to grand vistas of the floor of Death Valley. The canyon out-and-back hike has good highway access, requiring no four-wheel-drive vehicle. Narrow tunnels and sheer rock slots require moderate scrambling to dramatic views of Death Valley. Special attractions include several short slot side canyons that invite further exploration. The canyon also lies within bighorn-sheep habitat.

Start: About 34 miles south of Furnace Creek.
Distance: 4.6-mile out and back in main canyon plus short side hikes in slot canyons.
Approximate hiking time: 3 to 4 hours.
Difficulty: Moderate.
Trail surface: Dirt path, rocky alluvial fan, with short stretches of cross-country and moderate rock climbing.
Seasons: November through April.
USGS topo map: Gold Valley-CA (1:24,000).
Trail contact: Furnace Creek Visitor Center & Museum (see appendix D).

Finding the trailhead: From the Furnace Creek Visitor Center, drive 1 mile south to the junction of California Highways 178 (Badwater Road) and 190; turn south on Badwater Road and drive 33 miles to an unsigned dirt road that leads 0.2 mile left (southeast). This turn is easy to miss, but it is just before the highway makes a half-circle to the west (toward the valley). Proceed on the dirt road for 0.2 mile to a T that contains a short stretch of pavement. Turn right on

The narrows of Sidewinder Canyon at 2.2 miles. ▶

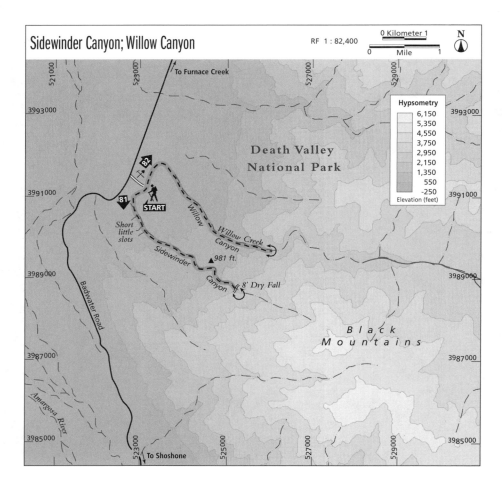

Sidewinder Canyon; Willow Canyon

RF 1 : 82,400

0 Kilometer 1

0 Mile 1

N

To Furnace Creek

521000 523000 527000 529000

3993000

Death Valley
National Park

Hypsometry

	6,150
	5,350
	4,550
	3,750
	2,950
	2,150
	1,350
	550
	-250

Elevation (feet)

3993000

3991000

82

81 START

Willow

Short little slots

Willow Creek Canyon

Sidewinder

▲ 981 ft.

Canyon

8' Dry Fall

3991000

3989000

Badwater Road

3989000

Black
Mountains

3987000

3987000

Amargosa River

3985000

523000

To Shoshone

525000 527000 529000

3985000

the T and drive to its end in less than 0.1 mile and park; this is the trailhead for both the Willow Canyon hike and the Sidewinder Canyon hike. The mouth of Sidewinder Canyon cannot be seen from the parking area, but it is straight south about 0.3 mile up and across a rocky alluvial fan.

The Hike

This excursion into the lower end of rugged Sidewinder Canyon provides a solid introduction to the wild canyon country of the Black Mountains.

Begin by hiking 0.3 mile southward across a rocky alluvial fan to the mouth of Sidewinder Canyon. The canyon opens to a broad wash exactly at sea level, but still high above the salt flats to the northeast. At 1 mile the graveled wash widens dramatically to a huge semicircle presenting a grand view of Death Valley and the Panamint Range beyond. A narrow, dark, cavelike slot canyon leads up to the right, enticing you to take a short side trip. At 1.2 miles another tight slot canyon enters from the right. This side canyon is also short and well worth a quick exploratory look. Thereafter, turn right up the main wash.

Continuing up Sidewinder, the wide wash soon funnels into a more narrow canyon. At 1.8 miles more "slots" appear in the rock with another slanted rock drop-off. Here the conglomerate canyon walls are steep with deep overhangs and little alcoves along the narrow passageway. This portion of the canyon is bound by high rugged mountains with markedly higher rhyolite walls along the face of the main uplift.

At around 2 miles the canyon hosts a series of steep, slanted rocks that can be readily climbed and descended with moderate levels of skill and agility. This stretch of Sidewinder has impressive slots in the rock, with narrows intensifying the canyon experience.

At 2.3 miles an 8-foot dry fall is encountered. An experienced rock climber could scale this dry waterfall and continue up the canyon, but most people would have a difficult time pulling themselves over the exposed ledge. The base of this short waterfall is actually an excellent turnaround point for this stimulating 4.6 mile round-trip exploration of Sidewinder Canyon.

Miles and Directions

0.0 The trailhead is just east of the Badwater Road.

0.3 Arrive at the mouth of Sidewinder Canyon.

0.9 A large side canyon enters from the right.

1.0 A gravelly wash widens to a huge circular amphitheater.

1.2 A narrow slot side canyon enters from the right.

1.8–2.2 More "slots" appear in the canyon, with slanted rock to traverse.

2.3 An 8-foot dry fall is encountered in Sidewinder Canyon (turnaround point).

4.6 Return to the trailhead.

82 Willow Canyon

Seasonal waterfalls provide a suitable home for bighorn sheep in Willow Canyon.

See map on page 278.
Start: About 34 miles south of Furnace Creek.
Length: 5 miles out and back.
Approximate hiking time: 2 to 3 hours.
Difficulty: Moderate.

Trail surface: Sandy trail with rocky sections.
Seasons: November through April.
USGS topo map: Gold Valley-CA (1:24,000).
Trail contact: Furnace Creek Visitor Center & Museum (see appendix D).

Finding the trailhead: From the California Highways 190 and 178 junction at the Furnace Creek Inn, go south on Badwater Road (CA 178) for 33 miles to an unsigned dirt road on your left. Drive 0.2 mile to a T-shaped paved parking area adjacent to a gravel pit used during the construction of the East Road in Death Valley. The unmarked trail leaves from the northwest corner of the T lot. This parking area is also the trailhead for Sidewinder Canyon.

The Hike

Although the ratio of hiking the alluvial fan to hiking in the canyon may seem lopsided, this hike features a gem of a canyon. Clearly a bighorn-sheep playground, Willow Canyon cuts short your visit at a 70-foot wall with a spectacular ribbon waterfall in season. Prior to that obstacle the canyon winds its narrow way like a street in a medieval city through sheer rhyolite walls, with a tinkling stream intermittently flowing down its center. Small falls, a shelf fall, and finally a long ribbon fall make the passage of the stream a delightful symphony of watery music.

The trip to this canyon follows a use trail that seeks the sandy sections of the fan and wash. Upon leaving the parking area, head northeast, staying below the eroding ash hillsides and their alluvial fans. The sloping forms of these latter features are the southern boundary of the Willow Canyon wash. Beyond their tilting faces, to the northeast, is a vertical wall of the same volcanic ash. This vertical wall is the northern boundary of Willow Canyon wash, and it is clearly seen as you wind your way up the fan following the sandy use trail, which takes you into the wash and on to the canyon itself.

Since you cannot see the canyon from the parking area—only the notch in the mountains beyond the volcanic ash hills suggests it—it is an exciting and abrupt change when the wash enters the canyon. Sheer rust-colored rhyolite walls tower above the gray gravel of the canyon floor. From the brightness of the open wash in the valley, you are suddenly enshrouded in cool shadows. The warm wind of the valley becomes a cool breeze within the canyon walls. And, if the season is right, the sound of running water cascading over the eroding canyon floor breaks the silence.

Ribbon falls punctuate the end of the Willow Canyon hike.

Plentiful sheep sign (tracks, scat, etc.) confirms that this is bighorn-sheep habitat, but it is unlikely that you will spot these elusive animals. If lucky enough to do so, please report sheep sightings to park personnel at the visitor center. The presence of water in Willow Canyon makes it a popular spot for the sheep.

Even in season, the stream in Willow Canyon is intermittent. At times it disappears underground, only to reappear again as another waterfall. Thus playing a hide-and-seek game, the stream brings visual and aural delight to the hiker. At 2.4 miles the stream drops over an extended shelf of rock in a 3-foot fall (easily climbed via a rock-step to the side). Immediately above the shelf, the stream vanishes again. The canyon narrows to less than 15 feet in width as the water-polished walls seem to close the canyon completely. Emerging from the narrows 0.1 mile later, you are confronted with the barricade that terminates the hike: a 70-foot sheer fall rising above you. The stream, when running, comes over this precipice in a silky ribbon. When dry, the fall is also striking for its marbleized water-smoothed surface.

The return trip from the canyon involves retracing your steps. Leaving the canyon's watery world is done with reluctance; Willow Canyon resembles an oasis at the southern edge of Death Valley.

Miles and Directions

0.0–0.7 Use the trail across the sandy sections of the alluvial fan to the mouth of the wash.

0.7–2.1 Use the trail up the wash to the canyon mouth.

2.1–2.5 Hike the canyon trail to the dry/wet fall (depends upon season).

5.0   Return to the trailhead.

83 Dante's View

This short, easy hike offers magnificent panoramic views of the highest and lowest points in the continental United States. Surrounded by some of the most dramatic and colorful relief found anywhere, you also enjoy the astounding vertical relief of being nearly 6,000 feet directly above the lowest spot in the nation at Badwater.

Start: About 24 miles south of Furnace Creek.
Distance: 1 mile out and back.
Approximate hiking time: Less than 1 hour.
Difficulty: Easy.
Trail surface: Clear trail; paved road access.

Seasons: October through June.
USGS topo map: Dantes View-CA (1:24,000).
Trail contact: Furnace Creek Visitor Center & Museum (see appendix D).

Dante's View provides breathtaking perspective on the amazing vertical relief between Badwater at minus 282 feet and snow-capped 11,049-foot Telescope Peak in the distance.

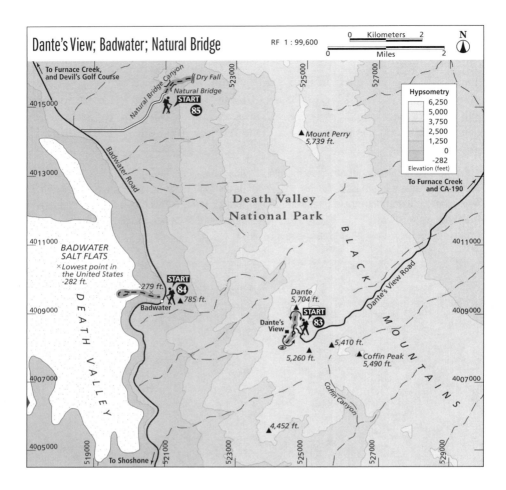

Dante's View; Badwater; Natural Bridge   RF 1 : 99,600

Hypsometry

	6,250
	5,000
	3,750
	2,500
	1,250
	0
	-282

Elevation (feet)

Finding the trailhead: From California Highway 190, 11.9 miles southeast of the Furnace Creek Visitor Center and 18 miles west of Death Valley Junction, turn south on the signed Dante's View Road (paved, all-weather). Drive 13.2 miles on this steep, winding road to its end at the Dante's View parking area. The unsigned path to Dante Point takes off to the north from the parking area and is clearly visible from the parking area as it climbs toward Dante Point.

The Hike

If at all possible, take this hike in the early morning so that the sun is at your back for better photography and for enhanced enjoyment of the superlative vistas and astounding 5,704-foot drop to the salt flats of Badwater, which sit at 282 feet below sea level. The temperature at Dante's View averages 25 degrees cooler than that of Badwater. This exposed location is usually windy, necessitating a windbreak garment during the hike.

This lofty vantage point in the Black Mountains enables you to almost see, or at least visualize, how the mountains are both slowly moving to the left (south) and rising relative to the surrounding terrain. Looking across Death Valley to the highest point in the park, 11,049-foot Telescope Peak, it is easy to note the major vegetative life zones stretching westward like a giant map. Bristlecone and limber pines thrive high in the Panamint Range. Below is the piñon–juniper zone. Dante's View is situated in a hotter, drier midslope of blackbrush and sage. Floods from the mountains result in graveled fans with spreading root species such as creosote bush. Fresh water displaces salt from the edges of fans, allowing mesquite to grow. Pickleweed gains a foothold in the brackish water below these edges. The muddy tans and grays of the valley floor grade into white beds of almost pure salt—a chemical desert.

From the parking lot, hike north along the road for 0.1 mile to where the Dante Point trail begins a fairly steep climb up the hill. Soon it winds to the left (west) and contours gently along the west slope of the mountain. This contour route provides an even more impressive view down to Badwater, with an almost overwhelming sense of vertical relief—more than a mile straight down! At 0.3 mile the trail intersects the summit ridge, then climbs the short distance to the 5,704-foot high point. Although unofficial, the trail is clear, well defined, and easy to follow. Return the way you came to complete this 1-mile out-and-back ridge walk—and don't forget your camera.

For a slightly different and highly worthwhile perspective, hike a well-used path 0.25 mile southwest of the parking area. The rock outcropping at the point of the ridge is especially welcome as a windbreak for setting up a tripod for early-morning photography.

84 Badwater

A perfectly flat hike on a boardwalk leads you onto the salt flats at the lowest point in the United States. This vast bed of salt lies 282 feet below sea level.

See map on page 284.
Start: About 17 miles south of Furnace Creek.
Distance: 1 mile out and back.
Approximate hiking time: Less than 1 hour.
Difficulty: Easy.

Trail surface: Clear salt flat.
Seasons: Late October through March.
USGS topo map: Badwater-CA (1:24,000).
Trail contact: Furnace Creek Visitor Center & Museum (see appendix D).

The view to the northeast from the salt flats of Badwater—282 feet below sea level.

Finding the trailhead: On Badwater Road, 16.7 miles south of the California Highway 190/Badwater (California Highway 178) junction at the Furnace Creek Inn, the signed parking area for Badwater is on the west side of the road.

The Hike

As bleak as it looks, a hike onto the salt flats at Badwater is arguably the ultimate Death Valley experience. If you have been to Dante's View or Telescope Peak, you probably saw the human "ants" on the white expanse of valley floor and wondered what could be so fascinating. Here you will find individuals, especially families, cavorting like they're at the beach or enjoying a spring snow. Just being out here on the boardwalk gives a genuine sense of the enormity of the salt flats.

The hike begins at the parking area beneath the cliffs that soar up to Dante's View, 5,755 feet above. There's a SEA LEVEL sign on the cliff face, high above Badwater, making very clear what minus-282 feet represent. Walk out to the salt flats on the boardwalk. Getting away from the highway is essential to get a sense of the magnitude of the salt flats.

Here fresh salt crystals are forming as groundwater percolates to the surface, bringing salt that crystallizes as the water hastily evaporates—chemistry in action. If you sit on the edge of the boardwalk and study the miniaturized terrain of the salt flats, you will find yourself among tiny salt pinnacles, a miniature mountainous world at the bottom of this mountainous basin. In close contact with the surface, you will also discover that salt is a tough commodity. The white flooring of the flats is only inches thick, but surprisingly firm. Salt's power as an erosive force is noteworthy in this desert, where it functions much like frost heaves and ice do in a wet climate. Salt crystals grow and force apart boulders, breaking them down to be further eroded by wind and water.

Above the microworld of salt, the world of Death Valley soars. To the west is Telescope Peak (11,049 feet), the highest point in the park, less than 20 miles away. The difference in elevation between Badwater and Telescope Peak is one of the largest in the United States.

A hike at Badwater is an essential introduction to the expanse of the valley floor. The emigrants and the miners who lived in this environment were a tough lot.

85 Natural Bridge

An easy, sloped canyon leads to a natural bridge that arches over the trail. The geological phenomena—faults, slipfaulting, chutes and dry fall, natural arch formation—are explained at the trailhead exhibits.

See map on page 284.
Start: About 13 miles south of Furnace Creek.
Distance: 2 miles out and back.
Approximate hiking time: 1 to 2 hours.
Difficulty: Easy.
Trail surface: Sandy canyon bottom.

Seasons: October through April.
USGS topo map: Devils Golf Course-CA (1:24,000).
Trail contact: Furnace Creek Visitor Center (see appendix D).

Finding the trailhead: From the intersection of California Highway 190 and Badwater Road (California Highway 178) in Furnace Creek, drive south on Badwater Road for 14.1 miles. Turn left (east) on the signed dirt road and drive 1.5 miles to the Natural Bridge parking area. The road is washboardy and rough but is suitable for standard two-wheel-drive vehicles. The trail begins behind the information kiosk.

The Hike

Death Valley's fascinating geologic history is featured on the kiosk at the trailhead of the Natural Bridge hike. Bedding and slipfaulting are explained on the board, so the canyon's display is even more impressive. Likewise, differential erosion is explained and illustrated, preparing you for the bridge. Fault caves, metamorphic layers of the Artist's Drive Formation, and mud drips are other topics covered in this condensed version of physical geology. The kiosk is worth a lengthy pause before embarking on the hike.

The canyon floor consists of loose gravel; that feature plus its sharp slope suggests this is a relatively young canyon. The Death Valley floor continues to subside while the Funeral Mountains rise. Geologic forces are still busy here.

The trail begins through deeply eroded volcanic ash and pumice canyon walls. The canyon gradually narrows. At 0.4 mile the bridge stretches over the canyon bottom. An ancient streambed is visible to the north of the bridge, where the floods swept around this more resistant section of strata before the pothole beneath it gave way to form the natural bridge.

Beyond the bridge, mud drips, slip faults, and fault caves appear on your journey uphill, reinforcing the information you picked up at the kiosk. A dry fall at 0.8 mile can be climbed with moderate effort, but a 20-foot dry fall blocks travel at 1 mile.

Retracing your steps down the canyon reveals even more examples of geology in action. The shifting lighting creates iridescent colors. Traveling in the same

The natural bridge—monumental gateway to the upper canyon. ▶

direction as the powerful flash floods and their load of scouring debris emphasizes the impact of water in this arid environment.

Miles and Directions

0.0 The trail heads northwest from the parking area.

0.4 Arrive at the natural bridge over the trail.

0.8 Carefully climb the smaller dry fall.

1.0 Where a 20-foot dry fall blocks the canyon, return to the trailhead.

2.0 Arrive back at the parking area.

86 Desolation Canyon

Desolation Canyon is a highly scenic but less crowded alternative to the nearby Golden Canyon. This short hike features moderate canyoneering to a high pass overlooking the Artist's Drive Formation. The deep, narrow, colorful canyon provides a feeling of solitude, with broad vistas from the overlook.

Start: About 5 miles south of Furnace Creek.
Distance: 5.2 miles out and back.
Approximate hiking time: 2 hours.
Difficulty: Moderate.
Trail surface: Clear wash with 3 short rock pitches.

Seasons: Early November to mid-April.
USGS topo map: Furnace Creek-CA (1:24,000).
Trail contact: Furnace Creek Visitor Center & Museum (see appendix D).

Finding the trailhead: From the Death Valley Visitor Center in Furnace Creek, drive south 1.2 miles to the junction of California Highway 190 and Badwater Road (location of the Furnace Creek Inn); turn right (south) onto Badwater Road (California Highway 178) and drive 3.9 miles to the unsigned parking area, which is to the left along the east side of the highway. The old road was washed out by the big thunderstorm flood of August 2004 and might not be rebuilt. Hike 1 mile to the end of the old road. Desolation Canyon is to the immediate left (northeast) of the old road. Follow one of several well-worn paths that lead northeast over the low ridge to the broad lower end of Desolation Canyon.

The Hike

This is an enjoyable and highly scenic canyon hike for anyone, but it is especially appreciated by those without a four-wheel-drive vehicle in that access is just off the paved highway. Despite its proximity to both the Badwater Road and Artist's Drive, the narrow canyon provides a deep feeling of intimacy and solitude. The entire out-and-back trip provides a superb opportunity to observe the dynamics of badlands erosion, which is everywhere, from mud-filled gullies to bizarre eroded shapes overlooking the canyon.

Hiking up the wash from the mouth of Desolation Canyon.

Because Desolation Canyon involves a short hike at low elevation, the recommended time of day for the hike is mid- to late afternoon when the cooler shadows fill the canyon. Upon return, late afternoon to early evening, brilliant light can be spectacular on the multicolored east-facing slopes above the canyon.

The main Desolation Canyon is just over the low ridge to the north from the end of the old road. Upon reaching the canyon in 1.1 mile, turn right and head up the wide wash that climbs gently to the first canyon junction at 1.3 mile, staying to the right. Continue right at the next junction at 1.4 mile. At 1.5 mile the canyon narrows with even narrower side draws. The next 0.1 mile brings a couple of stair-step rocks that are easy to climb, before the canyon again widens. At 2.1 miles what appears to be the main canyon to the left ends at a dry waterfall another 0.1 mile up. Continuing up the more narrow canyon to the right ends at a steep, unstable rock chute at 2.5 miles. This is a good turnaround point.

If you've still got the urge and energy to explore, climb up to the right on loose, deep gravel to the 740-foot elevation overlook at 2.6 miles. This relatively lofty vantage point provides a spectacular view of the varied colors of the Artist's Drive

Desolation Canyon; Golden Canyon/Gower Gulch Loop; Pyramid Canyon; Harmony Borax Works; Upper Hole-in-the-Wall

RF 1 : 198,500

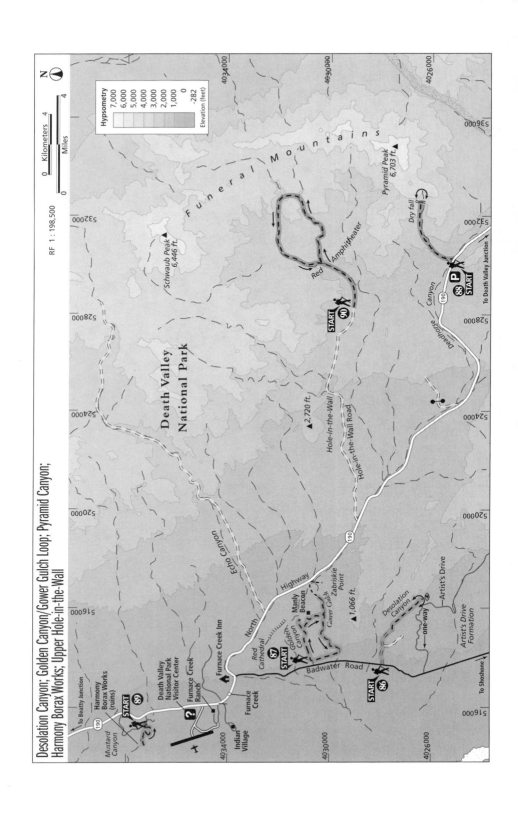

Hypsometry

	7,000
	6,000
	5,000
	4,000
	3,000
	2,000
	1,000
	0
	-282

Elevation (feet)

N

0   Kilometers   4

0   Miles   4

Funeral Mountains

Schwaub Peak ▲ 6,446 ft.

Pyramid Peak 6,703 ft. ▲

Red Amphitheater

Dry fall

Deadhorse Canyon

190

START 90

To Death Valley Junction

P 88 **START**

Death Valley National Park

▲ 2,720 ft.

Hole-in-the-Wall

Hole-in-the-Wall Road

190

Echo Canyon

To Beatty Junction

190 **START** 89

Mustard Canyon

Harmony Borax Works (ruins)

Death Valley National Park Visitor Center

Furnace Creek Ranch

?

Indian Village

Furnace Creek

Furnace Creek Inn

North Highway

Red Cathedral

START 87

Golden Canyon

Manly Beacon

Gower Gulch

Zabriskie Point

▲ 1,066 ft.

Desolation Canyon

one-way

Artist's Drive

Artist's Drive Formation

Badwater Road

START 86

To Shoshone

Formation to the south. From this point the Artist's Drive road is only about 0.3 mile west. Return by way of Desolation Canyon to complete this colorful 5.2-mile round-trip badlands/canyon excursion.

Miles and Directions

0.0 Start at the trailhead/parking area.

1.1 At the intersection with the Desolation Canyon wash, turn right up the canyon.

1.3 Where the canyon splits, stay right.

1.4 At the canyon junction, stay right up the main wash.

1.6 The canyon steepens with moderate scrambling.

1.7 The canyon widens to a junction. Go right up the steeper, less colorful canyon with more stair-step rocks.

2.1 At the canyon junction, stay right up a narrow gully.

2.5 The hike ends where the canyon reaches a steep chute. This is the turnaround point for the moderate hike.

2.6 Scramble up a very steep, unstable slope (right) to the overlook.

5.2 Return to the trailhead via the same route.

87 Golden Canyon/Gower Gulch Loop

A fascinating journey through geologic time passes through rocks of different ages as the elevation increases then loops back down to the floor of Death Valley past borax-mine tunnels. The first section is an educational geology nature trail. The scenery of the extended trip includes a colorful lake bed, exposed strata and alluvial-fan formations, and spectacular scenery of the Panamint Range from below Zabriskie Point

See map on page 292.
Start: About 3 miles south of Furnace Creek.
Distance: 6.5-mile loop (including 2 short side trips).
Approximate hiking time: 3 to 5 hours.
Difficulty: Moderate.

Trail surface: Sandy trail and rocky wash.
Seasons: November through April.
USGS topo map: Furnace Creek-CA (1:24,000).
Trail contact: Furnace Creek Visitor Center & Museum (see appendix D).

Finding the trailhead: From the north on California Highway 190, 1.2 miles south of the Furnace Creek Visitor Center, head south on Badwater Road (California Highway 178). After 2 miles, turn left into the Golden Canyon parking area/trailhead on the east side of the road. From the south, turn west on CA 178 2 miles north of the small town of Shoshone and continue into the park. From Ashford Junction, continue north on Badwater Road. The signed Golden Canyon parking area is 14.4 miles north of Badwater and can be seen just off the highway to the right (east).

The sharp point of Manly Beacon (left) is complemented by the dramatic amber face of the Red Cathedral (right background).

The Hike

An excellent interpretive trail guide to this Golden Canyon nature trail is available for 50 cents at the Golden Canyon trailhead. Ten stops in this geology guide are keyed to numbered posts along the trail.

Golden Canyon was once accessed by paved road. Then in February 1976 a four-day storm caused 2.3 inches of rain to fall on nearby Furnace Creek—one of the driest places on earth where no rain fell during all of 1929 and 1953. Runoff from the torrential cloudburst undermined and washed out the pavement so that today Golden Canyon is a wonderful place for hikers only. This pattern of drought and torrents follows countless periods of flash floods, shattering rock slides, and a wetter era when the alluvial fan was preceded by an ancient shallow sea—a land in constant flux. In the winter of 2004, heavy rains caused flooding, washing out sections of Badwater Road and further eroding these canyons and gulches.

At stop 2 it is easy to see how the canyon was carved out of an old alluvial fan made up of volcanic rock that predates the origin of Death Valley some three million years ago. Layers in the rock tell the tale of periodic floods over the eons. Just above, the canyon displays tilted bands of rock caused by faulting where huge blocks of the earth's crust slid past one another. As you proceed up the canyon, you are literally passing through geologic time. The Furnace Creek Formation is the combination over time of sediments from a lake bed that dates back around nine million years. Ripple marks of water lapping over the sandy lake bed hardened into stone as the climate warmed and are evident on the tilted rock. Weathering and the effects of thermal water produced the splash of vivid colors seen today.

Mountain building to the west gradually produced a more arid climate, causing the lake to dry up. At the same time the land tilted due to the widening and sinking of Death Valley and the uplift of the Black Mountains. Dark lava from eruptions of three million to five million years ago slowed down erosion, explaining why Manly Beacon juts so far above the surrounding badlands. These stark badlands rising above the canyon at mile 0.5 are the result of rapid runoff from storms on erodable, almost impermeable rocks.

Several narrow side canyons invite short explorations on the way up Golden Canyon, particularly opposite stop 2, and to the left and just above stops 6 and 7.

The nature trail ends at stop 10, about 1 mile up the canyon at an elevation of 140 feet. For a 0.8-mile round-trip to the base of the Red Cathedral, continue straight ahead up the broken pavement, past the old parking area, to a narrow notch, directly below the looming presence of the cathedral from where the highest point in the park—Telescope Peak—can be seen in the far distance.

Red Cathedral was once part of an active alluvial fan, outwashed from the Black Mountains to the south. The bright red results from the weathering of iron to produce the rust of iron oxide. The cliff faces are made up of the more resistant red rock crowning softer yellow lake deposits.

Upon returning to stop 10 (mile 1.8), follow the signed trail to the left (coming down) up a steep gully well marked with trailposts. The trail climbs across badlands beneath the imposing sandstone jaw of Manly Beacon. At 2.3 miles a high ridge saddle is reached below Manly Beacon. Follow the markers down a side gully to a wash/trail junction at 2.6 miles. The left-hand wash leads eastward up to Zabriskie Point. The right-hand wash/trail descends west to Gower Gulch. If you walk up the main wash, you will quickly come to the artificial cut made in the rock wall to divert Furnace Creek through Gower Gulch. This has resulted in speeding up erosion in the gulch. Note the gray color of the rocks on the bottom of the drainage washed in from Furnace Creek, contrasting with the red and yellow badlands.

Gower Gulch is partially the result of human construction to protect Furnace Creek from serious flooding. For a short side trip toward Zabriskie Point, turn left at the junction and follow the markers for about 0.5 mile from where you can select an excellent overlook of Zabriskie Point, the surrounding badlands, Death Valley, and the distant Panamint Range. Zabriskie Point is another 0.7 mile and 200 feet above and is accessible by road from the other side. It does indeed provide one of the most magnificent views in all of Death Valley, but its proximity to a paved road may detract from the hiking experience on the Golden-Gower loop. Thus, the overlook below Zabriskie Point is recommended as the turnaround point for a scenic side trip. Zabriskie Point is a popular starting point for those hiking 3 miles downhill through Gower Gulch then across to the mouth of Golden Canyon.

Back at the trail junction (mile 3.6), there is no marker post leading the way toward Gower Gulch. Simply continue down the wash toward wide, gray Gower Gulch, which drops below mounds of golden badlands. At 3.9 miles a side wash intersects the main wash; continue downward to the right. Early-day miners in search of borax have pocketed the walls of Gower Gulch with tunnels. These small openings are unsecured and potentially dangerous. A mile down, the wide gravel wash bends sharply to the left, narrowing dramatically with the bedding and faulting of red and green rock. The canyon floor then quickly drops 40 feet to below sea level.

At 5.2 miles the wash meets a 30-foot dry fall. A good use trail curves around the rock face to the right. From here the faint but easy-to-follow trail heads north 1.3 miles along the base of the mountains paralleling the highway back to the Golden Canyon parking area, thereby completing the basic 4.7-mile loop with an additional 1.8 miles of side trips.

Miles and Directions

0.0 Start at the Golden Canyon nature trail trailhead at 160 feet below sea level.

1.0 The nature trail ends at stop 10. Begin the 0.8-mile side trip to the base of the Red Cathedral here.

1.8 Back to stop 10 and the beginning of the trail toward Manly Beacon.

2.3 Arrive at the high point of the trail below Manly Beacon.

2.6 Arrive at the trail/wash junction between Gower Gulch and Zabriskie Point.

3.1 Arrive at the overlook below Zabriskie Point.

3.6 Get back to the trail/wash junction and begin the hike down Gower Gulch.

5.2 Gower Gulch reaches a 30-foot dry fall. Take the trail around to the right.

6.5 Complete the loop back at the Golden Canyon trailhead.

88 Pyramid Canyon

This is an easily accessible, waterless, out-and-back canyon hike with layered color-banded mountains. The mountains close into a narrow, dark chasm that is blocked in several places by boulders.

See map on page 292.
Start: About 14 miles southeast of Furnace Creek.
Distance: 4 miles out and back.
Approximate hiking time: 2 to 3 hours.
Difficulty: Moderate.
Trail surface: No trail but a sandy wash with loose gravel and moderate bouldering.
Seasons: October through April.
USGS topo maps: Ryan-CA and Echo Canyon-CA (1:24,000).
Trail contact: Furnace Creek Visitor Center & Museum (see appendix D).

Finding the trailhead: From the Furnace Creek Visitor Center, drive about 14 miles east on North Highway (California Highway 190). Shortly after passing an information kiosk/pay phone, you'll leave the park boundary on the south side of the highway. Drive another 1.1 miles and look to the north side of the highway for a prominent wash. The trailhead is unsigned, but there is a wide spot alongside the highway on the north side for parking.

The Hike

Some of the limestone in the surrounding Furnace Creek Formation is probably travertine that was laid down by volcanic hot springs. Travertine Point rises just east of the trailhead on the south side of the canyon. Pyramid Canyon is not an official place name on the map but is used here to identify the hike. When viewed from the mouth of Pyramid Canyon, the imposing, aptly named massif of Pyramid Peak dominates the skyline to the northeast. After 0.25 mile you'll come to an old rusted car body halfway buried in the wash—proof positive that you're in the right canyon. Barrel cacti dot the surrounding alluvial-fan conglomerate.

Continue hiking up the wide wash to narrows that define a dramatic gateway beyond. At 1.5 miles the canyon is blocked by a boulder, with dark cliffs ahead. Look back to the southwest for a great view of Telescope Peak. Climb to the left up a slanted rock to get around the boulder. At mile 1.7 reddish dark cliff walls soar hundreds of feet as the canyon again closes in. The next two boulder blockages occur in quick succession and can be readily climbed. But the fourth blockage at 2 miles is impassable. A gigantic chokestone sits atop a dry fall bound by sheer limestone cliffs. An alcove overhang juts out from the cliff high above the dry fall on the north side of the canyon. Retrace your route to complete this 4-mile round-trip canyon "teaser."

Miles and Directions

0.0 Start at the unsigned trailhead/parking area along the north side of the highway (2,560 feet elevation).

0.25 Look for the old half-buried car body in the wash.

1.5 At the first rock blockage, the canyon narrows.

1.7 Arrive at the second rock blockage.

1.8 This is the third rock blockage.

2.0 Turn around upon reaching the dry fall/chokestone.

4.0 Return to the trailhead.

Option: For added variety during the return route, look for a low ridge on the right side of the broad wash, about 0.5-mile below the dry-fall turnaround. Angle around the ridge and head up the left (west) fork for about 0.4-mile to a 30-foot dry fall. This two-pronged exploration of Pyramid Canyon adds about 0.8-mile round-trip to the hike.

89 Harmony Borax Works

This short hike on a loop trail leads to a nineteenth-century industrial site on the valley floor. The endless salt flats are an overwhelming sight.

See map on page 292.
Start: About 1.5 miles north of Furnace Creek.
Distance: 1 mile out and back.
Approximate hiking time: Less than 1 hour.
Difficulty: Easy.
Trail surface: Asphalt walkway to Harmony Borax Works (wheelchair accessible); sandy trail to overlook and to salt flats.

Seasons: October through March.
USGS topo maps: West of Furnace Creek-CA and Furnace Creek-CA (1:24,000).
Trail contact: Furnace Creek Visitor Center & Museum (see appendix D).

Finding the trailhead: The trailhead for the Harmony Borax Works Trail is 1.3 miles north of the park visitor center at Furnace Creek via California Highway 190. The 0.2-mile road on the left is signed. The asphalt walkway leads west of the parking area.

The Hike

This desolate site was the scene of frenzied activity from 1883 to 1888, not in the pursuit of gold like so much of the other mining activity, but of borax. Used in ceramics and glass as well as soap and detergent, borax was readily available here in Death Valley. Borax prices were highly mercurial due to soaring supply and moderate demand in the nineteenth century, so the industry was plagued by sharp

A 20-mule team wagon stands at the historic Harmony Borax Works trail.

boom and bust cycles. Here at the Harmony Works, the years of prosperity were typically brief.

Chinese laborers hauled the borate sludge in from the flats on sledges to the processing plant, remains of which are the focal point of this hike. There the borate was boiled down and hauled 165 miles across the desert to Mojave by the famed twenty-mule teams. One of the wagons that made this journey stands below the borax plant. Although the works were in operation only from October to June, working conditions for man and beast were harsh.

Although this is a short hike, be sure to bring water. It's a dehydrating experience.

Miles and Directions

0.0 Follow the asphalt loop trail west of the parking area.

0.2 A use trail leads south from the asphalt path to the hilltop.

0.5 The loop ends right back where you started. The use trail extends out into the salt flats.

1.0 Arrive back at the parking area.

Options: At 0.2 mile a 0.5-mile side trip takes you to a low overlook. Follow the asphalt path that intersects with the loop to the hilltop, which gives you an excellent vista of the central valley floor. From here it is easy to imagine the usual workday in operation here at the Harmony Works. To the east of the hilltop is an area that appears to have been a dump for Furnace Creek. A rusty antique car rests on the hillside, surrounded by desert.

For the 5-mile out and back to the salt flats, the trailhead is located at the far side of Harmony Borax Works, heading west from the loop trail. This hike likewise confirms the arduous conditions of life and work on the valley floor. An unsigned but well-trod path leads west from the end of the paved loop. It travels by a damp slough where groundwater is percolating to the surface, causing borate crystals to form. Farther out on the flats, mounds of borax mud remain where the laborers made piles to validate the works' mining claim more than a hundred years ago.

90 Upper Hole-in-the-Wall

This interesting cross-country canyon trek has lots to see, from marine fossils to grand mountain vistas. Short canyon narrows, geologic wonders, plant species found only in Death Valley, and moderate bouldering add variety to this long loop in the Funeral Mountains.

See map on page 292.
Start: About 12 miles southeast of Furnace Creek.
Distance: 11-mile lollipop.
Approximate hiking time: 6 to 8 hours.
Difficulty: Strenuous.
Trail surface: No trail but sandy gravelly washes and ridges.

Seasons: Mid-October through mid-April.
USGS topo maps: Echo Canyon-CA and East of Echo Canyon-CA (1:24,000).
Trail contact: Furnace Creek Visitor Center & Museum (see appendix D).

Finding the trailhead: From the junction of California Highway 190 and Badwater Road (California Highway 178) south of Furnace Creek, go southeast on CA 190 for 5.4 miles to the Hole-in-the-Wall dirt road on the left. The road is in the wash, near a sign recommending four-wheel-drive vehicles. The first 3.6 miles of the road is rough and rocky, but is often passable by passenger vehicles with slow, careful driving. Drive 3.6 miles to the Hole-in-the-Wall narrows (Split Canyon) and park there, unless you have a high-clearance four-wheel-drive vehicle. If so, you can drive another 2.5 miles to the end of the road just before the wilderness boundary.

Hiking up out of the narrows of the east canyon in the Red Amphitheater.

The Hike

At the trailhead you'll find remnants of an old travertine quarry. There is another quarry just over the ridge to the north in a small canyon of red sandstone. The quarries produced building stone for the Furnace Creek Inn. From the parking area, hike east for about 0.4-mile to the end of the travertine ridge on the left. You might find pictographs in this area. At this point the basin becomes wider and seems strangely remote, despite its proximity to busy Furnace Creek. Plants of this Mojave Desert ecosystem include creosote, rabbitbrush, barrel cacti, and sweetbush favored by bighorn sheep. At 1 mile you'll see a distinctive black rock outcropping on the left. Across to the south a side drainage leads up to an inner basin on the northeast side of Pyramid Peak. Scan the southern skyline for an arch. Schwaub Peak rises to the northeast, uplifted and tilted with almost vertical sedimentary bedding.

At 1.5 mile turn right (east) up a narrow canyon. Its easier to find the correct canyon if you stay on the right side of the broad valley, which is called Red Amphitheater. A sharp pointed peak marks the right entrance of the canyon. At 2.4 miles the canyon is bounded by dark limestone with moderate bouldering. Look for embedded marine fossils in the limestone. You'll pass through a canyon narrows with cliff walls marked with eroded ripples. These sedimentary rocks were probably mudstone from the floor of an ancient lake bed.

In the next set of narrows we spotted a perfectly camouflaged horned lizard. This is an uncommon reptile, so it pays to be observant. Death Valley goldeneye and napkinring buckwheat grow together in the wash. This secluded rugged terrain is heaven for desert bighorn. As you continue up the canyon, you'll see delicate little ferns clinging to rock walls, and you'll wonder how they can survive in this harsh, dry environment.

At 4 miles an arch sits atop tilted cliffs with eroded pockets used by nesting owls. Just beyond is an obvious gap on the left that leads to the next canyon north. At mile 4.8 a major side gully joins the main east canyon from the right. Continue left for another 0.4 mile and look for a route to the left that crosses the ridge to the next canyon north.

After cresting this divide you might spot another arch to the west as you descend to the north canyon. You might also see a light lavender flower with a yellow center known as rock nimulus growing from limestone cracks—these are endemic to Death Valley.

Upon reaching the main canyon floor at around 5.7 miles, turn left (west) and hike down the wash for the return leg of the loop. This stretch contains such wonders as beehive cacti, Death Valley penstemon, marine fossils, and great towering spires and cliffs. Try to avoid rock nettles or you'll learn the hard way why they're called "velcro" plants. The canyon walls are made of hard, sandy conglomerate, riddled with openings and alcoves. At 7.3 miles the canyon opens, with enticing side canyons to the right that invite further exploration.

When the limestone ridge on the left ends at about mile 8.2, you'll be looking straight south to the Black Mountains. The loop is completed at 9.5 miles. Continue down to the trailhead to finish this varied 11-mile canyon route in Death Valley's Funeral Mountains.

Miles and Directions

0.0 Begin at the trailhead/wilderness boundary.

0.4 Reach the end of the travertine ridge.

1.5 Enter the side canyon to the right (east).

3.2 With the low saddle on the left, continue to the right up the main wash.

4.2 This is the crossover point for the shorter loop option.

5.2 Climb the ridge to the left (north).

5.7 At the north canyon, turn left for the downhill (return) leg of the loop.

9.5 Complete the basic loop near the canyon junction.

11.0 Return to the trailhead.

Options: The loop can be shortened by 2 or 3 miles by crossing north to the next canyon at about mile 4.2. You can identify the spot by the color of the rocks: red on the left, white to the right, and black limestone straight ahead.

From the upper crossover ridge described in the hike, and before dropping to the next canyon north, climb up the steep ridge to the right (east) for expansive views of Amargosa Valley far into Nevada.

From the Hole-in-the-Wall narrows, 3.6 road miles above CA 190, a short 2-mile round-trip provides desert panoramas, majestic rock formations, and varied terrain. The hike begins at the Hole-in-the-Wall cliffs of differentially eroded volcanic ash. The narrows are also known as Split Canyon. The multitude of holes form enchanting shapes; some are precise, while others droop. To the north, beyond the alluvial fan, lie the Funeral Mountains. Travel north-northwest using the varnished desert pavement where possible since the wash winds a bit and is loaded with boulders that make hiking difficult. You gain 420 feet in elevation by the time you reach the canyon mouth. Here more towering limestone cliffs display the eyes and mouths of erosion holes. The canyon floor is a wide graveled wash. The canyon narrows and turns at 0.3 mile, only to be blocked by a 40-foot dry fall. The tempting sidehill to the west is too unstable and dangerous for climbing, so this is the terminal point of the canyon hike. At the canyon mouth, hike east 0.2 mile to the next canyon. This one is totally blocked by massive boulders. The return descent to Hole-in-the-Wall features magnificent views of the Artist's Drive Formation at the northern end of the Black Mountains, with Death Valley stretching out beyond. Telescope Peak stands on the far horizon.

91 Keane Wonder Mine

An old mining road in the Funeral Mountains leads to the historic ruins of mines, a mill, and tramways. The route is steep and rocky, and the scenic views down the canyon to Death Valley are dramatic.

Start: About 20 miles north of Furnace Creek.
Distance: 4 miles out and back.
Approximate hiking time: 2 to 3 hours.
Difficulty: Strenuous.
Trail surface: Rocky trail.

Seasons: October through April.
USGS topo map: Chloride City-CA (1:24,000).
Trail contact: Furnace Creek Visitor Center & Museum (see appendix D).

Finding the trailhead: From Nevada Highway 374/Daylight Pass Road at Hell's Gate Junction, head south on Beatty Cutoff Road going toward Beatty Junction. After 4.3 miles turn left on the signed Keane Wonder Mine Road, a good gravel route, and drive 2.8 miles east to the end-of-the-road parking area below the Keane Wonder Mill.

From the visitor center at Furnace Creek, drive north on California Highway 190 for 11.3 miles to Beatty Cutoff Road and continue right (north) on Beatty-Daylight Pass Cutoff Road for another 5.7 miles to Keane Wonder Mine Road. Turn right and drive the final 2.8 miles to the end-of-the-road parking area/trailhead.

The Hike

The Keane Wonder Mine was developed at a time and in a location of hundreds of gold, silver, and lead strikes. The relative success of this venture makes its history and today's ruins all the more intriguing. It all began in 1903 with an almost-unheard-of lucky strike by an unemployed Irish miner named Jack Keane and his partner. After months of futile searching for silver, Keane accidentally stumbled across a huge ledge of gold, calling the find the "Keane Wonder Mine" out of his total astonishment at being so fortunate.

The news spread rapidly, and by 1904 the local gold rush was on. The mine changed hands several times, making a fortune for its original partners, and was capitalized with stocks sold to an eager public. In 1906 Homer Wilson bought the mine and started a consortium that operated the mine for a decade. Wilson ordered a twenty-stamp mill to crush the ore and a gravity-operated aerial tramway nearly 1 mile long. Loaded ore buckets coming down the canyon from the shaft pulled the empty buckets back up. The tram contained thirteen towers, with the longest span being 1,200 feet, and a vertical drop from top to bottom of 1,500 feet. Lack of water prevented the mill from operating at full capacity. Even so, total gold production from the mine was around $1.1 million, most of which was extracted between 1907 and 1911.

The Keane Wonder Mine aerial tramway terminal overlooks a steep rugged canyon.

The Keane Wonder Mine was one of the two largest producing gold mines in the Death Valley region, the other being the Skidoo Mine. The artifacts and remnants of this mine have significant historical value and should not be removed or disturbed in any way.

From the parking area, climb 0.1 mile to the informative kiosk located just below the Keane Wonder Mill ruins. The sign contains a bit of the history of Jack Keane's amazing 1903 gold strike. From the trailhead, extensive mining debris can be seen in the wash to the left. At 0.4 mile the trail crosses under the tramway and begins a very steep climb straight up the ridge. In just 0.7 mile another 650 feet elevation is gained, at which point the trail contours and climbs more moderately to the right above the tramway canyon leading to the mine. At 1.7 miles the trail reaches the large aerial tramway terminal structure along with several shallow mine shafts.

From here a level trail extends another 0.5 mile around the canyon to an upper mine area containing additional adits. The view down canyon makes this short extension of the hike more than worthwhile. Another narrow trail climbs steeply 0.2

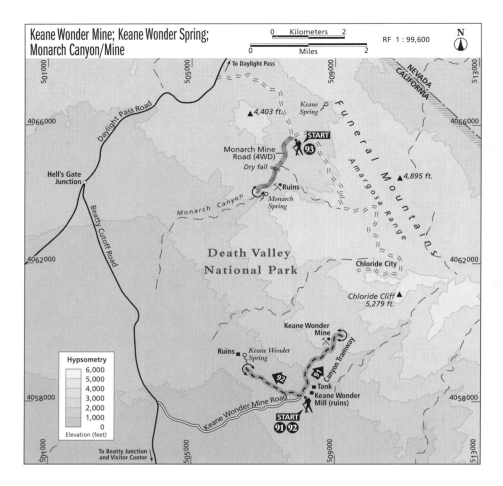

mile to the base of the main mine, which peers from the steep mountainside at around 3,000 feet elevation. Several stone building foundations are passed along the way. Around the bend and at the base of the mine, the area beyond is closed to hiking for public safety. Unsecured mine shafts present hazards and should definitely be avoided. Enjoy them from a safe distance before retracing your route to the trailhead, as you complete this round-trip hiking climb to one of Death Valley's largest and most interesting early-twentieth-century mining ventures.

Miles and Directions

0.0 Start at the trailhead/parking area.

0.1 Stop at the kiosk below the Keane Wonder Mill ruins.

1.7 Arrive at the aerial tramway terminal.

2.0 View the stone building foundations and mine shafts below the main mine openings.

4.0 Return to the trailhead.

92 Keane Wonder Spring

This nearly level trip takes you to the spring that was essential to the Keane Wonder Mine and mill operations. The area has many traces of mining activities of the last century.

See map on page 306.
Start: About 20 miles north of Furnace Creek.
Length: 2 miles out and back.
Approximate hiking time: 1 to 2 hours.
Difficulty: Easy.
Trail surface: Sandy, rocky path.

Seasons: October through April.
USGS topo map: Chloride City-CA (1:24,000).
Trail contact: Furnace Creek Visitor Center & Museum (see appendix D).

Finding the trailhead: From Nevada Highway 374, 19.3 miles southwest of Beatty, Nevada, turn left (south) on Beatty Cutoff Road and drive 4.3 miles to the signed dirt road on your left. Take the gravel road 2.8 miles to the Keane Wonder Mine parking area.

From Furnace Creek, go north on California Highway 190 11.3 miles north of the visitor center. Turn right (east) on the Beatty Cutoff and drive 5.7 miles to the Keane Wonder gravel road on your right. Drive 2.8 miles to the Keane Wonder Mine parking area. The trail to the spring begins at the northeastern corner of the parking area and heads north.

The Hike

The Keane Wonder Mine complex was at its height in the gold boom from 1906 to 1912. It was resuscitated by optimistic prospectors and investors several times. The most recent renaissance was in 1935–37 when cyanide leaching of the mine tailings took place on the site. The tanks used for that operation stand below the parking area.

Where the mine trail goes directly up the hillside, the use trail to Keane Wonder Spring goes left. The trail begins after you drop into the debris-strewn wash just north of the parking area. Emerging from the wash above the pair of settling tanks nestled together, you pick up the well-traveled trail. A broken pipeline lies 50 yards below on the hillside; it will lead you to the springs.

The trail travels by numerous mine openings and scenic travertine rock outcroppings. At 0.6 mile the trail merges with the trail coming up from lower on the hillside; you'll return to the parking area via this trail on the hike back. More mine openings and a stone foundation are nearby. The trail is meticulously bordered with rocks for most of the way.

Continuing northward, soon your nose will detect the scent of sulfur, even on a windy day. There, at 0.8 mile, the trickling stream from the spring crosses the road. Above the trail take a side trip to the spring. The salt grass marsh flourishes in the salt-encrusted soil 30 yards above the trail. A sign posted by the National Park Service warns of gas hazards in the mine shaft immediately above the spring. The area has many mine shafts, some flooded, all dangerous.

Salt grass thrives in the marsh at Keane Wonder Spring.

This mining wasteland is also full of wildlife. Heavy bighorn-sheep use is evident from the droppings on the damp spring banks. Birds and crickets create a symphony of sound in the desert stillness.

Continuing northward, the trail follows a crude aqueduct and curves around, now totally out of sight of the parking area and industrial sprawl there. More of the ubiquitous mine sites and another sulfurous spring bracket the trail. At your destination, 1 mile, you'll find a mine chute and a miner's cabin. Rusty cans, pieces of pipe, and the usual pieces of nondescript rusty artifacts litter the ground. In the dry desert air, the cabin is so well preserved it appears the miner left recently. Across the shallow gully to the west is a large rock outcropping atop a hill. Notice the stone walls built under the natural overhang. Did wind, heat, or both drive the miner to take refuge in such a primitive rock shelter?

Return the way you came, continuing on the wide rock-lined trail at the junction you passed on the way in. In sight of the parking area, the trail dissipates in the mine debris in the gully near the largest of the remaining tanks. From there you have to pick your way back to your vehicle.

The amazing thing about the Keane Wonder Spring hike is its plethora of mine sites. The Keane Wonder Mine was heralded to be the richest gold strike in Death Valley, attracting a multitude of hopeful miners. At its height nearly 500 prospectors were working in the area. Thus, everywhere you look, there's another mine mouth with its tailings dripping down the hillside. Mine tunnels like rabbit holes cut through the ridges and disappear into mountainside. Curious children and adults should avoid all mines.

Miles and Directions

0.0 The trail heads north above the pair of settling tanks.

0.3 The trail crosses a wash and continues following the contour of the hillside.

0.6 The trail merges with another trail from the lower hillside. Continue on the trail to the spring/mine site.

0.8 The first spring crosses the trail. An aqueduct ditch parallels the trail.

1.0 Arrive at a mine chute and cabin and another sulfur seep.

2.0 Return to the trailhead.

93 Monarch Canyon/Mine

This out–and–back hike takes you down a rocky canyon in the Funeral Mountains to an 80-foot dry fall, a well–preserved stamp mill, and a desert spring.

See map on page 306.
Start: About 27.5 miles north of Furnace Creek.
Distance: 3 miles out and back.
Approximate hiking time: 2 to 3 hours.
Difficulty: Easy.

Trail surface: Four-wheel-drive road, rocky trail, clear wash.
Seasons: October through April.
USGS topo map: Chloride City-CA (1:24,000).
Trail contact: Furnace Creek Visitor Center & Museum (see appendix D).

Finding the trailhead: From Nevada Highway 374/Daylight Pass Road 3.4 miles northeast of Hell's Gate Junction in Boundary Canyon and 15.8 miles southwest of Beatty, Nevada, look for a road to the south that is marked only with a small sign recommending four-wheel drive. Carefully driven high-clearance two-wheel-drive vehicles can negotiate this road for 2.2 miles to the bottom of upper Monarch Canyon. High-clearance four-wheel drive is required for vehicular travel beyond this point to Chloride City. The rough Monarch Mine Road takes off south from this point. This road junction can serve as the trailhead for the hike down Monarch Canyon. However, the hike can be shortened by 1.2 miles round-trip by driving down Monarch Mine Road to a point just above the dry fall.

The Hike

Hikers can start at the unsigned junction between the rough Chloride City Road and four-wheel-drive Monarch Mine Road (3 miles round-trip to Monarch Spring) or at the end of the Monarch Mine Road (1.8 miles round-trip). From the Chloride City Road junction, the trip starts out in rounded, low-lying hills. The four-wheel-drive road descends southwesterly, entering a rocky canyon after 0.3 mile.

At 0.6 mile the road ends above a striking 80-foot dry fall. A major side canyon enters from the left, bounded by high cliffs marked by folded multicolored bands of rock. Continue left around the falls on the old mining trail. After another 0.1 mile the trail drops to the wash, which is covered with horsetails and Mormon tea. This is favored habitat for quail and other birds. The base of the dry falls is definitely worth visiting, so turn right and walk 0.1 mile up to the precipice. In addition to the main wide falls, another smaller but equally high falls guards the canyon bowl to the left. The canyon walls are distinguished by shelf rock catch basins, overhangs, and contorted layers of colorful, twisted rock.

Proceeding back down the sandy canyon wash, an eroded-out mining trail crosses to the right and then drops back to the canyon floor at 1 mile. Rock cairns are in place for the return trip. At 1.2 miles the wood and cement ruins of the Monarch Mine stamp mill are reached on the left. The ore chute to the mill extends up an almost vertical rock face.

To further experience the rugged grandeur of Monarch Canyon, continue down the wash another 0.3 mile to the brushy bottom just below Monarch Spring. Here the canyon bends sharply to the right and begins to narrow. Hiking below the spring would be difficult due to dense vegetation and loose, rocky side slopes. Retrace your route.

Miles and Directions

0.0   Start at the trailhead at the junction of Chloride City Road and Monarch Mine Road in upper Monarch Canyon.

0.6   Arrive at an 80-foot dry fall at the end of Monarch Mine Road.

0.7   The mining trail drops to the bottom of a canyon wash.

0.8   Walk up the wash to the base of the dry falls.

1.2   Arrive at the Monarch Mine stamp mill ruins.

1.5   Arrive at Monarch Spring.

3.0   Return to the trailhead by the same route.

◀ *The base of the Monarch Mine stamp mill.*

94 Hungry Bill's Ranch/Johnson Canyon

This out-and-back hike follows a scenic stream up a canyon to the historic ruins of Bill's 1870s ranch deep in the Panamint Mountains.

Start: About 37 miles southwest of Furnace Creek.
Distance: 3.8 miles out and back.
Approximate hiking time: 3 to 4 hours.
Difficulty: Strenuous.

Trail surface: Primitive use trail.
Seasons: October through May.
USGS topo map: Panamint-CA (1:24,000).
Trail contact: Furnace Creek Visitor Center & Museum (see appendix D).

Finding the trailhead: From California Highway 190 at the Furnace Creek Inn, drive south on Badwater Road (California Highway 178) for 7.1 miles; turn to the southwest on the washboard/gravel West Side Road (closed during summer) and continue south for another 21.7 miles to Johnson Canyon Road; turn right (west) and drive 9.7 miles to a point about 0.1 mile before the end of the road at Wilson Spring. It is best to park about 0.1 mile below Wilson Spring to avoid driving through the riparian area and thick brush. The final 3.4 miles to the trailhead require a high-clearance four-wheel-drive vehicle. Those with standard two-wheel-drive vehicles should park at or near the burro pen before the rough road drops steeply into the canyon. This will add about 7 miles round-trip distance to the hike. The primitive use trail begins at Wilson Spring, following the stream drainage 1.8 miles to the upper ranch site.

The Hike

The original Hungry Bill's Ranch in upper Johnson Canyon was first developed in the 1870s by Swiss farmers who sought to grow fruits and vegetables for sale to the residents of Panamint City, over rugged Panamint Pass in Surprise Canyon. The mining camp had its brief heyday from 1874 to 1877. By the time the Swiss farmers were ready to sell their produce, bust had followed boom and the market had vanished! Later the ranch was occupied for many years by a Shoshone Indian named Hungry Bill, whose huge appetite matched his great girth. Today all that remains are fruit trees and extensive stone walls.

The road up Johnson Canyon is very rough, requiring high-clearance four-wheel drive in order to reach the road-end trailhead at Wilson Spring. Wilson Spring is a lush and lovely spot with water pouring from a pipe, huge willow and cottonwood trees, and an informal campsite—a true desert oasis. In the absence of four-wheel drive, plan on parking at the burro pen about 3.5 miles short of Wilson Spring, thereby adding 7 miles round-trip to the hike.

The South Fork of Johnson Canyon enters from the left 1 mile before reaching Wilson Spring. This canyon is wide and graveled and can be hiked up toward the crest of the Panamint Mountains as a side trip.

Hungry Bill's Ranch/Johnson Canyon; Surprise Canyon to Panamint City

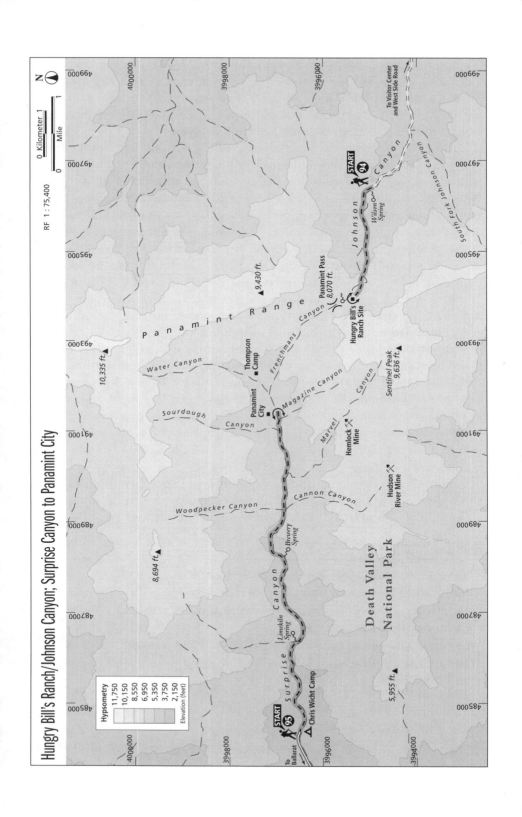

RF 1 : 75,400

N

0 Kilometer 1

0 Mile 1

Hypsometry

11,750
10,150
8,550
6,950
5,350
3,750
2,150

Elevation (feet)

Panamint Range

10,335 ft. ▲

Water Canyon

Sourdough

Canyon

▲ 8,694 ft.

Woodpecker Canyon

Cannon Canyon

Surprise Canyon

Limekiln Spring

○ Brewery Spring

START
95
△ Chris Wicht Camp

To Ballarat

9,430 ft. ▲

Thompson Camp ■

Frenchmans Canyon

Panamint City ■

Magazine Canyon

Marvel Canyon

Hemlock ✕ Mine

Hudson ✕ River Mine

Sentinel Peak 9,636 ft. ▲

Death Valley National Park

▲ 5,955 ft.

Panamint Pass 8,070 ft.

Hungry Bill's Ranch Site ■

Wilson ○ Spring

Johnson Canyon

START
94

To Visitor Center and West Side Road

South Fork Johnson Canyon

To reach Hungry Bill's Ranch from just below Wilson Spring, look for the use trail that heads up the canyon on the left side from the road end. Within 0.2 mile the trail passes the circular stone remnants of an arrastra used by miners for crushing ore. At 0.3 mile the trail fades out. Cross the canyon wash to the right side and look carefully for the continuation of the trail.

At 0.4 mile the canyon narrows, bounded by high rugged cliffs of volcanic rhyolite rock. The primitive trail crosses back and forth through the wash. The canyon again narrows at 0.6 mile; cross and climb around rock spires to the left. At 0.7 mile the trail climbs past hand-built rock walls and then loses 100 feet as it drops to the stream bottom. With a profusion of birds, frogs, lush vegetation, and water, this delightful stretch of Johnson Canyon is a refreshing celebration of life!

At 1 mile the trail reaches an overlook after contouring up and down along the steep rocky slopes. The trail then drops another 50 feet to the stream, crosses to the right, then the left, and continues up canyon to the lower ranch site on the right (north) side at 1.6 miles. Each stream crossing features well-placed stepping stones, so you are guaranteed a dry journey. At the lower ranch, the rock walls, fruit trees, and gurgling rivulet are overseen by massive cliffs toward Panamint Pass.

Cross to the left side and follow the primitive trail another 0.1 mile, where the stream has disappeared beneath the ground—a completely different and drier world. At 1.9 miles the stream resurfaces at the main Hungry Bill's Ranch—a huge open area on the left (south) side of the canyon. The site includes fruit trees surrounded by extensive rock walls. A rock-walled roofless house protected by a stone wall windbreak sits on a hill above the ranch. Hungry Bill certainly had a stunning view of an incredibly rugged cliff face, and down across Death Valley to the Black Mountains. It is interesting to reflect on the life he must have led.

You'll probably have an easier time following the use trail back down to Wilson Spring than you did on the way up. With the scenic canyon, rough trail, and ample exploration opportunities at the ranch, there is no need to hurry.

Miles and Directions

0.0 Start at the trailhead, located 0.1 mile below Wilson Spring.

0.3 Where the use trail fades, cross the canyon to the right side.

0.6 The canyon narrows. Cross and climb around the rock spires to the left.

1.6 Arrive at Hungry Bill's lower ranch.

1.9 Arrive at Hungry Bill's Ranch. After exploring, return by the same route.

3.8 Arrive back at the trailhead.

A bubbling brook flows down Johnson Canyon at 1 mile. ▶

95 Surprise Canyon to Panamint City

The hike to the ghost town of Panamint City follows a year-round canyon stream through a lengthy, dramatic canyon. Contemporary mining activity mingles with the historic in this remote Panamint Mountain location.

See map on page 313.
Start: About 65 miles south of Stovepipe Wells Village.
Length: 13 miles out and back.
Approximate hiking time: 4 to 7 hours.
Difficulty: Strenuous.

Trail surface: Rocky path.
Seasons: September through May.
USGS topo maps: Ballarat-CA and Panamint-CA (1:24,000).
Trail contact: Furnace Creek Visitor Center & Museum (see appendix D).

Finding the trailhead: From California Highway 190, 34.5 miles southwest of Stovepipe Wells and 2.6 miles east of Panamint Springs Resort, go south on Panamint Valley Road for 13.9 miles to the junction with Trona-Wildrose Road. Turn right (south) and drive 9.5 miles to Ballarat Road (signed) on your left. Turn left and go 3.6 miles to the tiny town of Ballarat. Turn left at the general store, which is a good stop for ice, cold sodas, and lively conversation with the proprietor. From the store, drive north on Indian Ranch Road 1.9 miles to Surprise Canyon Road on your right, which is marked by a signpost and by a large white boulder with a red S7 on it. Turn right and drive 4.1 miles to the road's end at the Chris Wicht Camp. Park on the side and speak to the occupant if he is around. Do not block the road or the driveway. Be considerate of those living here.

The Hike

The Surprise Canyon hike is located on the very western edge of the expansion area of Death Valley National Park above the Panamint Valley. The BLM Surprise Canyon Wilderness Area lies on both sides of Surprise Canyon Road off Indian Canyon Road. Here the BLM's open desert camping regulations are in effect; there are plentiful campsites along the first 2 miles of Surprise Canyon Road before it climbs the alluvial fan.

The Wicht Camp on the topo map straddles the end of the driveable road. The Novaks are living here. Please show respect and do not disturb the residents. The Novaks will keep an eye on your vehicle for the price of a six-pack. Don't, however, poke around their dwelling; there will be plenty to explore in Panamint City, 6.5 miles and 3,000 feet higher ahead.

A practical piece of advice is to waterproof your boots before hiking here—especially if the springs are running at full capacity. The trail/river combination makes for very damp hiking in the lower 3.5 miles of the canyon. This is a minor inconvenience in this adventuresome climb to Panamint City.

A mine mill site in Surprise Canyon just above the trailhead.

The vegetation and wildlife of Surprise Canyon is varied and plentiful, due to the presence of water and the elevation change. Birds and burros frequent the lower canyon. The hike will travel through several vegetative zones as it climbs, from the riparian willow groves to creosote scrub community to piñon-juniper forest. From your destination in Panamint City, the lofty cliffs of the mountain range soar above forested slopes.

Right from the start the hike up Surprise Canyon is a startling change from the drive through Panamint Valley. Even the bumpy ride up the road to the parking area does not hint at the water and greenery that greet you at Wicht Camp. The first 0.5 mile from the camp involves repeated zigzags along the shallow stream to dry sections of the largely washed-out trail. To enjoy the views of the rugged canyon walls, it is necessary to pause between stream leaps.

At 1 mile, hand and foot scrambling is necessary to get up the sloping gorge, where wet rocks are quite slippery. Another more challenging gorge lies 0.2 mile beyond, leading up to a broader valley. An amusing sight above the gorge is the deserted mine vehicle perched in the eroded trail. More vehicles lie in the brush, probably brought down the valley by the 1984 flood. During this lower third of the hike to Panamint City the watery trail periodically becomes dry, but the flow from Limekiln and Brewery Springs along the canyon revives the creek.

At 3.4 miles the damp trail bisects an arched willow grove and cuts by a rocky grotto. This is the last contact with the stream until the return trip. The next mile and a half of the hike climbs 1,000 feet, with rugged canyon walls of contrasting colors on both sides. Juniper, Mormon tea, and barrel cacti crowd the lower slopes, with barren cliffs bursting above.

By 5 miles you'll begin to spot remains of Panamint City's vast mining activities. Up to 2,000 people lived in the narrow city during its brief heyday in the mid-1870 silver boom. Even today validated mining claims exist here.

At 6.2 miles you'll arrive at the central city site, where it is evident that mining and residential activities have occurred recently. Several cabins are located in the valley above the smelter ruins. Respect private property during your visit. The interface of old and modern mining is also in evidence. Aluminum and plastic debris from the 1950s is mixed with the more traditional rusty tin cans and barrel hoops of ghost towns. Amazingly, much industrial equipment is located in this hard-to-reach spot: a 20-foot propane tank, two trailers, various trucks, and other heavy machinery. Some 1950s-vintage buildings are interspersed with remains of the last century's occupation.

The narrow valley floor below the modern mining outpost is overgrown with creosote and catclaw. Amid the shrubbery are the stone walls and foundations of the nineteenth-century dwellers. Near one of the larger building sites a garden of iris continues to spring merrily into life, a living artifact of Panamint City's brief but optimistic history. A large stone-walled livestock paddock remains on the north side of the trail; it is apparent that the wild burros of the canyon still like to hang out here.

Binoculars will enable you to explore the canyon visually without plowing through the dense vicious shrubs. Several other canyons branch out at the eastern end of Surprise Canyon. With topo map in hand, you can explore Frenchmans Canyon to the southeast toward Panamint Pass, or Water Canyon to the northeast. Thompson Camp, in the latter, is 0.5 mile beyond the upper end of Panamint City by way of an aqueduct trail. A couple of wooden-shell buildings and a water tank mark its 6,500-foot location. There is also a lush spring (Thompson Spring), with a large wooden cask cistern that used to supply the mining community. It is an excellent source of water even today.

Above the industrial city rise the peaks of the Panamints. The towering wall of the divide rises sharply 3,000 feet above the town, dwarfing the 100-foot chimney of the deteriorating smelter. The miners have come and gone, but the majesty of this desert mountain range persists.

Miles and Directions

0.0   Hike up the former road by Novak Mill. Do not linger near the mill site: The Novak family is wary of intruders.

0.1–0.5 The trail and river share the same bed, necessitating much stream-hopping.

2.8   At the junction with the canyon from the south, continue on the trail (left) up the main canyon.

3.5   This is the last willow grove—your feet will stay dry from here on.

4.9   Arrive at a mine opening on the right.

5.0   At this major canyon junction, Woodpecker enters from the north, Cannon from the south; continue straight up the main Surprise Canyon.

5.4   Marvel Canyon joins from the south at the trail junction. There's a low rock wall on the left. The chimney of the Panamint City smelter is visible a mile ahead.

6.2   Arrive at the junction with Sourdough Canyon from the north.

6.5   View the smelter ruins. The roads branch off to various other mine sites in Magazine, Water, and Frenchmans Canyons. This is the turnaround point for the hike back to the trailhead.

13.0 Return to the trailhead.

96 Telescope Peak

The trek to Telescope Peak is a strenuous all-day hike to the highest point in the park. From here you have spectacular vistas made even more impressive given the astounding elevation difference of 11,300 feet from the valley below.

Start: About 40 miles south of Stovepipe Wells Village.
Distance: 14 miles out and back.
Approximate hiking time: 7 to 10 hours.
Difficulty: Strenuous.
Trail surface: Dirt path with some rocky areas.

Seasons: Mid-May to mid-November. Check at the ranger station for weather information affecting the Wildrose Canyon Road.
USGS topo map: Telescope Peak-CA (1:24,000).
Trail contact: Furnace Creek Visitor Center & Museum (see appendix D).

Finding the trailhead: The trail begins at the south end of the Mahogany Flat Campground at the end of upper Mahogany Flat Road 8.7 miles east of Wildrose Junction. To reach the trailhead, take Emigrant Canyon Road 20.9 miles south of California Highway 190 to Wildrose Junction. Continue on Mahogany Flat Road. The upper section of the road is rough and steep for the final 1.6 miles after the charcoal kilns.

During winter Mahogany Flat Road above the charcoal kilns is often blocked by snow, adding 3.2 miles to the already long round-trip distance to Telescope Peak. If you are unable to drive all the way to the campground, start the hike from the Thorndike Campground (7.8 miles east of Wildrose Junction) or from the Charcoal Kilns parking area (7.1 miles east of Wildrose Junction). This will add 0.9 mile or 1.6 miles, respectively, to the hike each way, making an early start imperative.

The Hike

The 7-mile trail to the top of Telescope Peak is one of only two constructed backcountry trails in all of Death Valley National Park. Although no rock cairns or tree blazes mark the way, the clear trail is easy to follow throughout its length. After the snow melts by mid- to late spring, there is no water anywhere along the high, dry ridge route, so be sure to carry an ample supply.

An average 8 percent grade is maintained, but there are long stretches where no significant elevation is gained or lost as well as several very steep switchback pitches to the summit. This high-ridge trail hike is especially enjoyable during summer when temperatures are usually unbearable in the valleys on both sides of Telescope Peak—11,000 feet below. This lofty stretch of the Panamint Mountains catches and holds a lot of snow during winter, but the peak can sometimes be climbed without difficulty as early as mid-March with only a mile or so of deep ridgeline snow to "posthole" up just before reaching the summit. During winter it may be easier and safer to avoid the first 2 miles of steep sidehill trail by proceeding straight up the ridge over Rogers Peak. Winter climbers should register at the Wildrose Ranger

The 11,049-foot Telescope Peak rises to the south.

Station before and after the climb, and carry and know how to use ice axes, crampons, and winter clothing.

Backcountry camping is allowed 2 miles beyond the trailhead, but the first level and somewhat protected tent site is 2.6 miles in, along the edge of Arcane Meadows.

From the signed trailhead, the trail starts in a forest of large, old piñon and limber pines, thinning gradually as the elevation increases. A trail register is positioned at 0.2 mile. The trail climbs moderately for 2 miles with spectacular views into the rugged North Fork Hanaupah Canyon, which drains eastward to Death Valley. At 2.6 miles the broad plateau of Arcane Meadows is reached at an elevation of 9,620 feet. This high sagebrush saddle is on the north summit ridge of Telescope Peak, directly below and southwest of the communications facility on Rogers Peak. Twisted tree trunks add a distinctive foreground to the sweep of the high Sierras far to the west, with the wide Tuber Canyon dropping steeply at first and then more gradually into a broad valley.

At 2.7 miles the trail leaves Arcane Meadows as it wraps around the west- to northwest-facing slopes of 9,980-foot Bennett Peak. Expect that about 0.5 mile of this stretch of trail will be snow-covered into early May.

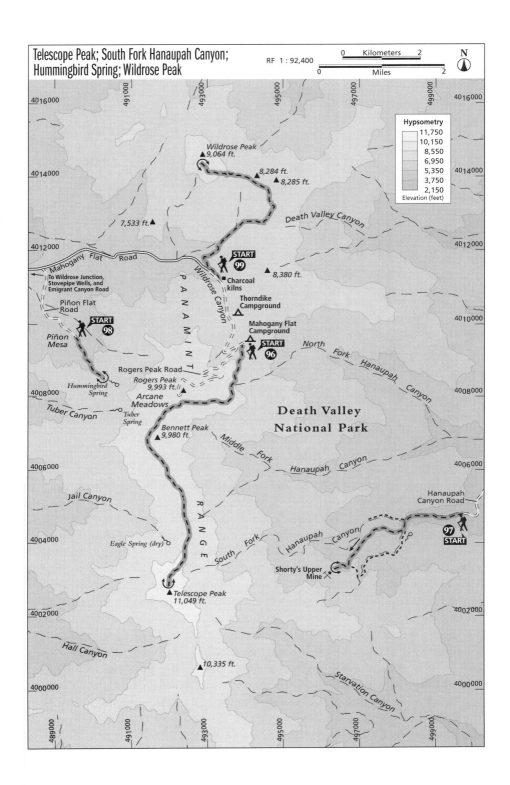

Telescope Peak; South Fork Hanaupah Canyon; Hummingbird Spring; Wildrose Peak

RF 1 : 92,400

Kilometers 0 — 2
Miles 0 — 2

N

Hypsometry
11,750
10,150
8,550
6,950
5,350
3,750
2,150
Elevation (feet)

Wildrose Peak
▲ 9,064 ft.

8,284 ft.
▲ 8,285 ft.

Death Valley Canyon

7,533 ft. ▲

Mahogany Flat Road

START 99

To Wildrose Junction,
Stovepipe Wells, and
Emigrant Canyon Road

Charcoal
kilns

8,380 ft.

Piñon Flat
Road

Thorndike
Campground

START 98

Piñon
Mesa

Mahogany Flat
Campground

START 96

North Fork Hanaupah Canyon

Rogers Peak Road

Rogers Peak
9,993 ft. ▲

Hummingbird
Spring

Arcane
Meadows

Tuber Canyon

Tuber
Spring

Death Valley
National Park

Bennett Peak
▲ 9,980 ft.

Middle Fork Hanaupah Canyon

Jail Canyon

Hanaupah
Canyon Road

Eagle Spring (dry)

South Fork Hanaupah Canyon

97 START

Shorty's Upper
Mine

▲ Telescope Peak
11,049 ft.

Hall Canyon

▲ 10,335 ft.

Starvation Canyon

PANAMINT RANGE

At 4.3 miles the trail reaches the 9,500-foot saddle south of Bennett Peak. In another 0.2 mile the nearly level trail intersects an unsigned side trail, which takes off to the right, climbing first then dropping 1 mile to dry Eagle Spring. Talus rock mixed with matted low-lying vegetation and prickly pear cacti add an unusual alpine tundra/high desert flavor. At the junction follow the trail to the left around the east side of the mountain and then back up to the summit ridge at 5 miles.

After another 0.5 mile the trail reaches the south upper end of the rugged cliffs of Jail Canyon at 9,970 feet. Huge bristlecone pine snags provide irresistible photo opportunities. The trail begins a series of steep switchbacks just right (east) of the sharp summit ridge, attaining an elevation of 10,400 feet at 6.2 miles. Gigantic gnarled bristlecone pines adorn these higher slopes. Some of these ancient trees have been bored and are around 3,000 years old. Members of the same species in the nearby White Mountains are among the oldest living creatures on earth at some 4,600 years!

The 11,000-foot mark is finally achieved at 6.8 miles. From here the trail climbs three mounds along the ridge before reaching the one farthest south at 7 miles—this is 11,049-foot Telescope Peak. The summit consists of a long rocky point, dropping off steeply to the south, west, and east. Mercifully, the actual peak is often less windy than the exposed ridge going up, so if conditions are tolerable, spend some time reading and signing the peak register.

The vertical relief is amazing, almost impossible to comprehend unless you make it to the top and look down on the salt flats of Badwater—the lowest point in the Western Hemisphere—more than 11,300 feet directly below. This monumental elevation difference is exceeded in the United States by only three other mountains: Mount Rainier in Washington and Mounts McKinley and Fairweather in Alaska. Telescope also affords a grand distant view of the highest point in the continental United States—14,494-foot Mount Whitney.

The vast desert basins of Panamint and Death Valley surround jagged canyons that emanate from Telescope Peak like spokes on a wheel. The remarkable contrast of basins and ranges that seem to stretch to infinity on a 360-degree arc is made even more dramatic when snow mantles the summit and higher ridges. Retrace your route to conclude a long, invigorating day on Death Valley's rooftop.

Miles and Directions

0.0 Start at the trailhead at Mahogany Flat Campground.
2.6 Arrive at Arcane Meadows.
4.3 Arrive at the saddle before the summit ridge to the peak.
7.0 Reach the summit of Telescope Peak.
14.0 Return to the trailhead.

Option: For an enjoyable 4-mile loop, hike to the end of the gated Rogers Peak Road, then up the ridge to intersect the Telescope Peak Trail, then north on the trail back to the Mahogany Flat trailhead.

97 South Fork Hanaupah Canyon

This vigorous hike on the eastern slopes of the Panamint Range includes a diverse canyon with springs, waterfalls, and a permanent stream, along with some of the most spectacular vistas in Death Valley. Other attractions include old mining artifacts and a chance to see wildlife.

See map on page 322.
Start: About 27 miles southwest of Furnace Creek.
Distance: 6 miles out and back from upper trailhead (add 6 or 7 miles if driving a 2-wheel-drive vehicle).
Approximate hiking time: 3 to 4 hours (plus another 3 to 4 hours if optional side canyon route is chosen).

Difficulty: Moderate (strenuous for option).
Trail surface: Old rocky mining road with rough sections of rock talus.
Seasons: Mid-September to mid-May.
USGS topo maps: Hanaupah Canyon-CA and Telescope Peak-CA (1:24,000).
Trail contact: Furnace Creek Visitor Center & Museum (see appendix D).

Finding the trailhead: From State Highway 190, drive 7.1 miles south on Badwater Road (California Highway 178); take West Side Road and drive 10.7 miles south to the rough Hanaupah Canyon Road. Hanaupah Canyon Road is also 25 miles north of the southern Badwater Road/West Side Road junction. Like all of the canyon roads on the east side of the Panamints, this road climbs up a rocky alluvial fan. The first 4.8 miles of this 8.3-mile-long road can be driven with a high-clearance two-wheel-drive vehicle. Then the road drops into the canyon and becomes four-wheel drive to the end. Once there, find a wide spot to park at the unsigned trailhead.

The Hike

Begin by hiking up the brushy bottom of the South Fork of Hanaupah Canyon. Hug the left side of the canyon wall to pick up a use trail next to the stream. The springs that feed Hanaupah Canyon discharge an amazing 250–plus gallons per minute, nurturing a diverse riparian corridor that attracts a wide array of wildlife. The old mines and cabin of "Shorty" Borden are on the hillsides above the springs. The trail cuts through an eroded alluvial fan and reaches permanent water at 0.6 mile, as evidenced by willow thickets. This is also the junction of an old mining road that leads to the upper mine. From here it's about 0.3 mile up the brushy bottom to a waterfall. Many of the granite boulders along the streambed are embedded with feldspar crystals, the same Little Chief granite found on Telescope Peak.

To continue the longer hike to the upper mine, head up the old mining road to the left. The next mile gains 1,000 feet, with breathtaking views of a side canyon waterfall and of Death Valley. The two-track is rough but provides a good hiking

Bouldering down a side canyon south of the
South Fork of Hanaupah Canyon.

trail. It continues climbing up a center ridge between the South Fork of Hanaupah Canyon and an unnamed tributary to the south.

Usually by March the road cuts are ablaze with cliffrose and Indian paintbrush. The trail keeps climbing with some very steep pitches, gaining more than 1,300 feet over the next 1.4 miles to the upper mine perched on an open ledge and strewn with old timbers and debris. The adit has an iron door leading to an ore cart on tracks. The adit is unstable and dangerous, so keep a safe distance.

Retrace your route to complete this scenic 6-mile round-trip in the eastern slopes and canyons of Telescope Peak.

Miles and Directions

0.0 Start at the upper trailhead/parking area 8.3 miles up Hanaupah Canyon Road.

0.6 At the springs and a mining road junction, climb to the left.

1.4 View the waterfall vista in the side canyon.

3.0 Arrive at the upper mine/adit.

6.0 Return to the trailhead for a round-trip hike. This doesn't include the distance required if you're using a two-wheel-drive vehicle.

Options: To turn this out-and-back hike into a diverse but strenuous loop, drop into the unnamed tributary canyon immediately south and east of the upper mine. Plan on three to five hours to descend this rugged and challenging canyon. It is so rugged that if you were going up, you'd quickly turn around. But with a down–canyon route, you have little choice but to keep going. You begin with a steep 500-foot drop to the canyon floor. Every twist and turn brings new surprises: sheer cliffs, formations, dry falls, and boulders that can be bypassed by climbing up, around, and back down. The midsection contains springs with pools of water in scoured rocks harboring frogs, long-eared owls, and other unlikely desert denizens. A 50-foot dry fall in the lower end forces a climb high on the left shoulder. Then more dry falls forcing more steep sidehilling. The canyon mouth intersects the trail below the upper mine and about 0.6 mile above the upper trailhead.

With its abundant water, the South Fork of Hanaupah Canyon could be used as a base camp for an extremely arduous cross-country climb of Telescope Peak (11,049 feet). The route for the gain of nearly 7,500 feet would be up the middle ridge between the South and Middle Forks of Hanaupah Canyon, intersecting the trail about 1 mile north of the peak.

98 Hummingbird Spring

An exploratory hike into a piñon-juniper canyon below Panamint Mountain cliffs takes you into a remote canyon within bighorn-sheep habitat, ending at a small spring.

See map on page 322.
Start: About 35 miles south of Stovepipe Wells Village.
Distance: 3 miles out and back.
Approximate hiking time: 1 to 2 hours.
Difficulty: Moderate.
Trail surface: Rocky path and rocky wash.

Seasons: October to mid-November, March through June.
USGS topo maps: Jail Canyon-CA and Telescope Peak-CA (1:24,000).
Trail contact: Furnace Creek Visitor Center & Museum (see appendix D).

Finding the trailhead: From California Highway 190, take Emigrant Canyon Road 20.9 miles southward to the junction with Wildrose Canyon Road. Continue east on Mahogany Flat Road, passing the ranger station and campground on the way up Wildrose Canyon. Four miles east of the campground, turn right (south) on Piñon Flat Road; there are JEEP (i.e., four-wheel drive recommended) and NO FIRES signs on a post. The gravel road becomes too rough for all but high-clearance four-wheel-drive vehicles at 1.5 miles. Park along the road and hike up the road 0.2 mile to where it bends sharply northeast and rises to the Piñon Mesa picnic area. To prevent vehicular use, stones block the old road that continues straight south. This is the trailhead.

The Hike

This hike provides exploratory opportunities for history buffs or anyone who might enjoy a destinationless ramble in a lovely remote canyon high above Death Valley. Although the spring is usually a mere trickle, the area contains dense piñon-juniper vegetation thanks to its mountainside setting. The elevation makes the hike suitable for a summertime outing in the Wildrose region of the park. Also, when the wind is intense on the ridges of the Panamints, the Hummingbird Spring valley offers some protection.

From the trailhead, the former road quickly deteriorates to a rocky trail. The area is a favorite of the resident feral burro population. Their tracks and droppings are everywhere. Avoid confrontations with these wild animals. It is unlikely that your paths would cross, since they are not interested in human contact. Whatever trail maintenance has been done in the last sixty years has been done by the burro pack that uses these pathways. The burros compete with bighorn sheep. As such, the park service will try to remove many of the burros from wild-sheep range.

As you climb the road/wash/burro path, you will spot remnants of prior human habitation: rusty cans, barrel hoops, lumber. Several pieces of galvanized pipe can be seen in the underbrush. Watch, too, for ax cuts on the pine stumps. This is a visual treasure hunt for the history detective. The actual site of the spring and buildings have vanished, but enough clues remain to suggest their whereabouts. Following the wash will bring you to a high junction of washes directly below a prominent 8,100-foot cliff face of the Panamints.

The immense value of water in the mining era in Death Valley is evident from the Skidoo Pipeline, which crosses the Mahogany Flat Road just before the Piñon Flat turnoff. This 1907 pipeline carried water from Birch Spring in Jail Canyon to the south of Telescope Peak to the town of Skidoo, 23 miles north. This project cost $250,000 (in 1907 dollars). Even a small spring like Hummingbird was important to the residents of the valley.

Exploring the various small washes and ridges that extend down from the towering cliffs of the Panamint Range behind Hummingbird Spring expands the hike and turns it into a rambling adventure. When you turn for the descent to your car, you will also enjoy vistas of Wildrose Peak and Canyon.

Miles and Directions

0.0 Head south up the eroded trail.

0.7 The trail and wash divide. Follow the one to the right.

1.5 The trail ends at a junction of three small gullies.

3.0 Return the way you came.

99 Wildrose Peak

The Wildrose Trail takes you to a high Panamint summit from which the highest and lowest land in the lower forty-eight states can be seen.

See map on page 322.
Start: About 38 miles south of Stovepipe Wells Village.
Length: 8.4 miles out and back.
Approximate hiking time: 4 to 6 hours.
Difficulty: Strenuous.
Trail surface: Dirt path.

Seasons: September to mid-November, March through June (depending on snow level).
USGS topo maps: Wildrose Peak-CA and Telescope Peak-CA (1:24,000).
Trail contact: Furnace Creek Visitor Center & Museum (see appendix D).

Finding the trailhead: From California Highway 190 at Emigrant Junction, drive south on Emigrant Canyon Road 20.9 miles to Wildrose Junction; continue east on Mahogany Flat Road (paved for 4.5 miles) and drive 7.1 miles to the Wildrose Charcoal Kilns parking area. In winter this road may be impassable; check with park authorities for weather and road conditions. The signed trail to Wildrose Peak begins at the west end of the kilns.

The Hike

Wildrose Peak provides panoramic views of Death Valley and the surrounding mountain ranges. This official park trail to Wildrose travels through classic piñon-juniper forest to a high saddle, then zigzags to the broad, open summit of this central peak in the Panamint Range. The meadowlike mountaintop is nearly always windy; appropriate clothing is a requirement, as are binoculars to enjoy the sweeping 360-degree view. Summer hikers will appreciate bug dope to combat flies and gnats.

In spite of its rather impressive elevation gain, the Wildrose Trail begins modestly. From the kilns at the trailhead, the trail charges 50 yards uphill to the northwest, achieving a 60-foot gain, but then follows the contour of the hillside for nearly the next mile. This section is a gentle warm-up for the hike ahead. Along the route, rock outcroppings extend to the west, hovering over Wildrose Canyon below. This is classic mountain-lion country.

Climbing only slightly, the trail joins another trail coming up from the canyon. Numerous pine stumps are a reminder of the logging done over a century ago to supply the charcoal kilns during their brief use in the 1870s. At the head of the canyon, the trail begins its climb. At 1.2 miles the trail bends north and steepens sharply, gaining over 600 feet in less than a mile. Rising to the first saddle, you will enjoy a magnificent view of Death Valley below through the evergreens.

The trail climbs around three small rises before emerging on a ridge above the saddle below the peak. Here, at 3.1 miles and 8,230 feet, you can pause and view the length of Death Valley. From here, a mile of switchbacks leads to the summit.

The trail snakes north, then south, then north, and so on, up the 800-foot climb. The changing direction enables you to enjoy a variety of vistas as you ascend the mountain, particularly as you near the windswept summit, which is clear of major vegetation.

A small rock wall on the peak was designed to give some protection from the wind. Or you can drop just a couple of feet down on the leeward side of the mountain to enjoy your stay and write a note for the peak registry. From Wildrose you can see the vast area of mining activity in the north end of the Panamint Range. Just to the northeast in the canyon below there is a massive mining camp. Farther along Emigrant Canyon Road, the mountainsides are crisscrossed with mining roads. Rogers (with the microwave station) and Telescope Peaks loom above to the south. To the west is the mighty wall of the Sierras. To the east, across the valley, are the Funeral and Black Mountains. This is an eagle's view of the Death Valley world.

The hike back down the mountain allows you to relax and focus on a new view of the scenery. Death Valley Canyon, extending eastward below the high saddle, is just one of the dramatic sights you may notice on the downward trip. Although this is a heavily used trail, its bending pathway preserves the sense of solitude for the hiker.

Miles and Directions

0.0 The trail climbs, then levels as it follows the contour of a hill.

0.9 Arrive at the head of Wildrose Canyon.

1.8 Arrive at a saddle, with views of Death Valley and Badwater to the east. The trail turns north and climbs to a second saddle.

2.9 Arrive at the second saddle, which offers more panoramas. The trail drops slightly, then switchbacks up the eastern side of Wildrose.

4.1 Reach the south peak, the false summit.

4.2 Reach the north peak, the genuine summit, where the register is in an ammo box.

8.4 Return to the trailhead by the same route.

100 Nemo Canyon

The Nemo Canyon hike takes you on a gentle downhill traverse hike through open desert and down a wide graveled wash, bounded by low ridges and multicolored badlands, providing a pleasing contrast to nearby mountain climbs.

Start: About 28 miles south of Stovepipe Wells Village.
Distance: 3.6 miles one way.
Approximate hiking time: 3 to 4 hours.
Difficulty: Moderate.
Trail surface: Cross-country; open graveled wash.

Seasons: October through May.
USGS topo map: Emigrant Pass-CA (1:24,000).
Trail contact: Furnace Creek Visitor Center & Museum (see appendix D).

Finding the trailhead: From Wildrose Junction (0.2 mile west of Wildrose Campground and Ranger Station), drive 2.2 miles north on the paved Emigrant Canyon Road and turn left (northwest) onto an unsigned gravel road that takes off from the paved road as it veers right (northeast). Drive 0.7 mile to the end of the road at a paved T next to a gravel pit. A USGS benchmark is adjacent to this spot, which is the trailhead/jumping-off point for the hike. The end point is the broad mouth of Nemo Canyon on Wildrose Canyon Road, down the canyon 3 miles southwest of Wildrose Junction and 1 mile southwest of the picnic area.

The Hike

This moderate point-to-point down-canyon traverse begins in open desert country dotted with creosote brush and Mormon tea. Nemo Canyon drops moderately to the southwest. To avoid walking toward the sun and into a stiff afternoon wind, make this a morning excursion if at all possible.

The canyon is wide open with low-lying hills and ridges. Soon, a few scattered yuccas begin to appear. At first the wash is braided and graveled, but it becomes better defined with a sandy bottom after about 1 mile. At 1.5 miles the valley narrows a bit. In another 0.2 mile red rhyolite bluffs rise on the left side. Around the corner the valley opens in a semicircle with several side canyons entering from the right. The white saline seep of Mud Spring is also to the right at 4,020 feet. At 2 miles 100-foot-high cliffs rise on the left as the canyon narrows slightly. After another 0.2 mile the wash parallels brightly colored badlands—red, white, black, gray, pink, and tan—with steep bluffs rising several hundred feet on the left. At 2.4 miles a huge valley enters from the right. At 3 miles and 3,550 feet, the canyon is marked by brown, deeply eroded conglomerate cliffs and spires. Soon large granite boulders appear, resting precariously atop spires of brown conglomerate. At times loose gravel impedes walking, but the steady downhill grade helps. At 3.5 miles the canyon opens to the wide Wildrose Valley. In just another 0.1 mile, Nemo Canyon meets the rough

Nemo Canyon

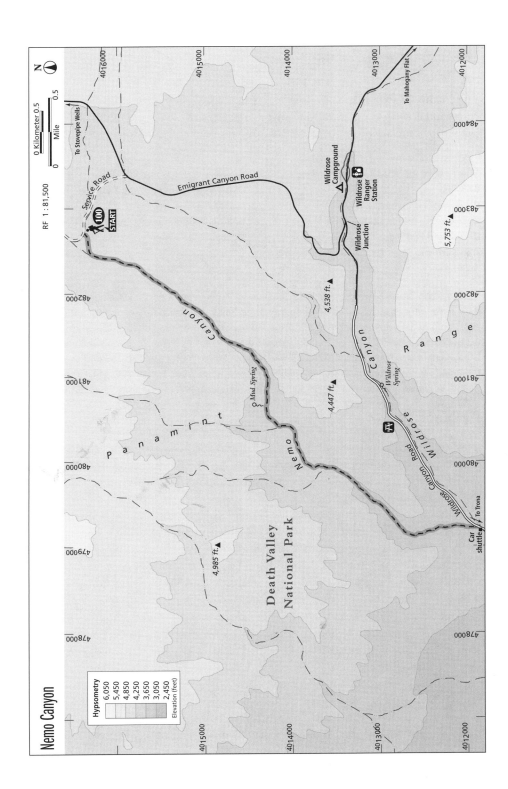

RF 1 : 81,500

0 Kilometer 0.5
0 Mile 0.5

N

To Stovepipe Wells

Service Road

START

Emigrant Canyon Road

4016000
4015000
4014000
4013000
4012000

4016000
4015000
4014000
4013000
4012000

484000
483000
482000
481000
480000
479000
478000

Canyon

Panamint

Mud Spring

Nemo

4,985 ft.▲

Death Valley
National Park

4,538 ft.▲

4,447 ft.▲

Wildrose Spring

Canyon

Range

Wildrose

Wildrose Canyon Road

Car shuttle

To Trona

To Mahogany Flat

Wildrose Campground

Wildrose Ranger Station

Wildrose Junction

5,753 ft.▲

Hypsometry

6,050
5,450
4,850
4,250
3,650
3,050
2,450

Elevation (feet)

Wildrose Canyon Road at 3,200 feet, thereby completing this point-to-point downhill traverse.

Miles and Directions

0.0 Start at the trailhead in the Nemo Canyon wash.

1.8 Arrive at Mud Spring.

3.6 Finish the hike at Wildrose Canyon Road.

101 Darwin Falls

A delightful moist microclimate with multitiered waterfalls is tucked away in a scenic canyon.

Start: About 31 miles southwest of Stovepipe Wells Village.
Distance: 3 miles out and back.
Approximate hiking time: 2 to 4 hours.
Difficulty: Easy to lower falls; strenuous to middle valley or overlook.

Trail surface: Dirt path to lower falls; some boulders to middle valley; primitive burro trail to overlook.
Seasons: October through June.
USGS topo map: Darwin-CA (1:24,000).
Trail contact: Furnace Creek Visitor Center & Museum (see appendix D).

Finding the trailhead: From Panamint Springs, 29.6 miles southwest of Stovepipe Wells on California Highway 190, drive west 1.1 miles to the first dirt road on the left. Turn left (south) on the dirt road and drive 2.6 miles to the signed side road on the right for the Darwin Falls parking area. You will notice a pipeline running along the road. The road is rough but passable for a standard passenger vehicle.

The Hike

Nestled at the western edge of Death Valley National Park, Darwin Falls was formerly a BLM Area of Critical Environmental Concern (ACEC). During its years of jurisdiction, the BLM took firm measures to protect the area against vehicular intrusion. Welded pipe barricades are still in place, along with stern warnings against such misuse. The BLM's 8,600-acre Darwin Falls Wilderness Area is immediately west of the park adjacent to the canyon.

Darwin Stream is the only permanent water in this area of the park. Flowing from the China Garden Spring, Darwin supplies the Panamint Springs Resort with water via a pipeline, which is visible on both the drive and the hike to the falls. This year-round water source sustains dense willow and cottonwood thickets in the valley and canyon as well as a thriving population of birds. Cliff swallows and red-tailed hawks soar overhead. Brazen chuckwalla lizards stare at intruders from their rocky lairs.

This hike is a radical change from the usual Death Valley outing. Right from the parking area, a streak of greenery and a glistening brook lead up the gently sloping valley floor. Hopping from one side of the stream to the other begins here and will continue throughout the hike. Steady footwork will prevent getting soaked, but care is especially required on the smooth, slippery boulders farther up the canyon. The Darwin Mountains of black rhyolite tower above the bright green grass, the willow saplings, the horsetails and cattails.

At the notch of the canyon's mouth, another welded barricade remains, as does a BLM sign reminding visitors of Darwin Falls' value to vegetation and to wildlife. Bathing and wading are prohibited. The high, dry trail is above the stream on the south side of the canyon. There are many bends in the narrow canyon. With the steep canyon walls, as well as the willow and cottonwood thickets, this is a shady hike, an excellent outing for a hot sunny day! A USGS gauging station is on the north side of the stream. With its aluminum phone booth architecture, it looks decidedly out of place in this Garden of Eden. Beyond the station you need to watch your footing when clambering over the smooth water-eroded boulders.

At 1 mile, after hearing them in the distance, you reach the falls. Double falls cascade over a 25-foot dropoff, surrounded by large old cottonwoods. Sword ferns, watercress, and cattails flourish in the pool below the falls. This is the turnaround point for the shorter hike.

To continue the recommended hike, retreat 50 yards downstream and pick up the use trail up the south wall. The best option (there are several use trails) takes off on a solid outcropping of greenish granite and traverses the canyon wall to the valley above the falls. Climbing the finely grained granite must be done with caution. It doesn't crumble, but it can be very slippery. From the trail, thread your way through the dense willows and cottonwoods to the upper end of the valley adjacent to a very loose talus slope. Here the three-tiered upper falls plummet 140 feet from the cliff above. This is not a heavily visited spot. In the narrow canyon your only company will probably be the cliff swallows swooping overhead.

To continue to the overlook, return down the valley to the same route and follow the burros' use trail on up the canyon's south wall. The trail emerges 140 feet above the valley. From the pinnacle at the point where the stream bends sharply from its easterly flow to a northern direction is the only view of the highest fall. Here the stream takes an 80-foot clear drop. This is the turnaround point for the longer hike.

Emerging from Darwin Canyon is an Alice-in-Wonderland experience. After being surrounded by humidity and greenery, the beige world of the desert looks one-dimensional. The valley below the canyon is a striking transition zone, with the soft greenery of the stream ecosystem juxtaposed against the jagged dark rhyolite cliffs of the mountains to the south. The hike to Darwin Falls is a carnival of sensory perceptions. The smells, sounds, feel, and sight of this watery world make this an exceptional experience.

Darwin Falls

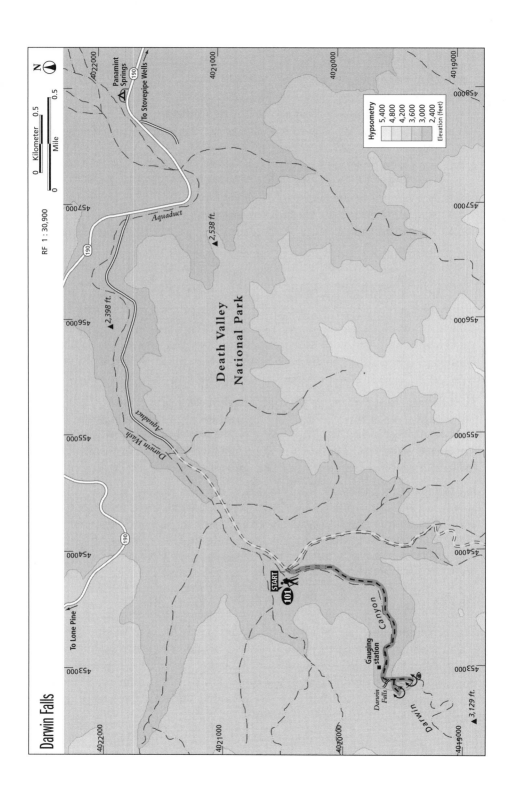

RF 1 : 30,900

N

Hypsometry

5,400
4,800
4,200
3,600
3,000
2,400

Elevation (feet)

Death Valley
National Park

Panamint
Springs

To Stovepipe Wells

To Lone Pine

Aquaduct

2,538 ft.

2,398 ft.

Darwin Wash

Aquaduct

START

101

Gauging
station

Darwin
Falls

Canyon

Darwin

3,129 ft.

Miles and Directions

0.0–0.4 The trail follows a stream up the narrow valley floor.

0.4 There's a vehicle barricade at the entrance to the canyon.

0.9 A USGS stream-gauging station is located on the right bank.

1.0 Arrive at the lower falls. Drop back downstream 50 yards to pick up the trail to the middle valley and overlook.

1.1 Arrive at the middle valley and thread your way through the willows to the high basin and pools below the falls (at 1 mile). Return to the same trail to ascend to the overlook.

1.4 Take the burro use trail to a view of the highest falls.

1.6 Arrive at the falls overlook and the turnaround point.

3.0 Return to the trailhead.

102 Panamint Dunes

This is a cross-country open desert hike on relatively inaccessible, high, star-shaped sand dunes in the expanded western region of the park. Spectacular views of the Panamint Valley and surrounding mountain ranges sweep in all directions.

Start: About 30 miles southwest of Stovepipe Wells Village.

Distance: 9 miles out and back.

Approximate hiking time: 3 to 4 hours.

Difficulty: Moderate.

Trail surface: Sand. No trail.

Seasons: Mid-October to mid-April.

USGS topo map: The Dunes-CA (1:24,000).

Trail contact: Furnace Creek Visitor Center & Museum (see appendix D).

Finding the trailhead: From Panamint Springs, drive east on California Highway 190 for 4.9 miles to the signed Lake Hill Road. Turn left (north) on Lake Hill Road and drive 6.1 miles to where the road begins to deteriorate as it bends east. This is the north end of the North Panamint Dry Lake bed. Park on the left (west) side of the road at the bend and begin the hike from here. The access road is rough and graveled but can be negotiated by standard vehicles driven slowly and carefully.

The Hike

The Panamint Dunes are clearly visible to the northwest from the trailhead/parking area. Because these extensive dunes rise several hundred feet, they appear deceptively close. In fact, they are 4 miles away across open desert, requiring a steady one-and-a-half- to two-hour walk just to reach the higher complex of dunes. This relative inaccessibility, as compared to most other dunes in the California desert region, accounts for their pristine quality.

Hiking the Panamint Dunes with a view to the northeast—star-shaped dune configurations are visible on the north side of these dunes.

These ever-changing mounds of sand are home to several endemic plants, dune grass, vetch, and more. The Panamint Valley is the site of mysterious rock alignments, some of which are called "intaglios." Intaglios are of prehistoric human origin and are huge animal shapes, perhaps hundreds of feet in size. These shapes, one of which is reported to be of a hummingbird, can be discerned from an airplane but not from the dunes. Fortunately, the park wilderness designation now protects these artifacts from the destructive impact of off-road vehicles.

At first the line-of-sight cross-country route to the dunes crosses a short section of rough, rocky alluvial fan. Don't be discouraged, for soon the open desert floor is made up mostly of well-compacted sand and desert pavement with more solid footing. The ascent is gradual, averaging only about 250 feet per mile. At 2.5 miles and 2,020 feet elevation, you'll reach the lower edge of the dunes, with large creosote bushes dominating the landscape. The going becomes a bit slower in the softer sand.

After another mile and 400-foot ascent, the base of the higher dunes is attained. Dune grass appears in sporadic patches with the indentations of animal and insect tracks seemingly everywhere. From here pick out a sandy ridge route to the apex of

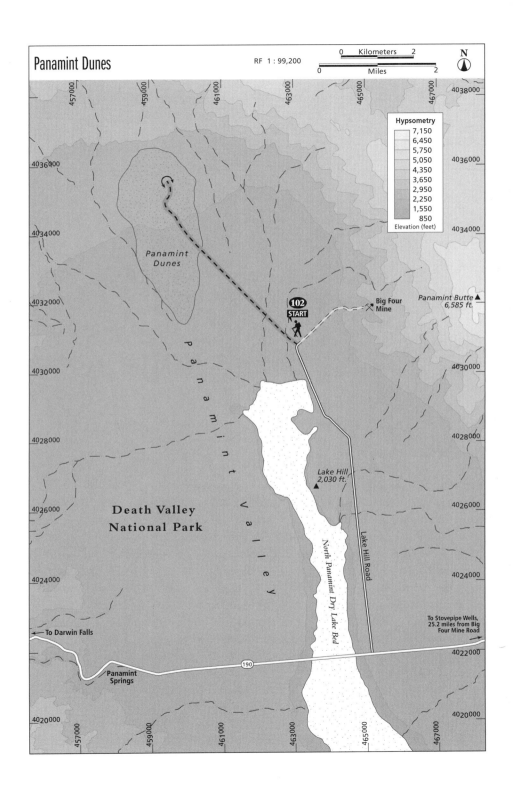

Panamint Dunes

RF 1 : 99,200

Kilometers
0   2
Miles
0   2

N

Hypsometry

7,150
6,450
5,750
5,050
4,350
3,650
2,950
2,250
1,550
850

Elevation (feet)

457000
459000
461000
463000
465000
467000

4038000
4036000
4034000
4032000
4030000
4028000
4026000
4024000
4022000
4020000

Panamint Dunes

102
START

Big Four
Mine

Panamint Butte ▲
6,585 ft.

P a n a m i n t

V a l l e y

Lake Hill
2,030 ft.
▲

**Death Valley
National Park**

North Panamint Dry Lake Bed

Lake Hill Road

To Stovepipe Wells,
25.2 miles from Big
Four Mine Road

← To Darwin Falls

190

Panamint
Springs

the dunes, attained after another mile, somewhere around 2,700 feet elevation. Depending on angle to the wind and relative moisture, climbing the nearly 300-foot-high dunes can be tiring, but the effort by way of a route of swirling, twisting ridges to the top will be well rewarded.

The star-shaped configuration of these dunes is especially apparent on the northern backside. Here swirls of sand wrap around small circular basins and bowls forming an intricate maze of shapes and patterns. Some of the sand basins resemble perfectly rounded craters. The view from the knife-ridge apex of the dunes is magnificent. Panamint Springs can be seen far to the southwest. The vast Panamint Valley stretches southward with the distinctive volcanic remnants of Lake Hill rising from the dry lake bed. Lofty Telescope Peak crowns the Panamint Mountains, with the multicolored bands of Panamint Butte dominating the immediate southeast horizon.

To return, follow a line-of-sight route toward Telescope Peak—by far the highest point to the south—and you'll end up at or very close to the trailhead, thereby completing this varied 9-mile trip to the Panamint Dunes. At first glance you might think that all dunes are somewhat similar, just another "pile of sand" as we heard one casual observer to say. Not so. Each of the four dune hikes suggested in this book, and their desert basin and range settings, is so different from the others that they can hardly be compared.

Miles and Directions

0.0 At the north end of the North Panamint Dry Lake bed, begin the hike across open, sandy desert.

2.5 After a gradual ascent you'll reach the lower edge of the dunes, with creosote bushes dominating.

3.5 Reach the base of the higher dunes (2,420 feet).

4.5 Reach the high point of the dunes (2,700 feet).

9.0 Return to the trailhead.

1○3 Marble Canyon

Marble Canyon is a long out-and-back day hike up a deep, narrow canyon in the Cottonwood Mountains. Here you will find colorful rock formations, petroglyphs, and expansive views of remote backcountry.

Start: About 14 miles west of Stovepipe Wells Village.
Distance: 9.6 miles out and back from the road closure 2.6 miles up Marble Canyon Road (if your vehicle is parked at the signed Cottonwood-Marble Canyon junction, add 5.2 miles to the round-trip hiking distance).
Approximate hiking time: 4 to 5 hours, or 7 to 8 hours for longer outing.

Difficulty: Moderate.
Trail surface: Rocky path for 1.1 miles; sandy wash thereafter.
Seasons: October through May.
USGS topo map: Cottonwood Creek-CA (1:24,000).
Trail contact: Furnace Creek Visitor Center & Museum (see appendix D).

Finding the trailhead: From Stovepipe Wells Village on California Highway 190, head west on Cottonwood Road. Cottonwood Road begins by bearing left at the entrance to the Stovepipe Wells Campground. The two-wheel-drive portion of this slow, rocky road ends after 8.4 miles when the road drops steeply into Cottonwood Wash and turns left up the canyon. High-clearance four-wheel drive is advised beyond this point due to soft gravel and high centers. The junction of Cottonwood and Marble Canyon Roads is 10.7 miles from the Stovepipe Wells Campground. Cottonwood Canyon is to the left. Marble Canyon Road continues to the right another 2.6 miles to the signed vehicle closure at canyon narrows, but park at the junction if you have any doubts about whether your vehicle can negotiate these final very rough 2.6 miles.

The Hike

The adjacent Cottonwood and Marble Canyons are as different from each other as night and day. Cottonwood is wide and open whereas Marble is a wonderland of intimate narrows and dark alcoves.

The recommended trip described below is an out-and-back exploration of scenic Marble Canyon all the way up to its junction with Dead Horse Canyon. However, a much longer 23-mile backpacking loop through both canyons can be undertaken by those willing to cache water on this dry route and commit a minimum of three days. The loop can start from the Cottonwood/Marble Canyon Road junction. Begin by hiking 8.5 miles up the Cottonwood Canyon road, cross over into Marble Canyon by way of Dead Horse Canyon, and descend 7.4 miles down Marble Canyon from the mouth of Dead Horse Canyon to the point of origin at the road junction. About half of this loop is on open four-wheel-drive roads, with

Marble Canyon contains several sets of petroglyphs— ▶
look but don't touch.

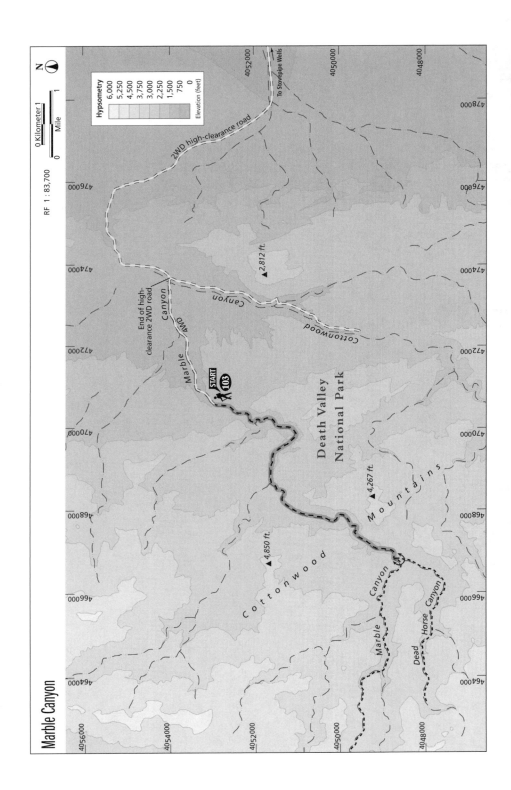

Marble Canyon

RF 1 : 83,700

N

0 Kilometer 1
0 Mile 1

Hypsometry
6,000
5,250
4,500
3,750
3,000
2,250
1,500
750
0

Elevation (feet)

4056000
4054000
4052000
4050000
4048000

4640000
4660000
4680000
4700000
4720000
4740000
4760000
4780000

2WD high-clearance road

To Stovepipe Wells

End of high-clearance 2WD road

Marble Canyon

4WD

Cottonwood Canyon

▲2,812 ft.

START 103

Death Valley National Park

Cottonwood

▲4,850 ft.

▲4,267 ft.

M o u n t a i n s

Marble Canyon

Dead Horse Canyon

the remainder being canyon washes and an overland cross-country route. Marble Canyon is susceptible to flash flooding with a corresponding danger of being caught in one of its steep chutes with no escape. Do not attempt to hike the canyon if wet weather appears imminent.

For the Marble Canyon out-and-back day excursion, the hike might start out of vehicular necessity at the Cottonwood/Marble Canyons Road junction, but the real adventure begins 2.6 miles up at the canyon gap/road closure. On the way up at mile 2.3, petroglyphs can be seen at the mouth of the canyon. Sadly, some of these irreplaceable cultural links to the past have been senselessly defaced by vandals. There are more pristine petroglyphs farther up Marble Canyon, readily seen going up but more difficult to spot on the way down.

At the trailhead the canyon is only about 6 feet wide, coinciding with the wilderness boundary, which is signed with a closure to vehicular travel. At 0.3 mile a canyon enters from the right, which leads quickly to a 15-foot dry fall. Continue left up the creosote–Mormon tea bottom next to great stair-step beds of tilted gray and red rock. At 1.1 miles a huge boulder blocks the canyon—it can be bypassed on the right by climbing up stepping stones. At 1.3 miles the canyon narrows to sheer, gray cliffs where graffiti mars still more petroglyphs. Here every turn in the twisting canyon brings new variety, with arches being formed from smooth, gently eroded gray cliffs. Overhangs create an almost cavelike effect.

At 1.6 miles the valley opens dramatically only to narrow again at 1.9 miles. Once more the valley widens with brilliant displays of reds, tans, and grays on both sides at 2.3 miles. Here a major canyon enters from the right; stay to the left (west) by entering dark-walled narrows, which soon give way to a long, open stretch. The canyon closes in again at 3.5 miles, marked by a distinctive semicircular alcove on the left. Soon white and gray bands of marble resembling zebra stripes border a wonderland of grottos in the narrow canyon. A second large boulder blocks the wash at 4 miles but can be easily bypassed by climbing a "staircase" rock on the left. A small side canyon, overlooked by buttes and pinnacles, enters on the right at 4.2 miles.

Dead Horse Canyon joins Marble Canyon from the left (south) at 4.8 miles, at an elevation of 3,110 feet. The wide Dead Horse Valley looks deceptively like the main drainage, but Marble Canyon cuts sharply to the right (west). There are several spacious and excellent campsites at this junction, above the wash, for those willing to pack sufficient water for an overnight stay.

Many years ago someone etched GOLD BELT SPRING 4 MILES into the desert varnish of a large rock with an arrow pointing up Marble Canyon. Another 0.2 mile above the junction a massive white cliff oversees the left side of Marble Canyon as it climbs steeply toward Goldbelt Spring.

As you return down the canyon to the trailhead, you'll appreciate having had the sun at your back both for the morning ascent and the afternoon descent. This trip is well worth a full day of canyon exploration.

Miles and Directions

0.0   The trailhead is at a signed vehicle closure 2.6 miles up the Marble Canyon Road, where canyon walls are only 6 or 7 feet apart.

0.3   Where the canyon (right) leads to a 15-foot dry fall, stay left.

1.1   A huge boulder blocks the canyon, ending the previously open four-wheel-drive road. Climb up the stepping stones to the right.

1.4   Overhangs here create a cavelike effect in the canyon.

2.3   At the major junction, continue left (west) into a narrow, dark-walled canyon.

3.5   The canyon again narrows, with a semicircular alcove on the right.

4.0   Another boulder blocks the canyon. Climb the staircase of rocks on the left.

4.8   Dead Horse Canyon enters from the south; turnaround point.

9.6   Return to the trailhead.

104 Mosaic Canyon

Patterned walls of multicolored rock and water-sculpted formations await you in this picturesque canyon near Stovepipe Wells.

Start: About 2 miles south of Stovepipe Wells Village.
Distance: 3.6 miles out and back.
Approximate hiking time: 2 to 3 hours.
Difficulty: Easy to lower dry fall; moderate to upper dry fall.

Trail surface: Dirt path with rock, then open canyon floor.
Seasons: October through April.
USGS topo map: Stovepipe Wells-CA (1:24,000).
Trail contact: Furnace Creek Visitor Center & Museum (see appendix D).

Finding the trailhead: From California Highway 190, 0.1 mile southwest of Stovepipe Wells Village, head south on the rough but passable Mosaic Canyon Road (signed). After 2.1 miles the road ends at the Mosaic Canyon parking area and the trail takes off immediately (south).

The Hike

The fault in the Tucki Mountain that produced Mosaic Canyon consists of mosaic breccia and smooth Noonday formation dolomite, formed in a sea bed 750 million to 900 million years ago. After being pressurized and baked at more than 1,000 degrees, then eroded, the resulting rock has startling contrasts of both texture and color.

Hikers make their way through the marbleized
watercourse of Mosaic Canyon.

Mosaic Canyon; Grotto Canyon; Little Bridge Canyon

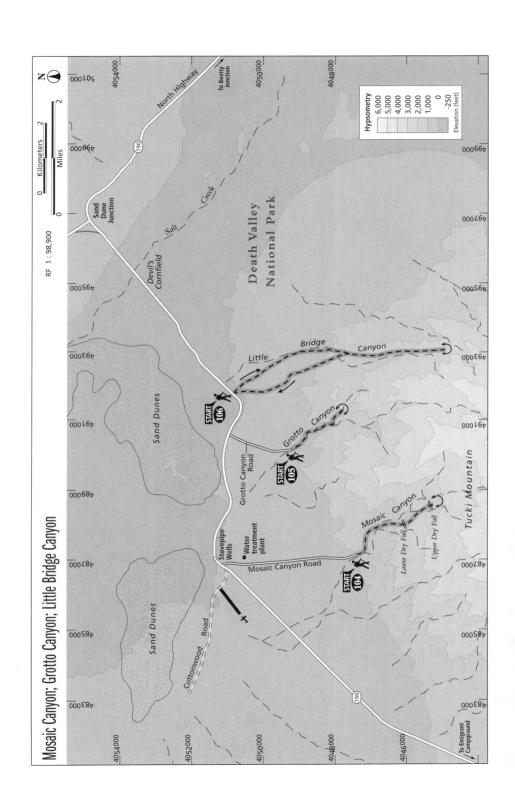

Mosaic Canyon drains more than 4 square miles of the Tucki Range, so it is to be avoided, like all canyons, in flash-flood conditions. Rushing water, carrying its load of scouring boulders, has created smooth marbleized waterways out of the otherwise lumpy breccia. Silky surfaces gradually change to ragged lumps from the canyon floor up its walls, reflecting the varying depths of floodwaters.

Like other canyons in Tucki Mountain, Mosaic Canyon is alternately wide and narrow. The wider spots are more numerous, and are broad enough almost to qualify as valleys. Often parties of hikers arrive at these open areas and turn back, figuring that the canyon excitement has ended. With plenty of water and a broad-brimmed hat, you can continue exploring the depths of Mosaic. If it's a hot day, be aware that this is not a deep, shady canyon like the ones in the Grapevine and Funeral Mountains.

The first 0.2 mile of canyon features the smooth marble surfaces that have made Mosaic a favorite destination of Death Valley visitors. After that, the canyon opens to a wide colorful amphitheater, swinging eastward to a broad valley with a 40-foot butte standing in the center. Use trails go in all directions, converging at the end of the valley where the canyon narrows again. To the right of this butte, a deep wash will eventually become a new branch of Mosaic Canyon.

At 1 mile a small pile of boulders blocks a narrow spot. A well-traveled path to the left provides an easy detour. After another wide spot, the canyon narrows again, where an abrupt 40-foot dry fall blocks your passage. It is possible to get around this barrier by way of a well-traveled and cairned trail. Drop 50 yards back from the dry fall to the trail on the sloping canyon wall to the south. This trail takes you to the upper region of Mosaic Canyon where another 0.5 mile of marbleized chutes and narrows awaits you. A steep marble chute, 50 feet high, halts the hike at 1.8 miles. It's a striking spot, with eroding, fragmented Tucki Mountain rising above the silky smooth waterslide.

The hike back down the canyon provides new views of Death Valley and the Cottonwood Mountains in the distance. Sliding down the short water chutes on the return to the trailhead increases the marbleized beauty of these breccia formations; generations of hikers have added to water's erosive force in creating these smooth rocks.

Miles and Directions

0.0–0.2 The trail begins in a wash from the parking area behind an information sign.

0.2 Hike through the wide-open canyon.

1.4 A 40-foot dry fall blocks the canyon; 50 yards back, cairns and arrows mark the side trail detour.

1.8 A 50-foot marble chute blocks the canyon.

2.8 Return to the trailhead from the lower dry fall.

3.6 Return to the trailhead from the upper dry fall.

105 Grotto Canyon

This out-and-back canyon hike winds through water-carved grottos and narrows of polished rock to a high, dry falls.

See map on page 346.
Start: About 3.5 miles southeast of Stovepipe Wells Village.
Distance: 4 miles out and back.
Approximate hiking time: 2 to 3 hours.
Difficulty: Easy.

Trail surface: Sandy rocky wash, then open canyon floor.
Seasons: October through April.
USGS topo map: Grotto Canyon-CA (1:24,000).
Trail contact: Furnace Creek Visitor Center & Museum (see appendix D).

Finding the trailhead: The Grotto Canyon access road heads south from California Highway 190, 2.4 miles east of Stovepipe Wells Village. The road is signed for Grotto Canyon and four-wheel-drive vehicles. After 1.1 miles the road ends for most vehicles above the wash, which is soft gravel. There's no actual trailhead, but the road/trail continues on up the wash to the canyon.

The Hike

With careful driving, a passenger vehicle can negotiate the road to the wash on the Grotto Canyon hike. The soft gravel of the wash for the mile to the canyon entrance requires high clearance and four-wheel drive. No signs or markers punctuate the end of the road, but severe washouts end vehicle access just before the first dry fall. Conditions in this canyon change with each flood. At times the gravel is deep and the dry falls are easy to scale, but often floods have scoured the gravel away, making exploring more of a challenge.

Like the other Tucki Mountain canyons, Grotto is a very broad canyon, up to 200 yards wide in many areas. Deeply eroded canyon walls stand like medieval castle ramparts, with short serpentine pathways in their lower reaches. The narrows at 1.8 miles bring welcome shade after the journey up the graveled canyon bottom. A pair of ravens nesting in the aerie alcove above the grotto may provide suitable visual and sound effects for the hiker approaching the almost cavelike section of the canyon. About 0.1 mile back down the canyon, a cairned trail on the eastern side leads you around this barrier to the canyon above. Another dry fall will block your travels there, so start your return trip.

Even with its proximity to Stovepipe Wells, Grotto Canyon is not heavily visited. Thus the adventuresome hiker can enjoy desert exploration and solitude without a lengthy drive. The high silence above Mesquite Flat rings in your ears—between cries of the ravens.

The narrows of Grotto Canyon.

Hiking back to the road, the dunes stretch out below, framed by the Cottonwood and Grapevine Mountains. Grotto Canyon is a desert wonder of a smaller dimension.

Miles and Directions

0.0–0.8 There's no actual trailhead, so from your car hike up the gravel jeep road in the wash.

1.8   Arrive at the narrows.

2.0   Turn back where another dry fall blocks your path.

4.0   Return to the trailhead.

106 Little Bridge Canyon

As its name suggests, this canyon has a natural bridge, as well as an arch. The hike can be done as either a loop or out and back across a broad alluvial fan.

See map on page 346.
Start: About 3 miles east of Stovepipe Wells Village.
Distance: 7 mile loop.
Approximate hiking time: 3 to 4 hours.
Difficulty: Strenuous.

Trail surface: Cross-country on rocky alluvial fan, open canyon floor.
Seasons: Mid-October through April.
USGS topo map: Grotto Canyon-CA (1:24,000).
Trail contact: Furnace Creek Visitor Center & Museum (see appendix D).

Finding the trailhead: The unsigned trailhead/route takes off to the south from California Highway 190 between Stovepipe Wells and the junction of CA 190 and Scotty's Castle Road. Little Bridge is the first major canyon east of the signed Grotto Canyon Road. The actual starting point/pullout on CA 190 is 3 miles east of Stovepipe Wells.

The Hike

Little Bridge Canyon isn't deep and narrow but it does contain several hidden points of wonder, making its exploration interesting and enjoyable. Unlike nearby Grotto and Mosaic Canyons, it is lightly visited, primarily because you must hike about 2.5 miles across a graveled alluvial fan just to reach the canyon entrance. One way to add a bit of spice to these first couple of open desert miles is to approach Little Bridge Canyon by way of a southeast-trending gully that parallels the steep mountain slopes on the right (west). By hiking up this gully, then up Little Bridge

The Little Bridge of the canyon of the same name about
1 mile up from the canyon mouth.

Canyon, and returning to the trailhead/parking area back down the alluvial fan, a loop of about 7 miles can be attained without increasing the round-trip distance of a less interesting out-and-back route.

Begin the hike by heading south to southeast across desert pavement then up the alluvial fan toward the power line and the Little Bridge Canyon entrance, which cannot be seen from the highway. Soon after passing under the power line at 0.5 mile, you'll enter a deep, graveled wash. At 1 mile the route reaches a high-walled wash where the walking becomes more difficult in loose gravel. Soon a major canyon enters from the right; continue southward up the left-hand wash. At 1.5 miles the wash narrows; climb to the left over a 5-foot dry fall. A 12-foot fall appears around the bend. Backtrack a short distance and take a faint use trail on the right side (going up), which climbs and then drops above the dry fall. Soon the wash narrows to only 3 or 4 feet.

At 1.9 miles large boulders block a narrow gap; climb around to the left with rock walls rising on the right. At 2 miles the canyon opens up, with its head being reached at 2.3 miles just south of Little Bridge Canyon.

The sand dunes of Mesquite Flat can be seen back to the north, with Little Bridge straight ahead and to the right. Drop 20 feet into the wide wash, turn right, and enter the red-walled Little Bridge Canyon entrance at 2.4 miles. At 2.5 miles the canyon narrows a bit, bounded by bright red walls. Compared to most Death Valley canyons, this one runs due north straight as an arrow. Striking clefts of white quartzite appear on the right at 2.7 miles, contrasting dramatically with adjacent dark rhyolite. Loose gravel makes for tiring walking, but the effort is soon rewarded with a small arch on the right (west) side at 3 miles.

At 3.1 miles a sizable canyon suitable for a side trip enters from the right. At 3.4 miles the main canyon again narrows, with a large cave high on the right side and the namesake natural bridge of Little Bridge Canyon also on the right side. This stunning sweep of white quartzite has a 20-foot-high opening bounded by a 40-foot-high arch. The notch above and to the right of the natural bridge ends quickly at a dry fall but provides a photographic angle for the bridge. With juniper clinging to the cliffs, this is indeed a tranquil and picturesque spot.

Hike up the canyon another 0.1 mile to a white quartzite gap for expansive views of the dunes northward and of great mounds of dark rhyolite rock overhead. The canyon narrows above but can be hiked for several more miles by those with sufficient time, energy, and water. To return, hike back down the canyon past the junction point with the side gully route. Continue to the right down the canyon and gradually angle left across the alluvial fan toward the sand dunes, aiming toward the highway/parking area starting point, to complete this adventurous 7-mile round-trip loop.

Miles and Directions

0.0 From the starting point on CA 190, head southeast up an alluvial fan toward Little Bridge Canyon.

0.5 Pass under a power line.

0.6 Enter a deep graveled wash.

1.0 At the high-walled gravel wash, continue up the left-hand side.

1.5 Where the wash narrows, climb left past a 5-foot dry fall.

1.6 At the 12-foot dry fall, climb a faint use trail to the right.

2.3 Reach the head of a gully just south of the mouth of Little Bridge Canyon.

2.4 Arrive at the mouth of Little Bridge Canyon.

3.0 Reach a small arch on the right (west) side of the wide wash/canyon.

3.4 Stop and observe the natural bridge on the right side of the canyon.

3.5 The canyon narrows above and can be hiked for several more miles.

7.0 Return to the trailhead.

107 Salt Creek Interpretive Trail

A nature trail on a boardwalk along Salt Creek features pupfish, pickleweed, and salt grass, and an optional 5-mile hike north to Devil's Cornfield.

Start: About 14 miles north of Furnace Creek.
Distance: 0.5 mile lollipop.
Approximate hiking time: Less than 1 hour.
Difficulty: Easy.
Trail surface: Boardwalk; use trail to Devil's Cornfield.
Seasons: November through April.

USGS topo maps: Beatty Junction-CA (Salt Creek Nature Trail), Stovepipe Wells Northeast-CA, and Grotto Canyon-CA (5-mile one-way hike), (1:24,000).
Trail contact: Furnace Creek Visitor Center & Museum (see appendix D).

Finding the trailhead: From California Highway 190, 2.4 miles northwest of Beatty Junction and 4 miles south of Sand Dune Junction, turn southwest on Salt Creek Road and drive 1.2 miles to the Salt Creek Interpretive Trail. From the park visitor center in Furnace Creek, drive north on California Highway 190 for 13.8 miles and turn left on the signed Salt Creek Road, 1.2 miles to its end.

The end point on the one-way hike to Devil's Cornfield is where Sand Dunes Road joins CA 190 from the north, 6.3 miles east of Stovepipe Wells Village and 1.1 miles west of Sand Dune Junction, on the south side of the highway across from Sand Dunes Road.

Salt Creek's boardwalk trail runs along the stream full of pupfish.

The Hike

Salt Creek Interpretive Trail is a fully accessible lollipop-shaped boardwalk hike, with trailside signs providing interpretive information. The extended hike continues 4.5 miles up Salt Creek to the Devil's Cornfield on CA 190. There is a beachlike quality to the short hike, not only due to the boardwalk designed to protect this delicate habitat, but also due to the aroma of salt water and the salt grass and pickleweed growing in dense clumps on the sandy stream banks.

The Salt Creek pupfish, endemic to Death Valley, are the stars of this hike. In the spring there are hundreds of them in the riffles and pools of the creek. In other seasons they are dormant (winter) or the stream is reduced to isolated pools (summer and fall).

The boardwalk runs alongside the creek and then crosses it in several spots, so it provides an excellent vantage point to watch the pupfish in the clear shallow water or the deep pools. Pupfish are small (not much longer than an inch) and fast, and enjoy zipping up and down the shallow riffles to bunch up in schools in the deeper

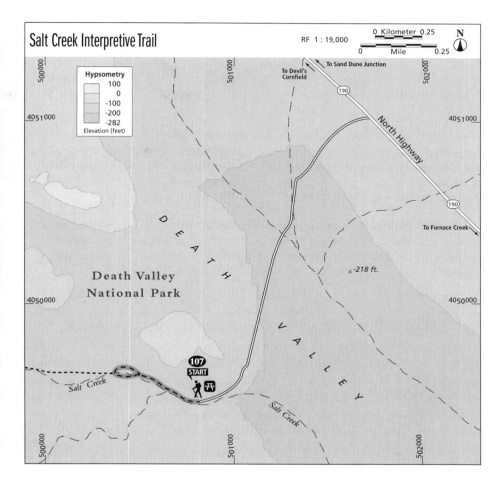

Salt Creek Interpretive Trail

RF 1 : 19,000

Hypsometry

Elevation (feet)
100
0
-100
-200
-282

To Devil's Cornfield

To Sand Dune Junction

North Highway

To Furnace Creek

×-218 ft.

D E A T H

Death Valley
National Park

V A L L E Y

107
START

Salt Creek

Salt Creek

terminal pools. As prehistoric Lake Manly dried up and grew saltier, these little fish were able to adapt to the new salty environment. Slimy green and brown algae, caddis flies, beetles, and water boatmen flourish here, too, providing an adequate diet for the pupfish.

The walk out along Salt Creek is a startling change from the usual Death Valley desert-floor hike. The sound of the merry running water in the winter and spring, with the flourishing growth of salt grasses, suggests a stroll on the beach. All that's missing are the seagulls. With the interpretive signs along the trail, you can enjoy the fish and birds as well as learn about the dynamic changes of the desert habitat and the ability of some species to adapt to its harsh conditions.

Option: To undertake the one-way hike up Salt Creek (which disappears at 2 miles), take the use trail from the far end of the loop, heading north to CA 190 at the Sand Dunes Road. Make sure your car shuttle is reliable because you won't feel like reversing your route to Salt Creek.

108 Titus Canyon Narrows

This narrow canyon cut deeply into the Grapevine Mountains is dominated by majestic cliffs and arched caverns.

Start: About 32 miles north of Furnace Creek.
Distance: 4.2 miles out and back.
Approximate hiking time: 2 to 3 hours.
Difficulty: Easy.
Trail surface: Rocky four-wheel-drive road.

Seasons: October through April.
USGS topo map: Fall Canyon-CA (1:24,000).
Trail contact: Furnace Creek Visitor Center & Museum (see appendix D).

Finding the trailhead: The two-way road to the mouth of Titus Canyon is 11.9 miles north of Daylight Pass Road (Nevada Highway 374) and California 190 junction, and 17.9 miles south of the Grapevine Ranger Station on Scotty's Castle Road. Take the signed dirt road northeast 2.7 miles up the alluvial fan to the Titus Canyon mouth, where there is a parking area.

The Hike

Titus Canyon is the longest and one of the grandest canyons in Death Valley. Titus Canyon Road was built in 1926 to serve the town of Leadville, an investor scam that became a ghost town the following year. This 26-mile one-way unpaved road was washed away by winter floods in 2004. The only way to visit majestic Titus Canyon is now by foot. The rough 2-mile portion at the western end of Titus Road still exists. From there you can park and hike the dramatic narrows of the canyon. Driving to the canyon mouth also enables you to omit the alluvial-fan hike that's so common in canyon hiking in Death Valley.

Titus Canyon is a slot canyon, immediately narrow at its mouth. From the brightness of the desert floor, you are plunged into the cool shadows of the canyon. Cliffs tower hundreds of feet above. Breezes rush down through the funnel of the canyon. The display of cliffs continues without intermission for 2 miles as you hike up the primitive canyon road. The variety of colors and textures on the canyon walls is immense and ever-changing. The limestone layers are twisted and folded; fault lines run at all angles. In addition to the power of the earth's surface to rise and fall and shift, the power of water is visible throughout the slot canyon. The water-smoothed walls indicate the level of flooding. The curves of the canyon's path reveal the erosive power of the swift floods as they roar down the narrow opening with their load of scouring boulders. Flash floods are a real danger in Titus, as 2004 demonstrated.

The 2-mile hike through the narrows is overpowering. Like walking down the nave of a European cathedral, hiking up (and later down) Titus is a soaring experience,

The canyon walls in lower Titus Canyon dwarf hikers.

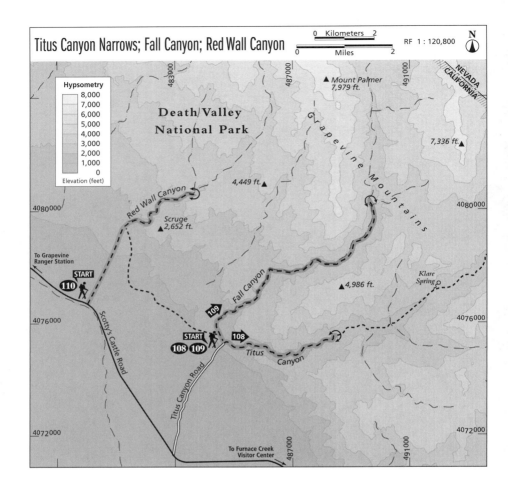

0   Kilometers   2

0   Miles   2

RF   1 : 120,800

N

Hypsometry

8,000
7,000
6,000
5,000
4,000
3,000
2,000
1,000
0

Elevation (feet)

Death Valley
National Park

▲ Mount Palmer
7,979 ft.

Grapevine Mountains

7,336 ft.▲

4,449 ft.▲

4080000

Red Wall Canyon

Scruge
▲ 2,652 ft.

To Grapevine
Ranger Station

START

110

4076000

Scotty's Castle Road

Fall Canyon

109

4,986 ft.▲

Klare
Spring

4076000

START

108 109

108

Titus   Canyon

Titus Canyon Road

4072000

To Furnace Creek
Visitor Center

4080000

4072000

NEVADA
CALIFORNIA

but also an immensely humbling one. The Titus Canyon Fault, which created the canyon, slices through the heart of the Grapevine Mountains, laying their innards bare for the geologist and layman both to enjoy.

Miles and Directions

0.0   From the canyon mouth, follow the four-wheel-drive road east into Titus Canyon.

2.1   The narrow canyon opens into a broader valley. Turn around here.

4.2   Retrace your steps to the parking area.

Option: For a longer and more strenuous hike—a total of 12 miles and five to six hours—continue up the road another 4 miles to Klare Spring. The canyon floor is considerably broader, although quite steep, after passing from the narrows at 2.1 miles, but the towering peaks of the Grapevines provide a spectacular backdrop for this canyon hike. The spring is on the north side of the road. It's a critical habitat for bighorn sheep, which gather nearby in hot summer months. Some marred petroglyphs are above the spring, a reminder that it is both unlawful and boorish to harm such artifacts. Return the way you came, enjoying your downhill trip.

109 Fall Canyon

This twisting, deep canyon in the colorful Grapevine Mountains features one of the most spectacular canyon narrows in the park.

See map on page 358.
Start: About 32 miles north of Furnace Creek.
Distance: 16 miles out and back.
Approximate hiking time: 4 to 5 hours.
Difficulty: Strenuous.

Trail surface: Sandy path and cross-country on a clear wash.
Seasons: October through April.
USGS topo map: Fall Canyon-CA (1:24,000).
Trail contact: Furnace Creek Visitor Center & Museum (see appendix D).

Finding the trailhead: The trailhead is at the Titus Canyon mouth parking area 2.7 miles north of Scotty's Castle Road on Titus Canyon Road. The two-way road to the mouth of Titus Canyon takes off 11.9 miles north of the California Highway 374/190 junction and 17.9 miles south of the Grapevine Ranger Station on Scotty's Castle Road. Proceed northeast on the signed Titus Canyon dirt road 2.7 miles up the alluvial fan to the mouth of Titus Canyon, where there is a parking area. Right behind the trailhead restroom, follow the distinct but unsigned trail north of the parking area 0.7 mile to an extensive wash leading to the mouth of Fall Canyon.

The Hike

Do not attempt this hike if wet weather appears likely. Fall Canyon is highly susceptible to flash flooding. You could easily be trapped in one of the narrow stretches of the canyon by a raging torrent if caught during a mountain storm.

From the parking area at the mouth of Titus Canyon, hike north on an unsigned but easy to follow use trail, climbing gradually across several low ridges and gullies. At 0.5 mile the trail enters a side wash and then swings to the right (north) toward Fall Canyon. At 0.7 mile the use trail tops out above Fall Canyon, drops into the wide graveled wash, and vanishes after another 0.1 mile at the canyon mouth. At first the canyon is wide, up to 150 feet in places. At 1.3 miles the walls steepen and close in; dark shadows fill the bottom, adding to a feeling of intimacy. The canyon quickly opens to a huge amphitheater–alcove, bounded by sheer cliffs on the left, bending tightly to the right. At 1.5 miles a large rock sits in a wide bottom that opens to colorful bands of red, white, and gray on the cliff faces. Continue left up the main wash. The canyon narrows again at 1.8 miles, its sides pocketed with a myriad of ledges and small alcoves, only to open again with

the west rim soaring 1,000 feet overhead. At 2 miles a narrow side canyon enters from the left just above a massive boulder that blocks much of the wash. Continue to the right up the main wash next to an isolated rock pinnacle.

Soon the canyon narrows once more with rock overhangs reaching out above. At 2.2 miles colorful folded rock dramatizes the powerful forces that continue to shape this rugged landscape. The canyon squeezes to a gap of only 8 feet at 2.6 miles, widens, and then narrows again at 2.9 miles. A sheer 20-foot-high dry fall is reached at 3 miles. The fall cannot be safely or easily climbed, so this is a good turnaround point for an exhilarating 6-mile out-and-back exploration of Fall Canyon. To this point, the difficulty rating is moderate.

To continue up Fall Canyon, drop back down the wash less than 0.1 mile and look for rock cairns on the left (south) side (right side of the canyon going up). This bypass route around the fall should only be attempted by those with at least moderate rock-climbing skills and experience. Begin by climbing a steep but solid rock pitch to a well-defined use trail that angles above and around the right side of the fall. Exercise caution on the loose gravel directly above the canyon. Immediately above and beyond the fall, the canyon becomes extremely narrow, bounded by sheer cliffs, folded layers of rock, overhangs, and semicircular bends of smooth gray rock. There are a few short rock pitches that can be easily scrambled up.

At 3.2 miles the tight chasm opens to more distant cliffs, but the actual wash remains narrow. At 3.4 miles a massive boulder blocks most of the wash, with the easiest way around being to the left. Here the hardest part about turning around is turning around; every steep-walled bend entices further exploration. The gray-walled canyon, polished smooth by the action of water, is left at 3.5 miles with the valley opening to reddish rhyolite cliffs and peaks.

At 4.1 miles dramatic cliffs rise above steep slopes punctuated with jagged columns of dark rhyolite. Anywhere in this stretch provides a good turnaround point, but it is possible to continue climbing northward for another 4 miles to the head of the canyon, where the country opens up into low ridges, high plateaus, and open desert. Retrace your route to complete your exploration of this enchanting canyon.

Miles and Directions

0.0   Start at the trailhead at the mouth of Titus Canyon, behind the restroom.

0.7   The use trail meets the Fall Canyon wash.

0.8   Arrive at the mouth of Fall Canyon.

◀ *A hiker sits above a 20-foot-high dry fall 3 miles up Fall Canyon.*

1.3	The canyon narrows dramatically.
2.9	Rock cairns mark a faint, scrambling use trail to the right that climbs above the dry fall.
3.0	Reach a 20-foot dry fall; turnaround point for the short hike.
3.1	The canyon narrows.
4.1	The canyon opens up to high peaks and ridges beyond.
8.0	Reach the head of the canyon.
16.0	Return to the trailhead from the longer hike.

110 Red Wall Canyon

Red Wall Canyon deserves its name. After crossing the open desert floor of Death Valley, this hike takes you into a rugged, brightly colored canyon in the Grapevine Mountains. The cool shadows of the deep canyon provide a respite from the glare of the desert outside.

See map on page 358.
Start: About 36 miles north of Furnace Creek.
Distance: 7 miles out and back.
Approximate hiking time: 2 to 3 hours.
Difficulty: Moderate.

Trail surface: Sandy rocky wash, gravel canyon floor.
Seasons: October through April.
USGS topo map: Fall Canyon-CA (1:24,000).
Trail contact: Furnace Creek Visitor Center & Museum (see appendix D).

Finding the trailhead: The main wash of the alluvial fan is 35.5 miles north of Furnace Creek, 17.4 miles south of Scotty's Castle, and 14.1 miles south of the Grapevine Ranger Station. The hike takes off from Scotty's Castle Road, 3.8 miles north of the Titus Canyon Road exit, and heads northeast across 3 miles of sloping desert alluvial fan to the mouth of Red Wall Canyon.

The Hike

Although rock-climbing skills are needed to proceed beyond a dry waterfall 0.5 mile up the canyon, this hike provides delightful vistas in the lower canyon region for the casual hiker. The trip can also be extended to a point-to-point excursion (with a car shuttle) by hiking from Red Wall Canyon to the Titus Canyon parking area, 3.5 miles to the south.

The approach to the canyon via the alluvial fan is not particularly challenging, but it is certainly not easy! The easiest hiking is on the dark desert pavement of the old alluvial fan. The wash route changes directions with its tributaries, so it's necessary to cut from wash to wash to maintain the route to the canyon mouth. Above the wash, the sections of smoother varnished desert pavement provide some respite,

The entrance to Red Wall Canyon.

but these sections are brief, interspersed with sections of cobbled, bouldered, and eroded washbeds.

The canyon mouth opens to the northwest; except for the red/black wall contrast, it is nearly hidden in the cliff faces. The canyon, which looked so narrow or invisible during the approach, is surprisingly wide, at least 50 yards from wall to wall. At the entrance, the north wall is a sheer red cliff face, while the south side is a black slope. The canyon takes a sharp turn to the north 0.2 mile farther, and suddenly the Red Wall towers 400 feet above you on the right. A narrow S-curve brings you to another red wall, now on your left. A short distance farther an even redder wall appears. The red walls, alternating with the black, provide a blast of sharp color on the beige desert palette.

At mile 0.4 in the canyon, water-sculpted narrows enclose an easily climbed low dry fall. Just beyond this obstacle is the 20-foot dry fall that blocks the canyon to all but seasoned rock climbers. Don't trust the knotted rope hanging at the dry fall. Using ropes of unknown origin, age, or strength is never recommended. So this is a good turnaround or lunch spot.

In Red Wall the variety of canyon architecture lures you onward as the canyon is constantly bending out of sight. Only upon turning around for the hike back are you aware of the elevation gained (800 feet in 0.5 mile). The descent from the dry fall provides numerous vistas of Death Valley in the distance.

The sharp slope of the canyon floor and its heavy gravel surface both indicate that this is a relatively young canyon. There is still a lot of erosive energy in the uplifting Amargosa Range, of which these Grapevine Mountains are a part.

Miles and Directions

0.0 From whatever point on Scotty's Castle Road you select, aim for the Grapevine Mountains. The canyon mouth is where the red and black rock faces meet. The alluvial fan emerging from the canyon forms a distinct triangle. Head up this alluvial fan, cross-country or via one of the washes.

3.0 Enter the canyon.

3.5 A 20-foot dry fall blocks the canyon. The use of the knotted rope of unknown age and origin is not recommended for scaling the fall.

7.0 Return to the trailhead by the same route.

Option: For the avid desert hiker, another approach (or exit) for the Red Wall hike is from the Titus Canyon/Fall Canyon trailhead. From the Red Wall Canyon mouth, you can see the most efficient pathway across the fan and the ridges to the south. Since the finger ridges hide sharply eroded dropoffs, aim for their lower western edges in your southward hike. A faint use trail is intermittent on this cross-country hike, visible only on the desert pavement ridges, and marked by a few cairns.

Like all rugged cross-country journeys, this hike does not allow a direct line. Detours are constantly required for steep ridges, deep washes, and high alluvial plateaus. Eroded cliffs of volcanic-ash badlands obstruct the shortest distance from Red Wall to Titus. With neither shade nor cover, this trip should only be undertaken with plenty of water.

In the midst of a busy section of the park, this canyon-to-canyon hike, 2 miles from the road below, provides a taste of true desert travel. The silence of the desert surrounds you. The difficulties of desert hiking abound. From your 1,000-foot elevation, you enjoy sweeping views of the valley below as well as the Grapevines above. Your destination dances in the distance as both Fall and Titus Canyons at once appear close but don't get any closer! A cooperative partner can let you off at the alluvial fan on the Grapevine Road then meet you at the Titus parking area several hours later. The 8.5-mile hike south to Titus takes twice as long (three to four hours) as the direct hike up the fan, but it is worth the effort.

111 Ubehebe Peak

Ubehebe Peak is one of the few Death Valley peaks largely accessible by trail. The steep out-and-back hike leads to a remote peak in the southern Last Chance Range from which you will enjoy spectacular views of surrounding basin and range country.

Start: About 81 miles northwest of Furnace Creek.
Distance: 6.2 miles out and back.
Approximate hiking time: 3 to 5 hours.
Difficulty: Strenuous.
Trail surface: Clear rocky trail, changing to good, then to primitive, and finally to no trail for the final 0.4 mile to the summit.

Seasons: October through June.
USGS topo map: Ubehebe Peak-CA (1:24,000).
Trail contact: Furnace Creek Visitor Center & Museum (see appendix D).

Finding the trailhead: From the junction of Scotty's Castle Road and Ubehebe Crater Road in the northeastern corner of the park, head northwest on the paved Ubehebe Crater Road. The pavement ends after 5.3 miles at the turnoff to Ubehebe Crater. Continue south on the washboard dirt Racetrack Valley Road 19.7 miles to Teakettle Junction. Here Racetrack Valley Road turns right; continue to follow it another 5.7 miles to the Grandstand parking area, which is opposite the "grandstand" of gray rocks in the dry lake bed east of the road. The trail heads west from the parking area toward the prominent Ubehebe Peak.

The Hike

Before climbing Ubehebe Peak, a short 1-mile round-trip hike east to the Grandstand is a worthwhile warm-up and also provides a good perspective on your journey to the top of Ubehebe Peak. From the Grandstand, a pre-climb visual orientation involves identifying Ubehebe Peak on the left with your route going up the east face of the north peak, then around the back side into the prominent notch, then left up the skyline to the peak.

The Grandstand is a large 70-foot-high mound of gray rocks rising in stark contrast to the surrounding white flatness of the Racetrack playa, or dry lake bed. For added perspective, walk around the Grandstand, then scramble up some of the large boulders. The Grandstand can be easily climbed 40 to 50 feet above the playa. Be on the lookout for the tracks of "moving rocks" streaked across the lake-bed sediment. The mystery of these mobile rocks is heightened by the fact that no one has ever seen them move. Most likely the rocks are swept by powerful winds when the lake bed is slickened by heavy rain. If time allows upon completion of the peak climb, drive south from the Grandstand another 2 miles. Walk to the east toward the base of Peak 4,560. This is where you will find the best view of the mysterious trails of the moving rocks. Please do not walk on the Racetrack if it is wet or muddy.

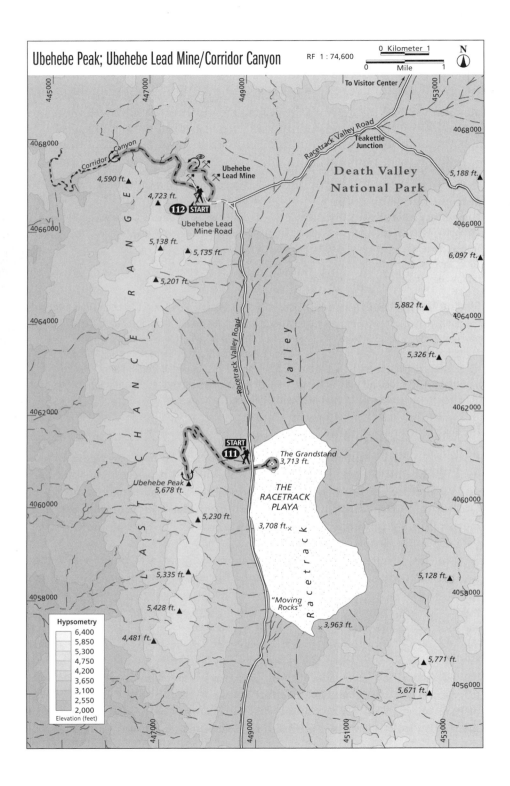

Ubehebe Peak; Ubehebe Lead Mine/Corridor Canyon

RF 1 : 74,600

0 Kilometer 1

0 Mile 1

N

445000
447000
449000
451000
453000

To Visitor Center

4068000

Corridor Canyon

Racetrack Valley Road

Teakettle Junction

4068000

4,590 ft. ▲

Ubehebe Lead Mine

Death Valley National Park

5,188 ft. ▲

E A S T

4,723 ft. ▲

112 START

4066000

Ubehebe Lead Mine Road

6,097 ft. ▲

4066000

5,138 ft. ▲

5,135 ft. ▲

5,882 ft. ▲

C H A N C E

5,201 ft. ▲

V a l l e y

4064000

4064000

5,326 ft. ▲

Racetrack Valley Road

4062000

4062000

R A N G E

START
111

The Grandstand 3,713 ft.

Ubehebe Peak ▲ 5,678 ft.

THE RACETRACK PLAYA

4060000

4060000

5,230 ft. ▲

3,708 ft. ×

R a c e t r a c k

5,335 ft. ▲

5,128 ft. ▲

4058000

5,428 ft. ▲

4058000

"Moving Rocks"

Hypsometry

	6,400
	5,850
	5,300
	4,750
	4,200
	3,650
	3,100
	2,550
	2,000

Elevation (feet)

4,481 ft. ▲

× 3,963 ft.

5,771 ft. ▲

4056000

5,671 ft. ▲

4056000

447000
449000
451000
453000

Ubehebe Peak (right) towers over the playa (dry lake bed) far below.

Be sure to carry sufficient water for this high, dry desert peak climb. The clear trail, originally an old mining path, begins by ascending gradually to the northwest up an alluvial fan clothed with desert trumpets and creosote bushes. Within 0.5 mile the trail begins a long series of steep switchbacks up the east face of the 5,519-foot north peak. This imposing buttress is made even more impressive with broken cliffs of desert varnish. After climbing nearly 1,200 feet in 1.8 miles, the trail reaches the north ridge of the peak, just after passing an outcropping of limestone where the blue-green copper of malachite rock lines a shallow mine digging. From this point, a trail takes off to the right, ending after 0.1 mile at an overlook above an old mine entrance. The summit of Ubehebe Peak can be seen in the distance beyond the north peak, which rises directly above.

Continue up the left-hand trail, which climbs steeply up the ridge through the rocks to 5,160 feet at 2 miles. The trail then wraps around the west side of the mountain, reaching an elevation of 5,440 feet at 2.4 miles. From here on, the trail becomes rougher and more faint, compensated somewhat by stupendous views of the playa to the southeast. The trail then drops for another 0.2 mile to the 5,220-foot saddle between the two peaks. Any resemblance to a trail ends at the saddle, which is a good turnaround point for those not wishing to scramble the steep rocky ridge another 0.4 mile and 460 vertical feet to Ubehebe Peak.

To attain the summit, climb southward straight up the rugged spine of the north ridge. Much of this route is marked by rock cairns. There are no technical sections, but care must be exercised in negotiating narrow chutes around steep rock faces. The quartz granite top of 5,678-foot Ubehebe Peak contains a summit register and is marked by a wooden triangle. Although narrow, there are lots of ideal sitting spots upon which to relax and soak up the incredible 360-degree vista.

The Saline Valley lies 4,500 feet below to the west. Beyond is the soaring 10,000-foot crest of the Inyo Mountains with the even higher Sierra Nevada looming farther to the west. The crown of Death Valley—lofty Telescope Peak—can be seen to the southeast, along with the vast wooded plateau of Hunter Mountain. Perhaps most impressive is the eagle's-eye view of the gleaming white Racetrack playa encircling the tiny dark specks of the Grandstand far below.

Miles and Directions

0.0 Start from the trailhead at the Grandstand parking area on the Racetrack Valley Road.

1.8 The trail switchbacks to the north ridge of the peak. Where the trail splits, stay left.

2.4 The trail reaches a ridge on the west side of the mountain, becoming rougher and more faint.

2.7 The trail drops to a saddle between the two peaks. Begin the route-finding segment to the peak.

3.1 Reach Ubehebe Peak (5,678 feet).

6.2 Return to the trailhead.

112 Ubehebe Lead Mine/Corridor Canyon

This exploration of a historic mine site with a tram will appeal to mining and history buffs. The longer leg in Corridor Canyon will enchant those who appreciate excellent vistas of cliffs and mountains.

See map on page 366.
Start: About 76 miles northwest of Furnace Creek.
Distance: 6 miles out and back.
Approximate hiking time: 4 hours.
Difficulty: Moderate.

Trail surface: Dirt path to mine; clear wash in canyon.
Seasons: October through March.
USGS topo maps: Ubehebe Peak-CA and Teakettle Junction-CA (1:24,000).
Trail contact: Furnace Creek Visitor Center & Museum (see appendix D).

Finding the trailhead: From Grapevine Junction, take Ubehebe Crater Road northwest 5.5 miles to the end of the pavement and the sign for Racetrack Valley Road. Turn right onto Racetrack Valley Road. Four-wheel drive is recommended but under normal weather conditions is unnecessary. Racetrack Valley Road is severely washboarded but contains no other obstacles as far as the Racetrack. Go south on Racetrack Valley Road 19.6 miles to Teakettle Junction. Bear right and continue 2.2 miles to the right turn to Ubehebe Lead Mine Road (signed). The dirt road leads 0.7 mile to the parking area at the mine site.

The Hike

The Ubehebe Mine has a lengthy history, beginning in 1875 when copper ore was found here. The copper mine was not fully developed until early in the twentieth century, but the profitable ore was soon depleted. In 1908 lead mining began and continued until 1928. Ubehebe Mine had another renaissance in the 1940s as a zinc mine. Mining activity came to an end in 1951.

After all this mining it is not surprising to find a plethora of mining artifacts in the valley and in the hills above. A miner's house is still standing. Its door and windows ajar, stripped of its plumbing (the range lies outside), it is a well-preserved remnant of its midcentury inhabitants. Remember that it may be unwise to enter deserted buildings due to deer mice and hanta virus.

In the wash above there are other traces of crude dwellings of miners. Stacked stone walls are still in place. The men worked inside rock walls by day and slept in them at night. Rusty debris and small, level tent sites are scattered about. The usual squeaky bedspring (burned and rusted) lies amid the creosote bushes. This is an appropriate place to pause and contemplate the bustle of activity and spirit of optimism that must have prevailed in this mining valley in its various heydays.

Below the housing area sits the ore chute, with rail tracks still leading from a mine opening. The area looks like it had been deserted only a year ago. The sagging

The chute at the Ubehebe Lead Mine.

old tram cable still hangs from the tower atop the hill to the valley floor. Unsecured mine openings dot the hillside. Although the National Park Service has not posted its usual warning sign, do not get close to the mines; the tram should also be given a wide berth.

The hike up the trail to the overlook gives you a magnificent aerial view of the mine encampment and the rolling hills of the Last Chance Range. Mine openings proliferate like rodent burrows. The rust-colored rock and earth in piles at each opening give the mining operations an eerie fresh appearance, as if the work here just stopped yesterday instead of 60 or 100 years ago. Numerous wooden posts mark the mountainside along the trail to designate claims of long-gone prospectors. Crossing carefully beneath the hilltop tram tower, you arrive at trail's end and a view westward of winding Corridor Canyon.

For this 5-mile out-and-back leg into Corridor Canyon, start at the mine chute and drop down the wide and graveled wash to the head of the canyon, generally westward. At 0.3 mile a tantalizing narrow stair-step chute of a canyon enters from the left, inviting exploration—although large boulders may prevent you from getting very far.

At about 1 mile impressive cliff walls soar high to the left, whereas the right side is marked by folded rock layers altered by fault lines. Below, as the canyon turns left, are colorful bands of rock. The cliffs are pockmarked with caverns and other small openings, some of which serve as active dens for animals.

The canyon is unique in that it provides both a closed-in experience as well as far distant vistas of cliffs, overshadowed by even higher cliff layers beyond, opening to expansive views of adjacent and faraway mountains. Hike another 1.5 miles in the wide wash before turning around and retracing your steps.

Miles and Directions

Mine:

0.0–0.1 Back up the road from the miner's shack, on the north side by a low stone wall, the trail leads up the hillside.

0.4 There's a tram cable tower at the hilltop.

0.5 Enjoy the view at the overlook.

1.0 Return to the trailhead by the same route.

Canyon:

0.0 At the mine chute, head west down the wash.

0.3 The chute canyon enters from the left.

1.0 View dramatic cliffs, continuing in the canyon until you decide to turn around at one of various turnaround points.

2.5 By this point you've seen what makes this canyon special. For more of the same, you could continue as much as 2.5 miles more.

5.0 Retrace your steps to the parking area.

113 Ubehebe and Little Hebe Craters

These volcanic craters are a fascinating geology lesson on the forces that helped form Death Valley. A short loop hike around the large Ubehebe Crater and the several smaller ones enables you to witness the complex erosion patterns that have occurred since the craters' birth.

Start: About 51 miles north of Furnace Creek.
Distance: 1.5-mile loop.
Approximate hiking time: 1 to 2 hours.
Difficulty: Easy; moderate to the bottom of the crater.
Trail surface: Volcanic cinder.

Seasons: Late October through April.
USGS topo map: Ubehebe Crater-CA (1:24,000).
Trail contact: Furnace Creek Visitor Center & Museum (see appendix D).

Finding the trailhead: From the Grapevine Junction of Scotty's Castle Road and Ubehebe Crater Road, 45 miles north of Furnace Creek, take Ubehebe Crater Road northwest. Drive 5.7 miles to the Ubehebe Crater parking area for the Ubehebe Crater/Little Hebe Crater trailhead. The parking area is on the eastern side on the one-way loop of paved road at the end of Ubehebe Crater Road.

The Hike

The volcanic region at the north end of the Cottonwood Mountains, near Scotty's Castle, is evidence of recent cataclysmic events in Death Valley, geologically speaking. The huge Ubehebe Crater was created around 3,000 years ago when magma heated groundwater and the pressure from the resulting steam blew the overlying rock away. This explosion covered 6 square miles of desert with volcanic debris 150 feet deep. Called a maar volcano by geologists, Ubehebe is a crater without a cone. The rim has been eroding ever since the explosion, gradually filling the crater with alluvial fans.

Little Hebe, directly south, is much younger. Having exploded about 300 to 500 years ago, it is one of the newest geologic features of Death Valley. Little Hebe's rim is neat and well defined, exhibiting little of the erosion that has reduced Ubehebe's edge.

Pausing at the parking lot to read the information on the board and glancing at these monstrous holes in the earth might seem sufficient, but hiking all the way around this monumental display of volcanic power provides a much better understanding of the dimensions of the Ubehebe complex.

The first fourth of the hike takes you along the rim of the main crater. The size of the hole is overpowering. It is almost 0.5 mile across from rim to rim. Alluvial fans have formed on the walls as the rains tear down the crater's edges.

The sharply defined rim of Little Hebe Crater is evidence of its youth, geologically speaking.

In the vicinity of Ubehebe, there are as many as twelve additional craters, all examples of more maar activity. You will see numerous craters in various stages of eroding deterioration. Little Hebe stands out as a jewel of a crater. Neat and trim, this volcanic chasm is only 200 yards across. The younger, fresher rim has barely begun to weather. Volcanic materials are very durable. Clearly visible on the walls of Little Hebe are the layers beneath the earth's surface. Especially noticeable is a thick layer of viscous lava that had oozed from the earth's interior prior to the explosion of Little Hebe.

After the tour around Little Hebe, continue your hike around the main crater, which seems even larger after visiting its younger neighbor. A well-defined trail leads around Ubehebe. At 1.3 miles pass the trail that slopes down into the crater—see the option below. The volcanic cinder trail descends nearly 500 feet to the floor of the crater, where creosote bushes flourish. After major rainstorms the crater also features a small lake. Most of the time it is very dry.

The power of nature to modify the terrain via volcanic action stands in sharp contrast with the more gradual erosive forces that are demonstrated elsewhere in

Ubehebe and Little Hebe Craters

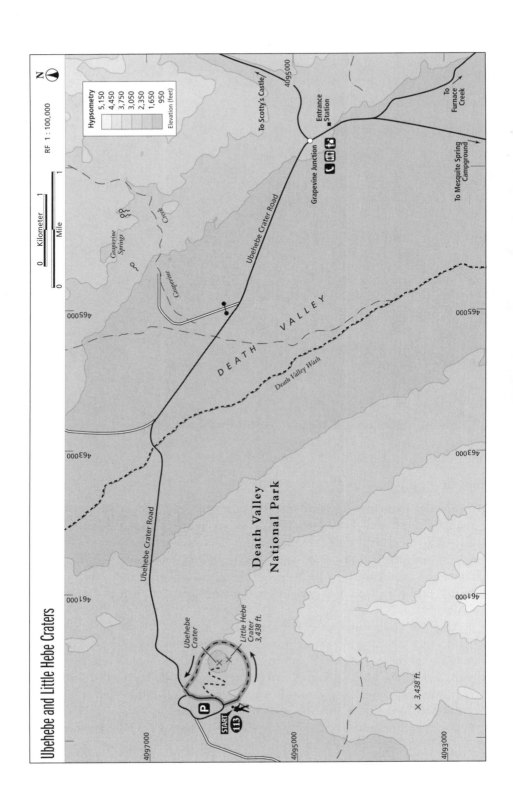

RF 1 : 100,000

Hypsometry

5,150
4,450
3,750
3,050
2,350
1,650
950

Elevation (feet)

N

0   Kilometer   1

0   Mile   1

4097000
4095000
4093000

4610000
4630000
4650000

Ubehebe Crater Road

Ubehebe Crater

Little Hebe Crater
3,438 ft.

START
113

P

X 3,438 ft.

Death Valley
National Park

D E A T H

V A L L E Y

Death Valley Wash

Grapevine Creek

Grapevine Springs

Ubehebe Crater Road

Grapevine Junction

Entrance
Station

To Scotty's Castle

To Furnace
Creek

To Mesquite Spring
Campground

Death Valley. The earth has not finished rearranging its surface here in Death Valley. The forces that created Ubehebe and Little Hebe are merely dormant, not dead.

Miles and Directions

0.0 The trail goes south of the information board at the parking area.

0.1–0.3 The trail climbs—bear left at the Y. The trail to the right is eroding on both sides and becoming hazardous.

0.4 Arrive at a maze of use trails on a small plateau between craters. A sign directs you to Little Hebe, directly south. Follow the trail around Little Hebe.

0.7 Back at the intersection, continue to hike around the large Ubehebe Crater.

1.5 Return to the trailhead.

Option: The 0.6-mile out and back to the bottom of the crater is a breathtaking outing into the earth. At the bottom you can imagine the force that blew off the earth to leave such a hole. The climb back to the parking area requires some exertion due to the skidding quality of the volcanic cinders.

114 Eureka Dunes

In a remote desert valley, against the scenic backdrop of the colorful Last Chance Mountains, lie the Eureka Dunes. These are the tallest sand dunes in California and the second-highest in all of North America, although their constantly shifting nature would make that tough to measure. Your cross-country walk to their summit will be a soft sandy stroll.

Start: About 90 miles north of Furnace Creek.
Distance: 3-mile loop.
Approximate hiking time: 2 hours.
Difficulty: Moderate.
Trail surface: All-sand cross-country route.

Seasons: October through April.
USGS topo map: Last Chance Range Southwest-CA (1:24,000).
Trail contact: Furnace Creek Visitor Center & Museum (see appendix D).

Finding the trailhead: From the south, take Scotty's Castle Road to Grapevine Junction and proceed northwest on Ubehebe Crater Road for 2.8 miles to Big Pine Road, which is also known as North Entrance Highway and Death Valley Road. The turnoff is signed EUREKA DUNES 45 MILES. Turn north onto the washboard, graded gravel Big Pine Road and drive 34 miles to South Eureka Valley Road, which is the road to the Eureka Dunes. Turn left (south) onto this road and drive 10 miles to the end-of-the-road picnic/parking area near the base of the dunes. From the north, Eureka Dunes can be reached from Big Pine via 28 miles of paved road and 11 miles of graded dirt road to South Eureka Valley Road. Turn right (south) and follow the narrow road for the final 10 miles to the camping and parking areas just north of the dunes.

The multibanded Last Chance Mountains provide a colorful backdrop to the 3,480-foot summit of the Eureka Dunes.

The Hike

The Eureka Dunes are a fascinating island of sand in a desert sea, within the recently expanded northern portion of the park. From a distance this 1-by-3-mile mountain of sand seems to hover over the remote Eureka Valley floor. Although not extensive, these dunes are the tallest in California and the second-tallest in North America after the Great Sand Dunes in Colorado. From the dry lake bed at their western edge, the Eureka Dunes rise abruptly more than 600 feet. Equally impressive is the sheer face of the Last Chance Mountains to the immediate east, with their colored striped bands of pink, black, and gray limestone.

If the sand here is completely dry, you may hear one of the most unusual sounds in the desert: singing sand. When the sand cascades down the steepest pitch of the highest dune, a rumbling sound comparable to the bass note of a pipe organ emanates from the sand. No one knows exactly why this happens, but the friction of smooth-textured sand grains sliding against each other probably has something to do with it.

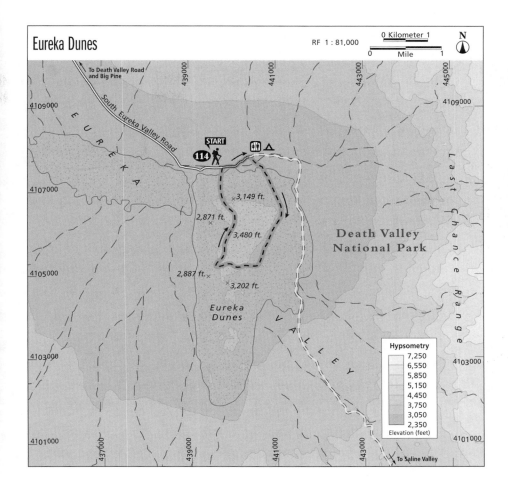

Eureka Dunes

RF 1 : 81,000

0 Kilometer 1

0 Mile 1

N

To Death Valley Road
and Big Pine

South Eureka Valley Road

EUREKA

START

114

Death Valley
National Park

3,149 ft.

2,871 ft.

3,480 ft.

2,887 ft.

3,202 ft.

Eureka
Dunes

VALLEY

Last Chance Range

Hypsometry

7,250
6,550
5,850
5,150
4,450
3,750
3,050
2,350
Elevation (feet)

To Saline Valley

These dunes receive more moisture than others in the park because they are positioned at the western foot of a high mountain range that intercepts passing storms. The isolation of the Eureka Dunes, far from any other dunes, has resulted in endemic species of animals and plants found nowhere else. For example, there are five species of beetles and three plants that have their entire range limited to these lofty mounds.

The three endemic plant species are shining locoweed, a candidate for endangered species listing, Eureka dune grass, and Eureka evening primrose, the latter two of which are listed as endangered species under the federal Endangered Species Act. The camping area and trailhead were recently moved off of the dunes to protect these species. Shining locoweed is a hummock-forming plant with root nodules that fix nitrogen from the air, a vital plant nutrient not available in the sand. When wind-blown sand covers the leafy flower shoots of the Eureka evening primrose, a new rosette of leaves forms at the tip. Large, white flowers bloom at night so that moths and other pollinators can avoid daytime heat. Usually Eureka dune grass is the only plant on the higher slopes of the dunes. Its thick roots hold shifting sand, forming hummocks. Stiff, spiny leaf tips discourage herbivores.

The Eureka Dunes are a small, ecologically unique place requiring our special care. Camp and keep vehicles a good distance from the base of the dunes, which is where most of the endemic plants and animals live. If possible, walk where others have in order to concentrate the impact away from pristine areas.

There are two basic choices for climbing the dunes, which can be hard work at times in the loose, shifting sand. The most direct route for the 600-plus-foot climb to the top is a 1.5-mile straight-up-and-back route by way of a series of knife ridges. Because of the long driving distance to the trailhead, a somewhat longer 3-mile loop is your better choice. In so choosing, you'll gain more intimacy with the dunes and their majestic Last Chance Mountains backdrop.

From the parking/camping area, head east cross-country along the base of the dunes toward the color-banded Last Chance Mountains, which rise an impressive 4,000 feet above the Eureka Valley floor. Hiking along the base provides a constantly changing perspective of this unusual landscape as well as a good warm-up for climbing the steep backside of the dunes. A profusion of animal tracks will appear as well as the circular paths of grass tips in the sand from the ever-changing wind.

At 0.8 mile the initial flat stretch becomes laced with up-and-down gullies, with volcanic "bombs" embedded in the sand. At this point begin curving around the base of the dunes to the right (south). This wonderfully wide-open trek stands in startling contrast to the closed-in feeling one gets when exploring the deep canyons of Death Valley.

At around 1.5 miles begin climbing westward up any one of the several narrow knife-edge sand ridges that converge at the apex of the dunes. A vertical gain of about 600 feet to the 3,480-foot high point is spread over about 0.7 mile, with most of the climb during the final 0.2 mile. The dry lake bed, expansive Eureka Valley, colorful Last Chance Range, and the dunes themselves combine to form a stunning 360-degree panorama. To complete the 3-mile loop, continue back down along narrow ridges and steep scooped-out bowls of sand in a north to northwesterly direction to the trailhead.

Miles and Directions

0.0 Start from the trailhead located at the picnic tables/parking area.

1.5 Begin climbing up the west side of the dunes.

2.2 Reach the top of the dunes.

3.0 Complete the loop back to the trailhead.

Afterword

As seasoned hikers accustomed to the high snowy mountains of the Northern Rockies, we were excited when the idea of exploring some of the California desert was presented to us. It would be hard to find two more disparate regions—the California desert and the Northern Rockies—within the lower forty-eight. We viewed the opportunity to learn more about such a different ecosystem as a tremendous challenge. And we foresaw many interim challenges along the way, such as the challenge of truly getting to know this splendid country and its hidden treasures beyond the roads. There would be the challenges of climbing rugged peaks, of safely traversing vast expanses of open desert, of navigating across alluvial fans to secluded canyons, of learning enough about the interconnected web of desert geology, flora, and fauna to be able to interpret some of its wonders for others to appreciate. These beckoned to us from blank spots on the park map.

But we each face a far greater challenge: the challenge of wilderness stewardship, which must be shared by all who venture into the wilderness of California's desert parks.

Wilderness stewardship can take many forms, from political advocacy to a zero-impact hiking and camping ethic to quietly setting the example of respect for wild country for others to follow. The political concessions that eventually brought about passage of the long-awaited California Desert Protection Act have been made. Boundaries were gerrymandered, exclusions made, and nonconforming uses grandfathered. Still, the wilderness and park lines that have been drawn in these four great parks represent a tremendous step forward in the ongoing battle to save what little remains of our diminishing wilderness heritage.

But drawing lines is only the first step. Now, the great challenge is to take care of what we have. We can each demonstrate this care every time we set out on a hike. It comes down to respect for the untamed but fragile desert, for those wild creatures who have no place else to live, for other visitors, and for those yet unborn who will retrace our hikes into the next century and beyond.

We will be judged not by the mountains we climb but by what we pass on to others in an unimpaired condition. Happy hiking, and may your trails be clear with the wind and sun at your back.

Appendix A: Our Favorite Hikes

Mountains

Table Top Mountain Loop (73) Plateau with sweeping view of Mojave National Preserve
Telescope Peak (96) Central peak with magnificent view
Clark Mountain/North Canyon (78) Twisting canyon, diverse forest, sweeping vistas

Open Desert

Alcoholic Pass (20) Alluvial fan and ridge climb to low mountain pass
California Riding and Hiking Trail: Covington Flat to Keys View (61) Crosses varied terrain, includes side trip to Quail Peak
Hole-in-the-Wall to Mid Hills (71) Dramatic features and views
Eureka Dunes (114) Highest dunes in North America, backdrop of Last Chance Range

Canyons

Pine City/Canyon (50) Dramatic canyon with boulder scrambling
Fort Piute/Piute Gorge (76) Gorge hike through heart of mountain range
Marble Canyon (103) Twisting walls with varied stripes and colors
Fall Canyon (109) Sheer walls above narrow canyon

Waterfalls and Streams

Sheep Canyon (24) Mountain valley with stream and fan palms
Caruthers Canyon (74) Seasonal brook with towering peaks
Surprise Canyon to Panamint City (95) Spring-fed stream, chutes
Darwin Falls (101) Hideaway canyon with compound falls

Oases

Mountain Palm Springs Loop (1) Series of palm groves, largest group of California fan palms
Borrego Palm Canyon Nature Trail (19) Falls, palm oasis in steep canyon
Lost Palms Oasis (26) Remote oasis, largest palm grove in Joshua Tree National Park

Interpretive Nature Trails

Borrego Palm Canyon Nature Trail (19) Excellent plant identification/bighorn-sheep country
Cottonwood Spring Nature Trail (29) Native American uses and processes for desert plants
Golden Canyon/Gower Gulch Loop (87) Geology of Death Valley
Salt Creek Interpretive Trail (107) Geologic changes and pupfish

Prehistory and History

The Morteros (8) Native American sites
Pictograph Trail (9) Native American sites
Barker Dam Nature Trail Loop (57) Native American petroglyphs, ranching
Fort Piute/Piute Gorge (76) Petroglyphs, Mojave Road, Fort Piute
Hungry Bill's Ranch/Johnson Canyon (94) Farm of 1880s

Mines and Mills

Lost Horse Mine Loop: Lost Horse Mountain (41) Well-preserved historic mine structures
Wall Street Mill (55) Gold-processing mill
Ashford Canyon/Mine (80) Numerous mine buildings in scenic canyon
Keane Wonder Mine (91) Extraordinary tramway, mine, and mill

Appendix B: Recommended Equipment

Use the following checklists as you assemble your gear for hiking the California desert.

Day Hike

- ❏ sturdy, well-broken-in, light- to medium-weight hiking boots
- ❏ broad-brimmed hat, which must be windproof
- ❏ long-sleeved shirt for sun protection
- ❏ long pants for protection against sun and brush
- ❏ water: two quarts to one gallon/day (depending on season), in sturdy screw-top plastic containers
- ❏ large-scale topo map and compass (adjusted for magnetic declination)
- ❏ whistle, mirror, and matches (for emergency signals)
- ❏ flashlight (in case your hike takes longer than you expect)
- ❏ sunblock and lip sunscreen
- ❏ insect repellent (in season)
- ❏ pocketknife
- ❏ small first-aid kit: tweezers, bandages, antiseptic, moleskin, snakebite extractor kit
- ❏ bee sting kit (over-the-counter antihistamine or epinephrine by prescription) as needed for the season
- ❏ windbreaker (or rain gear in season)
- ❏ lunch or snack, with baggie for your trash
- ❏ toilet paper, with a plastic zipper bag to pack it out
- ❏ your FalconGuide

Optional gear
- ❏ camera and film
- ❏ binoculars
- ❏ bird and plant guidebooks
- ❏ notebook and pen/pencil

Winter High-Country Trips

All of the above, plus:
- ❏ gaiters
- ❏ warm ski-type hat and gloves
- ❏ warm jacket

Backpacking Trips/Overnights

All of the above, plus:

- ❏ backpack (internal or external frame)
- ❏ more water (at least a gallon a day, plus extra for cooking—cache or carry)
- ❏ clothing for the season
- ❏ sleeping bag and pad
- ❏ tent with fly
- ❏ toiletries
- ❏ stove with fuel bottle and repair kit
- ❏ pot, bowl, cup, and eating utensils
- ❏ food (freeze-dried meals require extra water)
- ❏ water filter designed and approved for backcountry use (if the route passes a water source)
- ❏ nylon cord (50 to 100 feet for hanging food, drying clothes, etc.)
- ❏ additional plastic bags for carrying out trash

Appendix C: Other Information Sources and Maps

Natural History Associations

Anza-Borrego Desert Natural History Association
652 Palm Canyon Drive
Borrego Springs, CA 92004
(760) 767–3052/3098
E-mail: ABDNHA@uia.net
Web site: www.abdnha.org

Joshua Tree National Park Association
74485 National Park Drive
Twentynine Palms, CA 92277
(760) 367–1488
Web site: www.joshuatree.org

Death Valley Natural History Association
P.O. Box 188
Death Valley, CA 92328
(800) 478–8564
Web site: www.deathvalleydays.com/dvnha

Western National Parks Association (WNPA)
(covers Mojave National Preserve)
2701 Barstow Road
Barstow, CA 92311
(760) 733–4456
www.nps.gov/moja

These associations are nonprofit membership organizations dedicated to the preservation and interpretation of the natural and human history of the parks for which they are named. Membership benefits include book discounts, educational programs, and periodic newsletters.

Other Handy Maps

Although the "At a Glance" chart lists only the detailed 7.5-minute topographic maps for each hike, the natural history associations also sell additional maps that are indispensable for overall trip planning and for navigating around the park to and between hikes. These recommended maps are:

Anza-Borrego Desert State Park

- Anza-Borrego Desert Region Recreation Map (color)
- Topographic map set of eight 15-minute black-and-white maps covering the entire park, published by the Anza-Borrego Desert Natural History Association
- AAA map of San Diego County published by the Automobile Club of Southern California

Joshua Tree National Park

- Joshua Tree National Park topographic backcountry and hiking map, 1:78,125 scale, published by National Geographic Trails Illustrated
- AAA map of Riverside County published by the Automobile Club of Southern California

Mojave National Preserve

- The Bureau of Land Management (BLM) managed the East Mojave National Scenic Area before Congress awarded it national preserve status. The BLM 1:100,000 scale Desert Access Guides are valuable, not only for roads but also for determining land ownership. This is important because the preserve encompasses numerous private inholdings. Map guides covering the preserve include a California Desert District series from the BLM, 1999; the majority of the preserve is covered by the Amboy and Ivanpah maps. Books and maps can be purchased at Barstow, Kelso, and Hole-in-the-Wall.
- Mojave National Preserve, topographic backcountry and hiking map, 1:125,000 scale, published by National Geographic/Trails Illustrated
- AAA map of San Bernardino County published by the Automobile Club of Southern California
- Harrison map of Mojave

Death Valley National Park

- Death Valley National Park topographic backcountry and hiking map, 1:160,000 scale, published by National Geographic/Trails Illustrated
- AAA map of Death Valley National Park published by the Automobile Club of Southern California

Appendix D: State and Federal Park Management Agencies

Anza-Borrego Desert State Park

District Superintendent
Anza-Borrego Desert State Park
200 Palm Canyon Drive
Borrego Springs, CA 92004
Park information and administrative office, (760) 767–5311
Camping reservations, Destinet, (800) 444–7275
Web site: www.anzaborrego.statepark.org

Agua Caliente County Park (surrounded by Anza-Borrego DSP)
c/o San Diego County Parks and Recreation Department
5201 Ruffin Road, Suite P
San Diego, CA 92123
Information, (760) 694–3049
Campground reservations, (760) 565–3600

For information about wilderness and other public lands adjacent to the park, contact:
Bureau of Land Management
California Desert District
6221 Box Springs Boulevard
Riverside, CA 92507
(951) 697–5200
Web site: www.californiadesert.gov

Joshua Tree National Park

Superintendent
Joshua Tree National Park
74485 National Park Drive
Twentynine Palms, CA 92277-3597
(760) 367–5500
Camping reservations, Destinet, (800) 365–CAMP (2267)
Web site: www.nps.gov/jotr

For information about wilderness and other public lands adjacent to the park, contact:
Bureau of Land Management
California Desert District
6221 Box Springs Boulevard

Riverside, CA 92507
(951) 697–5200
Web site: www.californiadesert.gov

Mojave National Preserve

Superintendent
Mojave National Preserve
2701 Barstow Road
Barstow, CA 92311
(760) 252–6100
Web site: www.nps.gov/moja

Kelso Depot Information Center
Mojave National Preserve
1924 Kelso-Cima Road
Kelso, CA 92309
(760) 733–4456
(Open all year 9:00 A.M. to 4:00 P.M. Wednesday through Sunday.)

Hole-in-the-Wall Information Center
Black Canyon Road
Mojave National Preserve
P.O. Box 56
Essex, CA 92332
(760) 928–2572
(Open 9:00 A.M. to 4:00 P.M. Wednesday through Sunday from October through
April, then Friday through Sunday from May through September)

For information about wilderness and other public lands adjacent to the preserve,
contact:
Bureau of Land Management
Needles Field Office
101 West Spikes Road
Needles, CA 92363
(760) 326–7000

Providence Mountains State Recreation Area & Mitchell Caverns Natural Preserve
(within the boundaries of Mojave National Preserve)
P.O. Box 1
Essex, CA 92332-0001
(760) 928–2586

Death Valley National Park

Furnace Creek Visitor Center and Museum
Furnace Creek Resort Area on California Highway 190
Death Valley National Park
(760) 786–3200
(Open all year 8:00 A.M. to 5:00 P.M.)
Camping reservations, Destinet, (800) 365–CAMP (2267)
Web site: www.nps.gov/deva

Scotty's Castle Visitor Center and Museum
North end of DVNP on Nevada State Route 267
Death Valley National Park
(760) 786–2392
(Open all year 8:30 A.M. to 5:00 P.M.)

Beatty Information Center
Beatty, Nevada, on U.S. Route 95
Death Valley National Park
(775) 553–2200
(Open all year)

For information about wilderness and other public lands adjacent to the park, contact:
Bureau of Land Management
California Desert District
6221 Box Springs Boulevard
Riverside, CA 92507
(951) 697–5200
Web site: www.californiadesert.gov

Index

About the Authors

Polly and Bill Cunningham are married partners on the long trail of life. Polly Burke, formerly a history teacher in St. Louis, Missouri, now makes her home with Bill in Choteau, Montana. She is pursuing multiple careers as a freelance writer and wilderness guide and working with the elderly. Polly has hiked and backpacked extensively throughout many parts of the country.

Bill is a lifelong "Wildernut," as a conservation activist, backpacking outfitter, and former wilderness field studies instructor. During the 1970s and 1980s he was a field rep for The Wilderness Society and Montana Wilderness Association. Bill has written several books, including *Wild Montana,* published by Falcon Press in 1995, along with numerous articles about wilderness areas based on his extensive personal exploration.

In addition to *Hiking California's Desert Parks,* Polly and Bill have coauthored several other FalconGuide books, including *Wild Utah* (1998), *Hiking New Mexico's Gila Wilderness* (1999), and *Hiking New Mexico's Aldo Leopold Wilderness* (2002).

Decades ago both Bill and Polly lived in California close to the desert—Bill in Bakersfield and Polly in San Diego. They enjoyed renewing their ties with California while exploring the state's desert regions for this book. Months of driving, camping, and hiking, with laptop and camera, have increased their enthusiasm for California's desert wilderness. They want others to have as much fun exploring this fabulously wide-open country as they did.

Authors Polly and Bill sit on top of Ubehebe Peak.